Playing for Change

Playing for Change

Music and Musicians in the
Service of Social Movements

Rob Rosenthal &
Richard Flacks

Paradigm Publishers
Boulder • London

Copyright © 2012 Paradigm Publishers

Published in the United States by Paradigm Publishers, 2845 Wilderness Place, Boulder, CO 80301 USA.

Paradigm Publishers is the trade name of Birkenkamp & Company, LLC,
Dean Birkenkamp, President and Publisher.

Library of Congress Cataloging-in-Publication Data

Rosenthal, Rob, 1951–
    Playing for Change: Music and Musicians in the Service of Social Movements /
Robert Rosenthal and Richard Flacks.
        p. cm.
    Includes bibliographical references and index.
    ISBN 978-1-59451-789-1 (paperback : alk paper)
    1. Music—Social aspects.   2. Social movements.   I. Flacks, Richard.   II. Title.
ML3916.R67 2010
306.4'842—dc22

                                                                    2010013784

Printed and bound in the United States of America on acid-free paper that meets the standards of the American National Standard for Permanence of Paper for Printed Library Materials.

Designed and Typeset in Garamond 3 by Straight Creek Bookmakers.

16 15 14 13 12   1 2 3 4 5

Contents

♪

Acknowledgments

We are indebted to many friends and colleagues for their generous gifts of time, insight, and support:

Rosenthal's SOC 239 students, and in particular, Jorge Arevalo, Jacob Bricca, Amanda Chiu, Graham Griffith, Simca Horwitz, Sean Linehan, Joanne Maxwell, Zi Mei, Kathleen Ring, Chris Varmus, and Erik Vickstrom;

Rosenthal's colleagues in the Wesleyan University Department of Sociology;

The Humanities Center at Wesleyan for providing us the opportunity to begin our collaboration;

The Interdisciplinary Humanities Institute at University of California, Santa Barbara, for providing resources for a seminal conference on music and social movements that helped shape this project, and the Harburg Foundation for helping to fund that event;

Generous readers of earlier drafts, including Neely Bruce, Mary Ann Clawson; Reebee Garofalo, Larry Roberts, Bill Roy, and Mark Slobin;

The political activists and musicians who gave us our materials, and particularly Dar Williams;

Archivists, librarians, and music industry employees who helped us find and access needed materials, including Roger Manning, and Megan Saboura;

Dean Birkenkamp, for believing;

And most of all, our loving families: Sunny Banwer, Sam Rosenthal, Annie Rosenthal, and Mickey, Chuck, and Marc Flacks, whose musicking enriches our shared lives.

PART I

An Introduction to the Music-Movement Link

♪

Chapter 1

You Can't Scare Me, I'm Sticking to the Union

It was the summer of 1941. Four young musicians, the Almanac Singers, traveled west from New York City, stopping to play wherever they could help organize workers into the new unions of the Congress of Industrial Organizations (CIO). They believed they were part of shaping history:

> Each new day seemed more thrilling than the last.... They were caught up in the excitement, the *privilege,* of playing for huge crowds of men and women who were sacrificing everything to build the CIO. And they were entirely amazed by their own effectiveness: the four of them ... had the power to get thousands of workers ... up and singing, "Oh you can't scare me, I'm sticking to the union, ... sticking to the union, till the day I die." They could charge up a crowd, turn them around, weld them together, get them roaring. It was a transcendent moment....
>
> They glided west in their touring car, convinced they were an integral part of something very important.... [A] major change was taking place in the lives of American workers—one by one the big companies were caving in, submitting to the CIO—and it was being orchestrated in large part by radicals and, especially, by Communists ... and the Almanacs were helping it along.[1]

Songs, singing, and singers as an integral part of changing the world! Music shaking the foundations of an established order! This must have been what the Scottish political philosopher Andrew Fletcher had in mind when he declared, "Give me the making of the songs of a nation, and I care not who makes its laws."[2]

3

And yet, it turns out the Almanacs were often received with less than enthusiasm by organizers and political leaders: "Some CIO officials greeted them with open arms, but others were unfriendly or downright hostile, treating the Almanacs more like cheerleaders than consciousness-raisers";[3] The Communist Party "regarded the work of the left-wing folksingers in its midst as largely nonessential to the mechanics of its revolutionary struggle, if not downright spurious altogether."[4]

Such conflicting assessments are common to other movements and musics as well. In the late 1960s, rock and roll was declared (with glee by the Left, with alarm by the Right) to be the major conveyor of the social movements challenging the existing order;[5] as summarized by Simon Reynolds, "Serious rock's dream is that people can be changed, minds opened."[6] But Alex Ross, writing a generation later in the wake of the suicide of grunge star Kurt Cobain, argues that "Rock and roll has never been and will never be a vehicle for social amelioration, despite many fond hopes."[7] Rock musician Lou Reed, interviewing Czechoslovakian president Vaclav Havel after that country's "velvet revolution," says, "You obviously feel and prove that music can change the world"; but Havel responds, "Not in itself, it's not sufficient in itself."[8]

Which is it then? Is music a force that can change the world, or—at best—a little bit of entertainment that breaks up the real work of organizing? Often this question has been answered in polar terms: music as essential component versus music as irrelevant window dressing, and further, as inherently or universally one or the other.[9] We'll argue instead that there is no single truth about the music/movement nexus, but a range of connections. The uses, functions, and effects of music in movements are surprisingly and intriguingly complicated.

Those who claim an essential role for music in social movements can certainly point to a long history of their intersection. Most Americans are aware of the freedom songs associated with the civil rights movement of the 1950s, 1960s, and 1970s; the Reverend Jesse Jackson "once noted that while mass action—marches, sit-ins, boycotts and the like—created the body of the civil rights movement between 1955 and 1965, 'the music breathed its soul.'"[10] (This is not merely retrospective romanticism, but was a conscious strategy of the times. For example, Charles Sherrod, a renowned field organizer for the Student National Coordinating Committee [SNCC] in the 1960s, instructed fieldworkers that as soon as they felt settled in a community, their next task was to "teach the songs of freedom."[11]) But the tradition stretches back in the country's history: to John L. Lewis, founder of the CIO in the 1930s, who is reputed to have said that "a singing movement is a winning movement";[12] back to the "Wobblies" of the Industrial Workers of the World, who used music as an integral part of their organizing, printing their songbook, the so-called Little Red Songbook, in lots of 50,000 within four years of its introduction in 1909.[13] And even further back, to the union organizers, populists, suffragettes, and tenant farmers of the postbellum years; to the Hutchinson Family of New Hampshire, who toured the country from 1841 throughout much of the nineteenth century, singing their songs supporting the leading movements of the day. And, of course, there were songs that were part of the revolutionary struggle against England.[14]

In fact, music accompanies political struggles in much of the recorded and oral history of most of the world's societies: protest broadsides in Europe throughout the Middle Ages, a long tradition of traveling singer/poets in Latin America, singers of calypso in Trinidad arising in the 1920s, the pervasive mass singing in the South African struggle against apartheid, the nationalist songs of Irish rebellion, the *twoubadou* tradition in Haiti, *rai* in Algeria, and on and on.

One of our purposes in writing this book is to argue for the importance of culture in general and music in particular for social movements. We want, first of all, to document this—to say, "Look and see what music has contributed to the history of social movements!" But we want to go beyond a simple documentation of the frequent link between music and social movements to catalogue and illustrate the many uses of music claimed or suggested by analysts, performers, and movement members. And further, we want to assess such claims, to see whether and how music actually serves the various functions that have been claimed for it and to begin to determine how the functions and effects of music vary depending on social and historical contexts.

What Are Social Movements?

Social movements are historical moments when numbers of people, ordinarily living their individual daily lives, come together to make history. People occupying positions of political or economic power can make history—can take action that affects the lives of those "beneath" them—as a routine part of their daily work life. People not in such powerful locations can take historically effective action as well, but to do so they have to stop their daily routines, step out of their everyday roles, use time and energy in extraordinary ways. Such departures from everyday life by definition require sacrifice. The more one devotes time to activism, the less one has time or energy for activities that sustain personal and family life. Moreover, movement participation often puts participants at significant risk. Since movements typically challenge established authority, rules, or conventions, participants are likely to face a variety of possible reprisals.[15]

Indeed, the economist Mancur Olson argued that, from the perspective of individual rationality, it makes sense to be a "free rider" rather than an activist.[16] The logic is this: In social movement situations, what is being fought for are "collective goods," that is, resources or rights that will go to all members of the group, whether they personally fight for them or not. If women suffragettes win their battle for voting rights, for example, all women can vote. If a group of workers wins a union, all get union wages. Fighting for these things is dangerous. You can lose your job, your children may be ostracized, you may be attacked—even killed—in some struggles. Given that the rewards are yours anyway if the movement is victorious, why would anyone rationally risk his or her own individual well-being by actively participating?

Olson's free rider principle contains an obvious paradox: If everyone follows the logic of individual rationality, sitting on the sidelines while hoping others will fight for the desired collective goods, no collective goods will be won for anyone. But despite the apparent irrationality of collective action, throughout history relatively powerless people have, in fact, risked lives and livelihood to make movements for change.

A distinct academic field of social movement studies (SMS) now systematically tries to explain how such movements come into being, how they operate and develop, and how they affect history and social life. Until the 1960s, explanations typically put forth by social scientists in the United States lumped social movements together with "mobs" and "panics" in a field called "collective behavior," typically explained as based in the irrational, often pathological, motives of individuals. Those who joined social movements, it was generally argued, did so because crowds loosen moral control, or because mass society had left them without clear directions on how to act, or because they were, for various reasons, unable to live within the established framework of goals and roles. Moreover, the socially disruptive actions taken by movements were often deemed irrational, driven by ideological passion, blind allegiance to leaders, or magical thinking.

Such conceptions were hardly useful for interpreting the major movements for social justice in American history whose grievances and demands were demonstrably not irrational. In particular, the experience of the southern civil rights movement of the late 1950s and early 1960s led to an active search for a better paradigm for social movement studies. By the end of the sixties, a new generation of theorists began to picture social movements as rational responses to real problems, a different, but no less reasonable, approach than conventional forms of political organization and activity.

For the last several decades, social movement studies have aimed at theorizing and studying the interplay between social structures and the ways these threaten group interests or provide opportunities for collective action. We aren't going to review the ongoing debates that have helped shape SMS, or detail the conceptual apparatus that it has spawned,[17] but begin from a position we think represents a consensus among SMS theorists: While the political opportunity available through existing structural arrangements sets the stage and parameters for movement activity, making resistance and opposition more or less likely to occur and succeed, how people interpret and understand those arrangements—how they are *framed*—is crucial for determining whether potential movements become movements in reality, and how they will fare. The ability (or inability) of movement activists to create and popularize frames through which events are understood and contextualized by everyday people is critical for their collective action.[18]

"Framing" helps us conceptualize the ways in which belief, perception, and discourse affect the ways people understand their socially rooted troubles, but still doesn't adequately explain the willingness of individuals to participate in collective actions, that is, to defy Olson's free rider dilemma. Olson's emphasis on instrumental rationality ignored the possibility that the experiences of movement activity—the excitement, the sense of acting morally, the feeling of collectivity, the intellectual pleasures, the friendships formed, the identities adopted—might themselves be incentives for movement members.[19] In fact, in any movement there is a mix of "'instrumental' strategies and 'expressive' identities,"[20] self-interest and self-realization. Movements are often internally divided about the weight to give to the strategic and material versus the symbolic and expressive. But all movements, however "instrumental," must also be frameworks of expression—both collective and individual.

As theorists examined how cultural expression and social movements are intertwined, *identity* emerged as a central concept. Collective identity is understood as a crucial element in enabling movement participants to take the risks and make the sacrifices participation may acquire—to enable members to put the common good ahead of personal interest or to see the personal as fulfilled only in and through collective action. And whether or not a movement has succeeded in winning material gains for members, the movement can often achieve wider social recognition and acceptance for previously marginalized or scorned identities. At the same time, movements provide spaces for working out personal identities within frameworks for friendship and mutual caring and roles for personal development and fulfillment.

Movements in all times and places have shared certain essential needs: to attract and educate potential members about an alternative view of a situation, to get them to pledge a kind of allegiance and contribute time and energy, to mobilize them to engage in concrete (and risky) actions when necessary, and to *keep* them as members of the movement. At the same time, movements need to speak to nonmembers, to gain acceptance and support from bystanders, and to undercut or disarm opponents. Music and music making may play roles in all of these.

Music's Social Effects

There is a very long-standing debate within musicology between those who believe music—or at least so-called absolute music—is a pure and universal creation, removed from any particular social context of time and place and containing its meaning wholly within the music itself, and others who see all music as invariably tied to, and reflective of, the social context of its creation and reception.[21] This question is not going to preoccupy us here. As sociologists (and materialists), it seems to us beyond debate that music, like all human creations, reflects its time and place, whether explicitly or implicitly, consciously or unconsciously. In any case, there are already any number of works illustrating how music (even "absolute" music) reflects social life.[22] We're interested instead in exploring the *interaction* of social life (particularly social movements) and art (particularly music).

Many of those who have written about the music-movement link in the "reflection" tradition have been interested in exploring how a social movement affects the character of music that in some way derives from it.[23] Frank Kofsky, for instance, has spoken of jazz as "a vehicle for the expression of outraged protest at the oppression of Afro-Americans as a people."[24] Eyerman & Jamison's *Music and Social Movements* stresses as their "main point … that social movements are not merely political activities. Perhaps even more importantly, they provide spaces for cultural growth and experimentation."[25] Though they are interested in how the products of this experimentation eventually are absorbed into and alter the mainstream society (and sometimes play a role in the rise of subsequent movements), their main emphasis is on understanding social movements as frameworks for producing culture.

That question is important and pathbreaking, for it helps broaden our understanding of what social movements do, seeing them not only as vehicles for changing the material conditions of life but also as a source of art (and in Eyerman & Jamison's view, science). But in this work, we're less interested in how music *reflects* or is produced by social movements than in how it *affects* social movements and social life generally. The revolutionary German composer Hanns Eisler declared that his goal as an artist was to use "music as a weapon"; in the famous phrase of his frequent collaborator, Bertolt Brecht, "Art is not a mirror held up to reality, but a hammer with which to shape it."[26] Eisler and Brecht are expressing the key question that concerns us: How can music affect human action? How is music a *resource* for social movements?

"Music as reflection" and "music as causal factor" are very often confused or conflated.[27] The simple presence of music in or about a movement is often taken to show music's causal powers, when it might actually only demonstrate reflection. When Joe DiMaggio captivated the nation by hitting safely in 56 straight games for the 1941 New York Yankees, his feat was celebrated in many artistic creations, including a number of popular songs. It's unlikely, however, that the songs (and other artworks) helped him accomplish his feat. We're similarly wary when, for example, a contemporary songwriters' organization observes that "virtually all effective movements for progressive change around the world have been backed up by exciting sound tracks" as evidence in itself of "the power of music for peace and justice."[28]

The relation between art and society in general is best understood as dialectical, as interwoven: Music helps to create, sustain, and alter social reality as well as reflect it, sometimes in a single act. This is particularly pertinent when we try to understand the relation between music and political life. Yet it is useful to make *analytical* distinctions between cause and reflection in order to understand music's social effects. Music can be a reflection of an activity without in any significant way affecting that activity, as in the Joe DiMaggio example above. We want to inquire into *effects*: Under what conditions, and in what ways, does music contribute to social change?

When Hans Eisler and his followers called music a potential revolutionary weapon, they were trying to figure out how they could compose music that would be a resource for collective struggle. Such efforts to consciously create and use music for social and political purposes, as when the Almanac Singers sang *Union Maid* and *Talking Union* to help organize the CIO, are one important focus of our analysis. Alongside such deliberate creation and use of music in movements, a wealth of socially relevant music is created and performed in contexts outside of immediate arenas of struggle. A good example is the way socialist and antiracist themes were embodied in *Finian's Rainbow,* a Broadway show first presented in the late 1940s, with lyrics by Yip Harburg, one of those later blacklisted in Hollywood after being accused of communist affiliations.

Music may also have political implications and historical effects unplanned o not consciously perceived by composer, performer, or audience. For example, McClary has claimed that sonata music reinforces traditional gender roles;[29] various historians and musicians have claimed that the emergence of Elvis Presley singing "black music" may have facilitated white acceptance of the civil rights movement.[30] We're certainly interested in consciously created "movement music"—music intended by its creators, at least in part, to help support a movement. But whether the composer, producer, or performer intended the music to serve a movement is not all that we're interested in; it's the music as *used* rather than the music's function as *planned* that we most want to explore.

In summary: Music serves many purposes, and intersects with social movements in a wide variety of ways. We're interested in those uses of music that serve a function for a movement, consciously intended or not, at the micro or macro level, realized at the moment or at some time in the future. Denisoff declares, "the power of music as a weapon is historically unproven."[31] We aim to investigate that power.

The Music-Movement Link

Many established institutions make use of music to affirm the loyalty and guide the behavior of members. Patriotism is expressed in most countries by a body of songs, routinely taught in schools, used in ritual and sung at moments of national stress or celebration. Military formations use music, chants, and songs to demonstrate and reinforce troop unity, discipline, and morale. Students and alumni sing the alma mater of their schools (or at least pretend to) at commencement and other ceremonial moments. Music and religious ritual are almost always interwoven. Indeed, in Europe, much of the foundation of composed music was laid in church-related functions. There are even corporations that make use of anthems their employees are expected to sing, while the fact that their advertisers invest in the production of commercial jingles provides evidence that they too believe in the persuasive power of music. And, as folksinger Pete Seeger has been fond of saying, the lullaby is the family's propaganda song.

The interweaving of music and social movements explored in this book is, therefore, an example of how music is generally a resource for sustaining commitment to institutions and collective activity. But institutions typically use music to reinforce the hierarchy inherent in their structure. Such top-down production and use of music are not characteristic of social movements. Instead, grassroots cultural creativity are characteristic of social movements. Perhaps the most common form of this is the creation and use of songs, found in social movements across the world.

The Democracy of Song

Song—by which we mean lyrics and melody combined in a fairly simple structure meant to be performed by the human voice—is a particularly democratic art form. Since singing is close to ordinary speech, anyone who can speak can make a

g speech to melody. Of course, most of us doubt that we can create
nging and hearing, and yet we may create songs all the time, us-
) remember our to-do list or singing in our heads some line we've
onversation.

ჟongs are also easy to learn. Many can be acquired and reproduced at will by an
ordinary person with minimal effort and are more readily stored in memory than
unsung speech. Although poetry can be memorized and recited, most people don't
have a stored collection of poems that they can readily call up and reproduce. In
contrast, most people seem to have embodied a song database.

Songs are in this sense uniquely *portable.* We can reproduce songs (at least in our
heads if not out loud) in any circumstance we find ourselves. We can to some extent
reexperience a song even if we don't remember all of it or can't sing it ourselves. A
phrase or fragment running through our minds, or whistled, or hummed can evoke
the song as a whole. Each of us carries songs in such ways in our memories, where
the emotions and meanings associated with them are also retained.

Songs are also democratic because ordinary people can experience them without
the presence of their creators or skilled artists. Certainly many composed songs are
complex musically and/or lyrically and do require professional skill to be effectively reproduced. We may be able to quote a song's lyrics or hum its melody, but
we say we "know" it because we have experienced its live or recorded professional
performance. Such songs resemble other art forms. We appreciate and even love
them, but our experience is always mediated. But some songs that we first acquire
in mediated form, or in informal settings, become our own: We sing them for
ourselves, aloud or in our heads, or with others, and we need no trained performer
to experience them.

Finally, songs are easily adapted and changed to fit circumstances. What is sometimes called the "folk process" involves the ongoing tendency for songs transmitted
orally to be reworked accidentally or on purpose. Listeners mishear and change words
or tunes. Musical elements may get adapted to particular traditions with respect
to tonality, tempo, or rhythm. A familiar melody may be put to new lyrics, which
are readily learned and sung because of the familiarity of the tune. And there are
songs whose lyrics as well as melodies can readily fit a variety of differing social
circumstances. The "same" song can change its social and personal meaning and
the manner of its performance depending on who is making use of it. The more
vernacular a song, the more it will be changed and adapted by those who use it.

"Folk" Songs and "Movement" Songs

The democracy of song is exemplified by what are commonly called folk songs. These
are songs produced and reproduced in the context of everyday life by people who
don't live as musicians or artists. In their purest form, folk songs are disseminated
orally; people learn them from others whom they encounter in their daily lives,
rather than from professional performances, recordings, or other mass media. The
process of folk's informal dissemination results inevitably in modification of lyrics
and melody, if for no other reason than there is no "authored" version that ought to

be faithfully reproduced. Folk songs are changed as people in varying cultural and historical circumstances use them and make them their own. Songs whose authors are known can come to be folk songs when they are spread orally and adapted by people in diverse cultural settings.

Social movements provide occasion and opportunity for the production of such folk songs. An excellent and much discussed example is "We Shall Overcome," which originated as a black church song in the nineteenth century, and was adapted by southern tobacco workers during a strike in the 1940s. That version of the song was adapted by Pete Seeger for public performance, then carried and taught to civil rights movement activists in the early 1960s by Guy Carawan. Once sung in civil rights rallies, it continued to be spread orally as well as through performance around the planet to become a kind of universal protest anthem. In the last 40 years, it has been translated into many languages and used in a wide range of movement contexts.[32]

The story of "We Shall Overcome" illustrates that movement song production and dissemination are more complicated than the "pure" folk song model would suggest. The popularization of "We Shall Overcome" and other civil rights anthems involved organizers, activists, and supporters of many kinds and from many social locations. Pete Seeger and Guy Carawan were both politically conscious minstrels whose interaction with local activists helped the process of song production and dissemination. Carawan was a staff member at Highlander Folk School, an organization in New Market, Tennessee, whose purpose was to train and facilitate the work of local southern civil rights and labor activists. From its founding in the 1930s, Highlander staff deliberately collected and encouraged the use of song as a means of community and movement building. So this particular southern freedom song owes some of its life to the conscious, structured work of professional musician/organizers, whose use of the song built upon its folkish beginnings.

Other songs of that movement were created and spread in a more strictly "folklike" way. Local organizers, interacting with protesters assembled (typically in a black church hall) would adapt lyrics of well-known gospel songs and hymns on the spot, and lead call-and-response singing to prepare for mass marches and direct actions. Songs created in that fashion could be instantly sung by the audience, and readily introduced at other places and times by traveling organizers.

Thus, songs originally produced directly in struggle contexts became very widely known and sung. Without the creativity of local people reinventing songs drawn from their folk traditions, these freedom songs would not exist. Without the deliberate efforts by organizers and minstrels to disseminate them, they might have had but brief moments of use and impact. This interaction illustrates how movement cultural products can enter widening circuits of dissemination provided by the movement itself, by movement organizations and institutions such as Highlander, and, as well, through the established distribution channels of the popular culture "apparatus."

This formal apparatus—the companies that publish sheet music; produce recordings; book concerts; organize tours; manage, package, and publicize performers; and so forth—has always maintained its own sites for cultural production (Tin Pan

Alley, Motown Records, the Broadway musical theater, etc.), but these have never been adequate to fill the popular culture industry's insatiable need for material. Accordingly, the artists and enterprises of the culture industry ravenously seek out new material originating in more folklike ways. Urban neighborhoods (as in Kingston, Jamaica, the Bronx, or Greenwich Village) are places where street-level creation of new genres has been happening for decades. From these streets, the recording companies and music promoters capture the sound and recruit the performers who regularly revitalize the popular culture industry. Like those streets, social movements have been sites where music is created that then can be taken up and turned into materials of popular culture.

In the civil rights movement case, this absorption was complex. Freedom songs did not become commercial hits. But beginning in the fifties, a type of popular commercial performer known as the "folksinger" emerged,[33] as did a mass audience for recordings and live performances of traditional folk songs and new songs making use of traditional idioms. This so-called folk revival was defined by both the performers and their audiences as an alternative to commercial mainstream popular culture. In this emergent milieu, freedom songs created for empowerment of local direct action were introduced to mass audiences as a way to enable identification and support for the southern movement.

The dynamic results of the coming together of amateurs and professionals, movement activists, and music industry personnel in the 1950s and 1960s were unusual in the extent of their success in the commercial marketplace, but similar dynamics had a long history in the United States, as in many other countries. Jon Cruz has documented in detail the ways in which, in the nineteenth century, the songs of black slaves in the United States were taken up by various "outsiders" and in various transformations were made available to the wider world.[34] Abolitionists understood what Cruz calls the "ethnosympathetic" power of these songs: To get to know the slave songs by seeing them in printed compilation, or hearing them in concert, was to gain a window into the "soul" of the slave, and thereby to confront his/her humanity. As this body of song served the purpose of political ethnosympathy, it also became the basis for ethnology—the creation of a scholarly discipline aimed at the collection, cataloging, and analysis of folklore, and a foundation for anthropology and ethnomusicology as academic fields.

In the United States, active hunting and dissemination of folk songs were pioneered by John Lomax, an "amateur" ethnomusicologist, who began his work by collecting and publishing a compilation of cowboy songs and frontier ballads in 1910 that became widely popular. He continued this effort for decades thereafter, joined by his young son Alan. The Lomaxes created the Library of Congress Archive of American Folklife and published several popular song collections. By the 1920s, a number of collections of regional and national folk songs were in print in addition to John Lomax's, including Carl Sandburg's *American Songbag*.

The new technology of electronic recording was an enormous enhancement of the effort to preserve and disseminate American folk musics. The Lomaxes and other song hunters carried what was cumbersome recording equipment into the hollers and jails of the South, and were able to capture the voices and performance styles of folk song makers across the cultural spectrum. Many of the most important figures in the folk revival[35] were discovered and/or recorded, in the field or the studio, by the Lomaxes, including Lead Belly, Aunt Molly Jackson, and Woody Guthrie. Beginning in the 1940s, Alan Lomax, not satisfied to merely conserve this heritage, was able to promote the performers and their music on national radio, and through commercial recording opportunities as well.

These sorts of efforts by the Lomaxes were crucial pieces of a more general process of folk music revivalism that, during the Depression years, had begun to shape the cultural outlook and tastes of an urban, educated class. That class had previously privileged classical music (which itself was becoming popularized and more accessible through electronic media), and provided the audience for Broadway musical comedy. By the late 1930s, jazz was beginning to be heard in the concert hall as well. In the atmosphere of the times, it was not a stretch for sophisticated audiences also to lend an ear to various forms of folk music.

Folk music was professionalized in other ways that affected the cultural sensibilities of working-class, as well as middle-class, Americans. When Appalachian mountain musicians got radio airplay in the textile mill towns of the 1920s, they were, in a very local way, pioneering a similar process that was spreading throughout the South—the professional or commercial performance of southern folk musics. What came to be defined as "country music" came out of that process. Most influential in this transition were performers like the Carter Family, Jimmy Rodgers, and Hank Williams, whose repertoires included arranged performances of old gospel songs, blues, and ballads, but also self-created new songs using the idioms of the tradition. A similar evolution can be discerned in the translation of country blues by professional touring and recording black singers, and the subsequent representation of the blues in urban clubs up north. Muddy Waters was the prototype of this movement; recorded by Alan Lomax in Mississippi as a rural blues man, he moved up to Chicago, where he transformed the traditional form into amplified, urban dance club music.

In retrospect, it seems "natural" that all kinds of traditional folk music would become material for the insatiable demands of the popular culture industry. The rise of popular culture weakened the traditional social and cultural bases for folk cultures, while disseminating many elements of these cultures as commodities. Many of those involved in that folk process, such as Muddy Waters, the Carters, Lead Belly, and Alan Lomax, saw themselves as preserving and honoring the roots, and were themselves aiming to create and disseminate "art" rather than products. For many interested in playing and hearing music, the term *folk music* came to mean, by the postwar period, songs and performance styles that used roots forms for *artistic purposes* in contrast to roots-based commercial genres that subordinated art to market demand. To be "authentic" in that sense was not to claim faithfulness to the folk sources but to use such sources as resources to resist mass, commodified culture.

This perspective was expressed in the image of the folksinger that emerged in popular music in the fifties and became central to the politically influenced music that became so widespread in the 1960s: one foot in the streets and one in the market, telling it like it is, but still available through the commercial airwaves and on the largest record labels. That figure could be found not only in the United States, but in many other parts of the globe, in some cases developing out of similar trends, but in some cases also influenced by the U.S. example. It remains today as a model often invoked by contemporary musicians.

The Debate over "Popular Music"

The intertwining of folk and movement songs with "popular music"—i.e., music created as a product to be sold—leads us to a long-standing debate about popular music's general social and political impact. In the 1930s, 1940s, and 1950s, many theorists focused on the notion that mass culture in general and popular music in particular trivialized experience and diverted people from considering social life seriously. Although conservatives were prominent in attacks on popular music, the foundational critique came from Theodor Adorno, a leader of the Marxian Frankfurt School, who maintained that music in capitalist societies "has ceased to be a human force and is consumed like other consumers' goods."[36] Adorno wanted music that would aid the liberation of the individual and the society by engaging the listener's active participation. Instead, he argued, the popular music produced by the "culture industry" was a standardized product, much like any other commodity rolling off an assembly line, eliminating all possibilities of true creativity and requiring no effort from the listener. Such music did not call forth active engagement from its audience, but only a yearning for novelty within recognition, a participation just above the level of stupor. The result, for Adorno, was virtually fascistic, with listeners' response to the dance beat expressing "their desire to obey."[37] Although his criticism was mainly aimed at what he called jazz (by which he apparently meant the blander end of big band swing), Adorno applied this basic critique to all mass-mediated music, including "inferior" classical music and even the protest music of his day: "Those who ask for a song of social significance ask for it through a medium which deprives it of social significance. The use of inexorable popular musical media is repressive per se."[38]

Over the years there have been important criticisms of Adorno's approach: that he was elitist, that he was Euro-centric, that he knew little about the jazz he criticized.[39] But his approach contained two points that remain vitally important to consider: (1) The "message" of music is conveyed not merely by content, but also (and perhaps more effectively) by its form; and (2) the conditions under which music is produced and circulated—the social, political, and particularly economic framework—will significantly shape the music itself and how it is received.

From this perspective, if an artistic technique or mode of presentation discourages its audience's active participation, such work helps repress the very impulses that people must develop to engage in liberatory politics, whatever the intended message of the work's content might be. We can think of the typical rock concert in which the musicians on stage have nearly all the power—beginning with amplified sonic power. This arrangement is a microcosm of what C. Wright Mills defined as the essence of the mass society: few givers of opinion and many receivers.[40] Whatever the songs' lyrics might say, the mass audience is being reinforced in its passivity and atomization.

At about the same time that Adorno was writing, a less pessimistic argument about the effects of popular culture was being voiced by another Marxist critic, Walter Benjamin. While Adorno and his Frankfurt School colleagues feared elite and authoritarian control through atomization and standardization, Benjamin welcomed the technology of mass reproduction as enabling working people to seize greater control of art from the traditional domination by elites.[41] Although at times he too argued that form was more important than content—and therefore the role of the artist was to revolutionize the "production apparatus"[42]—Benjamin was less willing to accept that artists operating under capitalism invariably produced reactionary popular culture. Mass production, he argued, served to "democratize" art because it broke down the assumption that art was only for the upper classes.

The Adornian view was also challenged by a new group of commentators in the 1950s. The dominant critical tone of that time was a conservative version of Adorno—that culture was becoming "homogenized," falling generally toward the level of a debased mass culture that was threatening "high art" and reinforcing bad taste.[43] But there were some observers, notably Howard Becker, David Riesman, and others we call "Interactionists," who argued that consumers were not necessarily passive receptacles of cultural production. Such critics didn't deny that the conditions of production affect the cultural product (typically in adverse ways), but they argued that how consumers *use* these mass-produced products was crucial for understanding their effects. Popular culture, in this view, needs to be viewed as an interaction between producers and audiences: "The same or virtually the same popular culture materials are used by [different] audiences in radically different ways and for radically different purposes," noted Riesman. In his examination of popular music, for example, he identified a small group of "active listeners" who shared "a feeling that music is too important to serve as a backdrop for dancing, small talk, studying, and the like," as opposed to the many who used music as background for socializing.[44] Becker looked at the interaction of jazz musicians and their audiences, underlining the performance of the music as the product not only of commercial constraints or artists' intentions, but also feedback from the audience.[45]

These kinds of investigations were unusual at the time. Much of the debate regarding popular culture in the 1950s and early 1960s was concerned with who was consuming what and why; the Interactionists wanted to look at *how* consumption actually occurred. Careful examination of actual use, these writers argued, revealed that consumers of popular culture weren't simply manipulated by the culture industry; on the contrary, their active choice of particular artifacts and how they would use those artifacts demonstrated that, despite the power of the culture industries, at least some consumers demanded and received cultural products that reflected their interests and concerns.

In the 1950s, however, it was not assumed that this active involvement would connect with political action. Riesman argued that teenagers and members of other disadvantaged groups who understood how their cultural agenda was being manipulated by others became "cynical, not rebellious, and they are seldom even interested in the techniques of their exploitation or its extent."[46] But as the political activism of the 1960s and 1970s spawned a mass youth-based movement, apparently fueled in part by popular music, commentators became more optimistic (and in some cases romantically euphoric) about the ability of popular music to fuel radical thought and antiauthoritarian resistance. Observing (and often participating in) these movements, a new generation of writers believed they were witnessing the proof that Adorno and other left or right "mass culture" theorists could not have been more mistaken: Popular culture was not a tool of repression, but of liberation. Artists did not seem to be confined by the commodity form, but were apparently able to express radical, even revolutionary, ideas inside the existing commercial cultural apparatus, and particularly through popular music. Audiences weren't pacified by popular music but mobilized.

In a wide variety of fields, audience reception and use of popular culture began to receive serious study. Music critics argued that popular music in particular was more democratic and pluralistic than most other forms of art, and further, that its centrality in the lives of much of the population allowed—even required—politically progressive artists to use the form to challenge existing power arrangements. Particular forms—rock and roll, for example—were often depicted as *inherently oppositional*,[47] challenging established authority and embodying experiences of collective expression and liberation.

As the movement wave of the sixties and early seventies receded, however, it became obvious that the political and social effects of popular music were a good deal more ambiguous. The political turn to the Right in the United States and many industrialized countries in the 1980s certainly called into question whether popular culture was either intrinsically oppositional or politically effective; given the gains of the Right, it could hardly be both. Perhaps Adorno had been right to emphasize that the *appearance* of opposition in the manifest content of popular music masked its latent pacifying role.

On the other hand, it can just as well be argued that the 1960s had permanently altered the landscape, culturally and politically. The resurgence of the Right in the last two decades of the twentieth century was based in part on tactics, strategies, and even political beliefs learned from the Left; the legitimacy of protest and demonstration was firmly established for groups across the political spectrum. And though many national leftist movements and social movement organizations went into decline or became institutionalized as lobbying groups, populist political and social activity has continued into the twenty-first century. Music continued to be a part of most of that activity, often a central focus.

We say "political *and social* activity" because after the sixties, a new wave of academic interpretation—in "cultural studies" and by "Postmodernists"—was increasingly concerned with "subcultures," musical forms and related activities that were not necessarily avowedly political, and yet that seemed to represent resistance, typified by the emergence of punk rock in England and hip-hop in the United States. Postmodernists continued the Interactionists' emphasis on audience reception, but took it further: They were not interested in an audience's engagement with an artist's *intended* meaning, but emphasized how an audience deconstructs, reconstructs, and appropriates whatever commodified culture has to offer.[48] White racist skinheads in England, for example, adopted "White Christmas" as a theme song, a meaning and use not intended by songwriter Irving Berlin or singer Bing Crosby, but that nevertheless became the "true" meaning of the song for that subgroup.

Led by the Birmingham School in England, cultural studies explored how "subcultures present imaginary solutions to real problems," largely through the use of signs and symbols in what Dick Hebdige portrayed as "semiotic guerilla warfare."[49] The display of the swastika by English punks, for instance, was not an endorsement of Nazism, according to Hebdige; its use was outrageous, the ultimate in-your-face gesture given England's history, and it was *that* meaning—we stand for whatever you stand against, we stand against whatever you're for—that was attractive and meaningful for punks.[50]

The best of the Postmodernist work sensitized readers to the ways in which audiences may use the elements they encounter in popular culture in creative ways that don't necessarily reflect the conscious intent of the producers, but that nevertheless are meaningful to the consumers. But some postmodern work presented a picture of a world based on free-floating meanings applied to signs (words, gestures, songs, etc.), dismissing determinative connection to the intent of the artist, the framing supplied by the industry, or the environment of the listener. That pendulum swing toward indeterminacy went too far: It is clear that the meanings created by audience members are not wholly independent of what producers do. The images, sounds, and lyrical messages of popular artists; their delivery through a culture industry; and the settings in which these are received must at least be the starting point for audience interpretation. Each of these dimensions—what is made available, how it's framed, and the framework in which it's received—is crucial for understanding the social effects of music.

Postmodernists, and subcultural theory in particular, inevitably faced a host of other criticisms, only a few of which (thankfully) need concern us here. One was their focus on "style" as opposed to more traditional political activities. This was, of course, one of their great contributions: They pointed out how issues of style may in fact reflect and even help create oppositional tendencies that, given the right circumstances, might become more conventionally political. But both sides of this process were questioned. Critics like Sarah Thornton charged that the subcultural theorists had romanticized youth subcultures and overestimated their radical implications;[51] conversely, Keith Negus argued, the subcultural focus tended to neglect whatever real political activity was carried on by, for example, punks, in favor of discussions of art and style resistance.[52]

Perhaps more importantly, the emphasis of the Subculturalists (and their Interactionist predecessors) on audience seemed to conflate the activity and the groups engaging in it. That is, theorists focused on what they saw as the empowering, self-realizing, and democratic cultural expression of marginalized groups seeking a voice: punks, people of color, women, and so forth. But what if popular music is used by avowedly antidemocratic groups? What if those making or creatively listening to the music are not truly members of the group being sung about; how do we decide whether expression is "authentic"? And is "authenticity" a necessary feature of "progressive" culture?

Analyzing all this was made still more difficult by the fact that neither the musical categories nor the audience groupings were as clear-cut as some analysts seemed to assume. Few people truly give allegiance to only one group; few see their identity expressed by a single group membership. As we move from identified subgroups (rude boys, punks, riot grrrls) to larger categories (ghetto dwellers, working-class youth, women), the myth of homogeneity and a common vision becomes more difficult to defend. People's musical tastes, recent studies suggest, tend to cut across categories rather than be firmly fixed by a single demographic variable such as class or race, or even identification with a social grouping.[53] Even those groups with the strongest hold on their members' identities and loyalties are fluid affairs, a process spilling beyond the static moment that portraits of them tend to paint. The meanings attached to music, clothing, and activities of any form are constantly changing.

Music—popular music in particular—is also more complicated than a simple "subculture equals music" equation presumes. As John Street has written, "[W]hile some kinds of folk music do emerge from particular struggles, . . . [a]s soon as the nature of the political issues becomes confused and as soon as other factors (record companies, studio technologies, broadcasters) are involved in the making and distribution of the music, the links become blurred."[54] Virtually *all* cultural forms are contradictory, "composed of antagonistic and unstable elements," Stuart Hall points out;[55] the mixing of art with commerce, we can well imagine, makes interpreting popular culture even more convoluted.

Given all these difficulties, it seems obvious that notions of any inevitable effects of popular culture are untenable, whether the Adornian view that popular music will invariably be repressive, the 1960s "populist" position that popular music is inherently oppositional, or the subcultural studies/postmodern view that subcultures will use popular music (and other parts of popular culture) in oppositional ways. Popular music—like other forms of music—is neither inherently regressive nor inherently liberatory, though there are aspects of it that are inclined in each of those directions. We have arrived at a point, as writers like John Fiske, Richard Middleton, Simon Frith, and Lawrence Grossberg have argued, where our job is to specify *under what conditions* music is liberatory.[56]

Indeed, it is useful to see the uses and meanings of culture as an ongoing struggle among different interested parties. In these struggles, some groups certainly have greater power, as we explore throughout this book, and often this power is consciously used. Moreover, all social life has a strong tendency toward inertia, toward commitment to the status quo, toward maintenance of existing power arrangements. This isn't only because powerful interests have considerable control: Our own commitment to our daily lives and the demands of our everyday roles and relationships,[57] and our notions of what is possible (given the invisible but powerful structures of social life), all act to ensure that the default position of *any* activity—including enjoying music—is to preserve the status quo. Hence it takes special effort and circumstances for any activity to be truly oppositional, in form as well as in ostensible content.

Like all forms of social activity, then, popular music is struggled over, a "contested terrain." Its uses and meanings are not structurally determined (although they are certainly structurally influenced), but emerge through the concrete activities of

different groups. All parties—artists, record company executives, fans, performers, political activists, radio broadcasters, etc.—have some power at some time. As
Reebee Garofalo has written, "It is in the dialectic of production and consumption
that the politics of these events is realized."[58]

In carrying out these debates, academics, and particularly musicologists, have
spent a great deal of time trying to differentiate "authentic" folk music from "commodified" popular music, but the story we've told to this point suggests that the
music that is used by social movements can't be neatly separated into folk versus
pop, authentic expression versus commercial posturing. The polar distinctions are
certainly useful to consider since they point to important dimensions of why people
make music, and how; one of our questions is to what degree the music/movement
relationship takes different forms when the music is produced and/or received as
folk music (defined not as a genre, but by the absence of a market commodity aspect
to its creation) versus pop music. But we want to stress the tenuousness of these
classifications. A piece of music may begin as one thing and become another, and
it's the *use* of the music, rather than its origins, that most concerns us. Movement
members are not, by and large, concerned with questions of origin, and they freely
use resources from one arena in another. For example, participants in the early civil
rights movement routinely wrote new lyrics to current rock and roll hits, as well as
using gospel and labor songs. All of it was seen as "movement music."

What Counts as Political Music?

What do we mean when we speak of "movement music" or, more broadly, "political
music"? We'll begin with the deceptively simple word *music.* We use that term very
broadly, but it can be broken down into smaller elements. Frequently we'll speak
of *content*—meaning conveyed by the lyrics and the *sound,* which includes various
nonlyrical elements: melody, rhythm, counterpart and harmony, form, tone color,
dynamics, texture, and density. Neither lyrical meaning nor sound, of course, is
fixed or static: Different performers, different settings or framings, different audiences, and different combinations of all these will produce different experiences and
understandings of the music. As we'll discuss at greater length in later chapters,
we don't believe meaning is conveyed exclusively or even primarily to many audience members by the semantic content of the lyrics. Sound plays a major role, as
do a host of linked factors: the look of a performer, the expectations of a genre, the
social and political background of a performance, reviews and interviews, and so on.
When we say "music," we mean, at the least, sound, lyrics (if any), and performance;
often, we will be including the associated trappings, the linked factors, as well.

As Christopher Small has insisted, music is best thought of as both a noun *and*
a verb: "To music," according to his definition, is to play any role in a musical performance, from composing the material to taking tickets at the door.[59] We would
also include those who hum snatches of a piece heard the night before, or instruct
children in some mundane manner by quoting the lyrics to a hit song of our youth,
or otherwise weave music in some form into our lives—in short, virtually all of
us—as *musickers,* that is, those participating in musical experiences in some way.

But if music, or *musicking,* is everywhere, which of it might rightly be called "political"? (Again, as with all of the definitions we've been discussing, we think it less useful to worry about nailing down categories so tightly that every instance can be trapped inside one or the other, and more useful to have guidelines we can agree on for the discussion to come.) In one sense, as many have noted, all musicking—all social life—can be seen as political, since all activity reflects existing practices and arrangements (including power arrangements). To the extent it doesn't problematize those arrangements, it accepts and thus reinforces them. "Silly love songs," for example, which take conventional gender roles for granted, are political in the sense that they help reinforce those notions of "normal" gender relations. Yet, as John Street has noted, "applying the words 'politics' and 'political' to all aspects of popular culture adds very little to our understanding."[60]

Political music, for our purposes, is music that, first, engenders what C. Wright Mills called a "sociological imagination": It helps musickers to see the *social* roots in what might otherwise be felt as *individual* stories or problems. It identifies collective and structural arrangements—who has power? who does the work? who gets the payoff? who decides?—as the origin for much of what is usually felt to be one's personal situation. But further, political music implies, suggests, or openly states that existing arrangements are not natural, normal, or eternal, but the result of previous human decisions and arrangements, *and thus susceptible to change,* especially if those in a similar position band together to oppose those arrangements. And musicking is also political if it helps achieves the tasks necessary for mobilizing such opposition, whether or not it helped spark the original ideas behind that opposition.

"Political songs have a purpose that goes beyond entertainment—they are songs that are specifically useful for building a political struggle, not just to uplift the soul like any good song should do," says the political folksinger Fred Stanton.[61] When the legendary blues performer Robert Johnson sings:

> I got stones in my passway
> and my road seem dark as night
> I got stones in my passway
> and my road seem dark as night
> I have pains in my hearts,
> they have taken my appetite[62]

he acknowledges the meanness of his world, and perhaps lifts our spirits through that shared acknowledgment. But when the blues man Lead Belly sings (to an almost identical chord structure):

> Look-a here people, listen to me
> Don't try to find no home down in Washington D.C.
> It's a bourgeois town, it's a bourgeois town
> Got the bourgeois blues, gonna spread the news all around

Me and Martha was standing upstairs
Heard a white man say, "Don't want no colored up there"
It's a bourgeois town, it's a bourgeois town
Got the bourgeois blues, gonna spread the news all around[63]

he portrays one aspect of that meanness as created by humans (rather than an inevitable aspect of life), a more political stance. And when a group of people at a demonstration sing "We Shall Overcome" together (though the lyrics are less politically confrontational than the "Bourgeois Blues"), the result is even more politically charged. Political music treats what is occurring, from specific events to everyday routine, as open to question and change. A piece of music may become political not merely through its theme, but through the approach to that theme.

These themes, this approach, may be expressed or recognized in many ways. Gilberto Gil, founder of the Tropicalia movement in Brazil, which came to play an important role in opposing the Brazilian military's control of political life in the 1960s, notes that in the beginning he and his fellow oppositional musicians sang no lyrics about political matters, but saw themselves "as political through our attitudes. It was the way of dressing, of talking, of supporting the hippies and new ideas. And that was a challenge to the military, especially at a time when they wanted Brazilian society to do what they wanted, and to behave."[64] An avant garde composition without lyrics that calls into question conventional notions of melody or time may be political to the extent that it causes listeners to think again about the world around them that they usually take for granted.

Thus, the range of music tied to movements is quite large. Earlier we discussed "songs," a form we think especially important and notable because of its marked democratic character: easily created, easily learned, easily adapted, and very portable. But while song is an extremely common mode of expression by political actors, it is only one of many forms of music and music making that can be found in movements, as we'll document.

The political nature of a musical experience, then, may arise in one or more dimensions: It may be intended by the artist, perceived by the audience (whether intended by the artist or not), and/or engendered by the events and environment framing the artist-audience relation, or collaboratively created by participants where there is no artist-audience distinction. Any musical activity that is political in any of these ways is of interest to us here. This means, importantly, that music that may not appear to be created, performed, framed, shared, or even received as political at a given point in time may nonetheless be seen at some time as political. For example, some have argued that the pop singer Madonna's open insistence that she would define herself as she chose (however one evaluates the ostensible message of her music, stage show, and self-presentation concerning gender) may have been an important feminist lesson for prepubescent Madonna-wannabe girls, though at the time they may have been mainly interested in copying her look.[65] As the individual story can be traced to social roots, individual changes can become social changes.

A Few Last Issues

Resistance

Much of the argument we've traced in the literature up to now has revolved around whether we should see culture generally, and particularly popular culture, as *resistance* or *containment,* transformation or reconciliation.[66] That is, to what extent does culture—music in our case—aid those with less power to resist and challenge their situation, and to what extent does it instead encourage them to accept that situation?

As we've seen, Adorno characterized popular culture as generally regressive, and argued that even—or especially—the most explicitly political popular culture acts as a safety valve, letting off pressure and thus undermining capacities for resistance. In contrast, the populists of the late 1960s and 1970s, and the Subculturalists of the 1970s and 1980s, emphasized the fact that much of popular music has its roots in the cultural expressions of oppressed and marginalized communities. Because of those roots, and because popular music must win audiences drawn from those communities, it carries within it traces of the worldview of those groups, including feelings regarding their exclusion from real power in the society.[67]

These feelings, the argument goes, need not be expressed in conventional or narrow political terms, and usually aren't. Early rock anthems, Lipsitz writes,

> became anthems of rock and roll because they proudly and defiantly asserted group solidarity and rejected respectability.... These songs do not plot social revolution, but they do keep alive hopes for a better life. Like the mass demonstration and wild-cat strike, the good time in rock-and-roll songs elevates the world of play over the world of work, and it carves away a limited sphere of autonomy in an increasingly regimented world....
>
> If one views politics as only the public struggle for political power, then rock-and-roll songs were apolitical. But if one defines politics as the social struggle for a good life, then these songs represent politics of the highest order.[68]

The Subculturalists' celebration of punk similarly sees resistance in the creation of "a style that cannot be easily understood [by others] or erased,"[69] even where there is no conventional political content. Frith cites Paul Garon's work as illustrating that the power of the blues lies in its imaginative transformation—its "refusal"—of existing social life, rather than its directly political voiced sentiment.[70]

Many writers contend that the simple pursuit of *pleasure,* which is the theme of much of popular and folk music, is itself subversive since pleasurable activities—from sex to drugs to control of one's time—may in themselves conflict with the behavioral conformity a given social system demands.[71] Further, the pursuit of pleasure may be politicized when social and cultural activities are actively restricted, even banned, by a government that perceives them as conflicting with the values and behaviors it deems important. Then, as we'll see, these activities became weighted with a *consciously* political significance they did not originally possess.

These insights are crucial, but can lead to a comforting illusion that *any* activity at all qualifies as resistance as long as it exhibits agency—that is, autonomous control by those normally lacking significant social power. In some societies, particularly those with totalitarian states seeking control over all spheres of life, autonomy as such may be a form of resistance. But it's characteristic of our own society that asserting autonomy in one sphere may be entirely possible without challenging or resisting existing power relations. For instance, intense activity of poor kids in the Bronx organizing a New York Yankees fan club is in itself unlikely to foster resistance to prevailing power arrangements, by the organizers or by anyone else. Self-organization does create "social capital" (social ties and group connections) that may become a resource for mobilizing resistance. But it's short-circuiting the highly contingent processes that might have such an outcome to simply assume that resistance to existing power differentials will be the inevitable result.

Similarly, we want to distinguish between cultural activity that sustains an oppressed group's capacity to make it through the day and cultural activity that promotes active resistance. A correspondent wrote us from prison: "Thank God for the music here or two-thirds of these people would never make it through the day (or night)." But, as Frith asks, "How should we distinguish between the ways in which people use culture to 'escape,' to engage in pleasures that allow them a temporary respite from the oppressive relations of daily life (a functional use of working-class leisure that the bourgeoisie have always encouraged), and those uses of culture that are 'empowering,' which bring people together to change things?"[72] Making that distinction and exploring that question are critical to the analytic approach we make use of here.

We're interested, in this work, in active opposition, in attempts at "transformation" in Frith's words, and thus in the ways in which culture—directly or indirectly, immediately or over the long run, as a conscious project or as an unintended by-product—aids such activity. Rather than making a priori assumptions about the resistant or accommodationist character of music, we look for its actual uses by actual people in real movements to see how it has played one or another of these roles, or both.

Artist's Intent and Audience Reception

How should we determine these "actual" roles? In reading other accounts of the use of music in social movements, it strikes us how often analysts make a subtle but misleading move: They evaluate the impact of an artist or a piece of art by speaking of the creator's intent, usually deduced by the analyst's reading of the text, sometimes supplemented by statements of the artist.[73] This kind of information is, of course, interesting and useful, and we use this approach from time to time. But our primary interest is in understanding what the audience makes of a piece of music or performance (including the common folk process that involves the audience as the performers of the piece themselves). Understanding a composer's or artist's intent may be very important for understanding how making art affects *the artist* politically, but it tells us little in itself about the impact on others. We try to avoid substituting the artist's hopes or beliefs about that impact for what those who receive and use the music feel it to be.

The most common form of that substitution is to assume that we can understand what a song "means" by focusing on its lyrics.[74] While some scholars have pointed out the need to go beyond this to a more embracing vision of how meaning is understood by audience members, discussions of political music, in particular, still tend to establish an artist's meaning and significance predominantly or exclusively by citing the lyrics of their songs.[75] But meaning is conveyed and constructed in many layers and fluid contexts. We won't be arguing that lyrics play no role in establishing the meaning of a piece of music in the mind of a musicker, but that lyrics play only one part in the process, and that their role is larger or smaller for different artists, different audience members, different genres, different contexts, and even different eras.

Further, in the context of performance, each audience member constructs meaning somewhat idiosyncratically, transforming a performer's intended meanings in ways compatible with audience members' interests and personal experiences, including ways that have nothing to do with the artist's intent at all. A piece of music evokes the moment when we first saw the person who became our mate because it was playing then, or it reminds us of our mother who used to sing it, or we grin ruefully when we hear it because we got drunk for the first time to that song. Such evocation is part of the power that musicking has.

Whose Reception?

Our understanding of what a musical piece means to those who experience it may be even further confounded by the tendency of critics—like all of us—to assume that their own reaction to a performance or piece is shared by most or all audience members. Of course, few if any critics would actually defend that belief, but the implicit assumption makes its insidious way into much of what is written about music, popular or otherwise. We see this problem of overgeneralization most often when critics go for The Grand Pronouncement: "What Nirvana really means for their generation is X." "The ultimate source of pleasure in rock is Y," and so forth. But critics *don't* listen to music as the casual listener does, nor does the casual listener do so in the same way as the avid fan.[76] And this is particularly true of political interpretations of music, since the true fan and/or critic is often far more emotionally committed to the music as an expression of the movement than an average listener, who doesn't necessarily hear the music within the same framing.

Of course, if we're not prepared to simply accept the assessment of the performer, the critic, or the fan, neither are we willing to accept the judgment of those who *fear* the music. The fact that those with power seek to censor a song or punish a performer is often cited as conclusive evidence of a music's political importance. But even this must be seen as only circumstantial evidence of music's political *potential*. Whenever possible, we want to know how musicking has played an actual role in political action; the testimony of movement activists with respect to music's effects is crucial evidence in this regard.

What Is Success?

In a ditty called "The Folk Song Army," the satirist Tom Lehrer wrote:

Remember the war against Franco?
That's the kind where each of us belongs.
Though he may have won all the battles,
we had all the good songs!

Accounts of the use of music by various movements often claim it was used "with notable success" or "effectiveness," but, as Peter Yarrow (of the folk group Peter, Paul and Mary) asks, "What does effective mean? Does a song affect one human being or, on the other hand, do you say 'The Eve of Destruction' was a big hit, and for that reason it was effective?"[77] We often use terms like *significantly contribute* in our own evaluations, and we hope that's not simply a way of fudging this question. Music—of course—can't be discussed as if it operates independently of other social factors and conditions, but, when we talk about effects, we're looking for signs that music contributes something to the attitudes, feelings, and actions of members, sympathizers, and opponents that would not otherwise be there. If music reaches many but has no effect on the course of their struggles, we question whether it's a successful *weapon*. Whatever its effects aesthetically, a piece or experience that deeply affects one person and aids her movement activity is more *politically* successful; one that reaches many deeply and helps affect their movement commitment is even more successful from this standpoint. Unfortunately, there is no scientific or even consensual way to measure such matters. The investigative methods we've adopted, we hope, do give us some ways to make useful conjectures.[78]

Researching the Music-Movement Link

If we're right to say that much of what has been written about the music-movement link is plagued by vagueness, mystification, and confusion, there is a very good reason for this: Researching the link runs into serious methodological problems. Consider the task: We've argued that reflection and causality aren't the same thing, so we can't assume that the mere presence of music in a movement proves its effectiveness. We've argued that "meaning" is conveyed in many ways, so we can't just study the lyrics of songs. We've argued that composer or performer intent is not the same thing as audience reception, so we can't just interview artists or study the music itself.

This approach means we must somehow get inside the head of each musicker. How can we do that? We can, of course, ask people what music means to them, or how they have used it, or something along those lines. This is one of the main methods we've used in our work, but there are obvious problems with it. People may not realize how they use music or its effect on their thinking or behavior. They may romanticize it, or dismiss it, or in any number of ways distort its actual effect.

Further, they (and we) may easily conflate the effect of the music with other factors since music is typically experienced as one part of complex packages that may include romantic attractions, political allegiances, café discussions, and so on. While we think it silly to speak of music as if it's ever an isolated variable, *analytically* we want to isolate it as much as possible to avoid confusing its power with other factors present at the same time.

We also need investigative methods that recognize the heterogeneity of the audience(s), and thus the heterogeneity of the use and meaning of even a single piece of music. Similarly, we need methods that work across different genres, even different basic forms of music (for instance, folk versus pop, as defined earlier). Hopefully, these methods will enable us to explore *patterns* of meaning and effect, allowing us to begin to understand which functions music has played for which movements and why. Thus, these methods must allow us to gauge "effect," "success," and so forth more accurately than in the past.

Unfortunately, by and large, these methods have not yet been discovered, and perhaps they may always elude us, given the complexity of human consciousness and the vast array of factors potentially affecting it. In a researcher's fantasy world, the effect of music on individuals' political consciousness and behavior would simply be established by clear-cut reports of satori experiences: "I grew up thinking the United States should dominate the world. Then I heard the Incredible Fur Balls singing "Die Lackey Die," and I became an ardent anti-imperialist." Sadly for researchers, the actual link is far more complex.

As we discussed briefly above, the method of most of the early researchers in this field was to look at the *product,* the piece of music or performance itself. Content analysis of lyrics, for instance, assumes we can understand the impact of a piece by understanding the "true" meaning of what the author intended, and that intent is primarily or completely contained in the words.[79] Often this is supplemented with interviews with artists and/or analysis of their recorded statements about the product and its meaning. Both approaches import the methods and assumptions of traditional humanities studies, a focus on the text itself.

Other analysts have instead looked at the *production process.* Adorno and those in his tradition argue that the content is virtually irrelevant compared to how a piece is produced. Peterson & Berger altered this focus somewhat from production of music to its *distribution*—which music gets widely heard, which music is widely available for purchase, etc., which ultimately affects not only what consumers hear but what musicians subsequently produce.[80] Some researchers have looked at other institutional frameworks and actors that have impacted the production and circulation of music, from governments[81] to civic groups concerned with morality.[82] For all in this tradition, however, the task has been to investigate the *structural* environment—from the music industry to capitalism—from which the music emanates.

Beginning in the 1950s, the focus of some researchers changed from the art and the artists to the audience. Many of these investigations simply test the knowledge, taste, and so forth of audience members and then try to tie the resulting patterns to social background or some other explanatory variable.[83] Such studies often revolve around the "accuracy" of listeners' interpretations of a work compared to the "correct" interpretation (i.e., the researcher's determination of the composer's intent).[84] But Interactionists like Riesman, and later the Subculturalists, shunned the concept of a correct understanding, focusing instead on *how* audiences understood and used music (and other popular culture). Most of this work has been done by close observation of various subcultures, such as punks, skinheads, black ghetto dwellers, or marginalized women.[85] Interestingly, however, rarely have even these investigators asked audiences for *their* views regarding how they use music. Analysis remains the privilege of the outside observer.[86] The best of these have also contributed to our understanding, but whenever an investigation lacks direct testimony from the audience, there is always the danger that the critic will assume her interpretation of the meaning, importance, and pleasures of a piece of music is generally representative of the perceptions of the group being studied.

Our approach can best be understood by starting with the image of a medieval minstrel roaming from town to town, singing for his keep. He arrives in a new town, sets up in the town square, and begins to sing to a crowd, as seen in the figure below. [87]

The minstrel may have a message for the crowd: "The emperor has no clothes." There are (at least) three levels that need to be looked at in order to understand whether and how that message reaches and affects audience members:

1. The minstrel's contribution, including how the message is expressed lyrically and musically; how clearly the message is stated; what other clues and messages are provided in such contextual features as genre, dress, onstage comments, etc. We'll refer to all this as *transmission.*

The Minstrel Performs to His Audience

Courtesy of Walker Rutter-Bowman

2. The audience's receptivity, including such elements as expectations; their previous knowledge and interest in the topic, genre, and/or musician; their degree of sobriety, etc. We'll call this *reception.*

3. The processes and factors framing the interaction between minstrel and audience. Is there a lord who controls what music may be heard? What are the conditions under which music is played? What social and political events background the performance? And so forth. These we'll call *context.*

Without paying attention to all three levels and their interactions, we cannot hope to truly gauge the effect music—or any art—is having, and how and why.

At each level we've tried to let the experiences of real audiences and real artists guide our understandings, although we realize that musickers are not typically very analytical about their own experiences. A person may be totally captivated by the harmonies of the spirituals adapted in the early civil rights movement and be drawn to the movement through that captivation, but not realize the connection. As Lipsitz has written, studies need to be empirical (based on observations) but not empiricist (claiming the observations speak for themselves).[88] The researcher needs to observe and analyze the effect on the audience, as well as ask audience members for their own observations. We seek to understand meaning as it's created, re-created, and constantly negotiated, not as a fixed, intrinsic property of a piece of culture.

To do this, we've used a variety of (imperfect) methods of our own, recognizing that each presents, at best, a very partial reflection of reality, and thus we hope to combine them to get a better (albeit still incomplete) picture of what's going on:

1. We interviewed artists whose work was aimed at, or had been used by, a social movement, ranging from those deeply committed to political activism to those whose work or interests occasionally overlapped with movement concerns, but who didn't think of this as their focus. Our selection, of course, wasn't done for statistical sampling purposes, but we tried to get a good cross section along various dimensions: genre, age, race, sex, degree and era of fame, those recording on major labels versus those on independent labels, and so forth. (Throughout the book, interview excerpts that are not footnoted come from these primary interviews with artists or those with activists mentioned in method 2. Short biographies of the musicians interviewed may be found at the end of this chapter.)

2. We interviewed political activists about their relation to music. These were identified through an "author's query" sent to various journals and politically oriented Internet listserves:

I'm writing a book on how people use music in social movements and politics in general. I'd like to hear how music (broadly defined) has played a role in YOUR political experiences and development (no suggested readings, no lists of political songs, thanks). Send memories, anecdotes, your thoughts on what if anything music has contributed to your idea of politics and what you do or have done. Thanks.

Over a two-year period we received about 60 responses, 50 of which developed into interviews, occasionally in person or on the phone, but mainly through email. These were not "representative" of all activists, of course—it was precisely those who felt music *had* played a role who were likely to respond: "[Let me tell you] one individual's story of how he first came to taste, then to drink, then to cook the hearty soup of struggle and song that was then so elemental a part of our political nourishment," wrote one. "The singing and playing that took such a large place in my life have always been indistinguishable from my politics," wrote another.

Those who responded were fairly evenly divided into what one might call Old Left (those who came to political maturity in the 1930s and 1940s, although many have continued their political work to the present), New Left (1960s and 1970s), and Postmodern Left (1980s and beyond). A smaller number of queries sent to conservative and right-wing journals and websites produced only two responses, both abusive. (Our discussions of right-wing groups are therefore based on secondhand information rather than direct interviews.)[89]

3. We reviewed the social movement literature, including the more theoretical kinds of works on which the discussion of movements earlier in the chapter is based, but also including many case histories, looking for the role of music even when the authors hadn't raised that as a topic in itself.
4. We surveyed college students ourselves and supervised several student surveys of other students and friends. The two most important of these we'll call the Meaning in Music Survey and the Wesleyan Lyric Study. In the former, about 100 students were asked what music was meaningful to them and why. Questionnaires were distributed in 10 courses randomly selected at Wesleyan University. This survey was an effort to look at a broader population that included those not necessarily committed to a social movement to see if there were important differences in music use and notions of musical meaning between activists and nonactivists.

The Wesleyan Lyric Study is an ongoing study: Every year students in Rosenthal's course on Music in Social Movements ask five friends to tell them "the meaning" and then the lyrics to five songs they believe their friends are familiar with. Over the past 15 years over 300 students have carried out this assignment, each asking five friends about five songs, thus generating a total of over 7,500 possible responses. These have not been cumulatively tabulated—the differences in actual in-the-field methods used from one student to another preventing the kind of rigor a strictly quantitative investigation would require—but notes on the findings have been taken each year.

5. We drew on our backgrounds. Between us we have a combined total of over 100 years of participation in various social movements. Along with our political activism, we have both been involved with the music of social movements from our early youths. For the past 25 years Flacks has written and hosted a weekly radio program, *The Culture of Protest*, devoted to such music. For a similar period Rosenthal has been codirector of a small record label devoted

to producing such music, as well as a writer-performer-producer of several albums of movement music. Since our experience (as well as much of our previous research) has been in U.S. social movements, we focus on these, but bring in comparative information from other countries when we think it illuminates issues.

Can This Really Be Understood?

We're clearly cautious about any generalizations or definitive propositions that might emerge from our inquiries. Our survey samples weren't scientifically selected, and in any case, surveys and interviews have obvious limitations for eliciting reliable data about people's past experiences. But objections to our project may be more than methodological: Many would argue that the questions we're concerned with are impossible to answer with any degree of confidence. Dunaway, who has written sympathetically about such investigations, nonetheless notes that "music's effect on the political process is subtle and virtually impossible to measure."[90] Certainly the Big Questions lurking beyond the immediate questions have eluded precise answers: Why do people think what they do? And how is thought transformed into behavior?

People hardly understand these things—from the Big Questions down to our current concerns with music—about themselves, let alone others. Researchers face the same problem as those we interview: translating the liquid, abstract, ephemeral qualities of music and how we process these into the form we ordinarily expect knowledge to come in (at least in the Western academic world)—concrete, linear, testable, definitive.[91]

Even if we and those we question *could* translate into that form, critics argue, establishing definitive connections is just too difficult, given the wide array of variables that have to be factored in but can never be isolated as in controlled laboratory experiment settings. "Not only are there too many intervening variables," Street argues, "but ... there are no simple connections to be drawn between culture and action (and even to frame the question this way may be a mistake)."[92] "Social process," says Shepherd, "knows no strict or prime causation."[93]

But there's also another level of opposition to the kind of work we do, one we often hear from students but that only the rare academic is brave enough to admit:[94] the fear that closely examining music (or the music-movement link) undermines authentic response to the music. Deconstructing music, we often hear, replaces a felt experience with a cool, distancing mode of analysis. Fats Waller, asked to define swing, is reputed to have answered: "If you gotta ask what it is, you'll never know."[95]

Further (this argument often continues), those doing the analysis are extremely likely to distort the music and its essence in line with their own agendas. Intellectuals are always prone to overanalysis, to seeing more order and regularity than actually exists. "To apologize for the rambunctious edge of music or to substitute for this dimension some intellectually respectable justification that avoids the rhythmic impulse, to attempt to reduce apparent noise to rational order is to stifle the music," warn McClary & Walser.[96] The result, worries Tim Brennan, is that any genre studied by intellectuals becomes "a museum piece."[97] And the greatest perpetrators of this distortion, some conclude, are leftist scholars, who chronically display "a desire to find explicit political agendas and intellectual complexity in the art [the Left] wants to claim."[98]

We take these warnings of overanalysis seriously, but as warnings, not prohibitions. As Walser says of studying rock, "To argue that critical scrutiny of the ... music is inappropriate because people don't hear that way is like arguing that we can't analyze the syntax of language because people don't know they're using gerunds and participles."[99] Musicians themselves intensely study how music works by studying how music is made by other musicians, yet this doesn't inherently take the juice out of their appreciation or performance.

To be sure, there are dangers in conceiving of culture too narrowly, as simply a weapon or tool that serves a preestablished ideology and political program. Culture (including music) is much more than this, and analysts are understandably wary of oversimplifying what is a very complicated relationship. But all too often, the result of this well-merited caution is a mysticism about music's role in social movements. It's as if the scholars (and often activists and musicians as well) are saying, "It's too difficult to unravel the different factors, impossible in real life to isolate them, so we're not going to even try to examine them closely. We can't specify without distorting the reality, so from here on out we shut down the investigation and go on faith." The actual mechanics of the connection are assumed and implied, but not worked out.

We study these questions in part for the normal pleasures and professional payoffs academics get from pursuing an intellectual puzzle and trying to unravel it, but we'd like to think there's more at stake. We'll argue throughout this book that music has been, and is, a formidable weapon for social movements: an unpredictable, inaccurate weapon, hard to load and aim with any precision, but—at times—an extremely powerful weapon. Understanding the music-movement link will help musicians and movement members use it more wisely, we hope. As Susan McClary has argued, "Given its centrality in the manipulation of affect, social formation, and the constitution of identity, music is far too important a phenomenon *not* to talk about, even if the most important questions cannot be definitively settled by means of objective, positivistic methodologies."[100]

In a 1986 article in *The Nation*, Jesse Lemisch challenged leftists to think about popular music in new ways, arguing that the Old Left folk tradition was a dead end. In the heated exchange of letters that followed, he asked at one point, "Aren't we all still trapped in the stultifying old Communist notion of art as a weapon and failing to think in large ways about the connection between art and utopia?"[101] Our aim is to be aware of the dangers in attempting to categorize effects and processes into neat boxes that serve our theories, and to envision music-movement links in the broadest range of possibilities (and, by all means, to avoid being stultifying). But at the same time, we believe there has to be more than the mystical stance of "the music works in mysterious, unknowable ways" that many fall back on, the uncritical faith that music simply "helps" the movement in significant but unspecified fashion. In this area, as in all social life—which is to say, all human life—there are patterns of behavior, not necessarily universal, but common enough to be significant nevertheless. We want to look at those patterns and at least *ask*: why and how?

A Short Guide to Musicians and Music Industry Personnel Interviewed

PAUL BAKER HERNANDEZ: Scottish singer/songwriter, born 1939. A former Trappist monk, Baker Hernandez has worked as a "minstrel for peace" in the tradition of Victor Jara since the early 1970s. Since the mid-1980s he has been particularly involved in the struggles of Latin Americans, moving to Nicaragua in 1995. He is the founder and coordinator of Echoes of Silence, "an international network of artists and activists, with dirt under their fingernails, working to build a truly revolutionary world." He tours North America and Europe periodically, as well as performing in Latin America. His albums include *Hasta el aroma de la flor—To the Very Fragrance of the Flower* (2004) and *Twice Ten Thousand Years* (1999). He is the author of an autobiography, *Song in High Summer* (1989). Interviewed April 23, 1998, Middletown, Connecticut. Follow-up discussions November 17, 1999, Middletown, Connecticut; March 26, 2009, Middletown, Connecticut.

BILLY BRAGG: English singer/songwriter born in 1957. Mixing folk and punk sensibilities, Bragg was known early in his career as the "one-man Clash." Along with a commercially successful career since those days, Bragg is known for his support of many labor and radical causes, including the 1984 miners' strike, Red Wedge (a voter-registration effort in conjunction with the Labour Party in the election of 1987), and attempts to reform the House of Lords. In 1998 he released *Mermaid Avenue*, a collection of Woody Guthrie lyrics set to music written and performed by Bragg and the American band Wilco. A follow-up, *Mermaid Avenue Volume II*, was released in 2000. Among his other albums are *Talking with the Tax Man About Poetry* (1986), *Workers Playtime* (1988), and *Mr. Love and Justice* (2008). Interviewed September 29, 1998, Northhampton, Massachusetts.

GUY CARAWAN: U.S. singer, born in 1927. Carawan has been the music director and song leader for the Highlander Research and Education Center in New Market, Tennessee, since 1959. He is closely associated with the early southern civil rights movement, and is largely credited for introducing "We Shall Overcome" to that movement. He and his wife and frequent singing partner, Candie Carawan, were also involved as cultural workers in the Appalachian miners' movement in the 1960s and 1970s. They have issued important collections of songs from the struggles they've participated in, including *We Shall Overcome!* (1963), *Freedom Is a Constant Struggle* (1968), and *Voices from the Mountains: Life and Struggle in the Appalachian South* (1975). His albums include *Been in the Storm So Long* (1967) and *Songs of Struggle and Celebration* (1982). Interviewed September 12, 1997 (telephone).

ANN CHAITOVITZ: United States attorney and copyright expert. A longtime member of the advisory board of the Future of Music Coalition, Chaitovitz served as director from February 2008 to March 2009. She has served on the boards of SoundExchange and the Alliance of Artists and Record Companies, and as National Director of Sound Recordings for the American Federation of Television and Radio Artists (AFTRA). Interviewed May 8, 2009 (telephone).

CHUCK D: U.S. rapper, producer, and composer, born 1960 (full name: Carlton Douglas Ridenhour). As lead vocalist and primary writer for Public Enemy, he played a seminal role in the development and popularization of political rap in the 1980s. Important albums include *Yo! Bum Rush the Show* (1987), *It Takes a Nation of Millions to Hold Us Back* (1988), *Fear of a Black Planet* (1990), and *He Got Game* (1998). He has also been a pioneer in use of the Internet to bypass conventional record companies, launching the multiformat site Rapstation.com, an outspoken defender of peer-to-peer file sharing, and a host of the show *Unfiltered* on Air America Radio. He is the author of *Fight the Power* (1997). Interviewed August 18, 1998 (telephone). Follow-up discussion March 25, 2002, Middletown, Connecticut.

BARBARA DANE: Born in 1927, Dane forged a successful career as a blues (as well as jazz) singer in the 1950s and 1960s, playing with greats such as Roosevelt Sykes, Jack Teagarden, Earl Hines, Memphis Slim, Otis Spann, and Willie Dixon. Active in the civil rights and anti–Vietnam War movements, as well as the first U.S. musician to tour postrevolutionary Cuba, Dane founded Paredon Records in 1970 to produce music of liberation movements around the globe. Her albums include *On My Way* (1962), *Barbara Dane and the Chambers Brothers* (1966), *FTA! Songs of the GI Resistance* (1970), and *What Are You Gonna Do When There Ain't No Jazz?* (2002). Interviewed June 11, 1998, Boston, Massachusetts.

ANI DiFRANCO: Born in Buffalo in 1971, DiFranco has been the model of the truly independent recording artist, eschewing major record labels and releasing almost 20 albums on her own label, Righteous Babe Records, which she began in 1989 at the age of 18 with $50. Her material often combines personal and political themes, and she has been widely seen as an important musician for feminists and LGBT activists. Her albums include *Out of Range* (1994), *Not a Pretty Girl* (1995), *Dilate* (1996), *Living in Clip* (1997), *Little Plastic Castles* (1998), and *Knuckle Down* (2005). Interviewed October 12, 1998 (telephone).

MIMI FARIÑA: Born 1945, died 2001, first performed and recorded with her husband Richard Farina in the mid-1960s, and later, following his death, with her second husband, Tom Jans, and occasionally with her sister, Joan Baez. In 1984 she founded Bread & Roses, a nonprofit organization that presents over 500 shows a year to institutionalized populations, including those in nursing homes, hospitals, and prisons, which she ran until her death. Interviewed August 10, 1997, Newport, Rhode Island.

QUETZAL FLORES: U.S. writer, singer, instrumentalist, born 1973. In the early 1990s he formed the band Quetzal, which fuses traditional Mexican music with rock, jazz, R&B, and Afro-Cuban traditions. In addition to putting out a series of independently released albums (including *Quetzal* [2000], *Where Eternities Meet* [2000], *Sing the Real* [2002], *Worksongs* [2003], and *Die Cowboy Die* [2006]), the band has been heavily involved in local organizing and encouraging transnational dialogue, including their work in developing "Fandango Sin Fronteras," which fosters a dialogue between Chicanos in southern California and musicians from Veracruz, Mexico. Interviewed July 3, 2006, Middletown, Connecticut. Follow-up discussion June 18, 2008 (telephone).

JOE GLAZER: Born 1918, died 2006. Often called "Labor's troubadour," Glazer was closely associated with the AFL-CIO and was founder of the annual Great Labor Arts Exchange at the George Meany Center for Labor Studies. His best-known songs include "The Mill Was Made of Marble," "Automation," and "Too Old to Work"; earlier he was the author with Bill Friedland of the *Ballad of Sectarians*, songs parodying the Communist Party. His autobiography, *Labor's Troubadour*, was published in 2002. Interviewed June 23, 1997, Silver Springs, Maryland.

PETER JENNER: British manager and producer born in 1944. Jenner has managed many leading rock acts, including Pink Floyd, Marc Bolan, The Clash, Ian Drury, The Disposable Heroes of Hiphoprisy, John Wesley Harding, and Billy Bragg. In recent years he has served as secretary general of the International Music Managers' Forum. Interviewed September 28, 1998, Boston, Massachusetts.

CHARLIE KING: U.S. folksinger, born 1947. King has been recording and performing socially conscious music since 1976, as a solo act and in collaborations including Bright Morning Star and, in recent years, with Karen Brandow. His songs have been performed by Pete Seeger and Arlo Guthrie, among others, and include "Two Good Arms," "Vaguely Reminiscent of the 60s," "Our Life Is More Than Our Work," "Wrap That Rascal!" and "Are You Now or Have You Ever Been?" Interviewed June 11, 1997, Guilford, Connecticut. Follow-up discussions May 5, 2006, [Santa Barbara, California]; August 7, 2009 (email).

IAN MACKAYE: U.S. musician, born 1962. MacKaye is arguably, with Ani DiFranco, the most influential truly independent recording artist in the United States in recent years, as guitarist, singer, and songwriter for two seminal punk/hardcore groups—Minor Threat and Fugazi—and founder of Dischord Records. Fugazi was closely associated with many progressive causes in the Washington, D.C., area; it was also among the bands most outspoken in criticizing violent behavior at punk concerts. Their albums include *Repeater* (1990), *Red Medicine* (1995), and *The Argument* (2001). MacKaye is the author of the song "Straight Edge," but—he'd like everyone to know—not responsible for that movement. Interviewed October 12, 1998 (telephone). Follow-up discussions April 13, 2002, Middletown, Connecticut; November 25, 2008 (telephone).

TOM MORELLO: U.S. singer and guitarist, born 1964. As guitarist for Rage Against the Machine, Audioslave, and Street Sweeper Social Club, Morello has been one of the most innovative instrumentalists of his generation, combining the traditional role of a guitarist in a rock band with that of a DJ in a rap group. He also performs in a solo acoustic act as The Night Watchman, with original material that is primarily political commentary. He has been linked to many political causes and struggles, including immigrants' rights, abolition of the death penalty, the antisweatshop movement, and union campaigns. Along with Serj Tankian of the band System of a Down, he is the founder of Axis of Justice, created "to bring together musicians, fans of music, and grassroots political organizations to fight for social justice together." Interviewed November 1, 2005, Hartford, Connecticut.

HOLLY NEAR: U.S. singer and songwriter, born 1949. Near abandoned a career as an actress to pursue creating and performing politically conscious music, beginning with the 1973 release of her first album, *Hang in There*, on her own independent label, Redwood Records, formed to support "politically conscious artists from around the world." She has been involved with the anti–Vietnam War movement, gay liberation, and the feminist movement, among many others. Although known primarily as an interpreter of others' music, she has written a number of well-known songs, including "Singing for Our Lives" and "The Great Peace March." She is the author of an autobiography, *Fire in the Rain, Singer in the Storm* (1991). Interviewed October 22, 1997 (letter). Follow-up discussion February 21, 2002, Middletown, Connecticut.

ODETTA: U.S. singer, born 1930, died 2008. Trained as an opera singer and originally appearing in musicals, Odetta turned to folksinging in 1950. She was closely associated with the early civil rights movement, performing seminal versions of some of its most important songs ("Hand on the Plow," "Oh, Freedom," "I'm on My Way"), and an important influence on a generation of politically conscious performers, including Joan Baez and Bob Dylan. Among her most important albums are *Odetta Sings Ballads and Blues* (1956), *Odetta at the Gate of Horn* (1957), *Odetta Sings Folk Songs* (1963), *Blues Everywhere I Go* (2000), and *Gonna Let It Shine* (2007). Interviewed August 19, 1998, New York City. Follow-up discussion February 18, 2000, Middletown, Connecticut.

TIM QUIRK: U.S. musician, music journalist, and industry executive, born 1965. The former singer and lyricist for Too Much Joy, currently recording with Wonderlick, Quirk is the vice president of music programming for Rhapsody. Interviewed May 4, 2009 (email).

SANDY RAPP: U.S. singer/songwriter, born in 1946. Along with constant gigging, she is active in feminist and gay rights organizations, including NOW and Feminists for Free Expression. Among her best-known songs are "Remember Rose: A Song for Choice," "Everyone Was at Stonewall," and "White Men in Black Dresses." She's the author of *God's Country: A Case Against Theocracy* (1991). Interviewed October 8, 1997 (telephone).

BOOTS RILEY: American rapper and political activist. Riley has been an active socialist organizer since age 15, as well as a musician. His main musical group, The Coup, has released a series of highly regarded, politically charged albums, including *Steal This Album* (1998), *Party Music* (2001), and *Pick a Bigger Weapon* (2006). He has worked with and in a broad cross section of political groups on a vast array of issues, including the Progressive Labor Party, the International Committee Against Racism, California's Anti-Racist Farm Workers' Union, the Women's Economic Agenda Project, the International Campaign to Free Geronimo Pratt, and the Tell the Truth tour. He's a cofounder of the Mau Mau Rhythm Collective (which uses culture to publicize activist campaigns) and the Young Comrades, a revolutionary political organization. Interviewed Septmeber 29, 2003 (telephone). Follow-up discussion October 27, 2005, Middletown, Connecticut.

PETE SEEGER: U.S. singer and songwriter, born 1919. Since first learning banjo in the late 1930s, Pete Seeger has been a major force in preserving and developing folk music and linking music and progressive social struggles. Aside from his work with the Almanac Singers in the early 1940s and the Weavers in the 1950s, he has released dozens of solo albums, many of which have been heard around the world. He has written or cowritten many beloved songs ("Talking Union," "If I Had a Hammer," "Turn, Turn, Turn," "Where Have All the Flowers Gone?" "Waist Deep in the Big Muddy") and popularized many others ("We Shall Overcome," "Kisses

Sweeter Than Wine," "Michael Row the Boat Ashore," "Little Boxes"). He is the author or coauthor of many books, including *Carry It On* (1985, 1991), *Everybody Says Freedom* (1991), *The Incompleat Folksinger* (1972), and *Where Have All the Flowers Gone* (1993, 2009). Interviewed March 19, 1997, Beacon, New York. Follow-up discussions August 12, 2009, Beacon New York; July 28, 2010, Beacon, New York.

IRWIN SILBER: U.S. journalist, editor, and activist, born 1925. Active in the folk circles around the Communist Party in the 1940s and 1950s, he cofounded and edited *Sing Out!* magazine from 1951 to 1967, and later became cultural editor, and then executive editor, of the *Guardian*. He is the author of many books on music and/or politics, including *Songs of the Civil War* (1960), *Socialism: What Went Wrong* (1994), and *Press Box Red* (2006). Inteviewed June 11, 1998, Boston, Massachusetts.

FRED STANTON: U.S. activist, union organizer, industrial worker, and singer/ songwriter, born 1943. He began singing at antiwar protests and union rallies in the mid-1960s and continues to this day. Among his songs are "Hitler Ain't Dead," "Rollin' Thunder," and "Singing Cars," "a Bronx salute to car alarms featured on NPR's *Car Talk.*" Interviewed July 15, 1997 (email).

JENNY TOOMEY: U.S. musician and arts activist, born 1968. Toomey has performed and recorded with many bands (including Tsunami and So Low) as well as under her own name, and cofounded the indie label Simple Machines in 1990. In 2000 she cofounded the Future of Music Coalition, a think tank devoted to musicians' issues, and served as its director until November 2007. Interviewed April 13, 2009 (telephone).

SUZANNE VEGA: U.S. singer and songwriter, born 1959. Beginning in 1985, she has released a string of critically acclaimed albums spanning a variety of genres, from folk to industrial. Two songs from *Solitude Standing* (1987) yielded commercial hits, "Tom's Diner" and "Luka," the latter adopted by the nascent movement against child abuse. She has also been active in support of Amnesty International and the Save Darfur Coalition. She is the author of *The Passionate Eye* (2007). Interviewed September 26, 1997, New York City.

DAR WILLIAMS: U.S. singer/songwriter, born 1967. Williams has recorded exclusively for independent labels, beginning with *The Honesty Room* in 1993. Among her later albums, which mix folk, rock, country, and pop, are *Mortal City* (1996), *The Green World* (2001), *The Beauty of the Rain* (2003), and *Promised Land* (2008). She has supported a wide array of causes, from local art centers to Bread & Roses, as well as founding the Snowden Environmental Trust. She is the author of two children's books, *Amalee* (2004) and *Lights, Camera, Amalee* (2006), and coauthor of *The Tofu Tollbooth* (1998). Interviewed May 23, 1997, Middletown, Connecticut. Follow-up discussions November 6, 1998, Middletown, Connecticut; May 25, 2006, Middletown, Connecticut; March 26, 2009, Middletown, Connecticut.

PART II

The Meanings of Music

♪

Chapter 2

Aretha Franklin Sings to Charlie Manson

Christopher Small tells us, if we could survey all musicking in all societies across time, we'd actually find the active minstrel/passive audience setup pictured on page 27 to be a very rare arrangement.[1] Still, we begin there because, for better or worse, it's an extremely prominent model in the type of society we're looking at in this book, and an arrangement that has grown in importance and dominance over the last 150 years. And further, the way we learn all kinds of music and music making is found in this model: Someone else plays, sings, or performs while we watch, listen, and perhaps eventually join in. (Of course, this learning often goes on in much more informal settings: Your mother sings you a lullaby; your older brother's best friend sits in the kitchen and plays "Don't Think Twice, It's Alright" on his guitar; you hear a jingle on the radio.) So we'll start with the minstrel-audience model, and move on later to look at musicking that doesn't have a pronounced performer-audience split.

What's going on as the minstrel sings to his audience? As we read what others have written about the music-movement link, we're struck by how often a shortcut is assumed: Lyrics = content = minstrel's intended message = audience's received meaning (L=ARM, for short).

In other words, to understand what a piece means to an audience, we just need to look at the lyrics. If the minstrel wants to express that "the emperor has no clothes," he sings, "The emperor has no clothes," and the audience hears, "The emperor has no clothes." But in reality, the performer rarely says clearly, "The emperor has no clothes," or *only* "The emperor has no clothes," and even if he did, members of the audience are likely to hear and understand many other things.

An infamous illustration of this took place in August 1968. Disciples of Charlie Manson murdered eight people in three residences in Los Angeles, leaving forks in some of them, and writing the words "Pig," "Death to Pigs," and "Helter Skelter" in blood on the walls and doors of the victims' homes. Their actions, it was later reported, were intended to begin a race war in which African Americans would emerge victorious, and Manson's group would be among the few white allies to survive. The blueprint for this plan, Manson felt, was revealed through personal communications to him from the Beatles, contained in five of the songs on their *White Album,* particularly "Helter Skelter" (an English term for what Americans call a playground slide):

> When I get to the bottom I go back to the top of the slide
> Where I stop and I turn and I go for a ride
> Till I get to the bottom and I see you again—Helter Skelter![2]

This case, it might be said, is hardly typical, since Manson was apparently psychotically delusional. But most of us have had similar (if less gruesome) experiences discussing favorite songs with friends: We can't believe how badly they've missed the point—and they think the same of us. Textual analysis of lyrics may (at best) tell us something about what's on the mind of the composer or lyricist, but not much about what reaches a particular audience member. In order to understand how a listener determines the political or movement significance of a piece or performance, we need to understand how listeners arrive at *any* significance. How is meaning conveyed and apprehended, two acts that overlap but are not synonymous?

Looking for Meaning

It's a very hot day, mid-July in New England. One of the authors is driving home with his nine-year-old son, a budding music fanatic. Just as we enter the driveway, a shared favorite comes on the radio, Talking Heads playing "Psycho Killer"—a first-person narrative of a person coming apart at the seams, "tense and nervous," "a real live wire." It's easily 90 degrees out, and the car is an oven. We sit there, for four and a half minutes, sweltering but grinning like maniacs at each other, singing along at the top of our lungs each time the chorus comes on:

> Psycho Killer, Qu'est que c'est? Fa fa fa fa fa fa fa fa fa fa
> Better run run run run run run run run away.[3]

What could this song possibly mean to us? Do we really find the ranting of a dangerously deranged person attractive? Or do we appreciate the artistry in the off-center vocal, the way singer David Byrne is *drawing us a picture* of that deranged psycho killer? Do we take this portrayal to be sardonic, and if so, what do we think that attitude conveys? Maybe our pleasure has little to do with the words or vocals, our joy tied to the pumping of the rhythm, or the way the chord structure moves from a disquieting minor in the verse and early chorus to the familiar IV-V-I chord progression that rock inherited from the blues, only to fall back to the relative minor as the chorus ends? Or is the meaning simply the moment, the two of us sweltering together, sharing the heat and the music and our bond? As Susan McClary has written, despite the sophistication of the average listener in response to music, "very few people are able to explain verbally to themselves how music affects them."[4]

Music scholars, it turns out, aren't that much help either. Surprisingly, the question of how meaning in music (with words or without) is conveyed and apprehended has not often been their subject of investigation. "Musicology fastidiously declares issues of musical signification off-limits to those engaged in legitimate scholarship," McClary complained in 1991. "There has really only been one stipulation in the bargain—namely, that I never ask what any of it means."[5] But this is precisely what we want to ask: What does music mean, to its creators, but more importantly for our purposes here, to its audience? Despite the difficulties in translating the experience of music into words, people do so all the time, from academic critics arguing about Beethoven's intentions to teenagers debating who's being dissed by whom in which rap.

As we search for meaning in music, we'll need to broaden our search beyond just an intellectual reception to include emotional and physical levels as well. And we'll need to use a similar broad approach to *where* we search for meaning. Writers who look beyond the Western "classical" canon have criticized many in that scholarly tradition for assuming that musical meaning is always found in fixed objects, such as a musical score or a recording of a piece. But aside from this "embodied meaning," they say, there is the "engendered feeling" that is produced during *performance*.[6] As Small declares, "Music is not a thing at all but an activity, something people do."[7]

Meaning is itself a tricky word. Suppose someone says to us that Beethoven's *Pathétique Sonata* or the Kingsmen's "Louie Louie" is very meaningful to her. Is she using the word *meaningful* in the sense that this piece of music is very important to her, significant in her life—that it *matters* to her? Or is it a more literal use of the word: that it is full of meaning, that it conveys an idea or feeling? It will be important to keep both senses of *meaningful*—impact/importance and reference to specific ideas and emotions—in mind while we're trying to unravel where meaning comes from.

Meaning is also easy to confuse with a host of other terms, as they are used by different authors, including *message, content,* and *effect.* Looking at the minstrel diagram helps define the terms. For us, *message* is an intended meaning of the performer, while *content* is the sum of everything the performer (as performer and/or creator) transmits—conscious or unconscious, intended message or unintended static. *Meaning,* on the other hand, will be used to denote the significance *to the audience member.* This may be in "propositional" form (i.e., a statement in which something is denied or affirmed about a subject—"War is bad" or "The monkey chased the weasel"), but it can also include less specifically defined reactions—emotions, memories, and so on. And even this isn't the end of the line: The *effect* of this whole process on an audience member need not simply and directly mirror whatever he takes the meaning to be.

Meaning and effect arise not as intrinsic properties of a piece of music, but as relationships of the performer's transmission of content interacting with a range of characteristics, beliefs, and so forth brought by the audience member, interacting with a host of intervening variables. Music doesn't always translate into effective meaning—but when it *does*, how does that meaning arise?

The Limits of Lyrics: Aretha and "Respect"

If you ask people in the United States (as we have been doing for the past two decades) to name the piece of music that is the single most important feminist anthem, one performance of one piece comes up more than all other songs combined: Aretha Franklin singing "Respect." And this seems almost as true for people born years after "Respect" was recorded and released in 1967 as it is for those who heard the record when it came out.

"Respect" was written, recorded, and first released two years earlier by soul great Otis Redding. The lyrics in his version seem a fairly straightforward declaration of the conventional gender deal of the time: He'll work hard, come home, and give her his hard-earned money, and in return he wants "my proper respect" from her, including most particularly sexual fidelity while he's away working. When Franklin released her version she changed the gender of the speaker and added some lyrics for her background singers; some of the original lyrics also took on new meanings because of those changes. Most people are very surprised to read the lyrics as sung in this new version:

> What you want, baby I got it
> What you need, you know I got it
> All I'm asking is for a little respect when you come home
> Hey baby, when you get home, Mister
>
> I ain't gonna do you wrong while you're gone
> I ain't gonna do you wrong, 'cause I don't wanna
> All I'm asking is for a little respect when you come home
> Baby, when you get home.
>
> I'm about to give you all my money
> And all I'm asking in return, honey
> is to give me my propers when you get home
> Yeah baby, when you get home
>
> Ooo, your kisses are sweeter than honey
> So guess what, so here's my money
> All I want you to do for me is to give it to me when you get home
> Yeah baby, whip it to me when you get home

R-E-S-P-E-C-T, find out what it means to me
R-E-S-P-E-C-T, take care, TCB
(Sock it to me, sock it to me, sock it to me, sock it to me)
A little respect
(Sock it to me, sock it to me, sock it to me, sock it to me)
Whoa babe, a little respect
I get tired, keep on trying
You're running out of fuel and I ain't lying
Respect, when you come home
Or you might walk in and find out I'm gone
I got to have a little respect[8]

These lyrics seem to be proposing a somewhat different deal: If Aretha's man comes home and gives her satisfying sex, she'll be faithful when he's away (as well as giving him all her money). As Jerry Wexler (who produced "Respect") wrote in his autobiography, "For Otis, 'respect' had the traditional connotation," but in Aretha's version, "respect also involved sexual attention of the highest order. What else could 'sock it to me' mean?"[9]

Now certainly it could be argued that *one* feminist demand is for more equal, more satisfying sexual attention for women. But when people name "Respect" as the leading feminist anthem of all time, that's not the meaning they're generally referring to. Instead, they say the song is about a much more general respect for women (or women of color, or people of color in some interpretations), for the person as a whole. Some, in fact, say the message is to respect women as complete people and *not* just as sexual partners.[10]

"Respect" is, of course, far from the only example of a gap between the semantic meaning as apparently intended by a performer and that arrived at by audience members. Charlie Manson's interpretation of "Helter Skelter" is another. So is the adoption by white racist skinheads of Irving Berlin's "White Christmas" as their anthem, or the use of John Lennon's "Imagine" (a song that envisions an end to nationalism, capitalism, and organized religion) to greet Prime Minister Margaret Thatcher at the 1987 Conservative Party conference in England.[11]

These apparent disjunctions strike at the all too common L=ARM assumption. That assumption, as Frith notes, is at the heart of "contemporary moralists' claims that heavy metal lyrics make white adolescents suicidal and that rap lyrics make black adolescents violent."[12] Heavy metal "tells" white kids that the world is bleak and won't get better, and that suicide is the logical option, and therefore kids commit suicide; rap "tells" black kids that the world is stacked against them and that violence is the only rational response, and therefore kids become violent. Works discussing the use of Oi! music as an organizing tool for extreme right-wing groups in England and the United States have similarly stressed the role of lyrics as a tool of conversion:

While many adults find it hard to imagine being swayed by the lyrics of rock bands, the fact is that for many youths music does play just such a role. As dozens of people who have left the scene have testified, teenagers who listen to the songs hundreds of times actually are affected by the words. With the white supremacist lyrics echoing in their heads, a certain percentage of these still-forming youths are transformed into full-fledged haters.[13]

Those who write about politically oriented bands are particularly likely to equate lyrics with the audience's meaning. The opening debates of what we now think of as the culture wars spawned in the 1960s were frequently concerned with the question of what the lyrics of rock songs were *telling* young people, and there was remarkable agreement (if vastly different degrees of approval) between left and right ends of the political spectrum. In 1969, leftist jazz and rock critic Ralph Gleason proclaimed,

> Today, all over the United States, American young people are being spoken to by revolutionists in words they understand, in a style that makes those words acceptable, and through an invisible medium that old professional politicos have not yet picked up on. This medium is the phonograph record.[14]

A year later, rightist Susan Huck declared pop music was "spreading the doctrines of Communist revolution in America directly," based on the lyrics of songs, and quoted Gleason as evidence of the seriousness of the threat.[15] Responding to earlier charges by similar critics, Gleason gleefully declared: "When they talk of the Beatles as Communists, they are not hallucinating—they are merely mislabeling the contents. They correctly define the Beatles as their enemy."[16] The method of communication was branded brainwashing by rightists and education by leftists, but descriptions by leftists like Gleason hardly sounded any different from what rightists claimed:

> The millions who bought the Dylan albums ... have heard and absorbed all the lyric content.... In this country, innumerable people in high school and college (and some older) go to bed nightly, their phonographs playing with the automatic turn-off devices set. It is sleep-learning of a kind. As they drift off to sleep, the words of the prophet ring in their ears.[17]

And yet, from that time until this, there have been studies[18] that suggest that (1) most people don't know the lyrics of even the songs they say they know and love; (2) even when they do know the lyrics, most people have little conception of any meaning, either as intended by the artist or some alternative comprehensive interpretation of their own; and (3) by and large, most people don't care much about either lyrics or semantic meaning.[19]

Many of the studies that arrived at these conclusions have methodological problems. Most assume there is a single possible meaning to be arrived at—the meaning that the artist intended and the analyst has already "correctly" adduced—and so the studies are concerned with seeing how close to that "correct" meaning respondents come. Those respondents are almost always exclusively high school or college students. And typically, the studies suffer from the very problem we're discussing here: They assume meaning can be reduced to lyrics as written, completely neglecting any of the other factors we'll discuss below. But the degree to which they seem to agree on one point is worth our attention: "[T]he vast majority of teenage [and other] listeners are unaware of what the lyrics of hit protest [or other popular] songs are about."[20]

A coherent discursive meaning isn't even necessarily a goal of the artist. Words sound cool or fit rhythmically, but there may well be no theme to them as a whole. Michael Stipe, lead singer and songwriter for the popular rock group R.E.M., says:

> When we actually started writing songs ... I just didn't think it was important to have any kind of meaning. I was just trying to get words out.... The word *ottoman* is a beautiful word, so I put it into some song. And then there's a couch somewhere else. Meaning didn't matter much.... There's meaning to some of it. Some of it's just nonsense.... It has more to do with what you can do with language.[21]

In other cases, an artist may have a fixed traditional narrative or propositional message in mind, but it may be unintelligible to audiences because the artist must disguise it to avoid censorship or legal reprisals, or because her way of expressing herself—poetically, through use of rhetorical devices like sarcasm, and so forth—obscures her meaning.

The basic point we're making here is hardly a new one: Meaning includes far more than lyrics. Adorno made it implicitly when he chided leftist songwriters of the 1930s seeking to enter the commercial market for thinking they could "ask for a song of social significance ... [in] a medium which deprives it of social significance."[22] But beginning in the late 1960s and continuing to the present, an increasing number of academic analysts of popular music have stressed this perspective. A particularly wonderful demonstration appears in Robert Walser's book on heavy metal, *Running with the Devil*. Walser explicitly excludes consideration of lyrics in his introductory chapter on the meaning of heavy metal to vividly illustrate his point: "[V]erbal means are only a fraction of whatever it is that makes musicians and fans respond to and care about popular music."[23] Yet the average record review still devotes considerably more space to lyrics than to music.[24]

Still, it's best not to overstate the case against lyrics as a source of meaning. Listen to any "Golden Oldies" station and hear the constant allusions to famous lines from past songs that DJs assume will be recognized by listeners. Google any artist and "lyrics" and see how many sites pop up. Think how many times a day some phrase launches you into an internal performance of a song you grew up on. Clearly, for some people, for some songs, at some times, lyrics are very important. A number of recent studies suggest considerably more listeners value lyrics and message than the earlier studies found, at least among certain groups.[25] Some genres of music showcase lyrics more than others,[26] as do some artists within each genre. Some situations—sitting alone in your room with the lights low, or surrounded by thousands of comrades singing the same song—encourage processing of lyrics more than others—say, dancing to music in a loud nightclub.

As Frith points out, we rarely hear musical pieces from beginning to end, but instead in snatches.[27] It's a basic tenet of popular songwriting that the "hook line" of a song, usually found in a chorus that's repeated, and sometimes as the title as well, will be heard and remembered far better than any other line. Even shorter segments project meanings. Individual words or short phrases—"respect," for example, or "angel" or "blown away"—can carry an immediate charge that may resonate with listeners far more than any intended message of the song as a whole. Some artists believe lyrical meaning is *only* conveyed through short phrases, since following an entire song is, for many reasons, too difficult for most listeners:

> CHUCK D: I do my style of phrasing—I call it schizophrenic phrasing—where I will lay out a phrase, and then I might jump to another issue. But if you look at television, we're living in a remote-held society where people surf through channels. I like to deliver phrases through songs the same way, a lot of headlines.

There are also a variety of ways in which lyrics convey meaning aside from—sometimes even in place of—their conventional semantic connotations. We were sitting one Friday evening on the porch of a Santa Barbara home when a young man in his early twenties pulled up in a late-model convertible and parked across the street. By all appearances—dressed to kill, flowers in hand, etc.—he was there to pick up a date (a suspicion subsequently confirmed). But he didn't get out right away. Instead, he stayed in his car, listening to the end of Bonnie Raitt singing John Prine's song of marital despair, "Angel from Montgomery." In a world-weary voice, Raitt sings:

> I am an old woman named after my mother
> My old man's another child who's grown old
> If dreams were lightning, and thunder was desire
> This old house would have burned down a long time ago
>
> Make me an angel that flies from Montgomery
> Make me a poster of an old rodeo
> Just give me one thing that I can hold on to
> To believe in this living's just a hard way to go
>
> There's flies in the kitchen, I can hear them buzzing
> And I ain't done nothing since I woke up today
> How the hell can a person go to work in the morning
> Come home in the evening and have nothing to say?[28]

As the song ended, the young man whooped at the top of his lungs ("Oooooow-www!!!"), vaulted out of his seat over the door, and bounced up the walk to get his date.

Why does this sad, sad song fuel his exhilaration? Why does it bring us pleasure? How do these emotions arise from hearing the despair and depression of the narrator of "Angel from Montgomery"? We may simply be registering our appreciation for the excellence of performance, the same kind of rush we feel when we see Michael Jordan or LeBron James double-pump the basketball in midair before jamming it through the hoop. But beyond that, the expression of raw emotion per se found in a song like "Angel" seems to matter to us. Recognizing, and thus sharing the recognition of, an emotion make us feel part of something larger than ourselves, make us feel our connection to others, regardless of what particular story is being told. The meaning of a song sometimes may be simply that *something* is being communicated, and that human contact may be more important than any particular message an artist might want to convey. (This may be why there are so few instrumental hits: We like to be talked with.)

The *form* of the lyrics may also make a statement beyond anything those lyrics say. This is perhaps most obvious when singers speak in a language or accent that has traditionally been devalued, as when artists in colonized countries begin writing in their own languages instead of the mother country's tongue, or punks sing in working-class accents. Here an artist could write "nonsense" lyrics and still project a clear meaning: I am not ashamed of this language, this accent. In any language, use of the first person plural ("we") includes listeners in a way that using the first person singular ("I") or addressing a particular person by using the second person ("you") does not.

Lyrics can also project a message about the individual speaker (and/or the listener) that is peripheral to their discursive meaning and the ostensible topic at hand. Dense, poetic imagery about, say, the setting sun may tell us something about the sun, or the end of the day, or life, but the meaning we take from those lyrics may instead be: "What a deep artist she is! And (implicitly) what a deep person I am if I like this kind of art!" Any number of meanings may be sent or received in this way: I'm a poetry-lover, or angry, or hip to other cultures.

Finally, lyrics, like all words, have a life as sounds. These may convey intelligible meanings ("crash!"), but often do not; their impact is "sonic" rather than "semantic."[29] Keil & Feld point out how the singer James Brown uses the sounds of words as an instrumentalist might use different forms of attack on an instrument:

> KEIL: ... "mother popcorn," "mama come here quick, bring me that lickin' stick"—it's the pops and clicks, the /p/s, the /k/s, the sounds of the words, not that they mean anything particular to James, either when he utters them, or later. It's the sound of those words together.

> FELD: That's what's so compelling about each "Ow!"—those exclamatory vocal interjections where his mouth is articulating with the horn section, punching, riffing.[30]

Similarly, Christenson & Roberts suggest that for some (mainly middle-class) rap listeners, "lyrics [perform] more of a rhythmic function than a symbolic one."[31] Western scholarship has been reluctant to appreciate the role of "the sonority of words," more clearly appreciated in other cultures,[32] but Western musicians have often embraced words as sounds, perhaps most obviously in the scat singing of jazz vocalists such as Ella Fitzgerald or Louis Armstrong.

The studies of the 1960s and 1970s that first cast doubt on the importance of lyrics in conveying meaning made an implicit assumption: To understand intended meaning (the only kind they were interested in investigating), you must remember and retain the words. But the Wesleyan Lyric Study has often revealed a different situation. In that ongoing exercise, now almost two decades old, hundreds of students have asked five friends to tell them the lyrics and meaning of five well-known songs. Students have found, in the first place, that very few respondents actually remember more than a smattering of lyrics, even to those songs that they report are their favorites, and the meaning they attribute to a song is often tied more to a variety of other factors—the respondent's own characteristics and interests; the setting the song is heard in; external aids such as videos, movie tie-ins, or the band's image—than to a strict reading of the lyrics. Yet they've also found quite consistently that some people can give what the student investigators consider accurate renderings of intended meanings of some songs without being able to recall the lyrics. This may simply reflect that the respondent once knew the lyrics, understood an intended message from them, and subsequently forgot the former but not the latter. But it also has to do with our ability to understand intended meaning from many clues. In this, listening to music is like other forms of communication. For example, we understand much of what people say from their vocal inflections and timbre. When listening to someone with a heavy accent, or a low talker, or talking on the phone with our aunt while watching a game on television, we still have a pretty good idea when to murmur something, and the appropriate tone to adopt, even if we haven't heard many of the actual words.

Read off a lyric sheet, the words to Aretha Franklin's version of "Respect" don't appear to convey the message of respect that most people believe the song is about. The question here isn't whether their interpretations are correct or incorrect; the question is *how and why* audience members construct the meanings they come up with. If the semantic meaning of lyrics alone is not a sufficient explanation, we need to look at other contributing factors through which music conveys meanings, but that also shape what the music means. These can be best understood by dividing them (for the moment) into *transmission* factors coming from the performer, *reception* factors tied to the audience member, and *context* factors that frame the relation between performer and audience.

From the Artist: Transmission

Music

Music—the sound portion of the content of a piece—may strengthen a meaning we pick up from the lyrics of a song, as a movie score serves a film: setting a mood, emphasizing a moment, and so on, providing important clues about which words are important and how we should understand them. These musical clues range from abrupt rupture with the musical scheme—pay attention, something new is happening here!—to the comforting return of the chorus, which tells the listener, "here's the main theme." Most importantly, adding music to lyrics ratchets up the power and impact of the experience. Speaking of his highly controversial record *Cop Killer*, the rapper Ice-T points out the words alone are "just" an editorial, "but when it's done on a record, it's like in your face, and there's loud guitars playing, and it'll scare the shit out of you."[33] As McClary & Walser (less colorfully) argue, "[U]nless the sensual power of the music is dealt with seriously, the rest of the argument becomes irrelevant."[34]

Music can also convey messages of its own. This power has perhaps been most appreciated by those who have feared it, beginning with Plato's famous warning in *The Republic* that musical innovation was inevitably a danger to the state and therefore should be shunned. In 1983, authorities in China issued a booklet, "How to distinguish decadent music," that warned of "the dire effect of alien Western sounds."[35] From the earliest days of rock, many of its critics argued that its danger to morality was to be found less in its lyrics and more in its sound, particularly the beat, described as hypnotic, sexually insistent, jungle rhythms (with obvious racist overtones). In 1958, *Music Journal* editorialized against rock's "threat to civilization. ... Teens listening to rock were 'definitely influenced in their lawlessness by this throwback to jungle rhythms. ... [It is] entirely correct to state that every proved delinquent has been definitely influenced by rock 'n' roll.'"[36]

If such pronouncements make us smile today, it's in part because we scoff at the leap they make from a beat to an attitude such as disdain for the law. Does that mean we *don't* believe specific ideas and attitudes can be conveyed musically? Here we encounter a fundamental question of meaning in music: "How do we locate content, especially narrative content, in sounds—mere acoustical phenomena?"[37] And how explicit can such meanings be? Meyer argued that music could convey only general "connotative complexes" that frame what the listener would get; the exact connotation would depend on the listener.[38] Kivy follows in this tradition when he says, "Pure instrumental music ... possesses expressive properties, but not expressive content";[39] that is, music may express sadness, but not sadness about anything in particular. For there to be an object of sadness, he argues, a story, lyrics, or other guides are necessary.[40] And many rock and pop critics are similarly likely to say that pop music is about general moods and emotions rather than specific content.[41]

There are, however, examples of musical signs with very fixed meanings. Different modes (that is, different relationships between the notes of a scale)* were assumed by the Greeks to reflect different characteristics, and were named after the people who were supposed to exhibit those traits: The Dorian mode is "strong and brave," for example, while the Lydian mode is "soft, sweet, and effeminate."[42] Renaissance theorists and composers were very concerned "with developing techniques and codes for delineating various emotional types and thereby moving the passions of listeners";[43] writings appeared on how best to represent grief, joy, and so forth. Baroque composers had a highly developed system of denotations.[44]

Even without fixed systems of denotation, music may suggest meaning. Melodies that rise are often said to give us a sense of energy, of soaring, of freedom. Walser offers a fascinating analysis of Van Halen's "Running with the Devil" in which the

---

*Note for nonmusicians: Imagine the notes you would sing if someone asked you to sing a scale: Do-re-mi-fa-sol-la-ti-do. That's a major scale, and the kind of melody that's composed using those notes is said to be in the Ionian mode. Now sing those same notes again (or try this on a piano if it's hard to sing), but starting with the sixth note of that scale ("la", i.e., the note A in the key of C). If we compose a piece of music using that mode we get a different kind of melody, one we might characterize as sadder, which is using a minor scale (or in the "Aeolian" mode).

fantasy of freedom is most strongly conveyed in the chorus as every two measures the melody moves "out of the familiar negative Aeolian terrain into the perfect resolution of the major mode's tonic. Immediately thereafter, we are plunged again into Aeolian gloom and then carried up out of it once more.... This two-measure pattern of tension and release, negativity and transcendence, is the most important signifying feature of the song."[45]

Of course, as Kivy argues, none of these convey a message or meaning that is truly propositional. We may hear happy or sad or freedom, but that doesn't tell us who or why or what anyone might do about it. And a given listener might not even hear happy or sad or freedom; perhaps he hears madness, thoughtfulness, and a traffic jam. The point (so far) is simply that elements of a transmitted message or received meaning *may* be conveyed through melody.

When harmony is added to the melody, new meanings arise. Just the presence of harmony may convey a different message (as well as sound) than a single voice, a feeling of weaving different strands into a single garment, a feeling of *togetherness*. When the Hutchinson Family singers toured the United States in the 1800s, they were famous for "the closeness of their musical harmonies [which] authenticated the closeness of their family relationship."[46] Harmonic singing may evoke experiences of bonding and mutuality when done by a small group; harmonies performed by a large chorus or a mass audience can convey some sense of solidarity or collective power.

Rhythm sends messages as well. Emphasis on the beat, in itself, is seen as meaningful in Paul Willis's study of motorbike boys' culture:

> Most crucially this music allows the return of the body in music, and encourages the development of a culture based on movement and confidence in movement.... The absolute ascendancy of the beat in rock 'n' roll firmly establishes the ascendancy of the body over the mind—it reflects the motorbike boys' culture very closely.[47]

The *nature* of the beat, too, may be experienced as meaningful, as in the widely shared assumption that the "rhythmically insistent" beat of rock and roll, "built around techniques of arousal and climax,"[48] conveys sexual insistence, presenting physical love as desirable (as the term *rock and roll* is itself derived from a slang term for having intercourse). At the other pole, musicians in Nazi Germany were directed to use brisk tempos "commensurate with the Aryan sense of discipline and moderation."[49] The setting up of a solid pulse, from the military band to the heavy metal band, conveys a feeling of power, of invincibility.

The way a piece is structured may further convey messages and affect meanings. The call-and-response tradition in African American musical forms such as gospel and soul creates a feeling of collective involvement inviting participation. Songs in any genre that feature a repeated chorus between the verses invite participation, thus sending a message of unity between performer and audience, and between different audience members, which is why they were a staple of the "mass songs" in the postrevolutionary Soviet Union. Even when a listener isn't participating himself, hearing many voices singing together may evoke feelings of solidarity. In contrast, songs without a chorus (or other lyrics that are repeated) typically are performed only by the artist, sending a different message about the relationships involved. It's easy to imagine a crowd at an antiwar demonstration singing along with a performer on "Down by the Riverside," with its recurring chorus ("I ain't gonna study war no more" repeated six times). It's impossible to imagine them doing the same with Bob Dylan's "Masters of War"—no chorus, eight verses, 64 lines, not one of which repeats.

The particular instruments used also contribute to the meanings we arrive at: An organ signals piety; a lone acoustic guitar signals a minstrel speaking truth. The Nazi government prohibited the use of "instruments alien to the German spirit (so-called cowbells, flexatone, brushes, etc.), as well as all mutes which turn the noble sound of wind and brass instruments into a Jewish-Freemasonic yowl."[50] Further, how the instruments are played and the way the entire musical package is produced can signify. The uses of guitar distortion, extreme volume, and distorted vocals, Walser argues, are not only fundamental to identifying a song as within the heavy metal genre, but essential to a central meaning of metal: I possess power.[51] The difference in sound is pronounced between metal (and the other subgenres of rock sometimes referred to collectively as "cock rock"), which emphasizes a pounding, heavy sound that conjures up a feeling of stereotypical male sexuality, and Top 40 pop, which features a lighter, more polished sound that more often signals romance than the act of sex itself.

The sound of music has often been seen to convey even more directly political meanings. As the civil rights movement progressed from its early integrationist phase to an emphasis on black power, the glossy production of the Motown sound in black music (consciously developed to facilitate crossover to white audiences) was displaced in popularity among black audiences and performers by a "harder driving, grittier (and angrier) rhythm and blues ... consciously understood to signify the growing militancy of the Black Community."[52]

Many of these musical effects are very subtle, and so likely to escape most listeners' conscious recognition. Richard Middleton—among the most musically sophisticated of writers in this area—argues that the techniques of drone and repetition found in much of rhythm and blues "are particularly sympathetic to connotations having to do with 'collectivism': they play down 'difference,' privilege the 'typical.'"[53] Similarly, Street points out that the practice in reggae of mixing the various voices and instruments so that no one voice or instrument is the sole focus carries with it a message of democracy: "Its politics lie as much in its collective character as in its radical lyrics."[54]

Of course, these extralyrical connotations are speculative. Perhaps the meaning listeners in the United States take from reggae's lack of a single lead is "don't worry, be happy, there's no clear direction to life, so just take things as they come." Perhaps they read repetition and the drone in the blues as the echo of the slave's life. It's not necessary to agree with the specific interpretations to accept the basic point: the *sound* of a piece may be a factor in message transmission and meaning construction. Some intriguing experimental evidence to support this comes from a study by St. Lawrence & Joyner, who found that listening to "heavy metal music, regardless of whether its lyrics were violent or Christian, caused undergraduate males to express somewhat more negative attitudes toward women."[55]

Such evidence, while far from definitive, resonates with our own experiences, as well as those of other activists, in social movement situations. For example, consider "Street Fighting Man," released by the Rolling Stones in 1968. A careful reading of the lyrics reveals what is apparently a rationalization for *not* becoming involved in "revolutionary" activities despite agreement that they are necessary ("But what can a poor boy do 'cept to sing for a rock 'n' roll band?/ 'Cause in sleepy London town there's just no place for a street fighting man"[56]). Musically, however, it sounds like a soundtrack for fighting in the streets. And, in fact, it was used in that way, one of the songs movement activists would listen to before going out on demonstrations and street actions. The rock critic Greil Marcus greeted the Beatles' "Revolution," released at the same time, in much the same way. Though the lyrics were decidedly cautious in the environment of the day (the song seemed to call for revolution but "when you talk about destruction, don't you know that you can count me out"),[57] Marcus noted,

> [T]here is freedom and movement in the music.... The radio executives ought to be more careful, those men that smugly program "Revolution" every hour in the hope that it will keep the kids off the streets. Those men like the "message," but there is a "message" in that music which is ultimately more powerful than anyone's words. The music doesn't say "cool it" or "don't fight the cops."[58]

The Power of Genres and Musical Codes

We've been arguing that the sound of music can underscore a lyrical message, or augment it, or, in some cases, actually become the meaning. But it isn't only our immediate experience of a piece—lyrics, instrumentation, sound, production values—that provides us with clues for meaning. If someone mentions to us that she heard a punk band last night, we *already* know it sounded angry. Genres and other musical codes and conventions provide frameworks that guide our interpretations of what we're hearing. Though formal training might teach us a great deal more about these, just living in a society (and in subcultures of a given society) turns us into experts of a sort about the musics found there and their codes. We know that punk means angry, or that a single performer singing to an acoustic guitar means folk, i.e., personal and "authentic." Without conscious effort we absorb musical conventions; these often are linked to whole genres that guide our understandings of the meaning of what we're hearing even more strongly. And, of course, the composer/performer is also well aware of these codes, and of the audience's knowledge of these conventions, and so creates accordingly.

Where do these codes come from, and how do they arise? Why does punk sound angry to us? Why does an acoustic guitar signal a minstrel speaking authentic truth? As with everything we encounter in our lives, there's a tendency to assume that how we receive and understand music is simply natural and universal: Loud music sounds angry, soft music is restful, and so forth. In the former Soviet Union, some conservative nationalists have adopted heavy metal music, mirroring one of its core audiences in the United States.[59] Does the form itself have such a strong *intrinsic* message that audiences in two distant lands adopt it for the same reasons?

There's some evidence for this point of view. Philip Tagg, though an opponent of this perspective, concedes that "'nobody yells jerky lullabies at breakneck speed,' just as 'nobody uses *legato* phrasing and soft or rounded timbres for hunting or war situations.'"[60] The neurologist Mark Jude Tramo notes that a marked use of octaves and fifths occurs in many cultures, and this may be "a consequence of the way that our ears and brains are built."[61] Some psychobiologists have even suggested this natural and universal understanding of music extends beyond humans to other species, a Platonic ideal of "a universal music awaiting discovery."[62] But many of these studies are themselves flawed by precisely that ego- and ethnocentric tendency to think that how one personally experiences music is universal.[63]

Tagg's work, as Frith points out, shows that even the "appropriate" sound of as common an emotion as grief varies widely from one society to the next, "and can only be explained ... in terms of social attitudes. In fact, as Tagg makes clear, there are very few universally understood aspects of musical expression, and these establish no more than extremely general types of [meaning]."[64] The meanings we take to be natural and universal, these musicologists argue, are neither, but are *social* constructions: musical forms and symbols created by humans at a particular time and place, modified through practice, and eventually used so often that they *seem* to be natural and eternal.

The punch line, then, for this perspective is that we understand meaning in music as part of a tradition we're taught—only rarely purposefully and consciously, but that we learn nonetheless. This seems a much more convincing explanation of the connection between meaning and music than some version of the biologically universal, but, of course, it immediately raises some basic questions: If these associations—slow equals grief; organ equals piety—aren't simply natural and intrinsic, how did they first arise? And then, how do we learn them?

Some musical meanings do seem fairly directly drawn from our extramusical lives. Composers may directly copy sounds they hear—say, a train whistle—and the listener will likely hear the result as "train" or perhaps "travel lust" or "wandering hobo," though already the likelihood of each declines as we move from connecting a sound to its imitated source to more abstract connections. Other meanings are not derived from "contour" (as Kivy calls this first connection), but are simply conventions fixed over time. For instance, the organ does not actually sound like prayer or any other form of religious activity commonly carried out in Western society. The equation of "organ" and "piety" is simply the result of the organ long being the instrument used in Christian services throughout Europe. Though we hear these associations as eternal or natural, they are quite clearly neither; it was the harp, not the organ, that was associated with religious subjects in the Middle Ages, a connotation we no longer recognize.[65] In India, the sarangi, a three-stringed bowed instrument central to North Indian art music, is always played when a figure of national importance dies, although, Qureshi notes, "the sound of the sarangi is not funereal."[66] The tradition instead dates to a decision in 1964 by Radio India to play 12 days of sarangi music in place of radio programming when Jawaharlal

Nehru died (perhaps because it already had other religious connotations because of its extensive use by yogis). Through that period of mourning the connection became made and accepted, and it is now replicated in similar situations.[67]

Musical expressions are also consciously worked out in some cases. Baroque composers, as we've mentioned, had a complex system of representations. Wagner had his own intricate system of representations in which musical themes and melodies stood for specific ideas or characters.[68] In Sergei Prokofiev's *Peter and the Wolf,* different instruments stand for different characters, much to children's delight.

But regardless of the origins of a connection, it is only by repeated use that it becomes accepted by (and assumes that "natural" appearance for) listeners. Theories of musical meaning grounded instead in universal, natural, or biological explanations assume use follows from intrinsic qualities: Funk music *is* sexy because it gets you gyrating, to use an example of Frith's. But the social construction perspective we're siding with here instead suggests that no connotations are inevitable from a given music, since association depends on actual experience, grounded in a specific time and place, and thus a specific culture. If, for some reason, funk music had been played for 12 days in place of all programming to commemorate the death of an important American political figure, it's possible that funk would be experienced after that as funeral music.

In short, just as we learn spoken languages, we learn musical languages; these include not only our strictly musical expectations (e.g., a piece will have the same beat in each measure), but also conventions that signify extramusical meanings. And just as we gain most of our spoken language skills through informal interactions, most people's musical knowledge is gained informally, even unconsciously. We don't need to know what the "tonic" is to expect a piece to end on that chord. We recognize when the scary music begins on the movie soundtrack that something frightening is about to happen without any necessary understanding of what musical relationships are required to produce that feeling. The social influence is so great that even the way we *hear* sounds has a social component. A Dutch friend was describing a harrowing sailing trip he had taken. At the height of the storm, he told us, the mast actually broke in two: *"Tchock!!!"* he said, describing the sound—a sound we North Americans would have described as "crack!" or "bang!"

Whatever their origins, those connotations then take on a seemingly natural independent existence, a meaning listeners in a given culture will generally recognize and respond to. They become, more or less, statements. These may be the kinds of individual musical "gestures" (to use Christopher Small's term) we've discussed above—the organ signaling piety; a bouncy melody signaling happiness—but they also include whole genres. American radicals of the 1940s and 1950s heard the music of various folk traditions as embodying dissent and protest:

> IRWIN SILBER: We felt folk music itself was a democratizing force, that it was a way of rejecting the commercial Tin Pan Alley culture and democratizing the culture.... [My specific interest] was the political content, but with folk music I could feel that it was the music as a whole that was an alternative, whether it was explicitly political or not.

In much the same way, musicians in countries struggling against colonization or the legacy of colonization have often used native folk music to signal a rejection of the colonial power's domination. The musicians of the *nueva canción* (new song) movement in Latin America—Victor Jara, Violeta Parra, the group Inti-Illimani, among others—consciously used traditional folk melodies and instruments to establish a cultural identity independent of U.S. and European domination. Though new lyrics were frequently written to reflect contemporary problems, traditional folk music forms were seen and heard *in and of themselves* as opposition to foreign culture—and thus foreign domination in general.[69]

In the United States, similar meanings have been attached to African-based musics. The blues and its derivatives, despite lyrical content that is only rarely openly political, have long carried a feeling of resistance, of "underground communication against the oppressor," as Gleason characterized it.[70] Much of the attraction of R&B and the emerging genre of rock and roll for white youth of the 1950s seemed to be precisely that this music belonged to a culture that was in a daily confrontation with the dominant society. To listen to "black" music was to state: "I'm looking for something different from the future being arranged for me." For blacks familiar with their cultural history, there was a more nuanced signification system, as different forms of black music conveyed different meanings. The "new Negroes" of the Harlem Renaissance of the 1920s, for instance, challenged the older generation represented by DuBois over what should be seen as "authentic" black music, preferring the modernity of urban blues to the sorrow songs of slavery that DuBois championed.[71]

The most commercially successful of the blues-derived musics—rock and roll—has carried with it that sense of rebellion from its birth, again, irrespective of the lyrical content of a particular song, and despite a musical form that was not particularly innovative. As Eyerman & Jamison write,

> The particular sense of a generation in revolt against an anonymous Establishment—a generation in search of authenticity, peace, and even collective love—continues to fuel rock music, even when it has become one of the most important industries in the world. The revolutionary quest for liberation may have become big business, but it nonetheless remains the core meaning, or sign, of rock music.[72]

Other popular genres have come to stand for other core values. Country music, from World War II through the 1960s and early 1970s, became increasingly associated with a conservative, anticountercultural, antirock message. While the lyrics of songs such as "Okie from Muskogee" could be pointedly antihippie,*[73] listening to the genre itself was probably much more important in defining oneself as opposed to the peaceniks. For many people, particularly those who don't listen to it, rap has come to represent a general meaning—young, ghetto, hostile to older, official white society—despite the huge diversity in lyrical messages. When the rapper/singer Ice-T was being pilloried for his highly controversial song "Cop Killer," he

---

*"We don't smoke marijuana in Muskogee ... We don't burn no draft cards down on Maın Street.... Like the hippies out ın San Francisco do." By Roy E. Burrıs & Merle R. Haggard, Tree Publishing 1969.

noted that although the record was actually recorded with a thrash metal band, opponents invariably described it as a rap album because "politically, they know by saying the word *rap* they can get a lot of people who think, 'Rap-black, rap-black-ghetto,' and don't like it."[74]

The equation of a genre with a particular social meaning or grouping is often reinforced—or even, in some cases, first created—by the music industry itself and how it frames the product it's trying to sell. "Folk," for instance, was a marketing category first created by the industry in the 1930s and 1940s to promote artists like Jimmie Rodgers and Woody Guthrie. This framing, despite its manufactured nature, helps to fix the equation between a form of music and its prime audience. Such attempts are not always successful, but when and where they are, they further the identification of the music with a particular grouping and its assumed values.

Genres thus point to a framework of meaning that many listeners will understand even before lyrics or other elements become clear, providing a *likely* framework for meaning to be adduced rather than providing detailed significance. Walser argues, genres "have the power to organize the exchange of meanings";[75] we'd move back a half-step from that. We think of genres, as we think of all the factors we've discussed and will discuss, as *pointers,* literally pointing toward certain meanings. The sound of an organ *points* to a meaning of piety. The sound of punk *points* to a meaning of dissatisfaction with current society. In Walser's view, genre is a far stronger pointer than other factors, laying the basic framework that guides audience interpretation. We'd say instead that the strength of each pointer varies according to many factors within each stage of our minstrel-audience process of transmission, context, and reception. Not only do these vary by artist, setting, audience member, and so forth, but they act on each other, increasing the importance of some pointers while decreasing the strength of others. We'll return to this after introducing other factors that play a role.

Before leaving genre, however, we want to underline one aspect that's particularly important for the music-movement link: Some genres embody meanings that can make them particularly available for transplanting into a movement context, as was the case in the early civil rights movement's use of music from the black church:

> GUY CARAWAN: [We were looking for] something that would inspire people. Sometimes demonstrations or working in this movement had its hard moments or alone periods, and people would be stuck in jail for a period of time. And also times when people came together at large meetings, they could sing and lift their spirits. And, of course, people already knew the power of music in the church.... You can't talk about just the words, you've got to talk about the style in which it's sung. Some of this stuff grew out of historical forms or ways that people already expressed themselves musically in church or gospel.

Since genres are often associated with a particular culture, the use of a genre by a *different* social group will often be seen as meaningful. Much of the "revolutionary" feel and impact of rock and roll in the 1950s (and much of the resistance to it) was based on the fact that white kids were embracing a form of music whose origins were mainly African American. That embrace, albeit ambiguous, for many signaled a rejection of social norms that had consigned black culture and bl. Americans to a second-class status. Adoption of rock—the music of the West—in Eastern Bloc countries during the cold war was often seen by government officials as a questioning of life under the Communist Party.[76]

Similarly, *mixing* genres can suggest meaning. As Britain experienced increasing racial tensions in the late 1970s, bands appeared who played hybrids of musical forms previously seen as belonging to a single group—punk for whites, ska and reggae for blacks. The resulting souped-up ska was widely understood by audiences to mean "we can get along, we can work together," even when the lyrics made no mention of such ideas.

Breaking with the conventions *within* a genre may also be meant and/or received as meaningful communication. Hanns Eisler, the revolutionary German composer, wrote that when the atonal music of his teacher Schoenberg "is heard in the concert halls of the bourgeoisie they are no longer charming and agreeable centers of pleasure where one is moved by one's own beauty, but places where one is forced to think about the chaos and ugliness of the world or else turn one's face away."[77] (This view of atonal music was shared by many on the Right: Hans Pfitzner, the renowned German composer and Nazi sympathizer, declared atonality "the musical equivalent of Bolshevism and 'Jewish Internationalism,' ... a 'symptom of decay,' the danger threatened of a poisoning of the people."[78]) Working within classical music and traditional stage musical forms, Eisler and his collaborator Bertolt Brecht deliberately twisted the conventions of those genres to allow their audience to look more closely at the assumptions contained within the forms, and thus the assumptions of conventional life.

Jazz, too, has communicated new worldviews through challenging musical conventions; Miller & Skipper argue, its aesthetic history is best understood as meaningful musical reactions to different stages in black-white relations in the United States. For instance, the emergence in the 1940s of bop—a hard-edged, dissonant-sounding variety pioneered by artists such as Charlie Parker and Dizzy Gillespie, considerably more difficult for the average listener to comprehend and the average jazz musician to play—illustrates the change in philosophy among many African Americans: "Acceptance *per se* was no longer a goal." Later variations went even further: "a forum for protest of the strongest kind—complete secession."[79]

If working within a genre presents a framework that is one factor in guiding a listener's (and artist's) interpretation of meaning, challenging those conventions may be an even more obvious pointer for message and meaning. Conventions, after all, come to sound so natural that we don't remark upon them. The breaking of convention encourages the listener (and the artist in the act of creation) to work harder, interpreting the unexpected as opposed to processing a work on autopilot. At a certain point, the bending and challenging of conventions may become so great that the music being produced no longer seems to fit within already known genres, and this too conveys meaning. Some theorists have suggested that *any* musical form that doesn't seem to fit within established genres is oppositional in a social and political sense as well as a musical sense, since it implies that things as they are now are not as they necessarily should or could be (hence Plato's warning about musical

se who champion experimental music as a political weapon make
ument: While conventional music forms "reproduce the *past*, ...
music] frame of mind is totally future-oriented; its sole intention
n attitude of open-minded, open-ended discovery—the *future*."[80]
we might add that the same is true for any form that breaks with accepted
notions of what music should sound like, whether it's the newness of serialism in
1923, the loudness of rock and roll in 1956, or the public "sharing" of rap on boom
boxes in 1987. In doing so, each carries an implicit critique of the here and now,
questioning the ubiquitous assumption that the present order is both natural and
inevitable. Not surprisingly, new, "foreign," and/or experimental forms are often
repressed or banned in totalitarian states since these forms imply dissent by their
very existence. Not only do such musics question the status quo, but they provide
an *alternative* center of meaning to the state for groups of people.

Genre's role in meaning—whether its conventions are met, challenged, twisted,
or broken—again reminds us of the most important point Adorno raises, the question of how much of the message and meaning of a piece is contained simply in its
form. But form is delivered by concrete instruments, and these too contribute to
the message(s) in the music.

The Sound of the Voice

When a song is sung, the voice not only delivers the lyrics, but contributes something to the message in its sound and texture. "It is not just what they sing, but
the way they sing it," says Frith. As a result, "songs are more like plays than poems."[81] This is another clue to the mystery of the stature of "Respect" as a feminist
anthem: Aretha Franklin's voice isn't the voice of the submissive female, asking for,
pleading for, hoping for something. The grain of the voice embodies self-respect,
and therefore *commands* respect.

The voice is commonly understood to be an instrument in jazz, but this can
also be said of most genres. One of the vocal styles that appears repeatedly in new
forms of rock is the disdainful snarl, which conveys a bundled message beyond
the specific words it delivers: "The world is messed up and stupid; you are not as
smart/moral/good as you should be (or I am); I don't have to do what you want
me to." Cock rock vocalists express a different set of messages through vocal
timbre: freedom, aggression, sexuality. All of soul music, Perris argues, could be
regarded as a form of protest music due to "the immense anguish that the Black
soul singer 'owns.'"[82]

The sound of the voice in rap is clearly a large part of its message: young, street,
usually black, usually male, confidently and assertively telling other people what
the world is really all about—this is much of what makes it attractive and empowering to young people (especially black males) and, conversely, annoying to
some other people, even when they have no idea what the words are to a particular
song—"Where does this guy get off telling *me* what the story is?" (It might be
instructive for parents who feel this way to listen to the tone of voice of, say, the

young Bob Dylan: similarly young and male, similarly full of confidence that he's fully entitled and able to tell others what the real story is.) In these cases, the voice conveys a message by *not* displaying the tone of polite deference that a nice young man might be expected (by his elders) to adopt.

For some listeners, the sound of the voice is more crucial to the overall meaning and evaluation of performance than any other single factor. It vividly indicates who the character is in the "play" being staged in the song; but further, it's frequently taken as a sign of the personality of the singer herself, a window into her inner self. Many singing styles are valued precisely because the singer has not stripped away idiosyncrasies in search of some "perfect" delivery, but displays them: "Here is the real me inside the song, revealing my essence." The elements of this "grain," as Roland Barthes called it,[83] the embodiment of the physicality of singing in the sound of the singing, become evidence of *authenticity,* a crucial sign of truth telling for many fans.

In musics that stress performance (as opposed to composition[84]) as the primary source of meaning and pleasure, authenticity has been particularly valued as important to message and meaning. But how can it be gauged? In many forms, both authenticity and true feeling are often "proven" by physical effort, as wonderfully captured by Frith, observing the video of the recording session for "We Are the World": "Watch how the singers compete to register the most sincerity; watch Bruce Springsteen win as he gets his brief line; veins pop up on his head and the sweat flows down."[85]

But there is a contradiction in this, as summed up in soul giant James Brown's proclaimed title, "The Hardest-Working Man in Show Business." It *is* show business—even when nonprofessionals perform, entertainment of a sort—and therefore there is always some element of previous practice, of working on the material, that makes performance not altogether spontaneously authentic. The rock critic Greil Marcus once said that he judged a vocal by whether it sounded like it was the last time that singer was ever going to get a chance to sing it.[86] *Sounded like,* since clearly it wasn't really the last time. If the singer didn't like that take, she'd try another. On the road, that last time would come again tomorrow night, and the night after that, and the night after that. As Public Enemy's Chuck D raps in a moment of great candor:

> ... why is this verse coming six times rehearsed?
> I don't freestyle much, but I write 'em like such.[87]

Frith and others have argued that authenticity, at least for professional musicians, is *always* a myth to some extent. The genre distinction often drawn between rock's emphasis on authenticity and pop's emphasis on entertainment with little interest in the question of authenticity is really only one of style. Rock stresses *the illusion* of authenticity, while pop stresses *the illusion* of glamour. Rock stars sweat, while pop stars smile coolly behind their sunglasses, but both are just following a script.

And yet, even most of those with this somewhat cynical view seem to acknowledge moments when there is true—or truer—authenticity. Descriptions of these moments typically assume a different criterion for authenticity, one that doesn't stress artistic spontaneity or the sound of the voice, but the extent to which performers are representative of their audiences, indeed *part* of their audiences. This is most likely, of course, when music making is truly "folk" as we've been defining it: generated from a community and meant for consumption by that community. The musicians may even be professionals, getting paid for their work, but they are nonetheless truly part of that community. Folk in Greenwich Village in the early 1960s, rap in the South Bronx in the 1970s and early 1980s, grunge in the Pacific Northwest in the late 1980s—these are all examples of when there was little gap between artist and audience, when artists were (or seemed to be) conduits of community opinions rather than opinion leaders themselves.

> Q: Can music help move people to new ideas, to new ways of seeing things? That seems to be part of what you're interested in.
> QUETZAL FLORES: I think people are moving *us* to new ideas. We're documenting or mirroring what's happening, and we're also involved in what's happening on that level, so we're able to write about our experiences being involved.... Inspiration comes from the work, and then we put it out there and people get to see themselves in our work.

Performance

Performance, then, whether professional or casual, is another pointer for meaning. Bruce Springsteen's physical exertion through marathon concerts serves as a sign that he is authentically working-class (despite his wealth), that he is one of us, and that being working-class is a source of pride. For Cantwell, performance gives meaning to the music *for the performer*; in the folk song revival of the 1950s and early 1960s, nonprofessional folksingers reinvented themselves by mastering music from another time, place, and group.[88]

The very act of public performance can suggest meaning. Tricia Rose's important writings on hip-hop have emphasized that important part of its politics has been the visibility of groups normally excluded from certain public places.[89] The young rap fan blasting hip-hop from a boom box in the subway is asserting an important message beyond any explicit lyrical phrase: "My culture is important, I am important, I will not be silenced!" Within the world of hip-hop, the performance of women rappers can be understood similarly: Their mere presence onstage as the dominant performer says to both male and female fans, "Women can run the show."

The riot grrrl bands that arose in the Pacific Northwest in the early 1990s had a similar effect on audiences, shocking and liberating by showcasing an openness and rage that had been seemingly circumscribed by traditional notions of femininity and the conventions of public behavior for women performers. Corin Tucker, later guitarist in Sleater-Kinney, describes going to one of the early performances of Bikini Kill, the seminal riot grrrl act, at the age of 18:

> It was Feb. 14, 1991. And Kathleen Hanna was ... terrifying. People were just freaking out.... She was so powerful. People were crying.... For young women to

be doing that, basically *teenagers on stage,* to be taking that kind of stance, that kind of power, was blowing people's minds. And it totally blew my mind.[90]

In performance, as in other aspects of a music, meeting genre expectations or breaking them can convey fairly explicit propositional messages. The resistance to Elvis Presley was based more than anything else on his presentation, which conveyed two points fairly clearly: Black cultural styles are worthy of imitation, and sexuality is good. The heavy metal guitarist, male, long-haired, dressed in black leather with plenty of metal studs, handling his guitar strapped just below waist level, is sending a fairly unambiguous message central to the genre: "I am a *dude!*" As with mixing genres of music, messages can be sent by mixing, and thus confounding, visual expectations. When punk and ska bands began appearing together in the Rock Against Racism shows meant to challenge racism in Britain in the 1980s, the message of racial harmony was made most strongly, given the atmosphere of those times, just by presenting black and white bands on the same bill and, most strikingly, by the visual impact of the "2-Tone" multiracial bands. When public performances are framed by explicit political agendas, performance becomes a statement simply through the fact of an artist's presence. When Springsteen showed up at the MUSE (Musicians United for Safe Energy) megaconcert in 1979, it was his appearance at an avowedly antinuclear energy concert that displayed his political stance; the music he played was no different from any Springsteen concert of the time.

What happens *within* the performance, of course, may also convey messages and suggest meanings. Beyond the sound we've already discussed, expressed instrumentally and in the timbre of the voice, there are visual cues and statements, beginning with the appearance of the performers. The skin-revealing outfits of pop singer Britney Spears suggest interpretations of her music that have to do with conventional notions of female sexuality, while Melissa Etheridge's onstage dress, closer to Springsteen than to Spears, suggests that her music might be understood in ways that call into question conventional assumptions of female sexuality and heterosexuality in general. Trinidadian calypso singer David Rudder's refusal to wear the traditional fancy stage clothes that calypso singers wore was meant and interpreted, he felt, as "a sign that the people are fed up with the old order of things. So it could be seen as a political threat."[91] Grooming, hairstyles, cross-dressing, etc., illustrate the manifold ways that performers routinely manipulate their appearance, framing meaning construction.

Visual clues also include body language. Here again, different genres have different conventions of what is normal movement onstage. Bluegrass bands gather around one microphone to sing the chorus together, in line with bluegrass's traditional themes of the importance of kith and kin. In classic rock bands, bass players signify their traditional role as the heartbeat of the band—steady, essential, but not showy—by barely moving. In a fascinating study, Groce & Lynxweilier showed college students videotaped recordings of three local bands without soundtracks. Students were able to discern which bands played Top 40 music versus which played original alternative music purely based on visual clues.[92]

Aside from the way performers play, look, or situate themselves, audience members may construct meaning from what they say and how they act. Performers' patter between pieces sends messages about a wide range of topics, framing the reception of the music and/or making declarations independent of any specific piece being performed.[93] The way a band interacts with the audience also sends a message about their take on the nature of the performer-audience relationship.[94]

We've been stressing live performance, although most of us experience music most of the time in far more private settings, typically at home or in the car, listening by ourselves or with a small group of people. Even when we create music ourselves, it tends to be a private affair—singing to ourselves, playing on the fire escape, jamming with a friend. Yet the live, shared experience still seems central to our understanding of music. Much of the history of recording, in fact, has involved successive attempts to make recorded music sound and feel more like live music.[95] And particularly for the politically relevant music we're most concerned with, as we'll further explore in the following chapters, the collective experience of live musicking seems crucially important.

The Performer's Image

A key message in all live or recorded performances is the projection and reception of a performer's persona or image. Who we believe the performer to be is a powerful pointer for meaning. Image is established in many ways (not all, of course, in live performance). The way performers look, we've suggested, offers a first clue. The flamboyant clothes of some performers is intended to send the message "I'm different, I'm special." The workaday laborers' overalls and work shirt worn by the Almanac Singers was meant to say: "We're laborers too. We're just like you." (Ironically, some working-class audiences resented their dress, adhering instead to the belief that entertainment should create a special world removed from workaday life, and thus entertainers should be "dressed up."[96]) Body language speaks: Aretha Franklin's title of "Queen of Soul" extends beyond her voice to her entire regal bearing. This, too, affects how we interpret "Respect" when sung by such a person.

As in a play, a performer's props also signify. Particular instruments send a visual as well as an aural message of what an artist is about, based on previous uses and historical connections. In Latin American folk and popular culture, the guitar appears "as an icon of pathos, protest, and despair"[97]; in China in the 1980s, the electric guitar was seen as the symbol of Western freedom or decadence (depending on one's perspective). English singer/songwriter Billy Bragg stands onstage, alone, carrying just a guitar, tying him to the folk protest tradition of Woody Guthrie and (the early) Bob Dylan, but the guitar is electric, tying him (quite consciously) to the political punk of the Clash, the band that first inspired him.

Beyond the visual impact of appearance and props, artists' images are based on their reputations, established by a range of factors. Yogis, as religious personages, carry a reputation for spirituality that informs the listener's understanding of the music they perform; Ani DiFranco's reputation as a modern-day folk/punk minstrel who has refused to cooperate with the major record labels frames the meanings audiences construct of her message.[98] Image—built through the actions of musicians, the conscious machinations of publicity machines, the active imaginations of fans, or other factors—may, in fact, become the most important factor in constructing meaning in some cases. Elvis Presley as persona became a symbol of something new to young people, particularly young, working- and middle-class white people, a rejection of the *Ozzie and Harriet* futures they were supposed to be striving to attain.

Wayne Hampton's fascinating study, *Guerilla Minstrels,* argues that the greatest importance of political troubadours lies in their service as "totalizing agents" who serve as the embodiment of the movement, "the reification of the identities of those he represents, but ... also a model or ideal for the followers to emulate."[99] While it is conventional wisdom that we love our artists as well as their art, Hampton argues that what we see in our guerilla minstrel heroes is what we want to see in ourselves, and often what we need to find in ourselves in order for our movements to work. We worship in them the very characteristics we assume are necessary to bring about a vision that—we believe—we share with our minstrel and with all others who likewise love the minstrel.

In popular music, at least, the preoccupation with the performer has led some to suggest that the "primary text" audiences read is the performer, not the performance or the material performed. In many versions of this view, the impetus behind this emphasis is simple: "[E]verything in music—records, videos, performance, artist identity (image)—are [sic] all codified for one common purpose: consumption."[100] In the Adornian tradition, this is seen as thereby trivializing popular music and its trappings, and rendering any messages or meanings impotent, lost in the great wash of mindless consumption. But others suggest that the messages sent and the meanings received through performers' images may be powerful and effective in many ways despite the trappings. No artist has been so prominent in such analyses in recent years as the pop star Madonna, who suddenly became the topic of a spate of academic treatments in the late 1980s and early 1990s. Few argued that her lyrics or music contained profound messages, but her *image,* many argued, had a profound message that was enthusiastically embraced by young girls, a message of self-definition—of her musical product, of her sexuality, of being in charge of her life in general—that taught adolescent girls as much about feminism as any lyric ever could.[101]

Those who study communication have long argued that the impact of a message is highly dependent on what the receiver already thinks about the sender. Here we go further: The sender *is* the message as well as the bearer of the message, the product as well as the bearer of the product. As such, much care may be given to presentation. While some elements are not premeditated, most aspects of a professional performer's image are now carefully cultivated, and often constructed by industry professionals. In the early days of pop music celebrity, this included things like liner photos on albums or careful control of what one said in interviews. In recent years, music videos have been the overwhelming weapon of image construction.

The Role of Videos

Christenson & Roberts assert that available experimental research "shows unequivo-cally that exposure to music videos affects how teenagers and college undergraduates perceive, interpret, evaluate, and respond to a variety of social stimuli."[102] We're not willing to say the evidence is "unequivocal," but there's certainly enough evi-dence to strongly suggest that video viewing can be an important component of meaning construction.[103]

When marketing videos first became widely used by the music industry in the 1970s,[104] many critics feared their effect on audiences. Control of visual interpreta-tions of the music, they said, reduced the viewer's capacity for interpretation, an Adornian nightmare. (Of course, until not much more than a hundred years ago, audiences *always* had a visual image supplied with their music because all music was live; it was the advent of recorded music that, in a sense, broke that more "authentic" link between music and a performer-supplied image.) For others, the danger was not the imposition of a predetermined meaning through the visual link but the lack of conventional meaning characteristic of the postmodern style of most videos, the "substitution of *referential density* for *narrative coherence*," in Dick Hebdige's wonderful phrase, "a form designed to 'tell an image' rather than to 'tell a story.'"[105]

In the view of those who lacked Hebdige's enthusiasm for this shift, replacing the narratives (and thus, presumably, the messages) embodied in songs with free-floating images meant videos lacked any coherent meaning that was more than idiosyncratic to the individual listener/viewer. Their very style—"surface flash of images and rapid movement to the next more tantalizing or ecstatic scene"[106]—seemed incom-patible with conscious reflection. The kind of shared meaning envisioned by, say, Hampton's audience listening to a guerilla minstrel, seemed impossible to sustain.

The fears (or conversely, some Postmodernists' hopes) embodied in this critique now seem overblown. Christenson & Roberts's own summary of the available data suggests

> that most adolescents take music videos far less seriously than do either the music industry or its critics. Music video viewing commands much less time than either music listening or television viewing, and the time expenditure seems motivated less by a quest for deep involvement than a need for transitory, light diversion. For most adolescents, [video channels are] just a way station in the process of remote control grazing.[107]

The degree to which videos fracture and balkanize artists' messages (and thus audience meaning) may also be exaggerated. Despite the postmodern style of some well-known vidoes, most reflect the lyrical and musical messages of their song subjects, rather than disrupting those meanings or suggesting new meanings.[108] Even videos that offer a "postmodern" visual aesthetic seem to key their referential images to the propositional messages of the hook lines of the songs they promote. "[T]he *music* in music videos is largely responsible for the narrative continuity and the affective quality in the resultant work, even if it is the visual images we remember concretely," says McClary,[109] and this, too, is the final summation by

Christenson & Roberts: "One thing is clear ... : music, not music videos, is the heavy equipment of adolescent living."[110]

Comforting as all these reconsiderations of the power of videos may be to Adornian critics and the parents of teenagers, it's important to note that they all rest on a shared assumption: that impact and meaning depend on conscious reflection. Thus, if a teenager (or anyone else) isn't paying much attention to a video, or doesn't spend much time thinking about it, or doesn't even have time to reflect on any image because of the speed with which video images change, the conscious or unconscious messages of a video are not being received. But we don't yet have enough evidence to say that. Casual, unconscious, or fragmented attention to a video or anything else may in fact have a profound impact, though conventional assumptions emphasizing the importance of rational contemplation might lead us to overlook or minimize these. Meaning for the viewer may not come from conscious reflection, but from a general feel to a piece or a performer. And, of course, for some people, video viewing isn't casual or sporadic, but a central activity.

Other Media

Videos, live performances, the look of the performer, and so forth, are all visual sources of potential messages coming from the artist. Other extramusical sources of meaning and interpretation are even further removed from the central act of music making, and closer to traditional printed forms for conveying a message. Especially in modern times, music makers are likely to appear in the media as subjects of reporting, interviews, and so on. Through these, musicians further influence how an audience might interpret a given piece. For some artists this is an unplanned side effect of the necessary job of promoting the product, with sales as the objective and the message irrelevant, distracting, or simply a means to that end. Interviewers, too, are less likely to be interested in messages than in questions of style, gossip, and so on. But for some artists, particularly those with explicit political agendas, it can be a deliberately used tool:

> Q: Is it important to you that the people listening understand the song as you meant it, or are you just throwing it out there and you let them take it where they want?
>
> CHUCK D: Well, one thing that's helped ... is being able to articulate it and decipher it in the interview. When people ask me what did I think about the song when I wrote it, I give my description and that has to be taken into consideration [by listeners] too.... The interviews have helped me get a point across as opposed to just the song itself.... Just like if somebody looked at a Picasso painting and they're going to have their own take on it. Picasso's explanation might clarify things.

Other printed forms originating with the artist may play a role as well: Liner notes and photos establish a more or less explicit background for the music. In recent years, some politically concerned groups have gone so far as to direct fans to political groups and readings they thought important, linking the artists' message with "social consciousness" in general and those groups and readings in particular. Artists' web pages similarly may publicize and/or link to websites of activist groups.

The digital revolution has widened the avenues of direct communication between artists and fans enormously. Aside from record company websites, artists typically have their own websites as well as pages on popular social networks like MySpace, allowing them to speak directly to their fans. Such sites are sources of links, commentary, journal notes, and direct responses to fans' questions, as well as musical samples. (Artists' sites and pages also typically include posting boards where fans carry on discussions independent of the artist. These and other fan and participant online communities are discussed in Chapters 3 and 4.) Artists' blogs and Twitter "tweets" further allow the fan some kind of access into the artist's perspective. YouTube and other video-oriented sites allow artists (and others) to present visual images to fans that also frame the construction of meaning of any particular piece of music. The mediated relationship between fan and artist, as we discuss in later chapters, is increasingly replaced by a more direct (or what is presented as a more direct) relationship.

In this chapter we've reviewed a wide variety of possible elements in a performer's content, each of which may express or help express a message and contribute to an audience member's constructed meaning. In doing so, we hope, we've also illustrated the absurdity of the L = ARM (lyrics equal audience received message) equation. Artistic transmission is very complex, drawing from a wide range of factors. Lyrics are only one part of the content transmitted, and content isn't necessarily synonymous with a performer's intended message—assuming she even has a message she wishes to convey.

The performer, further, is only one part of the minstrel-audience relation. We turn now to other factors that affect the eventual construction of meaning.

♪

Chapter 3 •

Context

In the last chapter we illustrated how the meaning attached to music is in part a result of an artist/performer's content; in the next chapter we'll consider the role of the audience. But perhaps less obviously, the eventual meaning constructed is also affected by a host of factors that come between performer and audience (given, still, the minstrel-audience model) in what we're calling *context*. If we've broadened our understanding of "text" beyond lyrics to include music, sound, performance, and performer persona, we need to appreciate also the way in which that broader text is always "read" in a specific time and place, and under specific conditions. This context may support, amplify, distort, color, or negate any message—intended or unintended—sent by the performer's total content.

The Music Industry

The most important of these intervening factors for many forms of music is the amalgamation of people who produce, package, and sell music, commonly referred to as the music industry. Their organized presence and effect lie at the heart of the distinction we've drawn between *folk* music and *pop* music. Folk music is created within and presented to relatively homogenous, relatively self-contained communities, by people who usually differ in no significant way from their audiences in their daily lives. Pop, on the other hand, is created from the beginning as a commodity, something to be sold on the market to a wide, diverse audience; success is defined by "star power," i.e., being *different* from those in the audience. Note that *folk* and *pop* as we use them here are not genres but terms that define contrasting relationships between musician and audience. The commercial genre "folk music," as exemplified by people like Joan Baez or Bob Dylan, or even Woody Guthrie, is in this sense less folk than pop, since it's produced for a market. Conversely, hip-hop of the late 1970s would be defined as a folk music, generated within a community to be used within that community.

The difference between folk and pop turns out to be less clear-cut than this in practice. Bob Dylan releases "Blowing in the Wind" on an LP record produced and distributed by a major record company. Peter, Paul and Mary record it in a more accessible form and release it as a single, also on a major label, and it becomes a hit. Yet 40 years later, people gather in their living rooms or at a mass rally and sing the song, changing the words perhaps, or the melody, as suits them. Many have never heard the original recorded versions; the song has been adopted by "the people," its authorship now irrelevant if not anonymous. Has it become a folk song? Conversely, "In the Pines," a blues song of (now) uncertain origins, is adapted, performed, and recorded by Lead Belly, the great blues singer of the 1930s and 1940s, and thus made commercially available. By the 1960s it has passed into general knowledge among folkies and blues lovers, often disconnected from both its historical origins and its commodity form as a Lead Belly recording. But in 1994, the alternative rock group Nirvana records it on their *Unplugged* album, and it's again sold to a record-buying public.[1] Despite such ambiguities, however, the *distinction* between folk and pop remains important because it highlights the fact that pop music, the main (though by no means the only) source of music for most people in most industrialized countries today,[2] reaches us through the intermediary of an *industry*.[3]

When we speak of a music industry, we're discussing a huge colossus (albeit besieged, as we'll discuss below), a $12 billion industry in the United States at the turn of the twenty-first century, and over $60 billion worldwide midway through the next decade.[4] Aside from those directly involved in the creation of the music—artists, producers, studio musicians, and so forth—there are hundreds of thousands of people involved in the physical manufacturing of the product; its merchandising, promotion, and sale; and the discovery and care of the artists involved. Beyond those directly employed by the recording companies are many more working for an array of related industries: concert promotion, TV and radio, newspapers and magazines, and so forth. Many of these potentially have some effect on what a piece of music means to a listener.

One of the ongoing debates in the world of music scholarship concerns the role the industry plays in bringing music to the customer. Some argue that, in classic market fashion, the industry simply gives customers what they want, driven by competition to respond as well as possible to consumer demand. In a famous piece written in 1968, H. F. Mooney suggested that it was possible to read consumers' changing characteristics and taste from the 1920s to the 1960s by looking at how lyrics to popular songs had changed over that period,[5] presumably in response to what listeners wanted to hear. But others countered that this kind of interpretation missed the way the industry and its structure determine what's available for consumers to "want." Peterson & Berger declared that explanations of changes in lyrical content of popular music that only looked at "public consciousness" were insufficient; also crucial were changes in the structure of the industry and the available technology.[6] In work produced in the mid-1970s they argued that innovative and radical music (in all senses, not just the political sense we're most interested in) is always being created; what changes is how likely consumers are to hear it. This, they wrote, is largely the result of a cyclical pattern in the music industry: The market is dominated by a handful of very large companies; small, independent companies—"the indies"—appear in nooks and crannies, producing music that appeals to limited niche audiences. At some point the larger "majors" notice the most commercially promising of these musics—rock, reggae, and rap are all examples—and buy up the most important labels and talents in the field, adding these to their own stables.

In the process, however, the majors dilute and homogenize the new music because the amount of money they spend on producing and promoting acts requires much larger sales than the indies needed, crossing over from niche to mainstream. Reggae artists, for example, needed to "tone down" their Jamaican patois so that audiences in the United States could easily understand the lyrics. Thus, the music moves from a more or less folk status when first nurtured by the indies, aimed at a community—be it geographic, ethnic, political, or some other—to a pop status aimed at as large an audience as possible. As the majors, with their overwhelming resources, add a particular genre to their catalogue, the original indies are largely driven out of business or absorbed. This homogenization eventually leads to another cycle of development of new musical niches, the growth of new indies, their notice and eventual purchase by the majors, and so on.[7]

In their analyses of markets, economists have debated whether innovation and creativity are more likely in situations of competition (which spurs innovation as a way to gain a greater market share) or oligopoly (in which relative freedom from economic pressures allows room for innovations that may or may not pan out).[8] Most analysts of the music industry, like Peterson & Berger, have assumed the former: New and different music is nurtured by the indies, while periods of domination by the majors lead to stagnation and homogenization.[9] As Street observes, the majors seek "to ensure a constant supply of recognizably similar musicians and music, appealing to the same kind of audience and sold in much the same way. Anything that disrupts this pattern is relatively costly, presenting new types of sales, promotion, distribution, and packaging problems."[10] The archetypal story of this: In the early 1960s the U.S. division of Capitol Records initially refused to release the Beatles' recordings "because their music deviated from the corporate model of mainstream musical products" of the time.[11]

Developments in the record industry in the 1980s and 1990s altered this dynamic, but did not fundamentally change it.[12] The majors became less likely to buy up indies and/or their personnel, and more likely to enter into marketing and distribution arrangements (with both semiautonomous labels, which are actually divisions of the major, or with truly independent labels) in which a major becomes the distributor of an indie's products, using its contacts and economic muscle to get an album carried and heard in places a small indie would never be able to reach. Indies in this sense act as agents of innovation, finding and nurturing new sounds that are then brought to a greater market by the majors. Since the actual recording remains under the control of the indie, it might be assumed the dangers of homogenization and dilution Peterson & Berger warned of are no longer a problem, but the selection of which independently produced albums deserve serious support by the major still rests on determinations of how broadly an album can be sold. It would be naïve to think that indie executives and artists are unaware that their chances of being picked up and distributed by a major depend in some significant way on the majors' evaluation of their potential for crossover. The compromises, then, may be made in an earlier stage by an artist, her management, and/or the indie label, in anticipation of what may lead to the big payoff: a distribution deal with a major. Of course, there are exceptions where an innovative artist or music is supported by the major label, betting that this is the Next Big Thing, but these remain the exceptions in a much more common strategy of going with the familiar. According to this "production of culture" perspective, popular music is by and large shaped at each stage of the process by the shared assumptions and conventions of what will get it to the next stage—that is, what will be thought by those at the next level of the industry to be potentially commercially successful.

The same kind of institutional conservatism operates in the mass media, most obviously in radio. Here the basic job of a station is to deliver a selected demographic audience (males 18–34; World War II era, etc.) to advertisers, achieved through the standard practice of "negative programming," that is, *not playing* any record that seems too different from the station's normal fare. The point is not to excite audiences "but rather by not offending them ... [to] never give them a sufficiently strong reason to turn off."[13] Negus points out that there are parallel forces now operating in megastore chains, such as Wal-Mart, Target, and Best Buy: "Megastore retailers have influenced record company catalogues by restricting space for newer and less easily classifiable music (sounds that a retail buyer assumes will sit on the shelf for long periods before being purchased)."[14] Since megastores account for an increasing share of the retail market—over half of CDs sold, for example[15]—their power to affect the thinking of record executives about what music and musicians are worth supporting naturally increases, if not in a directly conspiratorial fashion. In recent years the policy of Wal-Mart (which sells about 20 percent of albums in the United States) to refuse to stock albums requiring parental advisory warning labels, as well as others with "objectionable" content, has led record companies to engage in self-censorship: "Record labels are now acting preemptively, issuing two versions of the same album for their big name artists. Less well-known bands, however, are forced to offer 'sanitized' albums out of the gate."[16] While some stores and stations may approach these decisions from an ideological perspective, industry practices are not, by and large, ideologically driven but simply based on bottom-line assessments. If and when "radical" music appears to be commercially viable—as in the late 1960s, for example—the industry will provide that product, but such moments are rare. Finding the Next Big Thing is a powerful lure, but pushing whatever is already known to appeal to the widest audience breeds commercial success far more often. "Crossovers" are the heart and soul of the industry, the cash cows that pay the bills. The soundtrack to *Around the World in 80 Days* outsold Elvis in 1957; the soundtrack to *The Sound of Music* outsold the Beatles in 1965. Sales of the Backstreet Boys' albums dwarfed those of the leading artists and innovators within more narrowly defined musical niches (e.g., Bob Dylan, Public Enemy).

These tendencies toward conservatism have been greatly reinforced by the wave of concentration and consolidation that has swept the music and communication industries in the past 15 years. Since the passage of the 1996 Telecommunications Act (which eliminated caps on radio station ownership and increased the number of stations a company could own in any given market), just 10 parent companies have come to own radio stations with two-thirds of all listeners.[17] Clear Channel alone went from owning 43 stations before the act was passed to over 1,200 in 2001, eventually owning over a quarter of all the stations in the country.[18] In that year, by one estimate, 30,000 CDs were released in the United States, containing about 360,000 cuts; *Rolling Stone* reported, "In one recent week the 40 top modern-rock stations added a total of 16 new songs, and the biggest 45 Top Forty stations added a total of 20."[19] The major record companies, too, have experienced consolidation: By 2004, the "Big 6" of the 1980s had been winnowed down to the "Big 4" of EMI, Sony/BMG, Universal, and WEA, often existing as "small subsidiaries of huge [diversified] corporations" and thus "even more risk-averse than ever."[20]

The industry affects what we hear, but also, less obviously, *how* we hear it, and thus may affect what meaning we give to it. Adorno's argument that the form of popular music conveys a message of conformity and uncritical affirmation of the status quo can be extended from the music itself to its presentation in the media, where it is mixed in with, and often virtually indistinguishable from, commercial advertising. Video television stations are the epitome of this, commercials breaking up a string of music promotional videos—which are commercials for music. In such settings, many have argued, *all* music is robbed of any meaning other than its status as a commodity.

It isn't necessary to adopt this critique whole cloth to agree that audiences' constructions of meaning are shaped by the way music is filtered and framed for delivery to consumers. Radio, for instance, especially in the modern era's extremely fragmented market, imposes strict genre segregation, telling us which music "goes" with which. The stations' need to package themselves primarily to advertisers rather than to consumers necessitates the use of negative programming, organizing their playlists around distinctions they feel relevant—genre, gender, race, lifestyle—and these thereby become part of the meanings audience members themselves attach to the music.[21]

The upshot of all this, according to many critics, is the inevitable corruption of radical music (or artistic creativity of any significant kind), which is twisted and bent to sell it to particular audiences. While the familiar criticism in this vein is that mainstreaming requires a dilution and "whitening" of edgy and unfamiliar sounds (as in 1950s covers of R&B hits by white pop singers), the opposite may sometimes be true: "[G]ospel and R&B and doo-wop were *blacked-up*. Thanks to rock 'n' roll, black performers now reached a white audience, but only if they met 'the tests of blackness'—that they embody sensuality, spontaneity, and gritty soulfulness.'"[22] Similarly some have argued that rap, far from being "whitened" when picked up by the majors, was pushed in the direction of greater pseudoauthenticity, particularly in the emphasis on gangster rap.[23] Reggae's politics weren't toned down when the majors moved in during the 1970s, but diction, sound, and packaging were all changed in the service of sales: "[R]ather than an indigenous music of Jamaica's poor and oppressed, 'international reggae' was sold more as a new brand of rock and roll."[24] What's common to all of these seemingly divergent outcomes is that the product is tailored according to industry notions of what will sell to the widest group of people who might conceivably buy it.

Musicians themselves may engage in this kind of calculated modification of their work, consciously trying to achieve commercial success—the dreaded "selling out." While doubtless some of this is fueled by desire for fame and fortune, some of it merely reflects the economics of the industry. Most bands are in deep debt to their record companies, at least until they produce a (fairly rare) second commercially successful album, and so their continued ability to record, tour, make videos, and so forth depends on pleasing their record labels.[25]

A good deal of this is also less conscious and less cynical: Musicians assimilate the expectations of the world around them, as we all do. In the early part of the twentieth century, rural blues musicians wrote and played both "lyrical" blues—the form we're familiar with today—and "narrative" blues, a much longer, story-driven form. The virtual demise of the narrative blues largely came about because the form was generally too long to be recorded on the primitive technology of the day, 78 rpm records, with their time constraints. Aspiring blues musicians, ears cocked to the new technology of phonograph machines and jukeboxes, stopped hearing narrative blues very often.[26] Two decades later, Craddock-Willis argues, electrified R&B took on its distinctive sound in part because "black people were now being influenced by radio, which was playing mostly white artists. The synthesis of the two modes of expression, white and black, would influence the future musical expression of both parties."[27] Such notions of creative synthesis, however, are dismissed by those who see the "commercialization" of a specific group's authentic cultural expression as a form of theft, including co-optation of the original music's oppositional image as the culture of underdogs, outsiders, or rebels.[28]

Finally, and most troubling in this line of reasoning, the ultimate result of the popularization of a crossover or copy version of the music is that it may ultimately wipe out the original music and musical scene on which it was patterned. In Peterson & Berger's original conception, indies producing the "real stuff" were commercially drowned by the majors, who not only could afford to buy the indies or hire away the best talent (who then were pressured to produce less authentic versions that could be sold to the mainstream), but took over the marketplace of that genre through their superior economic and institutional advantages, robbing the indie of even its niche audience. In Wallis & Malm's seminal writing on "world music," the danger is less one of competition than imitation: Indigenous street musicians hear their own genre played back to them on the radio in a diluted, mainstream-friendly version, and begin to imitate it, forsaking the original form.[29] At the same time, this mainstream version, "transplanted and torn from its traditional meaning context . . . loses its social effectiveness, though it may continue to diffuse internationally as a popular form."[30] Much the same thing happened within our national borders: The development of an American popular culture at the end of the nineteenth century borrowed heavily from older native and ethnic traditions but contributed to their demise as well. True, it frequently spoke a language working-class audiences understood. Yet it was a purchased form of entertainment that nonetheless left many previous vital traditions and practices—those that had shaped the ideas, values, institutions, and goals of workers for decades—by the wayside.... An industry of no small size had stepped forth to meet cultural and social needs once the preserve of workers and their neighborhood and community institutions and organizations.[31]

Similarly, Nelson George argues that the drive for crossover success in the 1970s effectively "killed" R&B that had authentically represented black cultural traditions.[32]

A Competing View of the Industry's Effects

Until the 1970s, as Lipsitz notes, "the best popular music criticism of this era tended to assume that commercial culture and mass media could only dilute and destroy the strengths of traditional forms of music."[33] Yet it's not clear that the development of a culture industry has been unequivocally damaging to the music. There are many examples of commercialization *aiding* the preservation and/or development of a music, for example, in providing the money that allowed some early jazz pioneers to give up their day jobs, allowing them to devote their time and energy to developing their art. Lipsitz points out that it was precisely the availability of a variety of musical traditions accessible through commercial radio that led young Mexican Americans to develop the rich hybrid musical form known as Chicano rock.[34] The music of U.S. soul giant James Brown and that of the Nigerian Afrobeat pioneer Fela were mutually enhanced because each was able to hear commercially made recordings of the other and incorporate aspects of what he was hearing into his own work.[35] Even the success of Elvis Presley—often presented as the archetype of an authentic (black) music being ripped off and then diluted to cater to a mainstream audience—"assaulted some of the 'standards' and conventions of popular music that served to exclude black styles" and thus "open[ed] up opportunities for both black and white musicians—though, of course, not on an equal basis."[36]

The lines between folk and pop, organic and synthetic, authentic and commercial are thus thin and porous. The commercial music of one era is transformed into the folk music of a later generation, its origins largely forgotten, and its form, words, and melody transformed through use; the folk music of an era is reworked into commercial material for another. Interest in a folk tradition is itself often the result of commercial recordings that make it available to those both within and outside the local group. The "folk revival" of the 1950s and 1960s in the United States became a mass cultural movement in the wake of the commercial success of the Kingston Trio's recording of "Tom Dooley," a pop recording of an old folk song; one result was that the sale of guitars skyrocketed[37] as millions of people began singing to and with their circle of friends—that is, becoming folk musicians.

As these examples illustrate, no single impact of the music industry is inevitable.[38] At times structural rearrangements within the industry may allow a music to be heard that might not be otherwise, as Peterson & Berger first argued; once it's heard, however, consumers and musicians may be spurred by their positive view of the new sounds to demand and produce more of the same, as in the market vision of Mooney. Concentration of production may typically produce homogeneity, but there are many exceptions. The industry, it's important to remember, isn't monolithic, but comprises a wide variety of work arrangements and workers. It's largely staffed (if not run) by people who love music and first became involved in the industry because of that love, some of whom have discovered and nurtured artists who might otherwise never have had a career in music. As Negus has argued, what gets produced isn't simply the result of a hierarchical winnowing out of suspect creativity, but reflects struggles between different levels and personnel over what should be produced and supported.[39] Once the music is released, the peripheral arms of the industry—DJs, journalists, record store employees, and so on—further affect the chance a consumer will hear a record, and what she will make of that record.

Art and commerce are neither easy companions nor inevitably at odds (or there would never be any great popular music). Since we can't assume a single predetermined effect the industry will have on music, inevitably "bad" or inevitably "good," our approach instead is to be aware in each case of the potential power of the industry to provide pointers for meaning, albeit often in ways that are not as obvious as lyrics or genre, for example, might be. Like all pointers, those supplied by industry framing are subject to contradiction and negation by other pointers; musickers aren't simply passive boobs slavishly following industry dictates. There are just too many variables to contend that industry structure alone determines what we hear, or that it alone determines what we make of what we hear.

The Role of Technology

Intertwined with the history of the commercialization of music is the history of the development of technology that has affected (and been affected by) the structure of the industry and that also affects how we experience music and the meaning we make of that music. Those living in industrialized countries in the early years of the twenty-first century are deluged with evidence of technology's enormous impact, particularly those of us who have made the ride all the way from a single family phonograph playing records to a car filled with teenagers, each listening to her own individual iPod. These technological advances obviously affect our social practices but, less obviously, also emerge *through,* and thus reflect, existing social practices.[40] iPods don't simply encourage more individualized consumption of music; their invention and development occurred in those societies in which individual consumption of music was already seen as a positive (rather than, say, antisocial) activity. Neither the invention nor effect of technology is value neutral: Some social practices grow while some disappear; some groups gain, some lose. The likelihood that one technology will be developed rather than another is bound up with the needs, values, and desires of actual groups and, in capitalist societies, with the perception that these can be turned into profit.[41]

The spread of commercial radio stations in the 1920s, for example, had profound effects on music, the music industry, and the greater society. Although music remained a minor part of the programming menu of most stations for years, what was played immediately attained a degree of exposure unavailable to music passed down only through live experiences. The choice of music reflected what radio staffs thought most popular with their listening audiences, but also helped to construct that popularity. Coupled with the choices made by the mushrooming independent record companies of the day, radio presented a picture to people of "their" music, which helped some genres and forms blossom while others fell by the wayside, as in the demise of the narrative blues. The development of the electrically amplified condenser microphones of the mid-1920s allowed and encouraged the crooner style associated with Rudy Vallee and Bing Crosby, a style that was simply not possible with the naked voice or the primitive megaphones used to amplify singers' voices in earlier days;[42] as aspiring vocalists heard this style on radio and records, it became their model of what a male singer was supposed to sound like. Peterson points out that the advent of the LP allowed jazz musicians to escape the three-minute limit of the 78 rpm format, allowing for far more innovation.[43]

The effects could be social and political as well as musical, as when the songs of mill workers were spread to isolated towns through the early radio stations in the South and the subsequent creation of a musician's circuit in the towns reached by those stations. Exposure to this kind of music, Roscigno & Danaher tell us, inspired and supported resistance and insurgency among mill workers who understood the tradition to be both an alternative source of information to what the mill owners and local newspapers said and an inspiration for banding into unions.[44]

Technology may invite creativity, as in enabling a new vocal style, but, in other ways and in other times, it may become a straitjacket constraining artistic expression. Adorno feared the standardization of the 78 rpm record would reduce all pieces to three minutes, minimizing complexity in composition;[45] the machinery of touring is now so complex, Goodwin points out, that live stage shows have become largely scripted affairs, out of the control of the artists who simply hit their marks and sing their lines.[46]

These technological developments inevitably take place in relationship to the music industry, shaped by and shaping its structure. For example, the explosion in FM rock-oriented radio stations in the late 1960s "resulted from the need to find a suitable outlet for the high fidelity, stereo rock records" that recording innovations made possible. Their growth, in turn, led to higher standards for recording fidelity, favoring the multinationals able to afford the most expensive recording equipment and disadvantaging the struggling indies.[47]

New technologies, however, don't always result in greater control for those already dominant in the industry. In the 1950s the advent of tape recording (replacing direct-to-disc recording) made the production process far simpler and less expensive. In five years the number of American record companies grew from 11 to almost 200, as independent record companies took advantage of the new technology to record niche music.[48] The creation of affordable digital recording equipment in the 1990s again fueled an explosion in the number of independent record labels; indeed, any band with access to a few thousand dollars could now turn out its own recordings with a sound quality that approached professional studios. Both cassette and digital technology have led to mass pirating of music that was virtually impossible previously. Since the culture industry is not a monolith, technologies that are profitable for one sector (the creation of CD burners, for example) may well adversely affect another sector (those who produce and sell prerecorded CDs). And as Frith has noted, generally "the devices that succeed in the market are those that increase consumer control of their music."[49]

The Digital Revolution: A Whole New Ballgame?

The conversion of music into digital (and therefore endlessly reproducible) form, the availability of affordable recording software that can be used on home computers, the spread of the Internet, the creation of software and websites devoted to file "sharing"—all these have combined to create what appears to be a break with much of what we've been discussing, a model of the music industry that lasted for more than a century but is now, according to some, on the brink of extinction. The most optimistic proponents regard this as revolutionary, "the most fundamental change in the history of Western music since the invention of music notation in the ninth century,"[50] according to one.

That old model was based on the creation of physical products—sheet music, LPs, CDs—and marked by limits and scarcity. Access was controlled by "gatekeepers"— most obviously record company executives who decided what would be recorded and distributed, but also those in similar executive positions in television, radio, print, retail, and touring. This system routinely resulted in vast differentials: A few megastars became rich and famous while most musicians hardly made a living; a few were able to assert control over their careers (based on their success) while most remained dependent on the various gatekeepers to such an extent that any shot at commercial survival required some level of acquiescence to the taste and opinion of those gatekeepers.

The new model, built on the digital revolution, is said to turn all of this around. It's not based on physical products and therefore embodies characteristics that fundamentally alter the situation: Digital music is "nondepletable," i.e., it's limitless. Unlike a physical record or CD, there isn't a finite number of them in a store or a warehouse that we can run out of. It's infinitely reproducible: Unlike previous forms—say, cassettes—making copies of digital music through burning CDs or downloading a file doesn't diminish the quality of the copy. Therefore it's "nonrivalrous": The supply doesn't diminish when someone "takes" a copy. And finally, it's "nonexcludable": Once created, access to the product can't be controlled for all practical purposes.[51]

Artists can now record themselves on digital equipment of their own at a fraction of the cost of the traditional studio; they can expose their music to consumers directly through the Internet, on their own websites, through social networking sites, or on the potentially unlimited number of Internet "radio stations"; and they can sell their music through mail order CDs or downloading, bypassing the need for record company distribution altogether.

The old gatekeepers, in short, are largely obsolete. Artists don't need a green light from record executives to record since they can do it in their own living rooms. They're not as reliant on print media because there are so many opportunities on the Internet to connect with fans. They're not as reliant on video television because do-it-yourself Internet sites—most obviously and prominently YouTube—allow the posting of all videos for free without any decision by programmers about what will be played and what will not be played.

The result is thus considerable empowerment of, first, the artist, who now can control his own career. Most importantly from our perspective of political music making, the new model permits musicians to create more of the music they truly want to create and less of the music they're told they need to create to advance in the industry. The economics no longer require the Holy Grail of crossover: In the old model, an artist might receive on average 8 percent of the consumer's price, requiring sales minimally in the hundreds of thousands to make a living income; in the new model she might receive 90 percent, requiring less than one-tenth the sales to make the same amount. The creation and marketing of "niche music" thus become far more possible; it's as if we suddenly had 10 million of the old indie record companies operating at once. Such conditions may be expected to allow the creation of a far larger "middle class" of musicians—not rich, not starving, but making a living—than the old model.

Audiences are also said to be empowered in the new model. They, too, are no longer affected by scarcity or the limits of physical products: Almost any music made anywhere at any time is accessible digitally, and copies never run out. And further, the digital model allows audiences to become participants in ways that would have Adorno smiling. Even novices can now easily make their own "mixes," choosing different songs to burn on a CD to create albums based on their own criteria. Those who are more technologically savvy and have the inclination can actually deconstruct existing recordings and then reconstruct them, creating new pieces from the old. Public Enemy's 2002 album, *Revolverlution,* actually featured four cuts whose mixes were created by fans from a cappella versions the band posted online.

But the most striking development in audience empowerment has been the creation of what are known as peer-to-peer (P2P) networks, which enable individuals to download each other's music files. Exploding at the turn of the century with the appearance and exponential growth of Napster, such file-sharing sites have become a main source of music for tens of millions ever since. Importantly, these P2P networks aren't simply music-sharing sites, but virtual meeting places for those who want to discuss music (and other topics).[52] Impassioned debate, tips on concert tickets, recommendations of other music, and so forth flow freely among fans who, in the process, become participants in a culture. Social networking sites like Facebook and MySpace, while not devoted to music, similarly allow virtual communities to form based on interest in a kind of music or particular artist, as well as an infinite range of topics, including political ideas. The democratizing effect of the digital revolution, it's argued, thus extends to grassroots person-to-person communication through the Internet to an extent that was unimaginable in previous days.

The social networking sites have become a major—perhaps *the* major—form of communication between young people with access to computers, and in recent years have become popular with their elders as well. But the netherworld of illegal sites for music downloading has also grown tremendously. While previous consumer duplication technologies—cassette dubbing, CD burning—were adopted by only a sliver of even the hard core of music fanatics, by 2005, 72 million people in the United States alone were estimated to be trading music online; a "2004 poll of children ages eight to eighteen by Harris Interactive showed that 56 percent of American teenagers with Internet access said that they download music on a regular basis, even though they know that they are breaking the law."[53] Even as legal downloading sites (such as iTunes) flowered, a 2006 study found that 43 percent of downloaders "say that they still do so illegally."[54]

The success of the new model, proponents argue, is in large part because it represents a far more democratic and egalitarian way of producing and distributing music. Some, however, fear that the popularity of this new model has less to do with democracy, egalitarianism, or empowerment of artists and audiences, and more to do with one obvious feature of the P2P networks: They provide music for free. Numerous studies find that consumers are largely (though not entirely) unconcerned about both the legality and morality of flaunting of traditional copyright laws. Most judge their chances of being apprehended as very small, and many feel that record companies have themselves been so unfair to both consumers and artists that bypassing them is an entirely justifiable action.[55]

The industry, obviously, feels otherwise. Free downloading, spokespeople often say, threatens the very existence of the industry. They point to significant drops in CD sales, the closing of perhaps 3,000 music stores in the past decade, and data that suggest that for every legal download of a song, there are somewhere between 6 and 12 illegal downloads.[56] These constitute nothing less than "piracy," industry representatives say, robbery from not just the labels but the artists. And the end result, they warn, will be the demise of the music itself, unable to monetarily support those who create it.

The loss of sales revenue the industry cites is undeniable, but the causes and effects are less straightforward than its spokespersons portray them as being. For one thing, as Kusek & Leonhard point out, it's not the *music* industry that's in crisis, but the *recording* industry; while CD sales dropped 26 percent from 2000 to 2003, for example, live concert returns were "soaring, rising four years straight" in the same time period.[57] While "about 800 music stores, including Tower's 89 locations, closed in 2006 alone[,] Apple Inc.'s sales of about 100 million iPods shows that music remains a powerful force in the lives of consumers."[58]

Further, there are other significant causes of the downturn in musical products. The "decline" is calculated from sales figures of the 1990s that were greatly inflated by the reissuing of albums originally produced on vinyl, a cycle that (coincidentally) came to an end about the time that P2P networks began to take off.[59] The dominance of big box retailers like Wal-Mart has lowered the per unit price of CDs, as music is used as a loss leader to draw in consumers to buy other products (and in the process driving out Mom and Pop record stores that can't match such prices and stay in business).[60] Doug Walters importantly points out that the number of total *units* sold—that is, counting "singles, CDs, digital albums, [digital singles], vinyl, and music videos as equivalent units"—has not fallen in this period, but gone up, for example increasing "14 percent in 2007 to a record-breaking 1.37 billion. In 2006, total sales rose 16 percent."[61] In his analysis, a leading cause of the drop in revenue is that consumers can now (legally) download the particular singles they want (for example at the iTunes store for $0.99) instead of being forced to buy the entire CD (for about $15) under the old system.[62] Further, organized piracy, that is, the production of physical CDs without paying royalties, may account for much of the loss of legal CD sales.[63]

Thus, downloader defenders argue, the drop in revenue from CDs is not as steep as sometimes portrayed, or attributable simply to illegal downloading.[64] Some illegal downloads are of music that's otherwise out of print; much is of music that listeners want to try out first before purchasing; that is, music, they claim, that they would not otherwise purchase if they couldn't first sample it, and so not a loss to the industry when downloaded. Certainly, there is some substantial loss of CD sales, but as Don Joyce of Negativland points out, audiences who are able to download for free still continue to buy CDs for "the dependability of physical formats, the desirability of packaging, the touchable portability of personal objects, and so on."[65] Empirical studies so far provide contradictory results regarding whether downloading on balance has led to the woes of the music industry, and if so, to what extent.[66]

Critics thus charge that the industry has greatly overstated the dangers of the digital revolution, and especially of free downloading of musical files. Importantly, they suggest that particularly for artists with modest total sales—that is, most artists—it has led to *greater* revenues, both through downloads and in encouraging fans to buy "hard goods" (CDs, clothing, etc.) and to attend live shows.[67] Some studies even appear to show that "collectively downloaders are not buying significantly fewer CDs than they would in a world without MP3s."[68] Singer/songwriter Janis Ian, publicly embroiled in this debate in the early years of this century, pointed out, "A conservative estimate would place the number of 'newly available' CDs per year at 100,000. That's an awful lot of releases for an industry that's being destroyed."[69]

If the music industry approached digital downloading and the digital revolution differently, it's then argued, it would be a boon, rather than a danger, to the industry. Ian continues:

> If you think about it, the music industry should be rejoicing at the new technological advance! Here's a fool-proof way to deliver music to millions who might otherwise never purchase a CD in a store. The cross-marketing opportunities are unbelievable. It's instantaneous, costs are minimal, shipping non-existent ... a staggering vehicle for higher earnings and lower costs. Instead, they're running around like chickens with their heads cut off, bleeding on everyone and making no sense.[70]

At first the industry seemed oblivious to the dangers of digitalizing music; instead, CDs seemed to (and did) offer the prospect of increased profits. Completely aside from whatever their qualities as products might be, CDs were attractive to the music industry because they meant the obsolescence of previous forms like LPs and cassettes, which ensured a certain amount of increased sales replacing already purchased albums in the new CD form. The price markup on CDs was also greater, particularly in the early years—by one account the profit margin was double that of LPs and cassettes for the labels.[71] Executives doubtless understood that digitalized music could be copied by consumers, but that had been true with the advent of cassettes as well, and yet only a tiny fraction of consumers had done so.

Through the 1990s, however, industry concern about consumer duplication grew, and spokespersons began to speak of the need to "protect artists." Some preventative measures were taken, such as backing the passage of the Audio Home Recording Act of 1992 and the Digital Millennium Copyright Act of 1998, both of which were attempts to outlaw or limit copying and clarify when such copying was a copyright violation. But, in general, the industry, awash in the CD boom, was watchful but not overly concerned.

It wasn't until P2P networks began to burgeon at the turn of the new century that the industry began to believe "that it was losing the ability to control its future through control of the physical distribution of the product."[72] Napster, the first widely known centralized P2P file-sharing site, was estimated at its height in 2001 to have "tens of millions of users downloading hundreds of millions of sound files."[73] The industry responded with a three-pronged strategy: (1) a public relations campaign around the theme of downloading as theft; (2) a technological approach that included both installing digital rights management systems (DRMs) on CDs to prevent duplication and "pollution" attacks that sent bugs and corrupted files into P2P networks;[74] and (3) a legal strategy of suing P2P sites like Napster, as well as individual downloaders, for copyright infringement.

The education campaign met with mixed results; the use of DRMs was widely condemned by consumers for interfering with legal duplications; the pollution campaign may have had significant results in increasing consumers' annoyance with P2P networks, but it's impossible to know how much of the disruption was due to deliberate industry sabotage. The legal campaign was highly successful in closing down particular sites (such as Napster) but hugely unpopular with consumers and certainly unable to keep up with each new P2P site that opened up as litigation shut an older one down. In recent years the Recording Industry Association of America (RIAA) has largely abandoned this legal strategy in favor of agreements with Internet service providers (ISPs) for their voluntary policing of illegal downloading.

The phenomenal popularity of file sharing, however, forced the industry to consider how it might be used in the industry's interest. Official record company sites began offering free downloads themselves as a way of encouraging interest in new music. Some of the most successful independently launched file-sharing sites—Napster, Rhapsody, etc.—have been bought by larger corporations and relaunched on pay-per-download or subscription status; the entry into the pay-per-download market of Apple through its iTunes Music Store in 2003 was only possible through agreement with the major labels to make their catalogs available. Illegal downloads still dwarf legal downloads—12 to 1 by one knowledgeable estimate in 2005[75]—but clearly the industry has made a basic shift toward understanding and attempting to monetize downloading.

At the same time, the industry has turned its attention to other components of the Internet revolution that had not been created with music in mind but that quickly became major new platforms for experiencing music: social networking sites—in particular MySpace—and video-sharing sites—in particular YouTube. MySpace, launched in 2003, reaches more than 110 million active users worldwide on a monthly basis.[76] Among its most popular features is the capability for musicians to upload MP3s, which are then available for fans to listen to, resulting in direct artist-to-audience delivery. YouTube, launched in 2005, allows users to upload and view video clips. Both seemed to hold the promise of increased democracy for artists and audiences, direct communication without the intercession of gatekeepers, but their very openness, of course, allows them to be used by corporations within the music industry as easily as by grassroots artists, and in recent years the industry has supplied content to both to push their artists.

As we write at the end of the first decade of the twenty-first century, we see at least three alternative visions for the delivery of music in the future. In the first, the industry successfully manages the shift from largely physical products to largely (but far from exclusively) digital products, with the iTunes store as the model: Consumers pay for individual downloads, while those who want a more inclusive product—cool cover art, a physical artifact, etc.—continue to buy CDs, or certain CDs. This, according to many in the field, will require establishing access to the vast inventory available on P2P networks while delivering something to consumers that they can't get through illegal (but free) downloading—quality of reproduction, virus protection, high-speed downloading, help with file management, recommendation engines, and so on. Further, for consumers to make this move back to legal downloading, at least in significant numbers, most analysts suggest the industry will need to figure out a way to drop the cost per download and still make a profit. So far, despite inroads, offering legal downloading hasn't been successful enough to predict industry survival in its present form. Kusek & Leonhard point out that "even Apple [iTunes store]'s one hundred million–plus legal downloads at the time of this writing are a mere drop in the bucket compared to the billions of downloads on the P2P networks,"[77] but at the same time they predict legal download services will eventually "outdo the existing 'rogue' P2P networks by developing their own delivery and customer interaction systems that employ superior technologies, recommendation engines, and customer service."[78] Some more recent variations of this model involve "revenue splitting" in which music files are sold for small amounts between peers on a P2P system with the server collecting half the fee, most of which is then paid to the copyright owner.[79]

A second model also assumes the music industry will reassert its control over much of the music produced and sold but envisions the delivery system as more like a public utility than requiring payment for individual products. In this "music as water" model, as advanced by Kusek & Leonhard, consumers will be charged at the point of access—i.e., their Internet service provider bill, probably—and then just "turn on" the music whenever they want, their subscription allowing them unlimited access to unlimited music available digitally.[80] In this vision, artistic control is greater and concentration in the record companies is less likely, but the basic model of an industry as conduit between artist and audience remains.

Finally, there is the radical vision of a drastic break with the music industry. In this vision, the dream of a democratic music, easily available directly from artist to audience—indeed, blurring the lines between artist and audience—is not colonized by the industry, but instead sweeps the industry into the ash heap of history, more or less. File downloading is universally available; consumers pay musicians out of respect or obligation or a sense of reciprocity, but musicians generally regard the musical product as a form of advertising and expect to make their money from concerts and merchandising. This scenario envisions many more artists able to make a decent—that is, middle-class—living, while the age of a few superstars becoming fabulously rich largely ends. In the words of Don Joyce, a member of Negativland, a band that has pioneered this kind of approach:

> The growing movement of musical self-sufficiency will change the nature of music. The Net could easily facilitate public awareness and access to new music. . . . [O]ur present cartel system's fixation with hit manufacturing, artist grooming, and exclusivity can be bypassed entirely.[81]

Despite their great differences, one belief remains common to all visions of the future—digital delivery will become increasingly common and therefore, whether this is accessed legally or not, the proportion of revenue that is produced by sales of the music itself will decrease, requiring greater revenue to be generated from other streams than in the past. It has been estimated that even for the digital music servers themselves, "as much as 50 or 60 percent of the future revenues will come in from selling other products and services, and from advertising, sponsorship, and marketing tie-ins."[82] In the past few years record companies have begun entering into "360" agreements with their artists in which the company takes a share of all revenue streams of an artist, including those that have nothing to do with recording, in return for providing money and services to support the artist's recording and extrarecording enterprises. For all musicians, live performing will return to its historical prominence as a main revenue source.

From the perspective of politically minded artists (and many other artists as well), the third vision of a less gatekeeper-controlled, more democratic, more middle-class system of delivery is, of course, the most attractive, but there are significant threats to its realization. The first, now increasingly unlikely, was that the industry would be able to simply crush it through regulation litigation, as it crushed Napster in its first incarnation. Though that strategy continues in less consumer-hostile forms, it's now fairly clear that downloading will not be stamped out and that the digital tide in general cannot be held back.

It's far more likely that the music industry will figure out how to adapt to these changing conditions in ways that maintain as much of their control and profits as possible. One tactic is to colonize precisely those platforms whose democratic format allows anyone to post content, such as YouTube and the social networking sites. Those with superior resources—including record companies—can potentially manipulate what look like neutral sites to create the appearance of demand for their product. Where prominence in a site is determined by site visitor demand—Google, say, or YouTube—it's obviously tempting to create that demand artificially, as has apparently been done on occasion by sophisticated fans and industry staff in the recent past.[83] All of the new avenues for artists to be noticed by fans can, in theory, be overwhelmed by hired employees acting as fans—writing recommendations on consumer sites, swapping playlists, creating "fan" iMixes to post at the iTunes store, and so forth.

A more blatant danger is the attack on open access and "Net neutrality," which simply means that companies providing consumers access to the Internet can't interfere with the content they provide or give preference to some sites over others. As summarized by Jean Cook of the Future of Music Coalition:

> The ISPs [Internet service providers] want to create what is essentially a fast lane on the Internet and charge websites extra to use it. Those that can't afford the fees will be relegated to a slower lane.... The Internet, by design, [currently] offers us a democratic, open structure.... This is good news for international artists. With over one billion people connected to the Internet, there is an audience for what you do. This is why it is so important to protect the openness of these systems.[84]

Ironically, the very openness of the Internet carries with it the danger of new gatekeepers arising. As all Net users experience on a daily basis, the astounding amount of available information creates a need for filtering out most of what we receive electronically so we can concentrate on those few items on which we want to spend our time. How can a consumer intelligently choose what to listen to when confronted by this avalanche of product, or alternatively put, how can an artist get noticed among so many others? One option is the advice of professional and amateur critics. Blogs have mushroomed that offer opinions on which artists are most worth listening to; the most popular of these are read by many hundreds of thousands each day,[85] with a dramatic impact on who gets listened to. The large digital service providers (DSPs) like Napster and LimeWire have regular columns of recommendations. These, clearly, can become the new gatekeepers. Defenders of digital's democratic potential point out that there are so many sources of opinion now that the power of each gatekeeper is diminished,[86] yet the popularity of a few dominant sources of recommendation is worrisome since it suggests the same kind—if not extent—of concentration of influence as in the past. A recommendation by Pitchfork, the most successful of "indie" review sites, for example, has led to thousands, even hundreds of thousands, more sales, according to artists themselves.[87]

Some DSPs, such as iTunes, also feature automatic purchase advice on the order of "if you liked this, you might also like that"; the Pandora Internet site offers automated musical recommendations based on a song or artist entered by a user. While these, too, conceivably could be manipulated to steer consumers toward certain artists and products, even those that simply reflect past consumer purchase patterns (e.g., those that buy Phish albums have also bought reissues of Grateful Dead material) may encourage consumers to remain locked into the artists and genres they've already explored, making it, again, more difficult to get them to hear "radical" music of any kind that doesn't fit easily into these preexisting patterns.[88]

There are certainly cases of new artists receiving attention based on the simplest forms of publicity, available to virtually all: local touring, word of mouth, a YouTube video that catches on, even becoming a popular ring tone on cell phones[89]—but these still remain unusual cases. Faced with the problems in attracting consumer attention in a digital world overflowing with product, many artists find themselves in a situation that greatly resembles the bad old days: relying on companies with greater resources to mount the kind of publicity that catches the eye of consumers and gatekeepers—the new and the old alike.

TuneCore, for example, is what's called an "aggregator," which takes musical files provided by artists and (for a very low annual cost) provides them to the largest digital service providers, such as Napster and iTunes. In March 2009, TuneCore's CEO, Jeff Price, estimated they were "releasing" 100–300 titles a day. This appears a great democratizing step forward. But, as Price admits, "Many bands say, 'okay, great, for 30 bucks I can have worldwide distribution [through TuneCore], but what does it matter if nobody knows I'm there?'" While Price's point is that the way "people know you're there has changed significantly," with open sources like YouTube replacing the old gatekeeper models, TuneCore itself offers all kinds of additional services (for a price) to get some artists more noticed than others.[90] As summarized by Kusek & Leonhard,

> [D]igital technologies have democratized this process, but they also have injected a good deal of Darwinism into the business. The more people record, produce, and publish their works, the more new releases will vie for our attention. And today, getting attention is the name of the game.... [U]ltimately the question of *what you pay attention to* will completely replace the question of how you get access to it. It's all about exposure and discovery.[91]

Finally, because the digital revolution (whether it is ultimately controlled by the existing record companies or not) seems destined to reduce the revenue that can be obtained by selling the music itself, the pressure to obtain revenue from commercial uses of the music grows. "Placement" has become the aim of many new artists, the surest way to support an act. While this may mean movies and other cultural settings, increasingly it means ads or video games. Kusek & Leonhard provide one example: "When Electronic Arts ships their new 'Madden' football video game, each song on the game will receive over 700 million spins in the first six months." As they then note, this means "Electronic Arts has become a gate-keeper and tastemaker for new music."[92] According to political economist Robert W. McChesney, a prominent part of the discussion for labels *considering* signing a band is what commercial uses can be made of their music.[93] As candidly laid out by TuneCore's Price,

> It sounds really horrible, too—if you break it down, you're leveraging music for corporate sponsorship, right, you're selling out to The Man. That's what you're doing. But then again, I see Iggy Pop, *Lust for Life,* as the Norwegian Cruise Line's

advertisement, and here's a song about heroin addiction.... I really do see corporations coming into the world and stepping in to help subsidize the fund of music, I really do. They need it desperately. And if you [as an artist] want it, it'll be there for you. And if you don't, you don't have to. You can choose to do things a different way.[94]

What is to be made of all these (often conflicting) potential developments? The digital revolution, like all forms of technology, is not by itself deterministic of the ends to which it will be put (though some become more likely than others because their logic is assumed or embedded in the technology itself); various futures are possible, and which come about will be the result of economic, political, and social struggles now going on. (The same could be [and is] said about the effect of the Internet on activism in general—it holds the promise of a great leap forward in democracy by allowing direct communication between peers in place of the top-down model of newspapers, television, and so on, but it carries with it the dangers of colonization by elites and/or the institution of new gatekeepers to act as filters of the avalanche of available information. This topic, however, would take us far afield.[95])

Writing in what we believe are still the early days of these battles, we're cautiously optimistic that the digital revolution will open new opportunities for artists, including politically motivated artists, to reach audiences more directly and with less fear of declaring their politics openly. Still, we don't expect the record industry or terrestrial radio to disappear, or the problems inherent in having culture delivered as a commodity in some form. The gatekeepers of the past have been challenged and weakened, without doubt, but they are far from dead,[96] and new gatekeepers stand ready to take their place should they succumb. The likely result for the foreseeable future is a combination of the three models we introduced earlier. As Jenny Toomey, past director of the Future of Music Coalition, told us:

There are some artists who can become very famous without a lot of management and without a lot of push from large institutions. And then there are a much greater number of artists who, in order to break to that next level, do it with the help of managers and large moneybags institutions. And that will ever be the case. There probably were famous artists who sold their own sheet music, and did very well with it, and other ones that paid people to sell it for them and became famous that way.

"Selling records involves the industry in a struggle to impose a particular meaning on music, and thereby to ensure a demand for their product," John Street observed 20 years ago. "Consumers and companies are engaged in an endless series of ideological skirmishes.... This balance of power is never fixed or absolute. The struggles for meaning and commercial success are never finally resolved."[97] As with all the factors affecting our construction of meaning, the pointers embedded in the status of pop music through its creation, status, and distribution as a product cannot simply determine meaning, but take their place with others that interactively shape what we make of a piece of music. Still, as Negus reminds us, "making meanings, actively using technologies and interpreting texts is not the same as having the power and influence to distribute cultural forms."[98] Given its centrality in the delivery of much of the music we experience, it would be naïve not to still grant that the industry provides a particularly powerful set of pointers that influence the meanings we attribute to the music we hear and the music we create, beginning with its simple power to make a given music available or not to us in the first place. But that simple power may be on the verge of disappearing.

Professional and Amateur Interpreters

Our understanding of a piece of music may be further framed by those whose job it is to report on and interpret culture; that is, the entertainment media. Armed with greater knowledge of the topic, far more time to explore it, and often access to artists the rest of us don't have, they make pronouncements of the meaning of a work that can be highly influential. These interpretations typically rely heavily on placing artists within already understood categories, placing them within a genre, comparing their sound to an already known group, and all too often exclusively analyzing their social or political orientation as understood through their lyrics (if any).

Other public figures may also help shape our constructed meanings. Government sponsorship of a music may tie its meaning to support of that government, while criticism or censorship tends to politicize music, making previously apolitical genres appear rebellious or oppositional. For example, as the Eastern Bloc began to dissolve in the late 1980s, the explicitly anti–Communist Party music played by Yugoslavian rock bands without any government interference was apparently not nearly as important a part of the organized opposition to the party as rock was in other countries such as East Germany or the Soviet Union, where it was heavily censored.[99] Government and other opponents of a music, ironically, are particularly likely to emphasize and thereby reinforce interpretations of a music's meaning that they object to and wish to prevent from spreading. "Nothing put the category *youth* on my own political map more resoundingly than a song called 'Eve of Destruction,'" writes Todd Gitlin, chronicler of the 1960s, citing the mood of that song and noting: "If there was any doubt left about what the song meant, the superintendents and interpreters of popular culture (including right-wing alarmists) went to work to clear things up."[100]

We further filter and interpret music through the eyes of friends, family, and others around us. As Riesman reminds us, even when we listen alone, we listen "in a context of imaginary 'others.'"[101] The meanings *they* construct influence the meanings we construct. To take an example familiar to most of us: the kid in your high school circle who knew the inside story about all the music.[102] That kid was not just a source of "factual" information (George plays lead, John plays rhythm), but a source of opinion (John's deep while Paul's clever; Ringo's a better drummer than he's usually given credit for). Some of this was based on intense scrutiny and firsthand knowledge, but much was itself based on reports of the media—that kid read *Rolling Stone* religiously. In this sense, some people in each social circle become opinion leaders, telling the rest of us not only who's good and who's bad, but the meaning of songs and artists, a link and a filter between the entertainment media and the general public. Fandom itself further draws us into contact, even alliances, with concentrations of such people with relatively firm ideas about what a band or artist we follow in common means. The same is true of folk music. We learn it in the context of kith and kin who also pass along—deliberately or not—what it's about, from the narrowest terms of a particular narrative to the broadest memories of the significance of this kind of music to the community. The virtual communities we discussed earlier, spawned by the Internet and particularly through P2P networks, are only the most recent of such communities. While the available technology allows such groupings to exist in far larger numbers and over far greater geographical areas, the dynamic within them—the sense in which we share a meaningful tie through our involvement with a particular artist or form of music—shares a great deal with the face-to-face gatherings of the past.

The Setting

We experience music—listening, playing, talking about, thinking about—not only with specific other people, but in more generalized groupings as well. At the broadest level, the basic social/political context of a society provides the backdrop against which we hear music (as it provides the context for all we do). Slave songs take on political meanings simply because they are sung within a greater context of a lack of access to fundamental rights. "Respect" resonated as a song about racial equality largely because it came in the midst of the ferment of the civil rights movement; it resonates as a song about gender equality largely because it was reappropriated and reused by feminists in the ferment of the women's liberation movement.

Adorno's critique of popular music treats the context in which it's made and consumed as the most significant factor in determining what it means to consumers. In his analysis, popular music in most countries comes to us in a general setting of commercialized entertainment that trivializes all content. As a result, the dominant meaning of *any* song is: "Don't listen actively—smile, bop along, but don't think!" Even if we reject this wholesale interpretation, it's certainly obvious that hearing music at specific times and places reserved for that purpose (as is the practice in more traditional societies) leads to different assessments of its meaning than hearing it as part of a ubiquitous low-level background hum emanating from elevators, radios, hidden speakers in stores, and so forth.

Within this general context, we experience music and musicking in very specific settings. Hearing music in a bar, a disco, a concert, a demonstration, a friend's bedroom at midnight—each of these greatly affects meaning. Setting frames the experience so that some factors of the music (and thus of meaning) become much more salient: the beat in a disco, the sense of solidarity at a demonstration, the lyrics when listening late at night in a friend's bedroom. But further, the setting may itself become the most important meaning of the piece, as in Small's observation that the revolutionary impulses of works by Beethoven and others are replaced in the minds of contemporary concertgoers by their use in the ritual of classical concertgoing that constitutes their main meaning: a "bedtime story" for the Western industrial bourgeoisie in which everything—the architecture, the dress, the use of music from a distant past—suggests that their way of life is permanent.[103]

In some cases, this setting isn't just symbolic, but a place where message is being quite consciously and purposefully presented. Aid concerts—Live Aid, Farm Aid, the Tibetan Freedom Concerts—typically encourage concertgoers to get information from people staffing booths outside the hall. Here the message is expressed twofold: Music attracts people to a particular scene or group that then provides very specific information (Tibet was independent until militarily occupied in the second half of the twentieth century), as well as a more general framing (people like us don't believe in oppressing other people).

The setting of the music within an event with its own narrative also impacts potential meaning. One of our students reported that some survey respondents asked to discuss the meaning of Janis Joplin's "Mercedes Benz"—apparently intended by Joplin as a criticism of commercialism and the American obsession with material goods—reported it to be an expression of desire for a better car. They had only heard the song, it turned out, as part of a Mercedes Benz commercial. Songs heard on the soundtracks of movies are often reported by listeners to be "about" the film's story, even when written years before the film was made.

Some pieces (or components of pieces) share a common meaning among many people because of a historical event or era with which they're associated. Both the event and the fact that it is a *shared* memory seem to give the music a particular charge. The songs of Thomas Mapfumo, bard of the Zimbabwean Revolution, had their political meanings buried so deeply in the lyrics that they were inaccessible to virtually everyone, but once they began being sung by ZANU, the force fighting to overthrow the white minority government, they became associated by friend and foe with standing for the revolution (and as a result, the Rhodesian government banned them and arrested Mapfumo).[104]

The stronger the narrative of the event itself, the stronger the influence on possible constructed meaning will be. In July 1990, six months after the fall of the Berlin Wall, an all-star group of musicians performed the Pink Floyd piece "The Wall" near what had been the demarcation line between West and East Berlin, an event viewed on TV or heard on radio by an estimated tens of millions. For many Europeans, "The Wall" became indelibly associated with the fall of the Berlin Wall, the mental soundtrack, despite its lyrics having nothing to do with that event (having been written 10 years earlier). Some swear it was actually playing as the Wall fell.

It's worth stopping for a minute to appreciate, again, this almost unique quality of music. There are certainly books or art pieces that have come to stand for a historical moment and specific struggle—*Uncle Tom's Cabin,* for example, or Picasso's *Guernica*—yet this is rare compared to musical examples. As we discussed in Chapter 1, a song's capacity to evoke historical events has something to do with the form itself, its portability and easy recall. Music in general frequently helps us to "shape popular memory, to organize our sense of time," as Frith says,[105] and also the converse: "[W]e tend to 'anchor' music with images, ... often in the form of memory of specific events or places when we had heard the music in the past."[106] In this role as soundtrack of our individual and collective lives, music not only takes part of its meaning from its setting, *but also organizes our memory of that setting,* the symbol that ties it together in an accessible package, thus contributing to the meaning we attribute to it in later recollections.

The shared past resurfaces in music; from specific pieces to whole genres, music carries historical connotations that inform the meanings of listeners familiar with those histories. Thus Amiri Baraka (then Leroi Jones) argued in *Blues People* that while many people could enjoy the surface qualities of the blues, listeners sensitive to the African American experience could still hear the "voices" of the first generation of Emancipation in blues songs.[107] John Street suggests that soul and reggae, whose origins are similarly linked to the African American experience, employ conventions that "call upon the language of liberation."[108]

Artists, of course, are also aware of these traditions and may consciously build on them, as labor troubadour Joe Glazer notes about Ralph Chaplin's writing of "Solidarity Forever":

> [A]fter observing a coal strike in West Virginia, he went back to Chicago and he decided to write a song. He says, "I wanted to pick a tune that was revolutionary," and he picked "Glory, Glory Hallelujah." And the words fit just right, and it became the great song of the American Labor Movement.

One of the fascinating things about hip-hop is the way, through sampling, it *consciously* calls upon past musical traditions to create new music. By recontextualizing past pieces in new settings, hip-hop changes the message sent, and thus affects the meaning constructed, as a conscious artistic device. But what hip-hop does consciously occurs in all music, precisely because of this linkage between music and collective memory: Significance is evolutionary. As historical perspectives change, the perceived meaning and use of a piece of music are likely to change.

Chapter 4

The Audience and Reception

In a concert setting focused on the music, audiences are distracted by a slew of competing stimuli—the person sitting next to you, thoughts of that confrontation with the boss today, I wonder if I can afford another beer at these prices? Attention sharpens and wanders; certain parts of the show grab attention more than others; a plaintive ballad is completely missed while you try to figure out how they get that orangey lighting on the drums. A single line or sound suddenly rushes into your consciousness, far more important than what came just before or what follows. If this is typical of a concert situation, think of what reception is like when we hear music in a noisy bar, or on the radio in the car, or as background as we do homework. Clearly, to assume a one-to-one correspondence between a performer's intended message—if any—and an audience member's received meaning is naïve.

For a long time (with some notable exceptions)[1] scholars badly neglected audience reception. Most of the classic works on musical meaning are not grounded in any research with audiences, and contain far more discussion of transmission (and sometimes context) than reception. In the 1960s and 1970s, however, the Interactionists began to stress the role of audiences, an approach carried much further by the Birmingham School, and then others in the postmodern cultural studies wave it pioneered, who emphasized finding the meaning of music in its concrete *use* by musickers, a shift "from a focus on cultural *codes* to a focus on cultural *practice.*"[2] In this perspective, a piece of music assumes meaning only when it enters the lives of audience members; the listener "finishes a song."[3] In the relationship among performer, setting, and audience, audience members aren't just the receptacles in which the various factors in meaning coalesce into intelligible patterns, but active participants: "'[L]istening' itself is a performance," as Frith says;[4] interpretation "is as much a process of construction as discovery."[5]

Part of this emphasis arises from the simple observation that audiences are not homogeneous, and how they receive, perceive, and construct a piece of music isn't uniform. Significant differences in taste and/or interpretations have been found by gender, race, nationality, political persuasion, and class;[6] beyond these there are groupings around allegiances to a specific music, "taste publics" as Gans called them.[7] But since our social identities are a combination of many of these dimensions and the virtually infinite differences in personal experiences, each individual within each grouping interprets culture and cultural objects—including pieces of music—somewhat idiosyncratically. Not only do we like different pieces, but we hear them differently.

A famous example in the United States was the attempt of Ronald Reagan's 1984 reelection campaign to use Bruce Springsteen's "Born in the USA." Although Springsteen subsequently made it very clear that he intended the song to be a critique of the country and specifically its treatment of Vietnam veterans, many heard it as a patriotic hymn. It wasn't just a random accident, of course, that people involved in the Reagan campaign were among those who interpreted "Born in the USA" in that way. As Christenson & Roberts say, "[W]hat an individual brings to a song is at least as important as the manifest content the song brings to the individual."[8]

Serge Denisoff reports a vivid example of audience determination of meaning occurring during student demonstrations in Berkeley in December 1966:

> [A]t a student strike meeting someone shouted, "Let's sing 'Solidarity Forever.'" According to one account, "No one seemed to know the words. Then from the back of the lecture hall, a hoarse voice shouted 'Yellow Submarine,' a song popularized by the Beatles. A thousand voices took up the song as the students floated from the building."[9]

The choice of "Yellow Submarine" was not random, though neither its singsong melody nor its child fantasy lyrics* might seem relevant to the occasion. "Yellow Submarine" tapped into some prior association for the students that made it seem appropriate for a demonstration, and it was readily usable for mass singing. Indeed, "Yellow Submarine" remained a standard protest anthem for Berkeley activists and came to symbolize the contrast of their politics with those of earlier generations.[11]

Such associations are an extremely important factor in audience construction of meaning. Asked to discuss their favorite songs, almost a fifth of the Meaning in Music study respondents cited not lyrics or music or performance, but simply the associations a piece held for them: a childhood memory of singing with a parent; a teenage memory of roaring down the highway with a friend, radio blasting. Couples have a special song tied to a particular moment in their courtship, and that meaning is far more important than anything said or otherwise conveyed in the song. Aspiring musicians remember the piece they played at their first public performance, and that significance marks the meaning of the piece forever. Perhaps for many in the Berkeley demonstration, the Beatles had become synonymous with the creation of one's own world, beyond the authority of parents or teachers, and it

---

*So we sailed up to the sun 'till we found the sea of green
And we lived beneath the waves in our yellow submarine[10]

was that feeling, based on the memory of previous (very different) uses of "Yellow Submarine," to which the protesters responded. And it's likely that hearing "Yellow Submarine" has recalled memories of that student strike ever since for those who sang it at the Berkeley protest. (These don't have to be movement or political associations, of course. One student wrote us that she "gets goose bumps when I hear any of the three songs that were played when the New York Rangers won the Stanley Cup in 1994. Silly but true!")

To properly appreciate meanings, we absolutely need to let go of the traditional assumption that the "real" meaning of a piece is what the artist intended, evaluating the audience's degree of "correctness" by comparing their meanings to the composer's or performer's intent (or, more often, the scholar's "deciphering" of that intended meaning). The point isn't to look for *the* meaning of a piece, but how a piece connects to each musicker's constructed meaning(s). Is "Born in the USA" a flag-waving, everything's-great-with-America song? According to its author, no. But for those who heard it that way, yes. Music is in this sense a canvas on which musickers paint their own visions.

These visions, however, are not completely free-floating, unattached to the materials at hand (as some extreme Postmodernists came to argue).[12] If all audience reception was simply individual and idiosyncratic constructions, we wouldn't have genres, niches, or musical movements. As Christenson & Roberts say in summarizing studies of lyric interpretations, "[A]lthough interpretations may be divergent, they are not random."[13] Audiences are not bound to particular interpretations, but they are *directed* toward particular meanings through transmission and context factors.[14]

Some theorists have argued that these framing factors—in particular the dominance of the point of view of the controllers of pop culture—minimize individual interpretations, particularly those that are oppositional in any sense.[15] Others, invoking Gramsci, see popular culture as a "contested terrain" in which different parties fight to control meaning. As in all such fights, however, some parties have more power than others. Negus cautions that while we shouldn't accept the simple vision of a "passive, gullible and easily manipulated audience absorbing values from outside," we can't forget the realities of power in production and distribution.[16] Still, as he also argues, our power to construct our own meanings limits the control of the cultural apparatus: "[H]ow we actually *listen* to the sounds, words and images and what these *mean* and how we then *use* these in our lives can surely be no more 'determined' than the language we have available to speak with will determine what we are going to say."[17]

Understanding audiences' construction of meanings requires appreciating music as process as well as product, as activity as well as object. The formal content of the music may be less meaningful (both in the connotation of "delivery of a coherent message" and that of "feeling of significance") to musickers than the surrounding activities: going to concerts, debating aesthetic questions with friends, reading about the artists, learning to play a piece, and so on. What's important is how use of music *invests* that music with a meaning constructed by the musicker, though not out of thin air, to be sure. We turn now to consider such audience uses, and how these shape what music means.

Identity

What something means to us is closely tied to who we think we are. Musicking may express a preestablished identity, as when Italian Americans gather and sing Italian opera arias, or surfers play Beach Boy albums. Musicking here serves as a way of identifying ourselves, to ourselves and others. Music and group identity may become so intertwined as to be synonymous in the minds of group members and outsiders, often through reference to a collective (part factual, part fictional) past that serves to frame the present. Paul Gilroy's writings on blacks on both sides of the Atlantic illustrate how "this musical heritage gradually became an important factor in facilitating the transition of diverse settlers to a distinct mode of lived blackness."[18]

This kind of musicking is a form of celebration, but also an affirmation and a valorization of identity that may not always be forthcoming in the normal run of daily life. The very existence of a public body of music reinforces the value of the identity. In this way, music is often an important resource for identities that are being redefined and reclaimed ("queer," "freak," "nigger," and so forth), resisting and overcoming stigma and stereotype. A punk fan writes, "Try to tell someone who finally feels understood, acknowledged, and affirmed that there is anything small or insignificant about that moment."[19] Hernando Ospina describes the impact of salsa in New York's Latino communities in the 1960s similarly:

> Few Latin musicians actively engaged in either the civil rights movement or their own communities' struggles. Nevertheless, the new type of music they began to play did give a sense of identity to all those condemned as "gangsters": workers, shop assistants, illegal migrants, delinquents. Now the bands were creating for the Barrio and no one else, for its street corners, its misery. [20]

Musicking may also be the nucleus of emerging identities and groups. Allegiance to a band or genre creates instant membership in a community, an important payoff. These loyalties are often felt as far more than simple taste preferences; they are not the same as declaring a preference for pizza over pasta. Especially among young people, debates over music involve not only what they like, but who they are. "Kids live for their bands, for hanging out, for their 'scene,'" says Donna Gaines, ethnographer of heavy metal fans in the 1980s.[21] "To embrace Led Zeppelin with all the trimmings was a declaration that you would have *no part of it*. Your place in town was set in stone. You flirted with evil, you were dangerous."[22]

This intensity of feeling comes about because the identities that are tied to music—headbanger, gangsta, folkie—typically embrace more than just a connection to the music. This is musicking's "totalizing" function, creating the feeling that various ideas, ideals, and lifestyles go together. Listening to, talking about, and actively creating music serve as forms of ritual that help to define one's identity in group terms. The grouping we now call the "hip-hop community," Tricia Rose argues, was created through a coming together around rap music (as well as break dancing and graffiti). Like most collective identities, there already existed some important commonalities among many who began to see themselves as hip-hop heads, but it was the music itself that cemented connection, leading to a communal history essential to creating that identity.[23] The youth counterculture of the 1960s recognized itself as a culture largely through the music, "which linked the youth of the world, a universal language they all understood, a musical badge of their brotherhood."[24] Participants and observers alike actually referred to the "Woodstock Generation," fixing its array of interests within a musicking context. (That this may not be the most stable basis for a political movement is something we'll discuss in Chapter 10.) The process is mutually reinforcing: Identity is understood in part by the music, and the music is understood in part by the identity with which it's linked.

Music, as Frith says, is a basic tool, especially for young people, in the "cultural map-making" that all people must do.[25] It helps us determine and express who we are—in part through helping us determine and express who we are *not*. Music and its rituals are, in other words, central to processes of social distinction. The love of some adherents for a music seems only equaled by their disdain for other musics, typically seen as representative of a lifestyle one wants nothing to do with. Belonging is defined in large part by those who may not join: parents, the unhip, posers who are not from the 'hood. Musical genres often introduce a vocabulary, a style, a whole way of being that is only accessible to those in the know. Your identity is *yours*; not everyone can share it or it ceases to be meaningful as identity. When appreciation or knowledge of a music is overlaid with demographic or other social differences, these distinctions often become even more highly charged. Part of the importance of the blues for many African Americans was that it was shot through with euphemisms that white people didn't understand. Young people who loved a particular heavy metal band, Gaines writes, entered "a secret society that excluded the adult world of parents, teachers, rock critics, and everyone else."[26]

In all these ways, music and musicking are not merely reflecting or expressing an identity; they are helping to *construct* an identity. On the one hand they provide materials to use in that construction and guidelines for how various pieces might fit together. On the other, by serving as a badge of that identity, they help determine a person's social world, and thus help cement that identity in place. To the extent that a form of music comes to represent an entire life view, we begin to adopt other seemingly related aspects of that ethos.

Identity (like music) isn't simply a product, but a process. We try on new ones, we discard them, we modify them, we play a role in redefining them for others we come into contact with, both within the group and those beyond its boundaries. By naming an identity and in part defining it, music and its ancillary activities help create and then fix that identity.

Typically, musical scenes first develop within more or less demographically defined groups, and they come to be identified with those groups. Hip-hop in the 1980s was for younger people of color; metal at that time was primarily tied to white working-class men. But there are always exceptions, and these, too, carry meaning. When an individual "crosses" into the music of a subculture not her own, she may be simply engaging an interest that doesn't affect her overall identity or self-identity, or she may be altering her identity in some important way. Frank Kofsky (writing in his typical apocalyptic style) foresaw a revolutionary future tied to the musical present:

> [W]hen it comes to the denouement, more than a few whites may find themselves on the "wrong" side of the barricades simply because a Ray Charles or a Miles Davis has been instrumental in giving them a changed perception of reality.... If the traditional Left in this country has fallen far short of its fundamental goal of imbuing white workers with a classwide consciousness, it cannot be said that Negro culture has failed to make its vivid imprint on those young whites fortunate enough to have caught at least a taste of it.[27]

When many individuals are involved, crossing is even more likely to become loaded with meaning, political and otherwise. Much of the opposition in the South to the emergence of rock was due to conservative fears of racial mixing resulting when black and white kids shared an interest in the same form of music. Similar fears had been voiced about earlier forms that attracted fans of more than one race, including spirituals, ragtime, jazz, and folk. Reflecting back on her tours of black campuses in the South in the early 1960s, folksinger Joan Baez recalled, "[I]t was still an enormous thing to have white people and black people sitting together in places like Mississippi and Alabama. It was probably my greatest contribution to the civil rights movement."[28]

When We Join In

Through most of our discussion of meaning in musicking we've assumed the original vision of the minstrel singing to the audience. But as we've suggested from time to time, this is a very incomplete picture of our relationship to music. Even as we listen to a recording of our favorite musicians we sing along, we dance, we play air guitar. And further, many of us play real guitar, or piano, or clarinet; we beat on tables; we write music; we sing to ourselves and with our friends. The range of participation is a continuum from largely passive spectator to full music-making participant. Even these distinctions are fluid: We may sit in an audience one night, silently observing—and yet the next morning start humming a song we heard, becoming a more active participant, more of a music maker.

   The performer-audience model we see in many instances of Western musicking is not typical of musicking in most times and places, and yet even that model contains far more audience participation than may seem evident at first glance. Audiences, we've been arguing, are always participants in making meaning, but even in terms of making music, audience members (in live venues or listening to recorded versions) are rarely entirely passive. Often we hum or sing along, or keep time with our hands or toes or heads; these all shift us toward the participant end of the spectrum. Some musicians and/or pieces emphasize audience participation as a primary goal, often becoming the most important meaning for those who participate. The German socialist composer Hanns Eisler wrote pieces in which the audience was expected to be the chorus.[29] Portia Maultsby points out how "the call-response structure of [James Brown's] 'Say It Loud' encouraged blacks to participate by shouting 'I'm black and I'm proud.'"[30] The core of Pete Seeger's concerts has been his effort to engage the audience in learning and singing (often in harmony) new songs.

Dancing is another way in which "spectators" become participants, cocreators of the musical performance, live or recorded, and of its meaning. We may just headbang along, or we may crowd the aisles, rush the stage, join the mosh pit, and engage in full-out dance, and these may represent the most important meanings to us as spectators/participants. Gaines describes the kind of dancing that often accompanied early hard-core band performances:

> Slamming (or moshing, dancing) was once a serious male-bonding ritual, a communal statement of solidarity. You dove off the stage into the arms of your comrades. There was nothing to fear. If you were falling, your friends, peers, scene brothers, your *generation*, would be there to catch you, pick you up, and push you forward. It was the strongest statement of intragenerational solidarity ever, thrilling to watch.[31]

William Tsitsos's fascinating work on dance in the punk scene reveals even more nuanced meanings, linking the general philosophy of three punk subgroups with their favored dance forms:

> Political punks advocate communal rebellion over more individualistic action, and their goal is the elimination of imposed rules in favour of a self-imposed order. These punks often reject slamdancing and moshing because aspects of these dances clash with both the means and the ends of political punk rebellion....
>
> Apolitical punks, on the other hand, find in slamdancing a reflection of their ideology of rebellion. The individualistic bodily display in the pit mirrors the apolitical punk emphasis on rebellion through individual, instead of communal, action. The seemingly chaotic atmosphere in the [dance] pit, moreover, is a small-scale realisation of the apolitical punk goal of a society without rules.
>
> The straight edgers who developed moshing as an outgrowth of slamdancing also value personal over group rebellion. However, these scene members do not aim to eliminate all rules. Rather, they rebel in order to impose their rules on others. This desire for control and strength brought about moshing, a dance with greater emphasis than slamming on individual dancers controlling the pit.[32]

Tsitsos's discussion not only is instructive in regard to dance, but also points to the ways in which audiences can sometimes participate so fully in the music making that they become major participants in the creation of the messages being generated (as well as constructing the received meanings). Again, some musicians have actively encouraged this, for example avant garde musicians who play particular phrases cued by what audience members are doing—coughing, stretching, standing—leading eventually to the audience catching on and then consciously directing the music through these cues. But more often it is the ethos of a particular scene that stimulates, even mandates, audience participation. For example, punk's DIY ideology—Do It Yourself—virtually required that the performer-audience split typical in "corporate rock" be overcome, and audiences seemed to be as important as performers in determining the direction punk took in its early years. At the other end of the spectrum, the advent of sophisticated copying technologies has allowed consumers to become participants in music creation of a sort. Those who create their own "dubs" and "mixes" from what's available commercially become part creators of a final product, which then means something more to them, a product of their own choices and labor.

When We Make Our Own Music

Let's—finally—get rid of the minstrel altogether, at least for a while. In many times and places, experiences of professional music makers have been few and far between. And even in North America in the twenty-first century, confronted by commercially produced music in stores, at work, in our cars, on our televisions, we still spend a great deal of time making music of some sort ourselves. The music we perform may come from many sources: popular music, ethnic and folk traditions, school band and childhood repertoires, our own creations. These origins may lend meaning to a piece, but whatever the origin, meaning is here tied to performing rather than observing performance.

Most obviously, performing music from a group tradition in itself establishes and/or reinforces group membership. In this sense alone, as Guy and Candie Cara-wan write, "cultural expression is unifying and empowering."[33] Especially in group performance, the words may contribute relatively little to the meaning: "[I]t's the experience of letting the rhythms of the music capture you, together, that affirms the group."[34] The importance of the songs of Bob Dylan, Phil Ochs, and similar 1960s protest singers, Eyerman & Jamison have argued, arose "not so much by being top ten hits as by lending themselves to shared performance."[35]

In specifically political settings, the feelings of unity and solidarity that arise out of shared performance are particularly powerful pointers toward a shared meaning. The civil rights movement was legendary for using music in predemonstration meetings as a way of establishing a common purpose, as described by Bernice Reagon:

> I can tell you that being a singing people during the organizing efforts of the Civil Rights Movement, the singing was everywhere. You will notice I make a difference between the songs and the singing, because it is not always a song that does it for Black people. It is when you use the song to experience what singing does, because the kind of phenomenon I'm talking about is a singing phenomenon, a collective experience that actually brings people together and holds them together as they move through something they decided to do. The singing is a sort of companion and glue and partner with a phenomenon that the people are involved in.[36]

While mass meetings, predemonstration gatherings, and demonstrations offer the most explosive of political settings, other more ongoing political settings also frame meanings of shared performances. Robertson, for example, points out the role of the Washington, D.C., Feminist Chorus as a "supportive family structure" for young lesbians. Here, singing in the midst of others who interpreted their participation as performing their solidarity with women-identified women helped provide "a sense of political and musical identity."[37]

Observing and appreciating art obviously can be very powerful, but actively participating in its creation—performing music, for example—may make it even more important to the individual, investing it not only with new meanings but with more powerful significance. Singing, Kerran Sanger argues, was a *transformative* experience in the civil rights movement:

> According to [activists'] descriptions, singing changed them, created strong positive emotion, banished fear and hatred, and charged them with a previously unexperienced sense of spirituality.... [I]t was described as a power capable of changing the very *being* of the activists. In other words, [Bernice] Reagon represented the freedom singing as having the power to recreate the people who sang.... "When I opened my mouth and began to sing, there was a force and power within myself I had never heard before. Somehow this music—music I could use as an instrument to do things with, music that was mine to shape and change so that it made the statement I needed to make—released a kind of energy I did not know I had."[38]

Activity, from this perspective, is itself a crucial meaning. "The more actively we participate, the more each one of us is empowered to act, to create, to display," declares Small, "then the more satisfying we shall find the performance of the ritual,"[39] and in this we hear echoes of Adorno's original argument: The music is meaningful to the degree it *activates* us rather than pacifies us.

Participation helps us construct meanings, and greater participation may well strengthen the impact of those meanings, at the time and onward. Performing music—whether that performance is for other strikers, for our daughter, for ourselves while we wash the dishes—helps make it ours.

Scenes and Cultures

While music may be experienced as discrete products—this song, that symphony— some music becomes connected to a grouping and lifestyle that seems to fit together, collectively standing for something in the mind of the individual. The Birmingham School, which helped found "cultural studies" as an academic enterprise, was interested in how music, style, identity, and other elements were drawn together into a more or less coherent—or coherent-*feeling*—package. Subcultures exhibit a style, but that needs to be understood as more than just fashion: as a sensibility, an ethos. Borrowing from the anthropologist Levi-Strauss, Burmingham School theorists stressed the "homology" of subcultures, the ways in which different parts of such subcultures seemed to fit together and reinforce each other.

Take punk, for example: The music was bare-bones, a minimum number of chords and instruments, stripped of the grand forms and virtuoso soloing that classic rock had developed. It sounded and seemed as though anyone could play it. The audience-performer divide was minimized, even abolished, as stage divers and mosh pit dancers became as much a part of the show as the musician. Punk fashion was similarly "democratic," replacing fashion dictated by expert arbiters of taste with a look that anyone could put together (it appeared) from a thrift store and hardware drawer. The do-it-yourself ethos of punk was evident in all of the subculture's manifestations.

The popularity of rock and roll in the fifties can similarly be better understood by the ethos that surrounded it than by its actual musical innovations, which were small in relation to the pop music of the time and minimal at best from already existing R&B. But rock and roll was understood by its fans to stand for more than music; it stood for rebellion and sexuality, for a different future from that already limned out for working-class and middle-class youth. For the white middle-class segment of the population, its roots in then marginalized populations (blacks and white hillbillies) gave it a sense of transgression that neither the lyrics nor musical structure alone could establish. For all youth of the post–World War II generation, it felt irresistibly present oriented, the celebration of "the sheer hedonistic joy of being alive"[40] as compared to their parents' generation's preoccupation with the future.

Some scenes have direct political connections and therefore an explicit political ethos. The folk music scene that was allied with the Communist Party in the 1930s and 1940s was dedicated to honoring and serving "the people," from an emphasis on folk and rural forms of music to styles of dress and even speech. Women's music in the 1970s and 1980s embodied a feminist stance in far more than just the content of the songs. Tours were run in which everyone—all performers, all stagehands, all promoters—were women; the audience that came was overwhelmingly people for whom feminism was a major concern in their lives. In the "counterculture" of the sixties it was common to link a love of rock with opposition to the war in Vietnam, support for legalizing marijuana, and the questioning of authority and conventional institutional arrangements. The salience of this feeling—that there were coherent, opposing camps, one in power and one forming around the rock scene—was so great that it hardly seemed hyperbole when the music critic Ralph Gleason wrote in 1969, "The whole body of rock music, spreading out from the center, with Dylan, the Beatles, and the Stones, involves its audience in an even more fundamental confrontation with the society. It says you are, all of you, wrong."[41]

The ethos developed in scenes and subcultures also functions powerfully to spread a worldview beyond their boundaries, particularly when there are avenues of communication, like modern mass media, that carry these outward. In Gitlin's phrase, "notions which had been the currency of tiny groups [begin] percolating through the vast demographics of the larger population."[42] What begins percolating isn't a coherent ideology, but what the Marxist literary critic Raymond Williams called "structures of feelings": part emotional, part rational, a heady brew of social ideas, fashions, music, and so forth, both precursor to a developing ideology and more than simply an ideology, involving "meanings and values as they are actively lived and felt" by each individual.[43]

Music is often the most visible part of the concoction, representing a whole culture to both friends and foes. Rap in the 1980s stood for a bundle of attitudes— "ghettocentricity," distrust of police, a claiming of the streets, and so on—that went beyond any single performer's persona. Musical pieces, genres, and artists are "that portion of the iceberg which is above the water and which is readily visible to the naked eye,"[44] as the folklorist Alan Dundes once said of proverbs. They owe their salience to the cultural frames they come from, but also summarize. One of the most important of music's functions for movements is to tie the emerging worldview of a movement to those cultural frames that can resonate with potential movement supporters.

♪

Chapter 5

The Meanings of Music

Some Reconsiderations and Implications

Music in Itself

As we've moved through the variety of ways in which musical messages are sent and meanings constructed, we've naturally been most interested in those that are politically motivated and/or carry importance for a movement. But we're mindful that very often music *does* seem to be about itself, rather than purposeful or referential to anything in the nonmusical world. When our young friend in Santa Barbara, arriving to pick up his date, howls in delight as Bonnie Raitt sings of futility and desperation in a loveless marriage, it seems much more likely that he is approving of the musical performance than responding particularly to the story being told in the lyrics or the emotions being expressed through the mood of the music. Friends sitting around in someone's living room singing "Long Black Veil" together are involved in playing folk music, not mourning the death of the protagonist who refused to expose his illicit lover, although the haunting mystery of the lyrics may contribute to the emotion of the moment. As Dave Laing writes of Buddy Holly, the appeal of some music "does not lie in what he says, in the situations his songs portray, but in the exceptional nature of his singing style and its instrumental accompaniment.... He uses it as an opportunity to play rock 'n' roll music, instead of regarding his role as one of portraying an emotion contained in the lyric."[1]

The enjoyment of music can't always be linked to some Big Idea the music "really" stands for any more than we can reduce all pleasure in baseball to an underlying Freudian narrative of sexuality, or our joy in dance to overcoming the specter of death. What makes hearing Aretha sing "Respect" thrilling isn't only suggestions of

103

freedom or feminism or sexuality, perceived in the lyrics, the genre, or the grain of the voice. There's a level of love for the music and performance itself. Music making and listening and sharing don't only reflect meaning; they also *constitute* meaning.[2]

Granting that we often find pleasure in the activity itself, however, doesn't mean there is no social context to that pleasure. What appeals to us about the music, even on an experiential level, is informed by our lives in a particular time and place, and thus always socially embedded. For example, John Shepherd has argued that functional tonality* *in itself* reflects and conveys the assumption of progress as a desired (and inevitable) goal, a notion that arose in the West in the wake of the scientific and industrial revolutions, and an accompanying assumption of hierarchy in which "certain relationships may be heard as more important or fundamental than others."[3] We don't need to believe that this is a conscious message of a composer or a perceived meaning of a listener to agree that commonly held assumptions in a society will be embodied in the creations of that society, making sense to creator and consumer alike without the need (or even likelihood) of conscious consideration. "[B]ecause *people* create music, they reproduce in the basic qualities of their music the basic qualities of their own thought processes," as Shepherd says,[4] and these, of course, are socially mediated. Even in pieces in which there is no deliberate attempt to say anything outside of strictly musical formations, the acts of creation, display, and reception are shot through with social assumptions.

The champions of absolute music have traditionally held it to be a higher form of art precisely because, they claim, it is *not* reflective of a given social situation but exists within its own realm, without narrative, timeless and universal. (Somewhat similar claims have been made for jazz and rock: that the "purest" examples of the genre are those that avoid the use of words with meaning.[5]) But some critics have argued that absolute music, on the contrary, does indeed contain narratives. McClary argues that Western symphonic music in its traditional sonata form "adheres ... thoroughly to the most common plot outline and the most fundamental ideological tensions available within Western culture: the story of a hero who ventures forth, encounters an Other, fights it out, and finally reestablishes secure identity."[6] These stories, McClary and others claim, are heavily gendered as well: The music identifies the hero as male (through social conventions of what sounds masculine) and the Other as female (through social conventions of what sounds feminine).[7]

Of course other interpretations are also possible. We might hear the sonata form as the story of class conflict, or of birth, or of "the great metanarrative: order is established, order is disturbed, and a new order grows out of the old," as Christopher Small hears it.[8] From this perspective, even if a composer were attempting to create absolute music with no conscious reference to anything in the extramusical world, she would still be influenced by the narratives with which she's familiar, the assumptions of her time about normality, gender, heroism, what is uplifting,

---

*Note for nonmusicians: Think of how you know what the last note of a song will be even before you hear it. That note, almost inevitably, is the root note of the *tonic,* the defining chord of the key the song is played in. Returning to that chord, and especially to that note, gives you that feeling of being back home, of being finished. Functional tonality means that a piece of music is organized in relation to that "home" chord, that it is the anchor for all that happens, and thus assumes greater importance than other chords and notes.

and so forth. And the same is true for listeners: Consciously or not, we tie our understanding of music to experience in the social world.[9]

The point is easily seen if we think about spoken language. We learn our native tongue without consciously reflecting on it for the most part. Within that language, however, are many assumptions about the world, assumptions that are not universal, we find, when we learn another language or travel to another society. So, too, the musical language we learn growing up in a given society *already* carries within it certain assumptions, links to prevailing beliefs about all sorts of issues. And just as the implicit assumptions of spoken language ("terrorist" is bad; "youth" is good, etc.) affect both speaker and listener, the implicit assumptions of our musical language, in a given time and place, will affect us as composers, performers, and audience members.

Some of these assumptions may be directly and obviously political, but many are not. Still, even music with assumptions and themes that appear apolitical may well have significant political implications and effects. Much of what we learn from music and its related activities is *incidental,* as Christenson & Roberts say about popular music—for example, "the rapid diffusion of a hair or clothing style following their appearance in a music video and the adoption of a new verbal expression after its use in a hit song."[10] In fact, they argue, it's precisely *because* it's incidental that audiences learn so much from what appears to be only entertainment: Audiences tend to critically examine information they perceive to be intended as persuasion, but don't resist information experienced as "just" entertainment. This is the point Bruce Springsteen and others have made about Elvis Presley: His effect on how whites thought about race was profound in large part because his audience didn't see race as even on his agenda:

> You could make an argument that one of the most socially conscious artists in the second half of the [twentieth] century was Elvis Presley, even if he probably didn't start out with any kind of political ideas that he wanted to accomplish.... [H]e was one of the people, in his own way, who led to the sixties and the Civil Rights Movement. He began by getting us "all shook up," this poor white kid from Mississippi, who connected with black folks through their music, which he made his own and then gave to others. So pop culture is a funny thing—you can affect people in a lot of different ways.[11]

One of the most important ways "apolitical" music engenders political or potentially political effects is simply through fostering of shared identity. We group with others who love the same music, and we think of it as *our music*—ours in contrast to someone else, whose music it isn't. Thus, even when the subject matter lacks explicit "us versus them" language, the very fact that some people like this artist/song/genre and some don't can set up a social distinction. What begins merely as difference, as Todd Gitlin points out, may become transformed into cultural *dissidence;* what seems on one level individual expression both reflects and becomes collective and alternative: "It didn't matter that Dylan's lyrics, for example, were celebrations of strictly private experience; by playing the music together we transformed it into a celebration of our own collective intimacy, love, hilarity."[12]

The more involved we are in the music, the stronger these effects are likely to be, especially the feeling of collectivity (which has great implications for social movement development). Those actually involved in the production and/or distribution of musics, for love or money (or both), are likely to have these feelings of solidarity actualized in the networks that develop from the music. In the early years of a new genre like rap, women's music, or punk, committed musickers form networks to support each other, trade songs, put touring musicians up in their homes, and create zines and other written materials. These networks are not only potentially available for political work, but serve an ideological and educational function in and of themselves. Watching young, radical people take over much of the world of popular music in the 1960s, Gleason wrote of their vast audience: "It has given them the vision that they can literally take over the world, as they see members of their own generation seizing the means of production in one area."[13]

Music's potential for encouraging dissidence is often found in the simple fact that music organizes our leisure time. Musical engagement typically competes with the demands of work time and the logic of work. Whenever authority—from medieval bishops to present-day corporate leaders—tells people to work hard now for the sake of the future, music that invites us to revel in the here and now of immediate sensations has an implicit, subversive political meaning:

> Popular music inevitably introduces uncertainty into the authorities' world, an uncertainty that sets the limits to state control by establishing an area of popular sovereignty in an area deemed politically important. ... The paradox built into the heart of [authoritarian] regimes is that to ignore politics, to have fun instead, to refuse to be involved, is to engage in politics. ... Music does not substitute for political dissent, just as gospel music does not replace religious faith, but the music does become the *form* of that dissent and not a mere appendage to it.[14]

Moreover, the conflict between music communities and government—authoritarian or not—is one of the ways in which musically fostered difference becomes first collective and then overtly political. Where governments seek to control all domains of life, as in totalitarian states, *any* deviation from what is considered normal in *any* sphere is defined as an attack on the state. The more repressive a state, the more charged unsanctioned music becomes with political significance. But in any form of state, the attempt by authority to control music in itself reinforces the *us-versus-them* feel of the music and its fans, and introduces overt politics where none were necessarily obvious before.

Banning music gives it an extra charge, a weight it might not otherwise have. In the wake of the fall of the Communist Party in the Soviet Union, many in that country's largely outlawed rock scene predicted it would never again be as important to its fans as it had been in those early years. "The best way to hear rock 'n' roll for the first time," says Boris Grebenshikov, of the leading Russian band Aquarium, "is when it's illegal."[15]

Multiple Meanings

Frith writes:

> In *The Composer's Voice*, Edward Cone asks whose voice we hear when we listen to a Schubert setting of a poem by Goethe. We hear a singer, Thomas Allen say, with a

distinctive physical voice; we hear the protagonist of the song, the "I" of the narrative; we hear the poem's author, Goethe, in the distinctive organization of the words and their argument; and we hear Schubert, *in whose voice* the whole thing is composed.[16]

And when we hear "Respect," we hear a singer, Aretha Franklin, with a distinctive physical voice; we hear the "I" of the narrative (and perhaps some of the person being addressed); we hear the song's author, Otis Redding. The cast of both examples could be expanded considerably, including the producer of the record, the conductor or musical director, a dominant instrumentalist in the band or orchestra, the important critic who criticized the artist's last performance, the owner of the record company looking to position his catalogue in a certain niche or cross over to a larger audience, and so on. This assemblage of artists and producers is joined in meaning construction by each audience member, each in her own context, which contains some features of ongoing duration and some that are immediate to the moment of *this* listening only.

The result is a thick stew, with flavors—meanings—blending together; occasionally one stands out; often one is altered, augmented, modified by another. Content is a factor, but so too is the medium in itself (for instance, the lessons and meaning in engaging in the activity of watching videos). Engendered feelings or embodied meanings, overt or concealed, intended by an author/performer, are understood, distorted, recast, recontextualized by an audience member/performer; at the same time *unintended* messages undergo these same kinds of transformations. Our reception of messages and construction of meaning blend conscious and unconscious reactions, emotion, and cognition in differing doses. How music makes us *feel* is just as much a "meaning" as what it makes us *think,* and these two levels of experiencing the music obviously affect each other.

It's not even simply a question of understanding that musickers are generally seeking pleasure rather than meaning, as some theorists have suggested. When we fall in love with a piece of music, as when we fall in love with a person, there's very little rational analysis going on. It isn't for its pleasures *or* its meaning, but because we can't help it. The piece haunts us; it gets into our head and won't let go. We've *fallen.* The reasons we fall may have to do with pleasures and with constructed meanings, but it's not a conscious plan: "Oh these are good politics (or a brilliant melody)—I should love this song."

Once we've fallen or, more commonly, once we're simply familiar with a piece, the case isn't closed. Again, as with people, our feelings and thoughts may well change over time. The meaning attributed to a piece when we fell in love with it may not be the meaning we attribute to it a year later. Our first experience of a piece is very different from our twentieth; the person we are at the time of the twentieth experience may be different, in a different situation, with different interests, with different concerns. The Beatles may have sounded like the soundtrack to the Revolution in Consciousness that we were sure was changing the world when we first heard them; those same songs now have a warm, fuzzy aura of "when we were young." Meaning isn't only multilayered but fluid.

As a final twist on meaning: How we feel about a piece, what we construct about its meanings, and the effect these have on us don't necessarily line up that neatly. We may get hooked on it for the joy of its creation or the skill of the performer, with no thought at all about its referential meanings or any other message, but the *effect* on us may still be political, for instance, linking us to a group with a shared identity or placing us in opposition to people who hate this kind of music.

One result of this extremely complex interaction is that we may receive competing, conflicting messages from a piece of music. This is most obvious when the lyrics and music seem to diverge, as when Marcus said of the Beatles' *Revolution* that though the words were cautionary and (relatively) conservative, "there is a 'message' in that music which is ultimately more powerful than anyone's words."[17] Dave Laing sees the same thing when rock pioneer Buddy Holly sings, "'if you knew Peggy Sue, then you'd know why I feel blue.' It seems to be the cry of an unhappy man, but the record radiates energy and enthusiasm."[18] The feminist writer Ellen Willis explained her preference for the often (lyrically) misogynist punk of the Sex Pistols to much of the folkie, introspective women's music genre of the 1970s: "Music that boldly and aggressively laid out what the singer wanted, loved, hated—as good rock and roll did—challenged me to do the same, and so, even when the content was antiwoman, antisexual, in a sense antihuman, the form encouraged my struggle for liberation. Similarly, timid music made me feel timid, whatever its ostensible politics."[19]

Form can also conflict with overt representations of political agendas. Consider right-wing skinhead music made popular in some Southern California suburbs in the 1990s. The form was extremely democratic—the line between performer and audience members (who, for instance, through moshing and stage diving became active participants in the show) was very thin—and yet the lyrics and general attitude of performers and audience members promoted a neofascist culture in which it was cool to be racist, sexist, and generally antidemocratic.

Similarly, the effects of a music may contradict its avowed purpose, as Perris observes of religious music:

> Music in all worship is expected to heighten the desired emotional effect in the listener, to emphasize the ritual text, especially certain significant words, and to focus the worshiper's attention on the rite. But the danger of so sensuous a phenomenon as music is that it may be more seductive than the rite itself, and that the musicians may evoke more interest than the priests.[20]

Having said all this, how can we explain the fact that musicians, critics, and listeners quite often try to reduce interpretation to a claim about *the* meaning of a piece (or even an entire genre) of music? At times the multiplicity of meanings may not be experienced as in conflict, but instead as producing what Feld calls "a special kind of 'feelingful' activity ... that unites the material and mental dimensions of musical experiences as fully embodied."[21] Whether expressed as feeling or thought, we often experience the "wash" of the total package as fitting together; fragmented meanings are "(re)constructed into a larger construct."[22] Much of the pioneering work of the Birmingham School involved arguing that subcultures—hippies, motorcycle boys, punks, etc.—were not chaotic (as they typically had been portrayed), but blended seemingly disparate elements into a homologous style. This interpretation stresses that music, as an element of lifestyle, seems to be about the core beliefs of a group, political or otherwise.

The resolution of potentially conflicting meanings may be aided and abetted by artists' attempts to cast their work as consistent. Gang of Four lyricist Jon King declares, "The whole thing is of a piece. It's impossible to separate the significance of the guitar break, say, in 'FMUSA' [1990] from the context in which the words occur. They live in the same thought or idea."[23] The "2-Tone" groups discussed earlier "presented a total package of sound and image so thoroughly integrated that the multiracial 'message' could be *inferred*"[24] in virtually every song played, whatever other messages or meanings were present. Where there is an authoritative source of information (artist, peers, context, media, etc.) declaring that the whole package fits together in a single meaning, that meaning will become more salient to those involved with the music. As Middleton says, such "coherence is 'unnatural'—the product of cultural work."[25]

We've used the term *pointer* to convey our view of the construction of meaning in music. Quite literally, each of the different variables in each of the different components of transmission, context, and reception may *point* toward certain meanings, making some interpretations more likely than others, but none absolutely guarantees a certain meaning being adopted or excludes other possible meanings. When there's agreement between many and/or the most salient of these pointers, some constructions become much more likely. If a feminist woman first hears "Respect" being sung together by those who have just attended a consciousness-raising session that was largely concerned with the need for men to respect women, she still may enjoy it primarily as an apolitical dance tune—but probably not.

Meanings are also cumulative, based on past experiences with similar sounds and what we have previously made of their meaning;[26] the same may be said of genre, performer's image, listener's ideology, and so forth. Each points us in a certain direction for constructing meaning. Some weigh more heavily than others, and their relative weight is idiosyncratic to our past history with each as well as the specifics of each experience.

Further, pointers are interactive; they don't simply add up cumulatively, but affect each other's impact. An audience member typically uninterested in lyrics, but hearing an artist known for her political music, playing just an acoustic guitar at a political rally, may construct more of his meaning from the artist's lyrics than he would otherwise; a friend's comments about how interesting the performer's finger-picking style is might lessen that effect, while being urged to sing along might increase the lyrics' salience. Pointers direct us toward likely meanings, but also toward layers of meaning that are most important in a given time and place, and thus affect the saliency of other pointers.

Sociologists like Erving Goffman or David Snow argue that our understandings of a situation are organized by *frames* we adopt that guide our interpretation of new information, fitting it into *schemas* we've created from past information. We use this kind of Structural Interactionist approach[27] to emphasize that although musickers seem to construct their own idiosyncratic meanings from a multitude of factors, structural forces—whether the commercial framing of Top 40 songs on the radio or the musical structures of genres—can be used to help understand how individuals arrive at meanings they share in common with others. Each structure—each pointer, in fact—doesn't *mandate* certain meanings but *increases the chances* of some meanings becoming salient while decreasing the chances of others. Charlie Manson can decide that "Helter Skelter" is about race war, but the chances of that interpretation being adopted by many people are slight, given all the pointers in other directions. As Hall wrote about television viewing, "Polysemy [i.e., the existence of multiple meanings] must not, however, be confused with pluralism.... Any society/culture tends, with varying degrees of closure, to impose its classifications of the social and cultural and political world. These constitute a *dominant cultural order*, though it is neither univocal nor uncontested."[28]

A Second Look at Artist's Intent and the Power of Lyrics

We began our exploration of music's meaning(s) by attacking the tendency to understand the meaning and impact of music simply by looking at what an artist intends (or seems to intend), best illustrated in the simplistic L=ARM equation. Now we come full circle: Returning to the minstrel-audience model, we want to argue that in the eventual meaning(s) constructed by an audience member through a complex amalgam of interacting pointers, the messages sent out by the performer typically remain among the strongest of these pointers.

Artist's intent will, first of all, inform many of the pointers we've discussed, from the artist's choice of music, words, and presentation to the venue in which the music is presented or the makeup of the band, all coloring audience members' interpretations. Music itself, as we said earlier, often conveys moods and emotions that most people in a given culture or subculture will recognize—anger, peacefulness, happiness, sorrow, etc. Additional hints from an artist can add to the specificity of these, directing audience interpretation in particular directions.

The most powerful of these additional hints, much of the time, are the lyrics (if there are lyrics).[29] Words, like all symbols, are far from absolute in conveying ideas, but they are the least ambiguous of the symbols humans use. When Aretha Franklin sings the word "respect," it gives us a pretty good idea of what ballpark we're in. If the key word in the chorus was "spaghetti," our understanding of the song would likely be very different.

But words, being symbols sent and received by different people, are still not precise. They retain ambiguity, or in a more positive sense, a richness of meaning beyond a single level. Lyrics serve as a kind of anchor of understanding, a strong pointer for meaning—and also for message, though, of course, the two need not coincide. The lyrics that most affect a given listener may not necessarily convey the lyrical intent of the artist, as Ronald Reagan's understanding of the hook phrase "Born in the USA" did not convey the message of that song as its author intended. The power of lyrics as pointers, in short, isn't *necessarily* harnessed in the service of matching an artist's intent and audience member's meaning, but it is a potent factor pushing in that direction.

There are those who regularly look to lyrics as a—or *the*—key component of any song. Pratt points out that if we take the rough estimates of "'only' 10 to 30 percent of listeners who are attentive to lyrics, there remains a massive population—indeed millions, in the case of some of the biggest-selling albums—who *are* reached by song lyrics or who may consciously seek out singers and songs expressive of their views."[30] Artists, responding to this need or out of their own belief in the importance of lyrics, have become extremely likely in recent years to print their lyrics as part of an album's packaging, making lyrics easier to access, even in genres like hardcore where discerning the lyrics as performed is often virtually impossible; lyrics of almost all recorded artists are available on websites. Of course, audience members may want to know the words for reasons other than to arrive at a meaning of a song (to be the authority, to be able to sing along, etc.); still, regardless of *why* they want to know the words, once they do, the words may become a potent pointer toward their eventual constructed meaning.

Sometimes lyrics are not the primary source of meaning so much as a fine-tuning of more general impressions audience members have already been (consciously or unconsciously) constructing based on other clues. Aretha's voice is confident and empowered but that particular attitude—"give me respect"!—would not have come through for most people without the word itself directing our interpretations of what that voice means. This may be of crucial importance for movements, which need participants to fix their emotions to particular ideas.

Perhaps paradoxically, lyrics have great power to shape our constructed meanings when they seem to contradict the meaning we believe we're getting from the other aspects of a piece—genre, performer image, etc. Just as in conversation we use the attitude, voice timbre, body language, and so on of the other person to guide us in our understanding of what we're being told, often we base our understanding of a song's content on the sound of it, the grain of the voice, the performer's look, and so on, rather than the lyrics. But just as in conversation, the words may suddenly tell us we were mistaken. Words of a song may disrupt expectations; their very conflict with our previous understanding may be what grabs our attention.

But this is rare: Words and sounds generally don't diverge because composers try to make them go together. As a result, the musical sound is often imbued with performers' and composers' understanding of the lyrics. "The words are very important," says singer Freedy Johnson. "They're key. But you have to sing the words. You can't just deliver them in a whispered voice.... The message is in the singing of the song."[31]

The composer knows the words, the singer knows the words, the producer knows the words, and the performance they seek to deliver will tend to be appropriate to that meaning. In this way, lyrical meaning, including the artist's intended message, is amplified, becoming more likely to be adopted by others, even those who aren't consciously paying attention to the lyrics. The lyrics to "Respect" as sung by Otis Redding *ask* for respect, and the tone of voice he sings in is that of a man not sure at all he's going to get what he's asking for. Aretha changes the lyrics in small but significant ways, and her tone of voice expresses these changes, a *demand* for respect. Her lyrical intent is reflected in the tone of voice she chooses to use for that particular song.

Understanding a song's lyrical message doesn't require knowing all the words; the intent of an artist may be conveyed in the smaller segments that *are* absorbed. The simple use of the word *we* in "We Shall Overcome" conveys a message (indeed, the early religious version of the song was "I will be all right"; the *we* was consciously used to transform the song's social purpose),[32] and this is generally true of the use of the word *we* instead of the word *I*. Main points tend to be repeated in the title and chorus and/or the "hook line" (for example, "We shall overcome" or "Ain't gonna study war no more"), further increasing their chances of being heard as significant by audience members.

It's a common belief among musicians and audiences that matching sound to lyrics increases a song's emotional punch: "Words make you think thoughts. Music makes you feel a feeling. But a song makes you feel a thought," said the famed lyricist Yip Harburg.[33] Of course, this isn't objective fact but a subjective perception of musickers, built on the musical (and other) conventions we've learned, subject to the many other factors in meaning construction we've been discussing. There's a feeling we get from our favorite music that goes beyond just liking the music—*it seems so right*, almost a moral or spiritual feeling. This may come from lyrics or any other component in particular, but in general we'd say it arises from a combination of many factors coming together for an individual at the right time and the right place. Whether that powerful charge originates with the lyrics or not, however, it may well be *transferred* to the lyrics, the most easily understood component for most people. Much as we tend to believe what a loved one tells us, we may believe what a loved song "tells" us.

The relative salience of lyrical messages may also vary based on cultural tradition. Some countries and cultures have a strong tradition of "truth telling" by "bard poets" that has been transplanted to music.[34] In such cultures, musicians are more likely to consciously send lyrical messages, and audiences are more likely to search for them. When Joe Hill or Woody Guthrie crafted new lyrics using familiar melodies, they were reenacting the social role of minstrels and bard poets. Bob Dylan deliberately brought that tradition into the mainstream of American pop, and his early fans responded to him as a poet with something crucial to say.

Such poets/singers become most salient in times and places where freedom of speech is abridged and censorship of some form is practiced. As one leading Soviet rock musician told Ramet in the years leading up to the fall of the Communist Party,

> We can't have any alternative parties or any alternative organized politics. So there are not too many places where you can gather large groups of people and communicate ideas which are not official. Rock 'n' roll is one of the most important vehicles for helping people in communist countries to think in a different way.[35]

The same can be said for situations where there is no official censorship, but where a group feels its particular concerns are not addressed in conventional forms of public forums. One reason why lyrics (and music generally) are so important to young people in the United States is that they have less access to mainstream public forums. "The lyrical content of underground music reflects kids' attempt at understanding things adults won't talk about," says Gaines: "suicide, alcoholism, incest, family violence, nuclear holocaust, alienation, street violence, police brutality."[36]

Lyrics take on a similarly heightened importance in cases of what might be called self-censorship, situations in which people don't trust their own ability to say what they want to say. Half a century ago Donald Horton pointed out the utility of the lyrics of popular love songs to those who were courting:

> In a culture in which skill in the verbal expression of profound feelings is not a general trait and in which people become embarrassed and inarticulate when speaking of their love for each other, a conventional, public impersonal love poetry may be a useful—indeed, a necessary—alternative.... This is undoubtedly one of the chief functions of the professional singer, whose audience of lovers finds in him their mutual messenger.[37]

Is Cognitive Processing Necessary?

Most treatments of political music assume that conscious comprehension is key to meaning construction and to retention of meaning. Such discussions largely assume that (1) meaning can be constructed only through conscious reflection, and (2) meaning is in the lyrics, i.e., the original L=ARM misconception.

For instance, Mondak argues that "true persuasion can only occur if the listener has cognitively processed the message." Further, since distraction of any kind is thought to interfere with "the receiver's ability to process the message, ... those features of a song which lead to an emotional response act to preclude cognitive processing."[38] Mondak is arguing here about the artist's presumed lyrical intent, but the same argument can be made about audience-constructed meaning; that is, that meaning depends on some conscious, cognitive "elaboration" that the musicker carries out. In contrast, much of what we've been arguing would suggest that while conscious cognition is a very powerful factor in meaning construction, music may impact muse·kers in other ways that are also significant, including politically significant.

The distinction between cognitive elaboration and "emotional" reactions is itself a questionable one. They are certainly hard to distinguish methodologically, and we tend to agree with Meyer, who questioned whether they can even be said to exist separately (let alone in opposition):

> [A]ffective experience is just as dependent upon intelligent cognition as conscious intellection, ... both involve perception, taking account of, envisaging, and so forth, ... [therefore] thinking and feeling need not be viewed as polar opposites, but as different manifestations of a single psychological process.[39]

But let's accept the distinction for a moment, thinking of it as useful for describing an imaginary continuum from purely conscious reflection to purely emotional reaction. Mondak was speaking principally of *persuasion,* that is, convincing someone of a position she had not previously held. In the following chapters on the functions of music for movements, we will discuss this kind of effect (which we call recruitment and conversion) as well as others: serving the committed, education, and mobilization. That discussion will illustrate that for some functions, such as what we here call "education," highly conscious cognition is generally more important and more common; for others, such as "mobilization," other kinds of response may be more crucial.

Meaning construction, we've been arguing, is complex, a dialectical process in which multiple factors interact. We've divided those into three "phases" (transmission, context, reception), but emphasized throughout that this is only a heuristic device to make some sense out of a fluid process. In this process, artistic intent may affect audiences, but audience intent affects artists as well. That is, performers are generally quite interested in what their audiences are thinking about their performances.

Meaning construction, then, even in the minstrel-audience model, is always a collaboration between artists and audiences, set within societal structures that exert their own influences. There is no single equation that can tell us how much each factor will contribute and how much each will affect the others. The effects of musicking will vary from setting to setting, from person to person, from Aretha Franklin to Charlie Manson. But patterns will and do emerge. Individuals make their own meanings but, to borrow from Marx (and Negus), "[T]hey do not make it just as they please ... but under circumstances directly encountered, given and transmitted from the past."[40]

The Expression and Construction of Political Meaning

We've gone on this extensive exploration of how musical meanings are constructed in order to look at how this plays out for social movements specifically. In the next chapter we'll begin discussing what *functions* musicking plays for movements, that is, what movement tasks musicking helps to accomplish. But before ending this chapter, we want to briefly summarize the different ways such meanings may be packaged and constructed. These, too, of course, are overlapping and interactive. We'll look at them one by one here, understanding that they don't exist in isolation from each other in the real world.

Propositional Information and Analysis

Through music and the full range of peripheral activities we're calling musicking, people may offer or obtain concrete, propositional information about social and political issues. Stories are told and interpreted, viewpoints are expressed, visions are presented. Musicking is in this sense a kind of living theory. The information may be new, or reinforce other information we've received in other ways, or simply crystallize or valorize ideas we've had spinning around in our own heads.

Although propositional meaning is generally constructed from information delivered in words—lyrics, onstage comments, written materials—that isn't the only possibility. The mixed-race composition of the British "2-Tone" bands of the 1980s, for example, was understood by many audience members to present an argument that race divisions were not inevitable, that there could be and was a movement against racism.

Reinforcing or Disrupting Basic Assumptions

Musicking may reinforce or disrupt common assumptions and the "schemas" or framing we use for understanding the world around us, and therefore the general feeling that life as experienced in a given place and time is or isn't natural, inevitable, and eternal. This form of contribution isn't the supplying of a concrete alternative vision or ethos that might be delivered as propositional information, but the understanding that alternatives are possible. Utopian visions, for example, are in this sense less important for the particular worlds they envision than for suggesting that alternatives exist at all.

As we noted back in the first chapter, the patterned nature of social life induces inertia. We tend to do what we've done before and what we see others around us doing; we tend to believe what we've always believed and what others around us believe. Musicking that follows well-understood (though not necessarily overtly stated) rules carries an implicit message that the status quo is normal; it's "propaganda for a way of life."[41] Music that violates the rules we've come to expect attacks this view of "the usual" as equivalent to "the only." This disruption may create a deeper level of questioning than just the political; it may or may not even have any direct relation to a particular issue or movement. But as Ralph Gleason wrote, observing the great sea change of cultural shift in the 1960s, "[O]nce you set up a situation in which sacred tenets of the social fabric are treated as obsolete or irrelevant, anything may be questioned."[42] Although this questioning of basic beliefs may occur in "strictly" musical terms, the implications are nonetheless politically charged and politically important.

Because societies are not completely engineered mechanisms, with each gear meshing perfectly, established beliefs can also be undermined and the naturalness of the existing order can also be questioned in some times and places through the contradictions inherent in "normal" life. Musicking, with its emphasis on pleasure and the here and now, can contradict the work ethic and delayed gratification that elites usually see as necessary for the masses to embrace. Thus, even in its most "apolitical" forms, musicking may undermine an existing order by claiming participants' passion, drawing their allegiance from other pillars of a society that those in control would like to see as the focus: work, state, family, and so forth.

The Organization of Coherent Packages

Whether specific to a particular issue or in the broadest societal terms, musicking may serve a political purpose by drawing together any number of ideas and events into what appears to be, what *feels like,* a coherent package, an ethos that links together a variety of ideas, emotions, and events. Music, it's often been noted, helps us organize memories of a time and place, but it also helps organize our understanding of the present confronting us. The great impact of mid-1960s music, according to

Gleason, writing at the time, was that "unarticulated protest is made specific, and applied to political subjects like Vietnam, for kids in remote towns who wouldn't otherwise know that they are a part of a vast movement or wouldn't connect their discontent to its sources in our social-political setup."[43]

In particular, the scenes that form around musical conclaves may convince participants and observers alike that music, style, and politics fit together, which is exactly what Subculturalists meant when they said punk or hippie culture was homologous. Construction of a coherent package is important for political movements in several ways. First, if it is true that much of musicking induces generalized emotions, an overall schema provided by a social movement can provide those emotions with an explicit social object. That is, it's quite different if our rage is attributed to, and then fixed on, a pointless cosmos, or Jews who are subverting the Christian world, or capitalists making money from workers' misery. Further, this coherent package can then be stored and accessed over time. Musicking connected to a movement may reinforce the movement's frame whenever it's recalled.

Identity and Solidarity

Musicking is central to developing and displaying collective identity. Musicking reinforces the feeling of being linked to a group in important ways; one of the powers of music is that it can evoke such links even when the group isn't present.

Moreover, sometimes musicking forges a sense of solidarity with outsiders, expressing and revealing linkages that hadn't been appreciated before. These potentially presage cooperation between groups who may not have seen each other as likely allies. In the latter decades of the twentieth century, various Irish rock and punk bands attempted to mix Catholic and Protestant audiences by playing venues on neutral turfs as a way of deliberately bringing them together to see and feel how much alike they actually were. The deliberate combination of punk and ska bands during the 1970s Rock Against Racism concerts in England was precisely intended to bring together young people of different races in a shared activity that might induce them to see their common identity as young music lovers as more important than their different racial identities.

Evoking Place, Creating Space

Sound, as Ray Pratt has written, evokes a sense of place and a "sense of space."[44] This may be a reference to some other particular time and place—Dixieland jazz evoking an older New Orleans, oldies radio evoking a time of youth. But often what's most powerful is simply the marking off of the activity itself, creating what Pratt calls *free space*: special and magical, where the "real world" has been banished, replaced by a different set of rules and relations. "In clubs, scenes, and raves, listening on headphones, radio, and in the concert hall, we are only where the music takes us," as Frith says.[45]

This is obvious in venues specifically meant for music, such as clubs and concert halls. A defined physical space is filled by a sonic presence and an audience that has come precisely for that sound; no wonder the rest of the world seems banished. Within these enclaves, groups gather and feel their identity and solidarity; further, because the space is intended for the sharing of music, the music and its culture define the activities and ethos of the space. Music gatherings thus provide opportunities for the sharing of the music, but also the growth of the scene around the music. For those whose identities are normally under suspicion or attack, in particular, this is incredibly powerful. Miller & Román tell us that in lesbian and gay theater spaces,

> [M]uch of the significant cultural work occurring ... results from the social dynamics of queer gatherings. The context and space of performance, for many queer spectators and participants, informs most forcefully their experience of the performance. In many ways, what is represented on the stage is beside the point.[46]

Sound makes claim to space in less physically defined settings as well. Music's effect, Pratt notes, is different from that evoked by other arts because it has no fixed physical boundaries, but nevertheless can define a space.[47] The late twentieth-century battle between urban adolescents with boom boxes and "adults" on the subways (largely won by the adults when transit authorities in most cities banned the playing of boom boxes) was a battle over who had control of the public space carved out by sound. As Tricia Rose has constantly pointed out, "It is not just what you say, it is where you can say it, how others react to it, and whether you have the power to command access to public space."[48] A similar process is seen in the Unionist marching bands that stage parades in Ireland, seeking to assert their right to publicly play their music in territories conventionally understood to be Nationalist.

Free space isn't only external. Music and the rituals around it are typically used to carve out what Gitlin has described as "inner space,"[49] an internal world that, too, feels removed and insulated from the everyday world. The stereotypical adolescent up in her room, playing her music and seemingly oblivious to the rest of humanity, is the poster child for this. In free space of all kinds, the meaning constructed by audiences may be simply "Here I am free, here I am me," though more particular meanings may also arise.

Crucially, our internal musicking may be connected to external free space experiences. The experience (and meaning) of temporarily living in a world that seemed to exist as an alternative to the normal world may be preserved and reexperienced as the music is used and replayed in the inner space of the mind. The private enjoyment of music can create an inner space where external freedom, otherwise limited, can be imagined. This process is reciprocal: Movements, once established, create free spaces (in each of the meanings we've just discussed) in which culture can flourish, engendering, as one result, free inner space.

Generating Energy

Adorno feared that popular music (in particular) induced a stupor in the listener; looking at classical concert audiences, Brecht said, "we see entire rows of human beings transported in a peculiar state of intoxication, wholly passive, self-absorbed, and according to all appearances, doped."[50] But these are in direct contrast to the experience most of us have of music much of the time: It energizes us, it makes us want to be active.

Certainly most music elicits a physical response. We tap our toes or nod our heads, get up and dance, or at least move around. When Bulgarian officials banned the local group Signal in 1982, they said it was because rock music in general stirred listeners to "excessive excitement."[51] Music helps create an energy that, in itself, may appear dangerous to guardians of the status quo because it threatens to overflow society's capacity to occupy it, leading to alienation, discontent, and so forth. But more importantly, that energy is available for any number of possible uses, including political use.

The energy of musicking, moreover, isn't just physically derived; music often stimulates an emotional response that seems to generate energy, as commented on by civil rights workers interviewed by Sanger:

> [A]ctivists depicted their singing as the *source* of much of the emotional force they brought to the movement. ... "I saw people in church sing and pray until they shouted. I knew *that* music as part of a cultural expression that was powerful enough to take people from their conscious selves to a place where the physical and intellectual being worked in harmony with the spirit."[52]

A number of authors have suggested that it is the mix of energy and emotion created by listening to white power rock that drives right-wing kids leading fairly ordinary lives "to become self-styled terrorists in their local communities,"[53] the fuel that drives theory into practice.

> "The music we listened to, how we talked, it got into your mind," says Randall Rojas, a 23-year-old in jail on a murder charge. "Then you'd start acting like that. You'd be doing speed and the lyrics would come into your mind, lyrics like 'Eating your insides, rah, rah, rah, smashing your brains, rah, rah, rah.'" ... Thomas Powell, 19, another California Skinhead and devotee of racist rock, describes it like this: "[T]hey talk about killing, and they just pump you up, you know."[54]

But clearly, it isn't simply energy and emotion that drive a member of the White Aryan Resistance to attack a person of color, or that enable African American activists in Georgia in 1962 to stand up to institutionalized repression and vigilante violence. These various aspects of music and musicking, once again, interact, with each other and with nonmusical factors, to support activism. For analytical purposes, we've presented them one by one, but many tend to mix together in any real situation. White power rock helps a young person identify his group; the words to the songs give him an analysis of where his problems come from, supplemented by the reading he's done in the magazines his favorite bands have recommended. On a given night, singing along to Skrewdriver roaring in the background, he takes the step into action that his ideology, his identity, his peers, his group, all seem to suggest is necessary. A 14-year-old girl hears music familiar to her from her church upbringing, but now accompanying words about the struggle for black freedom. She's drawn to the group's singing, by both the tradition and the new information it carries, and once inside it, draws additional strength from the circle of singing, a ring of protection that enables her to envision and then actually take part in a demonstration against segregation.

In the past few chapters we've explored how music and musicking play roles in the creation (as well as reflection) of the social world, conveying a dazzling array of messages, constructed into a dazzling array of meanings. Having explored *how* meaning is constructed, we return to our original question: How do these constructed meanings play a role in the development and sustaining of social movements? *What* is their contribution?

PART III

The Functions of Musicking for Social Movements

♪

Chapter 6

Serving the Committed

In the next few chapters we examine the ways musicking helps movements with the critical tasks of attracting members and supporters, inducing (and later maintaining) some kind of allegiance from them, and making it easier or more compelling for them to engage in actions when necessary. In the real world, of course, these aren't discrete stages but more or less interwoven. But here, to explore them more fully, we've divided these tasks up as (1) education; (2) conversion and recruitment; (3) mobilization; and (4) several related tasks we group as "serving the committed," which, although last in a chronological sense, are the most straightforward and widely recognized—and so we'll begin there.

Serving the Committed

Musicking, a contemporary political musician says, "encourages the encouraged."[1] Those people who identify themselves as members of a movement and engage in movement-related activities—"the committed"—are often the primary target and consumers of movement music. "People wrap themselves, sometimes, in song and singing," says Bernice Johnson Reagon, "and it helps them to do what they've already decided to do."[2]

Affirmation and Reaffirmation

Among the most important tasks of musicking, then, is helping activists honor a commitment they've already made—*affirmation, reaffirmation,* and *sustenance* are some of the terms that have been used to describe this. The songs of the civil rights movement, one participant wrote, "had an unparalleled ability to evoke the moral power of the movement's goals, to arouse the spirit, comfort the afflicted, instill courage and commitment, and to unite disparate strangers into a 'band of brothers and sisters' and a 'circle of trust.'"[3] "Singing is the backbone and balm of this movement," said another. "Somehow you can go on in the face of violence and death, cynicism and inaction of the FBI, the indifference of the federal government, when you can sing with your band of brothers."[4]

This function has sometimes been characterized derisively as "preaching to the converted," but this phrase misrepresents the dynamics of collective struggles. First of all, movements aren't homogenous, but groupings of heterogeneous individuals who agree about some things but may be at odds about others. Musicking often represents those shared beliefs that allow "disparate strangers" to feel they are indeed a band of brothers and sisters, and reinforces those beliefs when much of the world is working to break them down. "It is the sound of the Lambeg drum rather than the resonance of political ideology which brings tears to the eyes of a Loyalist," Bell says of the Irish Unionist movement.[5]

Movement loyalty is not simply achieved once and for all; it needs to be constantly re-created for a movement to survive. As Miller & Román have written,

> To claim that artists are only preaching to the converted implies a fixed position for the audience assembled that trivializes the ever-changing and never immediately apparent needs and desires of . . . [movement] spectators. . . . This charge assumes that a stable and static mass has arrived fully into an imagined state of conversion. Truth be told, however, the converted are never wholly converted.[6]

Solidarity—loyalty to the movement and its members—must be constantly reaffirmed, and musicking's role here is obvious and profound. One community organizer in Appalachia in the 1970s told the Carawans,

> It makes a big difference to have a whole group of people singing, dancing, clapping together. It gives you more strength and more courage within yourself. The music is one of the really important things in getting groups together. It puts people's minds at ease and helps them spread their love from breast to breast. It makes a connection.[7]

Solidarity is dependent in part on what sociologists call frame alignment, the perception by individual members that the movement's view of the world is consistent with their own. Such a view may be very specific ("The government is in cahoots with the logging companies to allow the rape of the Kalmiopsis Wilderness"), but more often musicking reinforces a generalized view (love and respect for Mother Earth). In the language of the behavioral sciences, music can serve as a "prime" that triggers a complex interpretive schema in which specific situations are linked to a framework of more general beliefs: Hearing "Respect" triggers a group of previously bundled beliefs about gender roles that are brought to bear on a situation at hand; singing about a single landlord in "Penny's Farm"*[8] triggers

---

*   Now you go out on Penny's Farm/Pick a little crop of cotton and a little crop of corn
         He'll turn around and plan and plot/'til he gets himself a mortgage on everything you've got
         Hard times in the country, down on Penny's Farm.

existing feelings about the system of tenant farmers working on the farms of the landed gentry. In this way, music seems to *embody* a movement, condensing and giving shape to an array of feelings and beliefs.

As musicking articulates these core beliefs, it also reinforces them. "If you sing 'Ain't gonna let nobody turn me 'round' enough times," says a contemporary song-writer, "you will begin to believe it."[9] Surrounded by others similarly restating their beliefs in music, the effect can be incredibly powerful. Hampton paints us a picture of Joan Baez leading 100,000 people singing "We Shall Overcome" at the rally ending the 1963 March on Washington: "At that moment, they all believed they could indeed overcome."[10]

Shared beliefs may be tied to particular identities. Singing along with James Brown as he says, "Say it loud! I'm black and I'm proud!" isn't just an expression of a viewpoint, but an expression of an identity, in this case embracing blackness as a positive characteristic at a time when "black" was often seen as a stigma. Listening to "Respect" may reinforce an identity as an independent, self-sufficient woman. Importantly for movements, that assertive identity may thereby be strengthened compared with competing—and less assertive—aspects of identity, often through the articulation of *collective* identity. The great accomplishment of the Industrial Workers of the World (IWW) in mass strikes such as Lawrence, Massachusetts, in 1912 was to emphasize to workers from many different nationalities and back-grounds that their identity as workers was more important at that moment than the ethnic or national backgrounds that divided them. In this, the Wobbly organizers' most potent weapon was often musicking, as a contemporary observer realized:

> The IWW has been quick to grasp the song as a band to hold varied nationalities together. It has become part of the new tactics, and like mass picketing, appeals to the imagination and gives those who take part a sense of solidarity and consecration.[11]

Music and musicking are often at the heart of activities and rituals in which movement members "perform" their identity, reenacting and reaffirming their core beliefs while celebrating and reinforcing members' ties to each other. When union members end a meeting by singing "Solidarity Forever," they are linking themselves to a set of beliefs about their shared situation and tradition, and their potential collective power. Sara, one of our activist informants, wrote us:

> I still am moved by the words and the memories of marching, swaying to [the music], and how the words, sung in unity and harmony, strengthened resolve. Music provided an expression of sincerity—you heard something in the singing voice that caused belief in each other.

Ritual helps manage disagreement and factionalizing by fostering an inclusive feeling that reinforces the links between participants. "There was almost no form

(note continued)
　　You go to the fields and you work all day/'til way after dark but you get no pay
　　Promises you meat and a little bit of lard/It's hell to be a renter on Penny's Farm!
　　Hard times in the country, down on Penny's Farm.

for people uniting around agreements, and no way that those agreements could fully be expressed," writes Michael Lerner of his experiences in movement organizations of the 1960s and 1970s, "[... but] song stated in ritual fashion what we all shared."[12] Ron, a current environmental activist, sees music providing "common ground" for "the boomers, Depressionettes, and youngsters.... It served to link the troops into a common drive." This is a strategy that established institutions have long understood as well. The singing of a national anthem promotes generalized love of country even in the face of internal conflicts.

Music also provides a link to unknown others who share your perspective, beyond those immediately present. By declaring and therefore externalizing core beliefs, musicking reinforces participants' feeling that the movement is *real,* that it's "out there" as well as in their own minds or small circles, giving the beliefs and the movement greater weight, a feeling of independent existence and objective reality. "'The music and the world it created,' recalled one former [1960s] activist, 'helped give us a sense that we were defining the culture, and the whole society was following.'"[13] Marty, now a university professor, says of his experiences in the 1960s:

> As a young, middle-class college student I quickly recognized that there were many others who shared the same idealism and dissatisfaction with the prevailing society as myself. Most of them were strangers, but the feeling was almost metaphysical. It was as if we had a role to play in history, even though as individuals we were unknown and powerless and the ultimate outcome was unclear.... There was a feeling of generational solidarity which I might compare to being an American traveler in another country who runs into a fellow American.... Songs such as "Ohio" and "Woodstock" by CSN [Crosby, Stills, & Nash], "Volunteers" by the Jefferson Airplane, and many other bands helped to verbalize our collective beliefs.

Because music is so portable, affirmation and reaffirmation can go on even in the absence of movement activity. This is obviously of great importance when movements go into ebb periods, appearing to die out and disappear, or when members have been exiled or otherwise dispersed. As Eyerman & Jamison emphasize, music is then the repository and bearer of a tradition. Folk music was one of the main avenues for the transmission of the ideals of the Old Left to the New Left of the 1960s:

> The Popular Front was dead, but the idea of it could be sung.... The political generation of the Fifties was missing, but folk was the living prayer of a defunct movement.[14]
> [T]he survival of a movement culture, of which the songs were an integral part, meant that the individual self-respect, collective self-confidence, and vision required to combat the dominant culture were in some ways passed on to the next generation concerned with similar issues. Folk song as a weapon reappeared in the 1960s, playing a significant role in building, and expressing the unity and determination of, a new movement culture.[15]

Vila similarly describes the reemergence of the political/cultural form *rock nacional* in Argentina in the 1980s after its repression by the military dictatorship in the mid-1970s: "fourteen- and 15-year-olds chorusing songs made popular a decade before, many of them banned and withdrawn from the record shops."[16]

The same is true for members of still-vibrant movements when they are not involved in movement work. Music allows activists to carry their beliefs and loyalties with them in their everyday routines; it provides a bridge linking yesterday's demonstration with today's workday, between "making history" and "making life."[17] During times of movement inactivity, music serves as one way that the identities and ties essential to future movement activity are not lost in the press of daily routines.

Johnston, Larana & Gusfield tell us: "The larger proportion of daily activities that movement-related roles occupy in a social actor's overall identity—that is[,] the sum total of his or her roles—the sharper the boundaries, the clearer the we-they distinctions, and the stronger the collective identity."[18] If leisure time is also reinforcing a political identity, through playing and enjoyment of movement music, rather than a neutral, irrelevant, or contradictory identity, identification with the movement is maintained, even increased, as the German Nazi movement understood: "Music [which 'glorified the Führer and the Fatherland'] was not to be viewed as an art confined to concerts, which would stand out in bold relief against daily living. Rather it should be an integral part of daily living and permeate every waking moment."[19]

Though this reaffirmation may come about through songs that are explicitly political in intent, other music may play a similar role. Music that reinforces an identity—gospel music as explicitly black, for example—maintains group identity that is then available for political uses at some future time. The enjoyment of certain kinds of music signifies an allegiance to others who share this preference, maintaining bonds of implied political similarity, even if these are not explicitly discussed. Two new roommates at college discover they both love the music of Ani DiFranco, and their mutual allegiance to some form of feminist perspective is assumed—and thus affirmed—even if no discussion of feminism ensues.

Spirit Maintenance

In the midst of mass action and high risk, music's affirmative power helps to maintain the spirits of movement activists. A voter registration worker, working in Mississippi in the fearful summer of 1964, wrote back to her family:

> I tried consciously to overcome this fear. To relax, I began to breathe deep, think the words of a song.... "We are not afraid. Oh Lord, deep in my heart, I do believe, We Shall Overcome Someday" and then I think I began to truly understand what the words meant. Anyone who comes down here and is not afraid I think must be crazy as well as dangerous to this project where security is quite important. But I think the type of fear that they mean when they, when we, sing "we are not afraid" is the type that immobilizes.... The songs help to dissipate the fear.[20]

Song has been a staple of meetings where actions are being discussed and planned, and particularly when activists are preparing to engage in immediate tasks, from the mundane (handing out leaflets) to the terrifying (challenging established and armed authorities by marching or demonstrating). David Crosby writes:

Belafonte, Seeger, Baez, Yarrow—all of them told me that at one point each saw a scene almost identical to this: a church basement full of black faces, terrified, sweating, afraid they would die at any moment, even afraid that their babies could be murdered. Then somebody in the corner would start singing "Ain't Gonna Let Nobody Turn Me Around" or some other spiritual. It was like a lightning bolt to the soul. People went from being so terrified that they were literally huddled in a corner, tears streaming down their faces—to where they could put that child on their shoulders, walk up those stairs, walk right out the front door of that church, and confront a line of policemen with police dogs and water cannons. They could look them right in the eye and still be singing "Ain't gonna let nobody turn me 'round/ God is standing at my shoulder/God is watching what we do here."[21]

To people faced with a hostile opponent with far greater power, the danger is real and the fear is great. Musicking helps to raise collective courage:

The freedom songs give the people courage to walk down the streets of Birmingham and face the dogs that are trained to kill on command. In Nashville, Tennessee, the students, returning from a demonstration, had to march up the center of the street between a mob which lined both sides. While the mob threw rocks and bottles at them, they sang "We Shall Overcome." This was not a pretentious display of nonviolence. The song was simply their only recourse at a time when nothing else would've helped.[22]

BRUCE: Then came the March to Montgomery.... The last camp site was in Lowndes county, which if Alabama and Mississippi are the depths, the nadir, the deepest part of American state racism, Lowndes county was the deepest part of Alabama racism.... Oh the rain, it was so muddy. The mud was so deep. You're trying to sleep in mud. The food arrives from Selma. It's in trash cans. Stone cold because they had to drive it 50 miles. Everybody is miserable. And so we get out on the road, and the rain comes pouring down, and then I don't know, it's so weird.... We start singing, and people's heads snap up, and our eyes take fire. Singing like crazy. This incredible frision [sic] of energy runs through us. ... [The march keeps] getting bigger and bigger, and everybody's singing, singing loud in the rain.[23]

As this last quote suggests, musicking raises spirit not only in the face of danger but in many situations of difficulty and frustration. After slogging through wretched weather at the famous Aldermaston (England) peace march of 1963, peace activist John Brunner wrote, "There's all the difference in the world between trudging through the rain with squelching shoes and your head miserably bowed, and trudging through the rain singing at the top of your voice."[24]

A dramatic example often cited by activists is imprisonment. Famously, in the early civil rights movement in the South, but in many other movements as well, musicking in jail cells has been a way of maintaining spirit in the face of fear, anger, physical hardship, and sometimes boredom. Hardin describes the arrest and jailing of environmentalists trying to prevent logging in Oregon's Kalmiopsis Wilderness:

Handcuffed in one hundred degree weather, packed into a metal paddy-wagon with barred windows, they one by one took up the Jim Stoltz refrain, "There's a power, there's a power in a band of folks who care." It grew louder until the entire vehicle was rocking from side to side....

... they found themselves jailed in separate cells, isolated and unable to communicate with one another.... Then, as by a common signal, they began to bang on the bars and walls with their fists, escalating in both volume and tempo. Some used the silverware from the packaged meal to tease a staggered scale from the differently tuned parts of their cages. While it began as a chaotic tantrum of rude sounds, within a few minutes every inmate of the jail was locked on to a single beat, entrained, in contact, in communication again: rhythm![25]

Jailed collectively, protesters use music to maintain spirit and solidarity, and even sanity. As Reagon says of her imprisonment in the Albany, Georgia, demonstrations, "When things would rub between people of different persuasions, someone would say, 'Sing a song, Bernice,' and I would. People were not necessarily changed, but singing collectively created more space to be together in a cell with no space."[26]

Musicking may also play an important role when activists are kept in isolation. One example is the kind of communication between isolated prisoners that Hardin describes above, but sometimes even this is not possible. Facing the disheartening loneliness and fear of solitary imprisonment, activists often turn to their music in one form or another to hold on to their spirit. When rock and roller Lou Reed interviewed Vaclav Havel, the new president of Czechoslovakia, shortly after the 1989 "Velvet Revolution," to his amazement "Havel handed me a small black book about the size of a diary. 'These are your lyrics hand-printed and translated into Czechoslovakian. There were only 200 of them. They were very dangerous to have.' ... Many [activists] told me of reciting my lyrics for inspiration and comfort when in jail."[27]

Musicking is a primary means to share and manage a range of emotions that affect commitment. Past and present victories are celebrated musically; music is also often central to rituals that deal with grief and despair—funerals, demonstration postmortems, and so forth:

> PETER YARROW: When people went to the basement of churches after their comrades had fallen, after they were set upon by dogs, after KKK cross burnings, the place where people went to heal was their music. They sang together and their courage reemerged with solidarity and their belief in one another solidified.[28]

> STAN: At the Gulf War protest in Washington, D.C. in March of 91 ... Richie Havens and Paul (from Peter, Paul and Mary) were on stage, and first they performed "We Shall Overcome." I, of course, knew the song as the civil rights anthem and had not heard it in any other setting. Along with hundreds of thousands of marchers, I felt "deep in my heart" that we would triumph. And then they finished with "Where Have All the Flowers Gone." I had heard the song many times before, but as I thought of my friends ... and people's sons, brothers, and fathers, the tears began to stream down my face. It's a cliché, but here it's true: There wasn't a dry eye there. At the time it was the most moving experience of my lifetime.

These collective efforts at spirit maintenance, like the expression of collective identity and belief we spoke of earlier, are essential for sustaining commitment. But there are many times when *collective* enactment is not possible, when the individual is isolated in her nonmovement routine and needs to deal with despair (or, more happily, with joy) by herself. Again, music serves here as a portable bridge, connecting the individual activist to the rituals, enactments, and spirit of the greater movement, providing "feelings of wholeness in a crazy personal and political world," as one told us, "a subfoundation to thought, the wind to stay afloat on, especially when the social support is not there," according to another.

> I recently moved from San Francisco to a suburb outside of Dallas.... As a liberal, antimainstream dyke, I have felt very alienated and alone living in this weird little suburb. Ani [DiFranco]'s music has made me feel connected to something that is like me when, everywhere I look, there is no one visibly like me. She helps me to keep the courage to be who I am and not be quiet about it. She reminds me of my social responsibility to question others and to stand up for what I believe.[29]

Themes of Reaffirmation

We've been illustrating how music serves the committed by providing a wide range of opportunities for rehearsing, sustaining, and reaffirming basic beliefs. Sometimes these are very specific to a movement. "Say it Loud. I'm Black and I'm Proud!" celebrated the then new black-is-beautiful perspective; "Meat is Murder" reinforced vegetarian values quite explicitly. But much of musicking concerns itself with more generic themes, adapted to particular movements or stated in general terms. Solidarity is virtually always a celebrated value of the movement, as in the words of the union classic "Solidarity Forever"[30] or the ritual of linking hands and singing "We Shall Overcome" as a group. Spirit maintenance—holding on, holding out, keeping on—is stressed, as in "Ain't Gonna Let Nobody Turn Me 'Round." Assertiveness and courage are frequently celebrated, as in the collective singing of the civil rights song "This Little Light of Mine":

> This little light of mine, I'm gonna let it shine
> This little light of mine, I'm gonna let it shine
> This little light of mine, I'm gonna let it shine
> Let it shine, let it shine, let it shine.[31]

Movement values are often emphasized through celebrations of past heroes. In "I Dreamed I Saw Joe Hill Last Night," a song that became a staple at movement funerals and memorials, sacrifice is sanctified by recasting the execution of the IWW martyr:

> I dreamed I saw Joe Hill last night, alive as you and me.
> Says I, "But Joe, you're ten years dead."
> "I never died," says he.
>
> "The copper bosses shot you Joe, they shot you Joe, says I.
> "Takes more than guns to kill a man,"
> says Joe, "I never died."[32]

Utopian visions of the future, of life after eventual victory, are also common:

I dreamed the world had all agreed to put an end to war
I dreamed I saw a mighty room, filled with women and men*
And the paper they were signing said they'd never fight again.[33]

Such themes may be most obvious in the lyrics, but, given our argument in previous chapters, we'd hardly stop there; other aspects of musicking are at least equally important. Participation in group singing celebrates solidarity quite apart from the lyrics being sung:

> BENNET ZUROFSKY: You really have not experienced political folk music if you have never sung "Solidarity Forever" with a group of angry strikers.[34]

> PETER YARROW: The Marches are so euphoric that you have the illusion that you've reached your objective by virtue of the fact that you just are standing there singing and gathering together. Everybody is feeling and saying, "We can do it. We can do it."[35]

As many musicians have commented to us, singing together serves as a model for working together, requiring give-and-take, listening to and learning from each other, and staying connected. Harmonizing or a call-and-response structure emphasizes solidarity and interdependence. Certainty in the eventual success of the struggle is signified in the melodic structure of "We Shall Overcome" as it is in the words; the tradition of singing it linking hands with the persons on either side of you expresses solidarity. The value that "black is beautiful" is expressed in the foregrounding of rhythm by James Brown in "Say It Loud," esteeming that African-derived tradition instead of following the European tradition of emphasizing melody above rhythm; the use of children to sing the chorus carries a message of intergenerational solidarity within the African American community as well. Allowing only women to play any role in any aspect of women's music concerts asserts a value of independence from male control that is central to the women's movement.

Internal Dialogue

Earlier we defended "preaching to the converted" as a valuable contribution to a movement, arguing that the disparate individuals who make up a movement are never uniformly committed, and therefore reaffirmation of shared beliefs is a continuous need. But even core beliefs are not static, and so another important role of culture is to offer movements a forum for internal dialogue where beliefs are constructed and reconstructed, strategies are debated, and issues are aired.

For example, questions of race have been debated within the labor movement for many years. From the beginning of the movement in the 1800s, the issue of inclusion and equal treatment of all workers was raised in the face of prevailing practices of exclusion of nonwhites; in later years the relation of the labor movement

---

*As originally written, the phrase was "the room was filled with men." It's rarely sung that way anymore.

to the civil rights movement and some of its goals (such as affirmative action) was debated. Phil Ochs, the 1960s political folksinger who identified with both movements, used one of the most famous lines of union song making—"Which side are you on?"—to sharply criticize union members for failing to embrace the young civil rights movement:

> The black man was a-risin' fast and racin' from the shade,
> And your union took no stand and your union was betrayed....
> Now it's only fair to ask you boys, which side are you on?[36]

Rap has notably provided this kind of forum in recent years. The hip-hop community is not a social movement per se, but displays some aspects of conventional movements (a shared identity, a feeling of collective fate), and certainly contains subgroups that are attempting to move it in a more overtly political/movement direction. Zook argues that rap in general has provided "in-house" intercommunication for blacks across a wide range of issues,[37] including gender relations, as seen in Queen Latifah's "U.N.I.T.Y.":

> Instinct leads me to another flow
> Every time I hear a brother call a girl a bitch or a ho
> Trying to make a sister feel low—You know all of that gots to go[38]

Tricia Rose, who has pioneered work on this topic, writes:

> [T]he subject matter and perspectives presented in many women's rap lyrics challenge dominant notions of sexuality, heterosexual courtship, and aesthetic constructions of the body. In addition, music videos and live performances display exuberant communities of women occupying public space while exhibiting sexual freedom, independence and, occasionally, explicit domination over men.... Through their lyrics and video images, black women rappers ... form a dialogue with working-class black women and men, offering young black women a small but potent culturally reflexive public space.[39]

Movements that have split into factions are particularly likely to develop and use this function of music, perhaps because internal criticism requires an audience educated enough in the issues to understand the critique. Among the funniest of these were the parodies written by American Trotskyists to criticize the policies of the American Communist Party (which remained under Stalinist leadership in the worldwide Stalin-Trotsky split), including "In Old Moscow" (to the tune of "Oh My Darling Clementine"):

> In Old Moscow, in the Kremlin, in the fall of '39
> Sat a Russian and a Prussian, writing out the party line
> Oh my darling, oh my darling, oh my darling party line
> Oh, I never will desert you, for I love this life of mine
> Leon Trotsky was a Nazi, oh we knew it for a fact

Pravda said it, we all read it, before the Stalin-Hitler Pact
Once a Nazi would be shot—see, that was then the party line
Now a Nazi's hotsy-totsy, Trotsky's laying British mines
Now the Nazis and Der Fuehrer stand within the party line
All the Russians love the Prussians, Volga boatmen sail the Rhine[40]

In addition to beliefs, internal dialogue often concerns issues of practice, questioning what members or potential members are doing and challenging them to do more. The Last Poets, forerunners of modern rap and proponents of race and class revolution in the early 1970s, often directed their poetry at those they felt should be pursuing the Revolution more diligently, as in their most famous cut, "Niggers Are Scared of Revolution":

Revolution is nothing but change, and all niggers do is change . . . .
Niggers always going through bullshit changes,
But when it comes for a real change, Niggers are scared of revolution.[41]

Several years later, Sweet Honey in the Rock issued this challenge to progressives in general:

Where were you when they killed Malcolm
Where were you when they killed Martin. . .
Do you hear them calling? Are you fighting today?[42]

Internal dialogues can be expressed musically as well as through lyrics. In the 1940s, the complex form of jazz known as bebop was favored by African Americans who saw the more accessible music of mainstream big bands representing a philosophy of integration and black assimilation that they rejected. Within the New York Puerto Rican community in the first half of the twentieth century, Glasser writes, music was not

a unifying force in a dividing or dissolving American ethnic community . . . [so much as] an ongoing source of diverse definitions for Puerto Rican ethnic identity and an arena of contention . . . with varying and ever-evolving ideas about their cultural identity and Puerto Rican or Latin music's relation to it . . . [Puerto Ricans debated, for instance], whether the *plena*, of black "lowlife" origins, was a fitting national music.[43]

Internal dialogue isn't always confrontational. Much of it is simply educational, resonant with the medieval minstrel's role of spreading the news. Music is one way in which different parts of a movement, separated geographically or otherwise, learn about each other's efforts. In El Salvador, the early albums of Cutumay Camones, a creation of the insurgent group ERP, brought news of other wings of the struggle to isolated liberation fighters. One song, for example, declared "the popular militias are active throughout the entire country, in all fourteen departments of El Salvador," and so insurgents far removed from each other gained a sense that the movement was growing ever more widespread, despite their own isolation at times.[44] Barbara

Dane describes a similar function she played doing gigs at antiwar coffeehouses that developed among GIs during the Vietnam War:

> [The army] ... did all sorts of things to keep the news from traveling so the GI in this place had no idea that there was a movement in this other place, and this other place. So I would start to talk about a chain of events: "I was just at Fort Benning, and the guys over there are talking about these things that happened to them, and this is a song we sang there. . . ." And each verse would get applause because they recognized something in it. . . . As I went along and heard them telling their stories, I would convert the stories into a verse that I would put in there. So at the next place I could say, "Well, back in Fort so-and-so, they had this incident happen and here's the verse that came out of that." And [singing] "Join the GI Movement" would reassure them that there *was* a GI movement, and something you could relate to.

Instruction

In some cases, musicking is instructional in the most concrete sense. "Steal Away" called slaves to secret religious meetings, held hidden and at night because they were banned by white owners.[45] "Follow the Drinking Gourd" was apparently a road map for riders and guides on the underground railroad out of slavery and up to Canada, always following the "drinking gourd"—the Big Dipper pointing toward the North Star. As the Salvadorian struggle moved into an overtly revolutionary phase in the late 1980s, the songs of Cutumay Camones began to provide basic military instruction:

> *Los helicópteros* provides directions on how to bring down a helicopter. . . . The same military-type tactics are repeated in songs such as *Los fusilitos, M-16* (e.g., lessons on how to arm, aim, fire, clean, and disarm this rifle), *Hoy nació el día del pueblo* [and] *La mechuda* (which tells how to build and use a popular armament). . . . Revolutionary organizations distributed cassette tapes to their members and supporters . . . as a way of preparing [them] for the November 1989 offensive.[46]

Similarly, Nicaraguan church leader Carlos Mejia Godoy supported the Sandinistan uprising against the dictator Somoza earlier in the 1970s with songs that were "musical lessons for trainee guerillas, describing how to make contact bombs, or clean, strip and assemble guns."[47] As Almeida & Urbizagastegui write, "In Third World rural regions and shantytowns with high rates of illiteracy and semiliteracy, popular music (and oral communication in general) may serve as a more powerful educator of movement strategy than written material."[48]

As the Focus of Activity

Music and musicking sometimes move from a supporting role in movement work to center stage; they become the focus of an activity, rather than an accompaniment. Sometimes this activity is simply a break from more arduous movement tasks. "Good organizers and union people knew that if people came out and had a meeting all night or all day, there were times when you had [to have] either somebody play some good music or have some time to dance," says Guy Carawan, based on his experience musicking in both the civil rights and Appalachian miners' community movements. "At certain times people were all talked out. And they might get some additional energy out of either sharing some songs they knew ... or having somebody there who could do songs."

Such breaks may mean more than merely entertainment and refreshment; the music that's shared and/or performed is usually expressive of the movement, reinforcing and reaffirming core beliefs. Moreover, sharing the music, particularly singing or dancing together, carries an important latent message, a model and reminder of community. Activists end these sessions refreshed, but also refocused on the bonds that tie them to others in their struggle. Bradley described to us a political gathering with a performance by Si Kahn: "[T]here was a revelation that stuck with me—that there was more passion to the movement than I had previously understood." Herb characterized movement music as "a joyous celebration of my [political] faith."

Musicking may also become a means of action in the field. Early Lutheranism was spread in part by the tactic of singing *at* opponents. The more ardent advocates of the Reformation would disrupt Catholic services by invading churches, singing Lutheran ballads that mocked the music of the service; orthodox clergy were often accosted on the streets by Lutherans singing ballads that "hurl[ed] scorn and derision" at them, and "many towns had to prohibit the singing of offensive songs against the clergy in their streets."[49] The same tactic has been used in modern-day labor struggles:

> [T]he practice of verbally abusing and ridiculing individuals with satirical songs in the Maritimes, whereby they are "songed," was also sporadically engaged in by the marching unionists against members of the management and staff of [the company they were striking].... The "effect" of the union protest songs in Buchans was not only the sense of solidarity generated amongst the singers, but also the feelings of anxiety, fear and hatred experienced by those persons on the receiving end of aggressive verbal barrages.[50]

In recent years, one of the most important movement uses of musicking has been as the focus of consciously created cultural events. With the rise of the cause-related "megaevents," first seen in the 1971 Concert for Bangladesh and then firmly established with Live Aid in 1985, these have achieved much greater prominence, though similar (if more modest) events have been a staple of mass politics for over a century. Some of the modern megaevents have aimed at raising support for charity rather than for change-oriented movements, but there have been a number of major instances where fundraising and social change have been fused, as in the antinuclear Madison Square concerts in the late 1970s or the 1988 Free Nelson Mandela Concert in London.

The more a political movement becomes intertwined with cultural groupings, the more *any* concert may take on the feel of a movement activity. This was often the case in the 1960s when movements against racism, the Vietnam War, and a host of other political issues commingled with changing ideas about music, sex, hairstyles, and so forth, resulting in what participants at the time simply called "The Movement." Robert Christagau reflects this melding when he claims, "The paradigmatic sixties experience isn't the demo, it's the rock concert—or the demo-like festival megaconcerts that start with Woodstock in late 1969."[51] Many such events are quite deliberately created for and tied to movement purposes, including the crucial role of reaffirmation of beliefs and spirit maintenance we've been discussing. In addition, the events themselves strengthen the networks of activists that movements require. By the early 1960s, Guy Carawan told us, activists/musicians in the civil rights movement were creating gatherings to share songs and musicking experiences. Women's Music concerts of the 1970s were places to meet other committed feminists. On the West Coast in particular, it is no exaggeration to say that such concerts were crucial in the linking of activists and thus in the growth and growing visibility of the women's movement. In recent years, hardcore concerts have played a similar (if less consciously planned) role for animal rights groups.

The same result may be found in musical networks that don't begin intentionally linked to a movement. Zook argued almost two decades ago that the most important contribution rap was making to a revitalized movement against racism was the creation of networks among black entrepreneurs for the commercial necessities of producing, promoting, and distributing what was then a marginal music, shunned by the white-controlled industry.[52] These networks not only facilitated the growth of the hip-hop industry, but greatly facilitated the emergence of a range of politically conscious hip-hop alliances in the late twentieth and early twenty-first centuries.

Gathering Resources

Cultural activities have been used to raise resources for movements almost as long as there have been movements in the United States, dating back at least to the Hutchinson Family's support for abolitionist organizations before the Civil War. In the late 1930s, the International Ladies' Garment Workers Union's production, *Pins and Needles,* became the longest-running Broadway show of its time, benefiting the union in garnering both support and funds (as the musical review's financial backer). The SNCC Freedom Singers' tours in the early 1960s were expressly meant to raise money and volunteers as well as public awareness for the southern civil rights movement; the sale of white power rock has been a major source of income for some white power organizations.

The rise of the megaevent in the age of global mass media has more than underlined the role musicking may play for movements in terms of garnering resources. Events featuring several different groups or musicians in a single concert have been used to raise several hundred thousand dollars at a shot; the largest have raised millions of dollars.[53] The Amnesty International tours of the 1980s are estimated to have recruited as many as 200,000 new members in the United States alone.[54]

The success of the megaevents, however, has spurred discussion among movement activists. To what extent are these supporting "charity" rather than activism and social change? Are musicians merely cynical seekers of favorable publicity rather than committed supporters of a movement—and does it matter? Are audiences oblivious to the issue at hand, treating the cause concert as no different from any other concert? And most importantly for our discussion, to what extent is music's potential contribution as a cultural force being sacrificed for its use as a cultural commodity—raising money in place of raising consciousness? Would it even make any difference if megaevents featured famous athletes playing sports for a cause instead of musicians singing?

Some say these questions themselves reflect an unrealistic view of the way movements need to work in the modern world. Will Straw argues, "[T]he most underrated contribution rock musicians can make to politics is their money or ways in which that money might be raised."[55] Others defend the megaevents in broader terms. Clearly they may serve as forums of reaffirmation and spirit maintenance for those already in a movement. But further claims are made beyond serving the committed: [M]egaevents "open up spaces for cultural politics" not previously possible in which "the development of a more politicized culture gets validated";[56] they provide alternative visions of what social life could look like; they educate previously ignorant individuals and inspire previously apathetic individuals. That is, they reach out and affect people *beyond* the committed.

The Denisoff Question

Serge Denisoff was skeptical about the ability of music to do anything other than reinforce existing beliefs and behaviors, to reach beyond the committed: "There is little, if any, concrete or empirical evidence that songs do in fact have an independent impact upon attitudes in the political arena," he declared.[57] This position draws support from an improbably wide coalition of theorists, from economic determinist Marxists (who see culture as simply reflecting the economic base of a society) to Weberian followers of what's called the "commercial laissez-faire model" of cultural life (who argue that, in a free market, the sovereign consumer demands and receives what s/he already wants, and disregards all else).[58]

The point such writers make is that there is *no evidence* of music's effects on beliefs and actions.[59] We certainly don't have the methods to definitively determine whether and to what degree music affects consciousness and activity, but that's not the same thing as saying there *is* evidence that musicking *can't* and *doesn't* perform this role. With an equal lack of hard evidence, some have concluded the opposite: that musicking has an enormous effect on the consciousness and behavior of those participating in political activities. Some commentators, as we've seen, viewed this power with profound suspicion. "Mass manipulation" theorists feared the brainwashing effects of music, whether they were leftists like Adorno, liberals like David Riesman and Jacques Barzun, conservatives like Allan Bloom, or far rightists like Gary Allen and Susan Huck.

Such fears haven't only been about political movements. Critics in the 1950s and early 1960s worried that the teen "car death" vogue of the time (e.g., "Tell Laura I Love Her" and "Teen Angel") would lead to glorification of death cults. The 1985 congressional hearings on popular music content, a direct result of the lobbying efforts of the Parents' Music Resources Center (PMRC), saw much testimony along the lines of this statement from Professor Joe Stuessy of the Music Department at the University of Texas, San Antonio:

> We have known intuitively for centuries, and it has been proven conclusively by scientific studies in recent decades that music does affect behavior. Music affects our moods, emotions, attitudes, and our resultant behavior. Music affects us psychologically and physiologically.... Any verbal message that you receive, you are more likely to remember if it is in a musical context....
>
> Today's heavy metal is categorically different from previous forms of popular music. It contains the element of hatred, a meanness of spirit. Its principal themes are, as you have already heard, extreme violence, extreme rebellion, substance abuse, sexual promiscuity and perversion and Satanism.[60]

Others have welcomed the purported power of music to affect behavior and communicate new ideas. Ralph Gleason trumpeted the effects of revolutionary popular music in the upheavals of the 1960s: "Students in schools and universities where the SDS hasn't a slim chance of penetrating hear this message loud and clear. And they believe it as they do *not* believe the history books in their classes and will never again believe their teachers."[61] Similar claims have been made on the Right: "Back in 1985, Skrewdriver *was* the skinhead movement," a skinhead activist told author Mark Hamm. "They provided the ideology for what we did back then."[62] And many without a particular overt political agenda have similarly attributed enormous powers of persuasion to art (and artists) in general, and music (and musicians) in particular.[63]

Contrary to Stuessy's claim to Congress, this isn't a question that has been definitively answered by social scientists. Whether looking at persuasion to engage in "positive" behavior (activism, altruism, etc.), or the more common studies of "negative" behavior (Satanism, suicide, etc.), the complexity of the connections and the difficulties in methodology[64] have made evidence of clear causal connections elusive at best.[65] If you ask musicians, you're similarly likely to find conflicting claims and understandings. When pressed, many artists express a belief that music can provide at least an entryway into alternative possibilities for living, as seen in this interview exchange between writer Jonathan Cott and Mick Jagger of the Rolling Stones:

> COTT: Keith Richards once said something to the effect that rock and roll really is subversive because the rhythms alter your being and perceptions.
>
> JAGGER: Music is one of the things that changes society. That old idea of not letting white children listen to black music is true, 'cause if you want white children to remain what they are, they mustn't.
>
> COTT: Look at what happened to you.
>
> JAGGER: Exactly! You get different attitudes to things ... even the way you walk.[66]

Some politically oriented musicians believe their work can have quite profound effects. Holly Near writes of her pioneering work with a few other feminist artists: "[O]ur music was completely changing the lives of thousands of women and their friends and families."[67] As the career of Peter, Paul and Mary skyrocketed, Peter Yarrow told journalists, "Do you realize the power of Peter, Paul and Mary? We could mobilize the youth of America today in a way nobody else could. We could conceivably travel with a presidential candidate, and maybe even sway an election."[68] For many, this kind of influence is their hope and their purpose. Eisler wrote that the arts "can become the great tutor of society."[69]

But most political musicians make smaller claims. Pete Seeger, for example, says, "Some songs help you forget your troubles, some songs help you understand your troubles, and—occasionally—a song comes along which can help you *do* something about your troubles."[70] Others claim even less, skeptical that music can do anything about changing attitudes and behaviors, restricting the role of music to reaffirmation for the committed and its use as an economic weapon for raising money, in boycotts and so forth.[71]

Many activist musicians are ambivalent, making limited claims and perhaps hoping for more. Billy Bragg often minimizes the role musicians can play in a struggle: "I think the political artist follows the political consciousness rather than the other way around." But when pressed, he admits seeking some role in facilitating as well as reflecting change: "You're just really reaching out to the widest audience to see if you can cause a larger ripple." That uncertainty is wonderfully illustrated in an interview with John Lennon and Yoko Ono, Lennon's last before his murder in 1980:

> Q: How does it feel to have influenced so many people?
> LENNON: It wasn't really me or us. It was the times....
> Q: For the sake of argument, we'll maintain that no other contemporary artist or group of artists moved as many people in such a profound way as the Beatles.
> LENNON: But what moved the Beatles?
> Q: You tell us.
> LENNON: All right. Whatever wind was blowing at the time moved the Beatles, too. I'm not saying we weren't flags on the top of a ship; but the whole boat was moving. Maybe the Beatles were in the crow's nest, shouting, "Land ho," or something like that, but we were all in the same damn boat....
> ONO: As I said, they were like mediums. They weren't conscious of all they were saying, but it was coming through them.
> Q: Why?
> LENNON: We tuned in to the message. That's all. I don't mean to belittle the Beatles when I say they weren't this, they weren't that. I'm just trying not to overblow their importance as separate from society.[72]

Asking those who are involved in political struggles about their own experience sheds more light on this process. When we've talked with activists, we've found quite a bit of anecdotal evidence that music does play a role in persuasion as well as affirmation. Those who become political musicians often cite their own "conversions" as audience members for their subsequent decision to follow that path themselves:

> FRED SMALL: I know for myself, that they can also persuade, and that they can really make a difference in how you think about something. I heard Phil Ochs sing "I Ain't Marching Anymore" when I was 12 years old. Blew my mind. Pissed me off. I was very upset. It challenged me to take all of American History and all of the wars and say, "They didn't do a damn thing. What's the point?" ... It upset my preconceived notions and it had a huge impact on how I thought about the world.[73]

CHARLIE KING: It was easy to go in and listen to the Charles River Valley Boys or Jim Kweskin and the Jug Band, or Dave Van Ronk, or Mississippi John Hurt, and come away with [my conservative] Goldwater idealism intact.... But, you know, when Pete [Seeger]'s *We Shall Overcome* album came out in '63, I got it, must've got it shortly after it came out, and I listened to it 'til all the grooves were worn out .... That might have been really what first created conflict because I did get this basic sense of sympathy for the civil rights movement, based on the music. Whereas at home, the official party line was that Martin Luther King was a communist and that he was a dangerous guy.

We can't know how often this happens, but we will argue that when it does occur, the impact can be profound, as found in some other studies[74] and illustrated by a number of students in the Meaning in Music survey:

Music was/is my primary method of formulating political ideas. Hip-hop serves as my dialogue with and perspective on the world. Through it I can learn and listen as well as teach and express.

I don't think music could have played a bigger role in my political development. The hardcore scene is very politically and socially active. One of its main purposes is to educate people and get them fired up to go out and make a difference.

Madonna is also pretty political in her views on sexual liberation and other sexuality issues and she's totally affected my views and identity issues.

Those who seek to censor popular music take its ability to affect minds, particularly of youth, quite seriously. In recent years some European governments have confiscated music and production facilities of right-wing groups producing music that glorifies Nazism or foments racial hatred. Germany, for example, has had a Federal Inspection Office for Writing Endangering Youth, with the power to ban objectionable cultural products. Within the United States, groups from the White Citizens Councils in the 1950s, to the PMRC in the 1980s, to the Wal-Mart Corporation in recent times, have warned of the "negative" influences of pop music, ranging from encouragement of racial integration to encouraging satanism and suicide, and advocated actions from economic boycotts to state censorship.

Ironically, the argument against censorship in any of these forms often rests on a *denial* of music's power to influence thought or action. "Music does not create the kind of society in which we live," declared the president of the Recording Industry Association of America testifying in one congressional investigation of rock's influence on drug use: "Music reflects our culture as interpreted by the artists who create the music." Rock is "a footnote to the events within society," another executive told the congressional committee.[75] "The PMRC seems to assume that adolescents listen attentively to music, pay special attention to the lyrics, and interpret both the explicit and implicit meanings of their favorite songs. Young people then apparently take these meanings and apply them to their daily lives in the forms of behavioral guidelines," say Verden et al., in the lightly sardonic tone of ridicule commonly used by the opponents of censorship to convey the absurdity of this naïve vision.[76] Yet this is precisely what many political musicians hope is happening.

Those who love a particular music often end up with contradictory positions: They want to declare music's power when it helps to support the "right" things (freedom, equality, resistance, etc.), but not when it's accused of supporting the "wrong" things (suicide, satanism, violence, etc.). They may want to honor the "consciousness raising" function of music in political struggles, but they are at pains to challenge notions that people are simply mindless zombies, dupes of the culture industry; that "[l]ike a hypodermic needle, rock music can change people's attitudes with just one fix."[77]

Music can have significant effects, we'd argue, but these are contingent and should be specified by context, situation, the individual, the type of music—in short, the many variables discussed in previous chapters. Musicking *alone*—like any factor alone—is limited in its ability to change minds and actions. "Music does not simply inflict its meaning upon helpless fans; texts become popular when people find them meaningful in the contexts of their own lives," says Walser,[78] and we agree. What is crucial to see is that music itself is a part of that context, not a separate entity that arrives after our context and thoughts are set and then finds a welcoming or hostile reception. Music, as all culture and indeed all activity, helps to create, sustain, and alter the social world as well as reflect that world.*

If this is correct, musicking can do even more than just serve the committed. We turn next to trying to determine ways in which musicking can help *alter* what we think and what we do.

---

*One implication of this view, though it's not our concern here: The argument against censorship can't be based on the ineffectiveness of art in affecting behavior. It needs to be based on entirely other principles, including most importantly the dangers in stifling any ideas, narrowing the boundaries of permissible discussion and setting the precedent for further narrowing of permissible discourse.

♪

Chapter 7

Education

Communication researchers tell us that most human communication simply express-es views that are already shared rather than introducing new ideas: "[P]erformance, not transmission of information," is the point.[1] We receive this communication through our preexisting frames, fitting information into patterns already familiar to us. These frames themselves, however, are built up from bits of information, and so remain open to alteration. Intellectual and emotional experiences may prove too discrepant to be incorporated by established frames, resulting in revisions of our existing frame or, in extreme cases, replacement by a competing frame. That is, though most of the time our habits and existing frameworks carry us through most tasks without much conscious thought, sometimes a situation calls for new analysis; new experiences move us, consciously and unconsciously, toward new ways of understanding the world.

Adoption of a new viewpoint begins with *education,* by which we simply mean exposure to and reception of new information. Whether a person accepts that in-formation, uses it to revise existing frameworks of understanding, or acts on it is a step we'll come to later. But for now we want to look at the role music plays in *presenting* us with new information. Can it actually reach out and touch someone who's indifferent or even hostile to some viewpoint?

Again we encounter that familiar dichotomy between those who see music and musicking's ability to educate as severely limited by a range of factors and those who see music as particularly suited to this role. "Rock and roll is not a means by which to 'learn about politics,' nor a wavelength for a message as to what is to be done, or who is to be fought," says Marcus,[2] and the same claim has been made about many forms of music at one time or another. In contrast, here's a passage from a statement by a contemporary political songwriters' group:

The popular song form has a unique ability to enter into the flow of time-driven events that dominate the mind of a listener ... and to draw that listener into a space that exists outside of time; a safe mental space from which entirely new approaches to society and personal living may be considered.... No other art form can do this as well.[3]

The classic statement of this viewpoint comes from Joe Hill himself:

A pamphlet, no matter how good, is never read but once, but a song is learned by heart and repeated over and over; and I maintain that if a person can put a few cold common sense facts in a song, and dress them up in a cloak of humor to take the dryness off of them he will succeed in reaching a great number of workers who are too unintelligent or too indifferent to read a pamphlet or an editorial on economic science.[4]

This viewpoint, of course, isn't restricted to those on the Left: *WAR* magazine, the in-house journal of White Aryan Resistance, declares, "music is one of the greatest propaganda tools around. You can influence more people with a song than with a speech";[5] Panzerfaust Records declares on its website that "it aims not to just 'entertain racist kids' but to 'create them.'"[6] A leading student of that movement declares, point-blank: "White power rock [is] the primary transmitter of neo-Nazism among American skinheads."[7]

The multilayered nature of musicking, combining entertainment with education, reason with emotion, the mental with the physical, gives it exceptional power to educate.[8] Of course, potentials for such efforts vary. Education is more of a possibility at a Free Tibet concert than at the neighborhood bar on a Saturday night. Audiences and participants vary in how primed to learn they are. Some genres may be more suited to educating.[9]

Many Audiences

Music may be aimed at and/or received by people with a wide variety of relations to a struggle (beyond the already committed). Most relevant are constituencies already expressing grievances relevant to a movement's goals: workers in the heavy industrial plants of the 1930s and 1940s, African Americans in small rural communities in the Deep South in 1964, young people entering the army in 2010.

Since aggrieved groups often lack resources, a second important audience for a movement's program is potential outside supporters. A particularly vivid case is the 1963–1964 tours of northern college campuses by the SNCC Freedom Singers. Those who attended their concerts were probably already favorably inclined toward racial justice, but largely unaware of the actual dimensions of the southern struggle then developing. Thousands were educated through those concerts; many of the hundreds of volunteers who later went south to register voters in the Freedom Summer of 1964 had seen the Freedom Singers in the North, "an initiating experience"[10] of education that led, eventually, to active involvement. In the 1980s, groups involved in Central American conflicts saw potential sympathizers outside their boundaries as key audiences. The Sandinistas of Nicaragua, locked in battle with the Somoza government, and then with the Contra rebels after the Sandinistas had come to power, sent musicians to Europe and North America to spread the word of their struggle and gather resources of money, volunteers, and political support. Concerts and recordings of such performers helped define how the Sandinistas were internationally perceived.

Uncommitted audiences, too, may be the object of education. For most of U.S. history[11] political campaigns have used songs to extol the virtues of their candidates or causes to the general voting public, from "God Save George Washington" in the late 1780s through the 1992 Clinton-Gore campaign's highly sophisticated use of the rock song "Don't Stop";[12] in the Obama campaign in 2008, dozens of songs were distributed on YouTube and other websites. Music-based megaevents are often designed to attract large numbers of fans of headline performers in hopes of educating at least some of these about movement issues, enlisting support or at least sympathy.

Education may also be aimed at those in the oppressor group. "There are things that white America needs to learn about us," says the African American rapper Chuck D.[13] When Fisk University, a black school approaching bankruptcy in the early 1870s, created the Jubilee Singers to sing black songs to mainly white audiences as a form of fundraising, the result was not only the financial salvation of the school, but, according to Andrew Ward, an educating of "white Americans and Europeans [of] the courage, dignity, and intelligence of African Americans."[14]

In theory, not only members of an oppressor group but even consciously committed opponents within it might be educated. "Years ago I wrote, 'Songwriters: you have to write songs so funny that people who disagree with you can't stop laughing,'" Pete Seeger told us. Singing in the civil rights movement, the Caravans claimed, "sometimes disarm[ed] jail guards, bystanders, and mobs of their hostilities."[15] According to Harry Belafonte,

> When we were incarcerated in the white prisons of the South run by racist sheriffs who had no qualm about snuffing out a black life—and things seemed to be the most desperate—someone would break into song. Not only did it take our spirits to places we never dreamed of, but what it did to the enemy was also a remarkable thing to behold. I watched men of power become impotent. I watched men of ruthlessness become tamed, I watched them become hypnotized.[16]

In our time, political musicians are acutely aware that education for all these groups can occur through the mass media.[17] One of the major aims of megaevents, for example, is to "get some press" for a particular issue, to bring it to popular notice through the media coverage that results from gathering pop stars in a large concert. Raising the visibility of an issue and a struggle can alter public opinion, allowing movement participants to make greater claims, enlarging the range of permissible tactics, and generally empowering participants vis-à-vis their adversaries.

One special audience—children—may most readily be educated through song. Many budding political activists recall being raised on political singing:

HERB: Both folk music and social justice have been part of my life, woven together, as long as I can remember. My parents were life-long left-wingers, in the Communist Party in the 1930s and 1940s. My father played guitar, and used to sing me to sleep when I was little. The house was full of books, from *Das Kapital* on down. But one book was the greatest, as well as the earliest influence on me: *The Fireside Book of Folk Songs.*

DALE: There is the old experience of my grandfather singing "Solidarity [Forever]" to me while he led me—at about age eight—to an ethnic bar, one of which was on his regular itinerary when he was organizing steelworkers in eastern Ohio just before WWII.... There were many other songs, all seeming to be labor lyrics superimposed on Protestant hymns. Another example was the song "Miner's Life Is Like a Sailor" ... in substitution for the original "Life Is Like a Mountain Highway with an Engineer So Fine" (Jesus), and the rousing "We Shall Not Be Moved," a song I was to sing many years later in the sixties in quite different circumstances.

MAUREEN: I was raised with the wonderful Seeger recordings ... that included "We Shall Not Be Moved," "I'm Stickin' to the Union," "This Land Is Your Land," and other rousing classics. The strong beliefs in social justice and economic equity which I cherish to this day were nurtured on these songs.

The educational power of song is often particularly evident in schools, summer camps, and other socializing institutions:

MARGARET: I went to elementary school in Brooklyn in the 1940s. A major part of the socialization experience was musical—and generally pretty eclectic. But I would like to single out several books that our 1930s generally moderately left teachers used on us, and with permanent results: Irving Singer's book on "brotherhood," ... *The Fireside Book of Folk Songs* taught us about the boll weevil and John Henry. Our teachers played "Ballad for Americans," even as Paul Robeson was facing HUAC [the House Un-American Activities Committee in Congress].... We were not part of a social movement, in that we were not playing and marching in the late [19]40s and early [19]50s. But we were being socialized into a left-liberal, sometimes progressive, culture that predisposed us to support the civil rights movement, root for Castro, protest against Vietnam, and vote for [antiwar Democrat] Eugene McCarthy in the 1960s.

Many Forms

Musicking may transmit information incidentally, as when teenagers learn new slang by listening to hit records. But education may be an express intent of the artist and/or participants, the minstrel spreading the news. The SNCC Freedom Singers saw themselves quite consciously as educators:

We told stories in song (sometimes we called ourselves a singing newspaper) that let our audiences know firsthand about racism in the United States and that helped them find ways for themselves to witness for freedom. Many people who went South were introduced to the possibility of becoming Movement organizers as a result of contact with the Freedom Singers or other speakers who covered the country telling the story that seemed to never make the paper or the six o'clock news.[18]

Some information that artists send can be quite specific. In the 1970–1971 electoral campaign that brought the socialist Salvador Allende's Unidad Popular (Popular Unity) coalition to power in Chile, the party platform was literally translated into songs performed and recorded by the group Inti-Illimani. Titles included "Song of Social and Private Property," "Song of International Relations," "Song of Agrarian Reform," and so forth.[19] Peter Gabriel's "Biko" introduced many listeners in England and the United States to the specific details of an activist's martyrdom in the antiapartheid fight in South Africa. The hardcore band Shelter's "Civilized Man" informs the listener that "(meat would be) $35 a pound but our taxes subsidize as 35 million starve."[20]

When other avenues for getting the news are absent, blocked, or censored, the arts often become a prime source of information for ordinary people. Slave songs are a well-known example of how subversive and oppositional lessons can be expressed musically, under the noses (or ears) of the masters. Today, Chuck D argues, rap plays a similar (if no longer so hidden) communicative role for African Americans largely denied control and access to the means of mass communication: "It's the black CNN we never had. . . . Rap records are direct speaking, unfiltered direct speaking . . . going to the black public, coming from a black source with no middleman."[21]

Musicking communicates most subversively when it seems to be revealing truths that can't be found elsewhere, a charged situation affecting both sides of the artist-audience relationship: Musicians feel a greater need and demand to express what can't be expressed in other ways, but audiences also show a greater inclination to read important meaning into the music.[22] Describing the almost religious attraction of metal for disaffected suburban kids in the 1980s and 1990s, Gaines says,

[I]t offered a worldview that made sense when nothing else did. Parents, the school, the town—they all had their version of things. But the kids could learn most everything they needed to know about the meaning of life from their friends, their scene, and, most important, their bands.[23]

Artists supplement information delivered in song lyrics through interviews, onstage patter, liner notes, and websites. The very sensibility embodied in some music seems to carry an educational message, a hidden agenda that is recognized by at least some listeners. As he immersed himself in jazz, writes Asian American jazz musician Fred Wei-han Ho, he came to feel that the music's aesthetic quality in itself conveyed "a profoundly revolutionary and liberational vision . . . [, a] cultural resistance to white supremacist/Eurocentric assimilation."[24] Rap embodies a worldview that originated in working-class communities of color. Whether or not those who live outside those communities understand all the lyrics, they can hear the anger and defiance in much of hip-hop. Hansi Biebl sings of the pivotal moment when he glimpsed an alternative to East German society as he knew it:

Suddenly a radio droned somewhere
And they played the rock 'n' roll music of Chuck Berry
Suddenly I was on my feet
and all at once there was something happening with me

> I felt so big, my knees shook
> My face started to glow, and the guy sang
> "If you wanna dance with me."[25]

At times, musicking seems to encapsulate a new ethos, providing entry into an alternative or oppositional culture. In the second half of the nineteenth century, vibrant workers' subcultures across the United States featured an array of "events, institutions, activities, and gatherings that proffered a set of values and ideals increasingly at odds with, and distinct from, the dominant society,"[26] and "song poems" presenting a specifically workers' view were an integral feature of such subcultures:

> Shall those who raise the fruits and grains,
> Who feed and clothe the race,
> Tramp through the land and for their pains,
> Starve, branded with disgrace?
>
> Shall idle drones still live like kings
> On labor not their own?
> While true men starve, shall thieves, and rings
> Reap what they have not sown?[27]

Much of rap presents (or is taken to present) a worldview in which ghettocentricity—esteeming the ghetto you come from as the wellspring of identity and creativity—figures as an organizing value for the way you live your life. When Bob Dylan sang in 1965, "'Cause something's happening here and you don't know what it is, do you, Mr. Jones?" he was singing a worldview—inchoate, but felt nonetheless as imminent—that millions of other young people in the world were feeling, the "fundamental confrontation" with adult, mainstream society that critic Ralph Gleason summarized as "you are, all of you, wrong."[28]

Recasting the Known

While music may present new knowledge, from isolated fact to global worldview, it can also recast taken-for-granted understandings in a new light, providing a different way of looking at something already familiar to us. Leon Rosselson offers a drastically revised view of Jesus, Judas, and Christianity in "Stand Up for Judas":

> The Romans were the masters when Jesus walked the land
> In Judea and in Galilee they ruled with an iron hand
> And the poor were sick with hunger,
> and the rich were clothed in splendor
> and the rebels whipped and crucified hung rotting as a warning
> And Jesus knew the answer, said "Give to Caesar what is Caesar's."

Said "Love your enemies."
But Judas was a zealot and he wanted to be free
"Resist," he said, "the Romans' tyranny."
So stand up, stand up for Judas and the cause that Judas served
It was Jesus who betrayed the poor with his Word.[29]

Publicly describing a situation offers the possibility that what previously seemed a personal trouble will be seen as a shared—thus, socially rooted—problem, fostering the "sociological imagination," the linking of private trouble to public issues, that C. Wright Mills argued is essential for understanding, and then changing, the world.[30] Simply by stating the onerous conditions of tenant farmer life and attributing it to one landlord's actions, hearing and/or playing "Penny's Farm" may have helped other tenants to reframe what seemed to be their personal misfortune as a collective problem created by actions of landlords, and thus rectifiable.

Re-presenting a previously devalued culture, way of life, or status as worthy of respect can be politically educational. The impact of black-based music on white audiences has been profound; appreciation of black-based music (jazz, blues, R&B, rock and roll, rap) has educated young whites to the cultural importance of black American culture, with resulting social implications. "Every time I have teenagers of European descent come to a concert and leave with a sense of wonderment about who these people were, then that's an act of activism," says the African American musician Linda Tillery.[31] Creating such enlightenment may be a conscious goal, but also occurs without specific artist intent. One self-described "upper-middle-class midwestern Jewish kid" wrote us of hearing

the Benny Goodman Band in 1937, which can only be described as a religious experience. Immersing myself in this exalted music, I began to explore its roots, leading me to early Louis Armstrong, Ellington, and in 1940 to Boston and New York to get into the center of the jazz life. Soon I was radicalized by the realization that the black pioneers and creators of this incomparable music were the systematic victims of appalling prejudice and discrimination. I began a lifelong practice of opposing racial inequity.

Self-worth is at stake as well. The African American folksinger Odetta told us:

I started getting clued into the history of us as blacks in this country when I got into folk music, and hearing about the history of those the songs were collected from—the rebellions, the whatever. We were never told those kinds of things in school.... We were told that the slaves were happy and singing all the time. And I received that information—it couldn't be in the book if it weren't true, so I believed it. And we were very ashamed.... When I got into folk music and I started learning the actual history, it straightened up my back and it kinked my hair.

Again, this involves more than the effects of just lyrics. The music that accompanied black pride movements in the 1930s, 1960s, and 1990s all moved toward a more "African" or "black" sound, asserting pride in that heritage as opposed to a desire to assimilate into a white culture held to be superior. When Fred Ho's Celestial Orchestra presented *A Chinaman's Chance* in the late 1980s, combining Western jazz instruments with Chinese opera percussion and featuring the orchestra onstage in the Chinese tradition rather than hidden from view in the pit as in the Western tradition, an educational point was being made beyond any specific lyrical content of the opera.

Alternative Visions

An existing situation can also be reframed by contrasting it to some alternative, often a utopian vision, as John Lennon invited his listeners to envision a "brotherhood of man" in "Imagine" ("Imagine no possessions—I wonder if you can/Imagine all the people sharing all the world").[32] Religious music has often presented visions of a utopian afterlife, which symbolized possibilities for emancipation in this life as well. Reggae frequently articulates Rastafarian visions that simultaneously envision eventual spiritual salvation and more immediate political liberation; North American slave spirituals were filled with such metaphors:

> Didn't my Lord deliver Daniel, Daniel, Daniel?
> Didn't my Lord deliver Daniel, then why not every man?
> He delivered Daniel from the lion's den
> Jonah from the belly of the whale
> And the Hebrew children from the fiery furnace
> Then why not every man?[33]

While visions of collective utopian fulfillment are common in movement songs, popular music typically deals in the currency of personal fantasy. But even the fostering of fantasy may have educational implications for movements, celebrating rebellion, calling on heroic qualities, and encouraging hope. This is the most important form of "free space" provided by music, Fiske and others have argued: It allows "the preservation of fantasy as an interior place" and "the ability to imagine oneself acting differently in different circumstances."[34]

If, as Gramsci famously argued, the hegemony of ruling ideas has to be constantly reestablished,[35] the specifics of any alternative view may be less important than the fact that it is suggesting that another world is possible. It's in this sense that some argue that avant garde music inevitably embodies a critique of the social status quo because it implies there are new frontiers to be explored; it's therefore rightly distrusted by authorities seeking to control acceptable thought. The great political contribution of rock in the late 1960s may have been simply to say: "Forget what you've been told are the boundaries. Anything is possible!" Punk's first attraction for many is not its assertion of a particular set of values but its very clear rejection of the normal rules of the game. The adoption of the swastika by early English punks, as we've mentioned, was not a declaration of allegiance to Nazism, but a claiming of the symbol most hated by the generation before them as a way of signaling a refusal to fit it. In style, in symbol, in sound, punk's most obvious and attractive initial declaration is "*Not* this! *Fuck* this!"[36]

Thus, while this glimpse of an alternative may be provided by lyrics, it also comes through the sound, style, setting, and use of the music. The lyrics of black rhythm and blues and early rock and roll presented white teenagers with a worldview that was not necessarily different from the one they already knew, but the scene and the sound generated movement and emotion that challenged mainstream rules and beliefs about physical pleasure and personal purpose. Women's music expressed feminist ideas not only in lyrics but often through the practice that all participants be female, from stagehands to performers, thereby modeling alternatives to the gender roles with which most people were familiar.

The young American communist composers of the early 1930s who tried to follow Hanns Eisler's lead to create revolutionary music for American workers first sought a new musical vocabulary that broke with musical conventions of the existing bourgeois society; their eventual interest in the kind of "people's music" that Woody Guthrie, Pete Seeger, and others were championing was also based on a feeling that such music challenged the codes of mainstream popular music (while, unlike the composers' Eislerian efforts, being accessible to ordinary people). A similar effort was embodied in the *nueva canción* movement that rippled through Latin America beginning in the 1970s, featuring new words set to traditional music and played on traditional instruments. Matta argues that a key meaning of this movement was the sense of "rupture" with the mainstream, the feeling that some new form of communication based on neglected traditions was being developed, beyond the dominant discourse that usually excluded "the popular voice."[37]

In our interviews with current and past activists, a number of those who came of age in the 1960s referred to the free-form jams of the Grateful Dead as among their most important musical/political experiences, a living demonstration that the usual rules could be changed. Musicking is "good for imagining all possibilities," as one said, engendering a belief that it was valuable in itself to explore "alternative ways of understanding the world." A free space is created—spatially, sonically, socially, psychically—in which new ways of thinking and behavior may be investigated.

One of the ways alternative ideas, specific or general, are most powerfully presented and received is through the minstrel himself. As Wayne Hampton illustrates in *Guerilla Minstrels*, "[T]heir public image has provided a vicarious gateway into the norms, customs, and conventions, the manners of dress and speech of the utopian lifestyle.... The listener is invited to soar with him vicariously into the realm of what might be."[38] "During the Black Power years," Van Deburg writes, "Afro-American recording artists not only served as conduits for the vital message of racial unity, but they also became significant role models for many young blacks."[39] The role was, in fact, the message; the artist embodied the idea of racial pride and solidarity, exposing music fans to this powerful political stance.

The artist's image may become the single most important factor in education, as Madonna's alternative model of being female may have been for young girls of the 1980s and 1990s; despite lyrics that largely adhered to conventional sex roles, she seemed to convey an aura of complete control over her career and life. Ray Manzarek, keyboard player for the 1960s rock group the Doors, noted that although they didn't play political benefits, "The existence of the Doors was such a profound political act that every gig we played was a political statement of us-against-them.... It was something about [singer] Jim Morrison—son of the admiral, college graduate—who, had he not gone into rock 'n' roll, could easily have gone into the diplomatic corps."[40] Some artists choose to play this role, but sometimes it's simply assigned to an artist by an audience seeking meaning. "Whether he liked it or not, Dylan *sang for us,*" says Todd Gitlin of 1960s activists. "We followed his career as if he were singing our song; we got in the habit of asking where he was taking us next."[41]

Musicking's contribution to education comes in one other way as well: It attracts or leads people to sources of information they might never have encountered otherwise. This is a time-honored political tradition: Offer music as enticement, and then launch the speeches. The Wobblies did it on street corners as early as 1908; the Aid benefits of recent years have a similar hope that people will come to hear the music but, while there, make a connection to one of the groups doing something for change. "Tabling"—providing literature, petitions, sign-up sheets and so forth—is now common at concerts in many genres, from folk to hardcore. Fans come to see Sting at an Amnesty International concert and pick up literature on prisoners of conscience at a booth in the lobby.

Bands of the 1990s such as Crass, Consolidated, MDC, and Rage Against the Machine used booklets and pictures with their CDs to explicitly direct listeners to political works and groups they thought important, which some fans then sought out. Today, the websites of politically conscious performers are filled with information and links about their favored causes, issues, and authors. Matt, 15 years old when he wrote us, said,

> When I listen to the songs, I usually read the lyrics and when something in the lyrics strikes me as interesting I want to find out what they are talking about so I look around on their websites, etc. And by doing that, I have found out a lot of info that I would have never known about.... [O]n Rage Against the Machine's second album they had a bunch of books pictured and *Johnny Got His Gun* was one of them, so I read it—after getting some info on what it was about. *In the Spirit of Crazy Horse* I started reading (and still am—very long book) because I heard about Leonard Pelletier [Peltier] and the AIM movement from some of Rage's songs.

Phil, now an extremely committed activist/musician, told us, "Sitting down and reading the material that came with MDC's 7" [CD] made me think, 'Hey, I really don't need to be eating meat,' and so I stopped." Gianpaulo, a high school senior, son of a chief of police and a "more conservative" mother—yet himself now active in the Anarchist Liberty Union—told us:

> I had, really, no political interests until I discovered punk rock through a friend of mine.... Through the music I became familiarized with the works of Marx, Proudhon, Bakunin, Goldman, and many of their contemporaries.... I don't feel it is impossible I would have come to my current political beliefs [without music], but until my involvement in punk, I—like the majority of people—had no idea what the principles of anarchism and anarcho-syndicalism were.

In general, attachment to a music and the scene around it—concerts, magazines, websites—may put a fan in ongoing contact with people who have an alternative worldview. "I latched on to songs and postures of protest the way other people latched on to sports, consumer goods, lifestyles, or career goals," said Hank, "but I wasn't alone, and this antidote to loneliness and anomie always led me to the more serious dissidents among whom my brain cells could get a workout as well as my hormones." A punk/lesbian activist student wrote us of

> a time in my life in which the music I loved was, in essence, all I had. The discovery of punk, independent and underground forms of rock music during my early teenage years was crucial to my development, involving me in a network of individuals who would create the backdrop to my personal revolution.

Alternative Identities

The most significant educational impact of a music may be to announce that a subculture or a cause exists at all, and in this musicking excels. The great political significance of the Newport Folk Festivals of the late 1950s and early 1960s was that "it provided for the eruption into day-lit social space the hidden underground life of an emergent youth culture."[42] Writing in 1950, David Riesman noted a small oppositional minority among young people, but declared that it had "no awareness of itself as such, no direct political consciousness, and, on the whole, no specialized media of communication."[43] Within a decade, the folk revival, and then the explosion of rock and roll, had provided an avenue for that self-awareness.

At first, such affinities may be hardly defined, and then typically as a social rather than political bond. Bruce Springsteen recalls:

> That's a lot of what music did for me—it provided me with a community filled with people, with brothers and sisters who I didn't know, but who I knew were out there. We had this enormous thing in common, this "thing" that initially felt like a secret.... There are very real communities that were built up around that notion— the very real community of your local club on Saturday night.... And then there is the community that it was enabling you to imagine, but that you haven't seen yet. You don't even know it exists, but you could feel that, because of what you heard or experienced, it *could* exist. That was a very powerful idea because it drew you outward in search of that community—a community of ideas and values.[44]

Musicking thus not only creates and provides free space for social alternatives; it alerts isolated people that a space is there, which they may then understand to be open to them. Salsa, Ospina argues, helped create a pan-continental Hispanic identity, tying together a great number of nationalities in a greater Latino identity that celebrated salsa as "our" music.[45] The Women on Wheels tour of 1975 provided a vivid demonstration to isolated feminists and especially lesbians that there were many others like them.

Further, musicking can let people know that those they now see as belonging to their group therefore have concerns and issues in common, which is what "Penny's

Farm" did for some rural tenants in the late 1800s. That is, musicking may help a group develop from a social to a political emphasis, as Ian MacKaye discovered when he first encountered the punk scene as a teenager:

> Punk rock was the first time that I found like the porthole to this underground where *everything,* all conventions, were challenged.... Here people were confronting philosophical issues, confronting musical issues—they're confronting conventions all across the border. Saying music doesn't have to be the way that it's being presented, they're saying that art doesn't have to be that way, right down to sexuality.... Suddenly it was like, wow, *everything* is being confronted.... I realized, wait a minute, here it is, here are the people who are confronting political issues.

Crucially, musicking can inform the uninformed that *a movement exists* that deals with these issues and concerns (just as earlier we noted it can reinforce that idea among those already committed to a movement). When the SNCC Freedom Singers toured northern campuses in the early 1960s, their most important message wasn't that segregation was unfair (which, even then, most audience members of all races already understood), but that there was a vibrant movement of resistance to segregation sweeping through the South. Singer David Crosby saw the same benefits for the antinuclear concert tours of the 1970s and 1980s: "No Nukes and Peace Sunday showed people that they could do something about a particular problem. That's the underlying truth of every one of these events: that you are not alone and you are not powerless. That message is as important as the primary message."[46]

By saying things *out loud in public,* musicking can confer an aura of reality and legitimacy on previously suppressed ways of thinking. Just as one of the first things civil rights organizers of the 1960s did upon entering a community was to begin to teach freedom songs, white power organizers today report that among their first acts upon entering a new community is "to get the kids into racist music, get them onto the mailing list of a distributor like Resistance Records ... [because music] gives the movement legitimacy. It is a subculture just like hip-hop is a subculture."[47]

The public declaration of a movement or ideology helps to *crystallize* currents of feeling and belief already present in the society at large and in the mind of an individual. Through music and musicking, random, inchoate, nonspecific, or unfocused feelings, "vaguely formed or mildly simmering,"[48] can be made concrete. Further, musicking provides emotional substrata to conscious thought; "music helps people to feel the things they are thinking," writes one musician.[49]

The term *homology,* favored by cultural sociologists, underlines how subcultures develop worldviews in which fashion, personal politics, music, and so on are all felt as part of a coherent scene and identity. Music and musicking can fix emerging sets of beliefs as a collective identity—this is Oi!, this is rock and roll, this is X—and what X is then becomes a matter of discussion, debate, and therefore refinement. "You write a song like *Luca,*" says Suzanne Vega about her pop hit that tells a story of child abuse, "and then people have a tool to talk about it with."

In this chapter we've argued that an important contribution musicking makes to movements, in some times, places, and situations, is its educational role. It's contextual, it's contingent, it's typically part of a greater picture—but it's significant nonetheless. Music carries suggestions of new ideas and identities, fixes others as something to be considered, ties these to other ideas and identities in ways that suggest they belong together, and does all of this with an emotional power that other forms of education only rarely achieve. "Not until the theme has been articulated, not until the tensions have been formulated ... can a social movement come into being," write Eyerman & Jamison, and musicking often helps focus that articulation.[50]

Chapter 8

Conversion and Recruitment

Politically engaged musicians are often hoping to do more than just acquaint an audience with certain ideas and perspectives—they're hoping to win us over to those ideas, to engender commitment to a perspective and the group that holds that perspective. They want us to become part of a movement.

Can music have this kind of power? Street writes: "A song, however powerful its performance, cannot win an argument."[1] But this was clearly the intent of the Almanac Singers as they drove from city to city in that summer of 1941. They weren't just calling attention to a problem, commenting on a situation. Their songs told workers: "This is what you should think and do about your situation."

> Now, if you want higher wages, let me tell you what to do
> You got to talk to the workers in the shop with you.
> You got to build you a union, got to make it strong ... you'll win.[2]

Musicking in this tradition has moved beyond the "diagnostic," as Snow & Benford call framing that draws attention to a problem, and into the "prognostic,"[3] suggesting what the audience might do. A song like "Which Side Are You On?" is "a challenge to anybody who hears it," says singer Fred Small. "Whose side are you on? You have to choose. You can't straddle the fence."[4]

Here we're drawing a (largely analytic) distinction between *education,* in which people are exposed to, and become acquainted with, certain ideas or feelings they haven't previously considered (or considered in a particular way), and *conversion and recruitment,* meaning an allegiance to those ideas and feelings and a sense of belonging to the movement. In a sense, this is the Great Divide. Now we're at the nitty-gritty of whether music can play a significant role in actually *changing* ideas and behavior. Olson's free-rider dilemma returns with a vengeance: Given the sacrifice of time, energy, and perhaps even personal safety, why become a publicly identified participant or supporter, even if you think the movement's view has merit?

Movements include both activists, who are consciously committed to political organizing as central to their everyday lives, and others who participate during the mass mobilizations that turn a cause into a movement.[5] Such participation depends fundamentally on conditions of opportunity and threat that compel many to break out of the routines and demands of their everyday lives. But there are also individual cultural experiences that turn a previously uninvolved person's ignorance or indifference toward awareness and adoption of alternatives: "Seeing Ani DiFranco perform live was one of those life-changing experiences that crept up on me when I wasn't looking," Vickstrom writes. "Her songs introduced me to topics and viewpoints to which I had never been exposed. They gave me a starting point from which I could structure an understanding of the world and my place in it."[6] Charles Hamm claims that the Hutchinson Family's "singing of 'John Brown's Body' converted more people to the antislavery cause than all the speeches and sermons of the time."[7] A student activist wrote us: "I joined Amnesty International at age 13 because my favorite band at the time, U2, sang about human rights issues and attached info about AI to a lot of their paraphernalia. This was the beginning of my activist life."

Some musicians we talked to reported evidence of conversion from their own lives:

> Q: You believe music can . . . convert or mobilize people as well?
> SANDY RAPP: Absolutely.
> Q: What's your faith in that based on?
> RAPP: Things people come up to me and say after a concert confirm it.

> TOM MORELLO: My last 14 years [are] peppered with stories of people who began as "that [angry, apolitical] guy" and ended up in their local chapter of [groups] from Amnesty International to the RCP [Revolutionary Communist Party]. I've seen that time and time again; I know that it can have that effect.... What we would hear constantly from the local grassroots organizations who kind of coattailed around with us was that there had never been anything like it. It was an unprecedented opportunity for the Left to burst into Peoria, Illinois, and, you know, sort of challenge the way things worked—the school board meeting, this high school classroom. Because there was twelve thousand kids a night who came [to the Rage Against the Machine concert], and a thousand of them or five hundred of them were ready the next day to act.

The late Utah Phillips, a modern-day Wobbly, argued that musicking was the *main* recruiting tool for the IWW of the early 1900s.[8] One Wobbly recruited in just that way later wrote, "[W]hat first attracted me to the IWW was its songs and the gusto with which its members sang them." While he welcomed their humor and liveliness to "break the monotony of long-winded speeches," it was the stories told in the songs themselves that attracted him to the Wobbly worldview. The success of the *Little Red Songbook* in communicating that vision, he writes, "was a hard blow to those who believed that the theory of industrial unionism could only be explained by pamphlet and book couched in language beyond the average workingman's comprehension."[9]

As always, causation is very difficult to determine, and accounts of the chronology suspect. Mark Hamm provides data that seem to indicate that exposure to the White Power band Skrewdriver is the greatest single factor explaining recruitment to the American skinhead movement.[10] But the data are actually ambiguous: Does attraction to and experience of Skrewdriver lead people to *become* the most radical, committed, and violent skinheads (as Hamm postulates), or are those already on the path to becoming fanatic skinheads the ones most likely to enjoy listening to Skrewdriver? Hamm does provide occasional pieces of anecdotal evidence from skinheads, but the evidence (as so often) establishes plausibility rather than probability.

Most musicians and theorists are skeptical about the conversion potential of music. Some see music as largely incapable of aiding conversion at all, unable to move anyone beyond the already committed. Lieberman, writing of the 1948 Progressive presidential campaign of Henry Wallace, perhaps the most musical presidential campaign ever mounted, says:

> The Wallace campaign songs most likely had no effect at all on those who were undecided about how to cast their votes. . . . Songs probably did not convince anyone to vote for Wallace, just as singing at hootenannies probably converted very few people to another worldview.[11]

Indeed, given that the Wallace vote turned out to be much smaller than early polls had indicated, there was probably a sizable number of people who experienced the campaign and its songs and ended up voting for Truman rather than Wallace.

"It becomes rapidly apparent that the mere hearing of protest song X will not turn the listener into being a supporter of X ideology or group," Denisoff declared; *mere hearing* is the key term. If mere hearing was convincing, the mid-1960s "listener to Top Forty Radio would be a Green Beret supporter of pacifist causes who takes drugs and beats up long-haired youths for opposing the Vietnam War," as he pointed out.[12] By the same logic, we would all buy every product we ever heard about in any commercial jingle advertising and agree with every side of every argument we ever heard about anything.

Those who envision a significant role for musicking in effecting change are thus less likely to speak of instant enlightenment than of its contribution to a process:

> FRED SMALL: I don't think anybody changes their mind just like that [snaps fingers]. You hear a song, or speech, or an editorial, and you are all of a sudden 180 degrees on the other side. But it's part of a sequence of incremental changes, and then something shifts. I know that my songs have been part of that sequence and in some cases they have been the element that made the shift.[13]

> TOM MORELLO: I don't know that it's accurate to say that there's the Paul-on-the-road-to-Damascus kind of thing, you know, where something comes from above and fills the glass, but I think it resonates with something inside you—in the same way it did with me.

Those available for recruitment are, in the vast majority of cases, people already educated and interested in the issues. The northern students who were spurred to support (and in some cases, join) the 1964 Freedom Summer voter registration campaign in Mississippi after attending a SNCC Freedom Singers concert were obviously already at least curious about the southern civil rights struggles, if not outright sympathetic. But the emotion, the commitment, the visible (and aural!) presence of the Freedom Singers moved many beyond interest to commitment to the movement.[14] The folksinger Phil Ochs proclaimed at that time,

> We're trying to crystallize the thoughts of young people who have stopped accepting things the way they are. Young people are disillusioned; we want to reinforce their disillusionment so they'll get more involved and do something—not out of a general sense of rebellion, but out of a real concern for what's happening—or not happening.[15]

Music's place in the processes of conversion and recruitment may often serve as a "point of entry," as Temple says of punk.[16] Musicking can help shape amorphous ideas into something like a coherent perspective, and by doing so help to bond "near-groups" into groups.[17] It's not just the coherence of the vision but the pleasure that the musical expression of the vision provides that helps the recruitment process. The aesthetic appeal of the music and the scene around it moves us toward what appears to be its source, cementing our allegiance to the movement.

As the National Miners Union battled the mine owners in the Appalachian hills in the 1930s, Aunt Molly Jackson sang:

> Come all of you good workers, good news to you I'll tell
> Of how the good old union has come in here to dwell.
> Come join the NMU! Come join the NMU!

The basic educational message—things don't have to be this way—is now extended: Join us and you can play a role in changing them.

Enacting the Collective

One way of urging this allegiance is to tie a group or movement to an earlier tradition that people feel is theirs. Eyerman & Jamison see this "mobilization of tradition" as a fundamental process in movements; music remains "as a memory and as a potential way to inspire new waves of mobilization."[18] This past, of course, is one chosen and constructed from among many possibilities. Musicking helps to create a form of collective memory, a shared vision of the past, and thus (perhaps) a shared vision of the future. Carl Gunther, organizer of a contemporary political songwriters' group, wrote us,

> I was born a bit late for the sixties, and so did not experience the important confluence of music and politics that occurred in that period. However, many of the people who I have met since founding Songs for Social Change (SFSC) were active in the move-

ment for civil rights, and so you could say that my involvement with political music has brought that influence in a more focused way into my own life and attention.

This tie to the past, however, doesn't have to be to an earlier movement. The Carawans found that singing commonly known songs of any kind helped forge commitment to the task at hand in the movements they worked with.[19] In Sanger's review of activists' musicking in the civil rights movement, it was their childhood (often lapsed) ties to the church that many felt infused their organizing: "Activists suggested that their singing was bound up with a spiritual part of their lives that had, perhaps, lain dormant before they began singing.... The traditional songs, almost always bearing some religious or spiritual references, became a way to tap into the preexisting spirituality of the activists and the people they sought to reach."[20]

In this example, as in many others, it is the active shared performance, rather than simply the words or music, that is at the heart of the experience. A member of the Sacramento Labor Chorus told an interviewer:

[I]n our society and culture just singing together is radical in that it breaks from the norm. It's unique and it gives a sense of collective spirit. I remember the first time I heard Pete Seeger get a crowd to sing.... [J]ust to hear my voice with a whole auditorium was just so exciting. It changed my sense of my voice.[21]

Such participation, Sanger suggests, sustains an emotional vulnerability to those around you that's valuable, even necessary, for successful organizations: "[I]t implied a risk taking, an opening of the self, and a trust in others that activists felt were necessary for the movement to succeed."[22] At the same time, the collective nature of the musicking is protective, allowing those taking part to express belief within a supportive atmosphere without fear. Collective musicking offers a way to try on ideas and identities in a kind of rehearsal.[23] And by joining the collective voice we are, at least at the moment, helping to reinforce the shared identity of the group and expressing our membership.

We began this book by describing the 1941 tour of the Almanac Singers, playing whenever and wherever they could to workers thinking of joining the CIO. Imagine one of those rallies. You come as a worker, interested but afraid. If you join the union, there may well be dire consequences: You may be fired from your job, you may lose your friends, you may be physically attacked, you may be killed. What will it take to get you to decide the gamble is worth it? Perhaps it's an inspiring speech, or the logical arguments made by a CIO organizer. Perhaps it's the size of the crowd, a feeling of safety and power in numbers. But perhaps it's also the music: singing along—and thus saying *out loud*—"You can't scare me, I'm sticking to the union," allows you to hear yourself saying those words, allows you to try out that idea and that identity. This was exactly what the young civil rights activists who developed into the SNCC Freedom Singers saw in Albany, Georgia, in the early 1960s:

The spirit of the songs could sweep up the crowd, and the young leaders realized that through song they could induce humble people to say and feel things that otherwise were beyond them. Into the defiant spiritual "Ain't Gonna Let Nobody Turn Me Around," Sherrod and Reagon called out verses of "Ain't gonna let [local police] Chief Pritchett turn me around." It amazed them to see people who inched tentatively into the church taking up the verse in full voice, setting themselves against feared authority.[24]

These rehearsals of a new and weighty commitment are possible because the situation and the activity are supportive, and yet demanding. We simultaneously experience the potential power of a unified mass, and the need to affirm our continuing relationship to these people. All the elements—what the lyrics are saying, what the music evokes, the act of singing together, the environment surrounding the singing—allow, sometimes even compel, trying on that new commitment. When the Almanacs sang "Union Maid," those in the audience sang with them. When they imparted the dry humor of "Talking Union," the audience laughed together. When they emphasized the rhythm of "We Shall Not Be Moved," the audience clapped along. The shared nature of the public performance created the solidarity called for in the lyrics of "Talking Union."

Group Formation

In addition to the role music plays in reinforcing preexisting groupings, musicking can serve as the basis for the *formation* of a group, cutting across other divisions, creating "a commonality of cultural experience"[25] that can form the basis of new community. Your song links you to others who also see it as their song.

Punk subculture in England first surfaced and coalesced around a musical style; in the Soviet Union, beginning in the late 1960s, "rock music provided the essential underpinning for an emergent youth counterculture."[26] Liking punk implied, in very short order, questioning authority, embracing a "do-it-yourself" (DIY) ethic, and adopting an "antifashion" sense of fashion. Liking rock in the Soviet Union was bundled with wearing blue jeans, a desire for greater individual freedom, and, eventually, a disdain for the Communist Party. Of course, those who already had these sensibilities, at least in embryo, were likely to be attracted to the developing musical scenes in the first place. As Hennion says of pop in particular, "[M]usic organizes youthful mobile social groups still in the process of forming. It draws together potential groups still ignored by the politicians, whose members share the same unspoken frustrations."[27]

In some cases, the social grouping becomes a political grouping. As we've often said, all musicking carries an implied political message of some sort, and musical movements may have political effects without that being their primary intention, or their intention at all (think Elvis and the civil rights movement). But in some times and places, groups formed around music become overtly, consciously political,[28] aiding what social movement theorists call "bloc recruitment" to the movement by constructing and reconstructing group boundaries. "Youth" was solidified as a meaningful category in the 1960s by what appeared to be a generational music, temporarily minimizing divisions of race and class that had been seen as more important just a few years before. Musicians active in peace groups in Northern Ireland in the late twentieth century trying to draw Protestant and Catholic youth to the same venues attempted to make "youth" feel like a more significant category than religion; those in Rock Against Racism sought to replace race with age. If you love a music, if you ally yourself with the community formed around that music, you become a member of a group that—at times—becomes more important than any other grouping you or others place you within.

Obviously, such efforts don't need to be intended as political, and very often they're not consciously interpreted that way by participants. Christenson & Roberts note that while the music of teenagers is often described by others as a weapon of identity and solidarity in their war against the adult world, adolescents themselves rarely describe it as such.[29] What we're suggesting is that identity and solidarity have a number of potentially political dimensions that may be available for movement purposes under the right circumstances. Van Deburg argues this was the contribution of soul artists to the civil rights movement in the 1960s: "When authentic soulmen asked if they could 'get a witness' or begged an audience to 'let me hear you say yeah,' they were nudging listeners toward a feeling of oneness that, in a somewhat different venue, might be adapted to more 'political' ends."[30]

The transformation of subculture into political grouping is especially likely when the music itself is repressed by government officials who fear what they perceive as its corrupting influence, or simply its power to create groups involved in activities not sanctioned by the state. The Czech revolution of 1989 had roots in the rock scene and its repression: The Charter 77 Human Rights movement that eventually toppled the Communist Party grew out of a campaign to free the Czech counterculture's leading band, the Plastic People of the Universe, who had been arrested in February 1976 for organizing a concert not sanctioned by the state, and then jailed for subversion. Intellectuals already discontented with restraints on individual freedom were joined by a much larger group of young music lovers who protested this particular act of censorship, but then moved to a more encompassing critique of censorship in general, and eventually of the party that imposed such restrictions.[31] Wicke argues that much the same thing happened in East Germany. Friction began with the Communist Party's sporadic attempts to repress rock music; in response, "rock musicians were instrumental in setting in motion the actual course of events which led to the destruction of the Berlin Wall and the disappearance of the GDR."[32] In the late 1930s, jazz served as a rallying point for youth opposition to the Nazi regime in Germany after it was banned by authorities.[33]

Sometimes, as we noted in the last chapter, music is the only channel of communication open to people who are repressed in all other avenues of life; the very lack of alternatives may elevate musicking from one of many voices—as in education—to the most trusted avenue of information, facilitating recruitment. In Argentina in the 1970s and 1980s, the military dictatorship banned virtually all collective activities except for cultural events. The result, according to Vila, was that the social scene that grew up around *rock nacional* "proved an original form within which the young created and inhabited a space of their own, symbolically protected from the assaults of the military dictatorship (which had made them its principal victims), and [came] to constitute ... a counterculture and a social movement."[34] Similarly in Brazil during the military dictatorship, the national musical festivals known as MPB (*Musica Popular Brasileira*) "became public forums, places to raise or debate issues—through song, performance and response—that the military's suffocation of free speech and political activity had disallowed in normal channels."[35]

Rock in the United States was a source of bloc recruitment in the 1960s. Conditions of repression were certainly not anywhere near as severe or total as in Eastern Europe or Latin America, but the music served a similar function as a major channel of communication for expressing the antiauthoritarian resentments of the young, rooted in part in experiences in family, school, and street, but much heightened by the draft and the Vietnam War. As the society increasingly came to feel like two opposing camps, a person's attitude toward rock felt to many like a declaration of allegiance:

HANK: In the time of cliques and dress codes, I escaped those into the bosom of political rallies where ... the stream of poetry set to music ... echoed my most profound feelings, feelings that found scant welcome among my parents, neighbors, most teachers and peers.

Some political groups have deliberately attempted to facilitate bloc recruitment through music. Tom Metzger, the visionary of the white supremacist movement, strategically invaded the punk scene through his group White Aryan Resistance's sponsorship of Skrewdriver; later, in the early 1990s, WAR and other radical right groups targeted the black metal scene as a source of new membership. But such recruitment is more often simply the by-product of the music and its scene. When fan loyalties—to the music, to the musicians, to each other, to the scene as a whole—conflict with societal arrangements that affect the musickers *as musickers,* some in the scene will adopt a political stance that addresses that conflict. Our midwestern Jewish jazz fanatic interviewee, whose "lifelong practice of opposing racial inequity" was the result of his "realization that the black pioneers and creators of this incomparable music were the systematic victims of appalling prejudice and discrimination," is an individual example of this. But often there is a group process as well, a segment of the scene exerting a pull toward a political stance, with an implicit or explicit expectation that a certain set of political beliefs accompanies this particular musical and social orientation.

When we enter a musical scene that is already explicitly linked to oppositional politics, the pull toward movement participation is even stronger. The *nueva canción* movement in South America in the 1960s and 1970s combined a rediscovery and reinvigoration of traditional music forms with "nationalism, anti-Americanism, and the related drive for economic, political, and cultural independence."[36] Lieberman tells us that in the United States in the 1930s, "Many people made their first connection with the Communist movement through culture.... Young people were exposed to a political outlook and a style of music at an impressionable age. They embraced both the music and the politics, from then on viewing them as inseparable."[37]

"From the beginning I associated folk music with left-wing politics since I had gone to a left-wing [summer] camp," Irwin Silber told us; Odetta told Karroll,

> [T]he people who were interested in folk music were also those people who were interested in social problems and trying to fix those social problems. I remember when I came into the area of folk music, we were at that time taking around petitions to save Ethel and Julius Rosenberg. So, already around this music there was the left bent, the socialistic looking at ways human beings could live.[38]

The folk music scene in New York and some college towns in the late fifties and early sixties was similarly formative; many of the first wave of white civil rights supporters in the early sixties were politically and culturally incubated in the hootenannies, concerts, and coffeehouses where the descendants of the Almanacs were playing.[39]

If some come to music scenes like this precisely because they find a combination of the cultural and political preferences they already possess, this mix also plays an important role for those aware of, or drawn to, a movement who haven't yet made a commitment. Hamm presents a vivid example of this in the development of Oi! in London's punk scene in the late 1970s:

> [A] number of hard-core London punks were still flirting with the vacant but violent and reactionary images of Nazism.... Suddenly, Ian Stuart was in the right place at the right time. Breathing intendment to the otherwise meaningless punk symbols of Nazism, Stuart and his skinhead associates created a subculture that was homologous.... The Skinhead Nation was born.[40]

But often politics are less central to the scene, less concrete and more in the process of emerging as many similarly minded people interact and evolve a common view. The greatest contribution of punk to political groupings, R. H. Rosenthal writes, was as "social legitimizer":

> [I]t brings many adolescents together who have some of the same political and social leanings and provides peer acceptance by creating a subculture that might not exist if the music did not exist. While the music creates the bond, the listeners of punk may then be motivated to carry out their political ideals not because the music "says" they should but because many others feel the same way and that it is acceptable to express those opinions.[41]

Constructing Collective Identity

What is common to all these scenarios is the crystallization of identity, particularly collective identity. Musical scenes define social boundaries, and valorize the identity of those who are included. Within the safety of these boundaries, musicking is used to construct, display, and reinforce each person's personal version of the collective identity he or she is embracing.

This kind of identity exploration is particularly likely when old identities no longer seem sufficient to deal with a person's circumstances. "They have to be in the context of some sort of questioning of their own views, or discomfort with their own views," singer Barbara Dane argues, speaking of her organizing work among GIs during the Vietnam War:

> The majority of the kids had not been exposed to anything outside of their own community, their small town, maybe their church, their parents. . . . Someone brings them to a GI coffeehouse, saying "Let's go down, they got pictures of Jimmy Dean, the rebel, on the wall, Jimi Hendrix, the guitar rebel, on the jukebox, and whatever on the turntable. It's a cool place!" So the guy goes—it's a cool place. But why does he go in the first place? Because he's curious—curious about the world outside of his own thing. In pain because of basic training and all the distorting. . . . Basic training in six or eight weeks is designed to totally take apart your mind, your preconceptions, and put them together in a new way. They've just been through that, so they're in this state of discomfort with this new thing and have left behind the old thing.
>
> So they come to the hangout there, the GI coffeehouse, because of all the discomfort that's going on and then they see something new: "Oh, there's a third way to look at this whole thing. Not the way my parents did, not the way the army wants me to, but the way these other guys are beginning to look at it." They have different things that reinforce that. You can look around the room and see the pictures, the books, the newspapers that the other GIs have written, and then they're all singing together pretty soon, you know? And the look on their faces, [laughs] singing words they would never have dreamed of singing before, is amazing to see. "Oh here I am singing 'Ain't gonna study war no more.' They've just taught me last week that I'm a killer, but what do I really want to do?" And so then it opens up room emotionally, intellectually, to debate that.

Identity processes are inherent in all movements. Commitment to a movement is synonymous with taking on the identity of movement member or activist. And musicking, we've been arguing, is the way many first try on that identity, facilitating commitment and recruitment. The GIs singing "Join the GI Movement" along with Barbara Dane, the industrial workers singing "Oh you don't scare me, I'm sticking to the union" with the Almanac Singers, the northern college audience hearing the SNCC Freedom Singers sing "Been Down into the South"—all of these were occasions in which a new identity could be tentatively worked out and tried on.

Indeed, music is a major resource for identity construction in contexts that are remote from the political. Musical tastes form the basis of adolescent subcultures, and help structure social distinction in the society at large. But because collective identity processes are crucial in movement creation and maintenance, music is a particularly important resource for social struggles. Civil rights activists consciously thought of songs as celebrations of new identities. In the words of one, "We sang . . . songs affirming the joy of coming alive, of becoming new persons."[42]

Song lyrics are often central as identity resources. James Brown's music was already implicitly celebrating African and African American sensibilities before he recorded "Say It Loud (I'm Black and I'm Proud)," but it was those lyrics that turned "Say It Loud" into a movement anthem of black pride; in much the same way, "The Farmer Is the Man," although musically similar to other songs of the 1880s, became widely used in the agrarian populist movements of that era because of the collective pride asserted in the lyrics. Still, as always, musicking's elements go beyond words (which is why musicking has been far more important to movements than poetry), or even music as such. The ritual of performance, Eyerman & Jamison write, conveys "a sense of movement in an emotional and almost physical sense";[43] at the core is often the impact of the performer, serving as movement "totalizer."[44] Fans and activists frequently cite their favorite musicians as role models who made movement activity seem desirable, or natural, or necessary:

> My favorite band at the time was Into Another. I was reading a bit about them and found that they were a vegan band—at the time, I had no idea what "vegan" even was. So I decided to find out, and theoretically the concept made sense to me, so I became a vegan. So, in essence, the reason I originally became vegan was split—it was partially because it was the right thing to do, but also ... that I wanted to emulate these people that I respected.[45]

The political messages being produced by music and minstrel are echoed, complemented, and amplified in the social scenes that give context to the musicking. Says another hardcore enthusiast: "It was more the music scene that I was a part of ... than the bands ... because a lot of the kids that went to shows were vegan and I looked up to them a lot."[46] A reader wrote to *The Nation*:

> As my husband and I try to raise an enlightened child in a society still in the Dark Ages, we're trying to impart to her the passion we found on the punk scene—which is far more than the music. It was on the punk scene that I was first introduced to {radical scholar} Noam Chomsky, where I saw people creating their own art and politics without any help from the "experts."[47]

The sense of homology that the Birmingham School theorists observed in the punk world is typical of musical/political scenes generally: Everything seems to fit together into a coherent, unified worldview that often includes prescriptions about political attitude and commitment.[48] When we dress like others in the scene, or buy the music they listen to, or become like one of them in any way, we take a step toward the political identification and commitment typical of the group.

The live concert is often a critical experience for turning fandom into group commitment, as Eyerman observes of the white power movement in Europe:

> Concerts sell records and introduce performers, which is important, but such collective performances, where the distinctions between players and listeners break down and all are performers, are more vital for creating group solidarity than for any status they may provide.... All who participate are co-conspirators, creating an even stronger bond with the experience of the music.[49]

In Small's wonderful declaration, "Whoever engages in a musical performance, of whatever kind, is saying to themselves and to anyone else who may be taking notice, *This is who we are,* and that is a serious affirmation indeed."[50] Many potential recruits, sympathetic but not allied with the movement, are normally invisible and isolated, committed to their daily routines, unaware that others feel the same way, or afraid of repercussions from public identification. Live performances allow these potential members to become visibly part of the movement, declaring their membership to others and to themselves.

Live performances create free space: a physical area, marked out by auditory and physical boundaries, with an attached social/psychological meaning. Within this relatively protected space—surrounded by others who appear to feel much as you do, perhaps transported to a micro model of what relations in that new world might be—the decision to actively commit to an oppositional movement is facilitated. The enormous impact of the 1975 Women on Wheels tour on the West Coast feminist movement was simply that it allowed feminists and lesbians to feel the strength of their numbers, to congregate in a place where positive feelings about feminism and/or lesbianism were shared by many others. Self-identification and commitment to the movement became much easier in such an environment.

Of course, not everyone who attends public performances, even of politically charged genres like women's music, arrives with a desire to link up with a greater movement. Many come primarily for the music and social bonding. But recruitment is encouraged when the event as a whole frames the music as movement related. In European white power rock concerts in recent years,

> Songs are usually introduced with short, highly ideological statements and ended with a series of collective gestures, a raised and pointed right arm, and the shouting of slogans. This ritualized performance/text links the individual to a symbolic past, as the experience links the individual to a movement, a movement with a history, its own story, its own heroes and habitus.... There is a moral exclusiveness in this defensive community.... The concerts re-member the groups and give a physical sense of belonging to a movement, to a collective.[51]

Although emotionally quite different in tone, the hootenannies sponsored by left groups in the United States in the 1930s and 1940s likewise greatly facilitated recruitment of those already interested in Progressive politics, as some from that time explained to us:

> SONNY: I spent the summer I was 18 in Woodstock, New York, living in a more bohemian way than I'd ever known. It was the summer of the Henry Wallace presidential campaign [1948], to which the greatest asset was Pete Seeger.... The hootenannies held by the campaign, the campfires, Pete's extraordinary energy and enthusiasm, and the clear message that the two old parties were beyond hope marked a turning point in my passage to adult life. I became a banjo player and folksinger. I registered for the draft as a conscientious objector. I have never abandoned the leftie politics I took up that year, nor have I forgotten the old left songs I learned from the *People's Song Book* ...
>
> I'd have been some sort of leftie without the music, sure, ... and I'd have been into music ... without politics. I guess the reason that summer was so important, though, was the conjunction of the music with real accessible people who talked about politics as though it too were real. Which made it so.

For the last half-century at least, recorded music has played an important role in recruitment as the technological ability to disseminate music through recordings expands the potential audience. A recording can serve as a concrete and renewable reminder of how the live music-movement experience felt. Recordings preserve that link as we go about our daily lives, nodding our heads to Propagandhi's "And We Thought Nation-States Were a Bad Idea" while we ride to school, or rapping "The Revolution Will Not Be Televised" along with Gil Scott-Heron as we wash the dishes. For those who haven't had the live experience, recordings may serve as a substitute. "Recordings make possible participation without apparent commitment.... This first step opens the door for more contact, and for more committed participation," writes Eyerman of European skinheads,[52] and this is just what Hamm found in his study of skinheads in the United States: Listening to white power rock was for many their first identification with a specific political image and/or group, providing contact with a political subculture that didn't physically exist in their area. Inspired by the music and the networks it led to, they sought out and became full-fledged members of White Aryan Resistance or other such groups.[53]

A few activist informants reported striking moments of conversion:

JOHN: In high school I was very attracted to racist/far-right thought.... I was a senior in high school and was also experimenting with "a certain herb" [one night] alone in my room and I played [Bob Marley's] "Redemption Song" pretty loud. The contradictions began to fade away—it's very hard to explain. Being an agnostic, I don't believe (really) in moments of revelation, but that's almost what it felt like. I thought, "this man singing this song is not only *not* inferior to me, but a better human being."
Q: You really felt this one hearing began to wash away your racist attitudes?
JOHN: Yes. It was all *very* subjective and strange. I guess my mind/spirit couldn't stand the cognitive differences between my prior attitudes and the connection I felt with the music and its maker.

CRAIG: I used to be from the right [i.e., conservative] side. I saw welfare as a place for undesirables to soak off of me. I made black jokes ... I hated gays ... [Someone I met at work] took me to a hardcore show.... The rest is history. Through bands like Struggle, Chokehold, Downset, and Battery, I saw that my life was fucked. I started reading zines, especially *Retrogression* and *Inside Front.* I began going to protests.... Through hardcore, I changed my own life.

Outright conversion reports, however, were relatively rare. As Craig's testimony hints, respondents more typically recalled that music of some kind helped them start down a political road. Rather than a moment of satori, a thunderbolt of enlightenment that leads us to see The Way,[54] recruitment through music is typically a process, framed and altered by the contingencies we've discussed: the times, the musical product, the preexisting level of political activity, the audience member himself, and so forth. But the core of that experience is a process by which a music becomes *your* music, the scene around it becomes *your* scene, the movement it springs from and represents becomes *your* movement. Your personal identity becomes aligned with an alternative way of seeing the world—musically, socially, politically—that implies, even mandates, a different way of orienting your life.

HANK: Without music, I'd been introduced to U.S. politics when my eldest brother brought me to the local Republican storefront to stuff envelopes on behalf of Barry Goldwater. I was 11 years old.... By the time of the next presidential campaign, I'd found in music the life-saving vehicle to dance to and the quixotic (and romantic) slogans and perfected poetry to hang my heart upon and hope that my mouth would oblige me by following along.... With *Hootenanny* and *The Smothers Brothers Show* and radio-played anthems and ballads against the Vietnam War and all war, I found the perfect melding of meaning and melody that embraced me as much as I did it, for the next decade of adolescent turmoil. At the time I had no direct experience of labor unionism; my Dad was an advertising copywriter for the largest agency in the world and we resided in what was then the wealthiest community in Michigan. But the nobility of unionism reached me, almost solely and convincingly through the songs I heard on TV and, more rarely, on radio and, most often, at rallies and festivals that I ran to, sometimes every weekend for months at a stretch.

PHIL: There wasn't a "moment of truth" when the light just went on; generally the songs I was listening to resonated with some feelings I already had and was working out in my mind and influenced me in a particular direction.... Hearing the Clitboys singing "gays ok" made me realize it really *was* in a way I hadn't understood before.... But most of the time it wasn't so dramatic and "enlightening"; the music was a significant part of the many influences shaping me, but certainly not the only one.

Just as with social groupings that aren't overtly political—skater kids, say, or metal heads—musicking tied to a political movement both helps to construct the identity of the movement member and serves as a constant affirmation of that activist identity, a badge a person wears that signifies to herself and to others where her loyalties lie. This is particularly important in the formative stages of recruitment, when identity is still unstable, subject to the tug-of-war between an activist identity and those offered by more conventional paths. Whether and how this new identity can coexist with other basic identities (student, daughter, artist, girlfriend, etc.) have to be worked out, conflicts resolved or repressed. Commitment to this new identity may well require a rejection of some familiar mainstream conventions, a drawing of boundaries as Taylor & Whittier have portrayed it, "highlighting differences between activists and the web of others in the contested social world."[55]

The music that highlights these differences may overtly and lyrically draw these boundaries, or express them in more subtle fashion, as an attachment to folk music in the early 1960s—more often ballads of murder and mayhem than anything overtly political—often engendered an allegiance to the emerging movements of that time. "When I started to drift to the left politically, to the pacifist wing politically, there was a culture waiting for me there that I was very comfortable with," political folksinger Charlie King told us. "And I was comfortable with it because for three or four years before that I had been sitting in coffeehouses and listening to this music without really thinking a lot about the politics that maybe the people who were singing had." Music, then, sometimes aids recruitment not by drawing boundaries but, conversely, by transcending them. When musicking spreads familiarity with ideas and worldviews beyond the confines of a select group to the population in general, it contributes to a general "sea change" that makes movement involvement more thinkable, to both the potential member and those around him. This was clearly occurring in the 1960s when popular music helped make antiwar sentiments familiar, and thus less alien and threatening. When a young man announced he was going to burn his draft card, the change in the reaction of kith and kin—from uncomprehending horror at this act of treason to (perhaps grudging) acceptance of this as a contemporary form of political activity—was in part due to the music, the general spreading of at least an awareness that such defiance was in the air. The wide-scale adoption of an antinuclear power stance by pop musicians in the 1970s and 1980s helped turn the image of antinuclear activism from the militant civil disobedience of a few to a fairly conventional position, removing most of the social costs from joining the movement.

Of course, falling in love with a music doesn't guarantee a loyalty to whatever scene or politics other fans of that music may feel is part of the experience. Overtly political musicians often report that many of their fans apparently enjoy their music while disagreeing with or ignoring the political views expressed in their songs.[56] Even fans who link their chosen music with particular social or political groupings are not inevitably destined to feel a deep loyalty to the group. People drop in and out, the implicit and explicit meanings of the group are in flux, and the focus itself may become unfashionable, replaced by the next genre, fad, or cause.

But for some people, musicking does become loaded with social and political significance, and our interest is precisely with those people:

TOM MORELLO: What tied me to the outside world were the Clash and Public Enemy, who made me feel less [alone]. I had my suspicions about, you know, the nightly news, U.S. policy in Central America, and apartheid. And it seemed like it was kind of just within the four walls of my own house until I got the Clash's *London Calling*. And I'm like, "Well, here are these guys who are halfway around the world who view the world the same way." It made me feel like there may be more of us out there, it made me feel part of a community. And there was a truth that I heard in the reporting in those songs that struck a chord that no textbook had ever struck with me and that no news footage had ever struck with me.

MARILYN: Learning folk music (hearing/singing Bob Dylan, Phil Ochs, Pete Seeger, and Joan Baez at the age of about 12) definitely contributed to both my sense of self and my sense of being in the world. . . . I'm aware that music actually generated that sense of feeling connected in a way that I might not have felt connected if the music wasn't there. And it makes me wonder about the next "story," that of coming out as a lesbian in the seventies. . . . The women's music movement was absolutely an integral part of my coming out. I have often thought that there are certain songs that I listened to (and I think I was aware of this at the time) that contributed to a better sense of self, that somehow explained certain things to me, and most of all gave me a better sense of self-esteem and self-acceptance. . . . If I think back, I can clearly see myself on the floor of the living room, belting out "The Woman in Your Life" by Alix Dobkin; I can see myself at countless concerts; I can see myself lying on the floor with earphones on and listening to "Waterfall." Somehow they feel like defining moments in my life, that definitely would not have been there without the songs.... Whether it really *informed* my coming out, I don't really know. But I'd venture to say it nudged me along the way. I think the most important part of my story, and probably others, is that music helped to form a composite picture of myself, and that it helped me grow into who I became as an adult.

Chapter 9

Mobilization

This item appeared in the alumni notes section of the *Swarthmore College Bulletin* of May 1994:

> Phil Ochs' song "When I'm Gone" helped Clinton Etheridge make a fateful decision in the spring of 1968. The late Sam Shepherd '68, a founding father and chairman of SASS [Swarthmore Afro-American Student Society], was graduating. Shepherd wanted his friend and roommate, Etheridge, to succeed him as SASS chairman, but the shy, soft-spoken engineering major was ambivalent, agonizing over the decision.
>   Shepherd used "When I'm Gone" (from *Phil Ochs in Concert*) to persuade Etheridge. The song, which rhapsodizes on the importance of making your contribution while you are "here," has two lines that particularly hit home with Etheridge: "Won't be asked to do my share when I'm gone," and "Can't add my name into the fight when I'm gone."
>   "I heard that song and became convinced of the obvious—that I couldn't escape my duty, my responsibility, perhaps my destiny," he remembers.... He became SASS chairman and helped take Swarthmore College through the most transforming few weeks in its history [including SASS's occupation of the Admissions Office, suspension of classes, a hunger strike, and other activities leading to increased black enrollment at Swarthmore].[1]

Etheridge is making a claim here that music was the catalyst that led to a change in his behavior. Musicking, he's implying, can help move people beyond knowledge of a movement and its claims (education), beyond agreement and identification with those claims (recruitment), to taking that crucial step into concrete public movement activity we call *mobilization.*

In describing their goals, politically conscious musickers often question claims that they can move people to take action: "I suppose I am trying to offer audiences a different way of looking at and thinking about the world," writes the English political songwriter and performer Leon Rosselson. "But as for inspiring them to act—that's an overlarge ambition for a rather small art form."[2] "I used to think that the civil rights movement happened because Bob Dylan wrote 'Blowing in the Wind,'" Billy Bragg similarly told us. "I now realize it was actually completely the other way around. Bob Dylan wrote 'Blowing in the Wind' because he was inspired by the civil rights movement."

But others describe music's contribution to mobilization as extremely powerful. Listening individually or in small groups to the music of Skrewdriver and other white power rock groups is, according to Hamm, "the backbone of the transmission process" that leads some skinheads from simple allegiance to a racist ideology to outright racist violence in the name of the cause.[3] In July 1991, Simon Bikindi, Rwanda's most famous modern musician, was arrested in the Netherlands and charged with war crimes: "In essence," Donald McNeil wrote in the *New York Times*, "Bikindi is accused of inciting genocide with his songs.... According to eyewitnesses, many of the killers sang Bikindi's songs as they hacked or beat to death hundreds of thousands of Tutsis."[4] Certainly many, many factors go into a person's decision to participate in movement activities. Musicking, we argue here, can be one important factor, as Etheridge claims it was for him, and as others claim it was for those charged with genocide in Rwanda.

As the military has always known, music helps the troops rev up for battle,[5] engendering both energy and unity, and many activists consciously use music for the same purpose. Wyatt told us:

> I used to listen to Propagandhi's *I'd Rather Be Flag Burning* album ... before going to demonstrations because it helped me plug into all the outrage and anger at the establishment I felt I was up against and made me feel like I was not alone. It's helpful to know that there are a lot of people out there that believe the same thing as you and that are as angry as you. Makes you feel more empowered and really gives you presence at demonstrations.

Intuitively we might expect mobilization to be linked to songs conveying great excitement, combining high-octane music with politically inspirational lyrics— imagine Zach de La Rocha chanting "Killing in the Name"*[6] while the rest of Rage Against the Machine rocks hard enough to bring down the walls of Jericho. In the right setting, even music without political lyrics—or any lyrics at all—can aid mobilization, just by juicing up the energy level of a group contemplating or about to engage in political activity.

Beyond this immediate rush, music may also aid mobilization through an underlying confirmation of the necessity of what movement members will be required to do. While this may mean accompaniment or prelude to a specific activity, activists often speak of music as the general background to the major life commitment they've made. Barry wrote us from a prison cell where he'd been for the past fifteen years:

---

* Killing in the name of!
   Some of those that were forces are the same that burn crosses...
   Some of those that were forces are the same that bore crosses...
   And now you do what they told ya, now you're under control...
   Fuck you, I won't do what you tell me! (eight times screamed/shouted)

[While] much of my activity was not directed by music, it was at least a major emotional energizing force. Country Joe and the Fish, Jefferson Airplane/Starship, and a host of others had a profound impact on me just as I was reading anarchist and socialist theory and history. Between these forces and my personal experiences, I ended up dedicating myself to some rather extreme political goals. Much of this is a direct contributing factor in my current living arrangement.

Music in this vein tends to encourage activity through emphasizing a deeper level of connection to others and a vision of a better day, as in "We Shall Overcome."[7] Movement participants are reminded of and reconnected to the ideas, values, and emotions that mean the most to them, providing motivation to *act* as well as think in a particular way.

IRWIN SILBER: I think the sense of solidarity with a larger community lets people get out there....
Q: Are you saying that songs that emphasize solidarity may actually do a better job of mobilizing people than songs that just say "go out and do it"?
SILBER: Hard to say, each one has its function. But "Solidarity Forever" has moved more people to do something than some picket-line chant.

Mobilization has often been the explicit aim of political artists. In a sense, the music created for this purpose is not "protest music," which complains about what exists, but "solution music," which suggests concrete changes. When the Almanacs sang "Talking Union" to workers considering joining the CIO, they had a specific action in mind they wanted workers to take: "You got to build you a union, got to make it strong." Some songs of the IWW urged mounting a general strike of all workers as a viable strategy for bringing on economic justice.[8] This approach may emphasize the practical necessity of action, appealing to reasoned self-interest, as "Talking Union" did, or may take a more universalistic moral approach—now that you know the facts, how can you fail to act?—as in "Blowing in the Wind." One of Chiu's informants reported: "I had been leaning towards becoming vegetarian for months, but just could not force myself to take that giant leap. After I heard ['Squeal Time' by APPLE], I knew that I had a moral obligation to do what I knew was right, and that was that."[9]

Other music that helps mobilization is less specific. When Bob Marley urges listeners to "Get up, stand up, stand up for your rights," or Public Enemy says, "Turn it up! Bring the noise!" they're urging their listeners to do *something* rather than suggesting a specific course of action—though in a particular time and place, these songs can be used to propel immediate activity. When Thomas Mapfumo sang songs like "Butsu Mutandarika," with its chorus about an "oversized, long, pointed shoe," black Africans revolting against the white minority Rhodesian government understood very well that the music was meant to encourage armed struggle, despite the vagueness (due to censorship) of the lyrics.[10]

Here, too, lyrics are not likely to be the whole story, as we've seen in two songs frequently associated with 1960s-era demonstrations and street actions: the Rolling Stones' "Street Fighting Man"[11] and the Beatles' "Revolution." The lyrics of the former rationalize singing rock and roll instead of fighting in the streets while the latter contains cautionary warnings against militancy, but both feature high-energy music. When contemporary students were asked to rate how likely these were to inspire them to political action compared to Thunderclap Newman's "Something in the Air," which combines much more radical lyrics*[12] with a dirge-like rhythm, "Street Fighting Man" and "Revolution" were overwhelmingly preferred.[13]

The personal inspirational and role-modeling impact of minstrels is another factor in encouraging mobilization:

> PAUL BAKER HERNANDEZ: My being drawn into [Latin American solidarity activities] to this degree, my moving to Latin America and living in a barrio, a shanty town, and all the rest—that was clearly largely the result of Victor Jara and what his music was about and still is about, 25 years later.... [And] I have had the experience of people saying "I was vaguely interested in this, then my friend brought me along [to one of Baker Hernandez's concerts], and this is really exciting and interesting, and maybe I'll go down to Nicaragua next year." ... I think that's what I would like people to come away with: the feeling that, "Hey, this is a magical thing, and I can make a difference. And I'm going to choose to do that in whatever way right here and now makes sense."

Concrete activity is most likely to be encouraged when the various elements—lyrics, music, artists' stance, audience background, the immediate setting, etc.—all come together to stress action. Rage Against the Machine playing "Killing in the Name" is a good example, and never more so than in August 2000, when they performed it to close their free concert held outside the Democratic National Convention to protest the lack of choice between the major parties. In the nonviolent phase of the civil rights movement, where demonstrators were called on to exhibit stoic patience under attack, the music, lyrics, and ancillary elements (such as quasi-sermons by leaders) instead all aimed for an atmosphere of steadfast resolve.

An ex-activist recalled for us a crucial moment in her teenage years when she was deciding whether to join others on a peace walk that planned to trespass on an air force base, a decision that was likely to lead to significant consequences:

> I had prayed about it during the entire walk, and did not know if I would actually cross the line or not. I knew that if I did that I might go to prison for 6 months and/ or have to pay a $500 fine. I was 19 and supporting myself and I didn't want to go to prison, and since I am a fairly emotional person, I was challenging myself, wondering if I was just getting carried away by the walk....
>
> There was a big gathering (40–50 people) in Knob Noster State Park, about a mile from the air force base. We all ate and then gathered in a circle, standing with our arms around each other, and [a leader] asked if anybody would lead a song. I just started singing "Let there be peace on earth/and let it begin with me," and it was then I knew for sure that I would go across the line.... Just a moment of singing a song that I didn't even know I knew until I opened my mouth and started singing. And everybody joined in. And it felt right. So: I went across the line.

Musicking is often a consciously planned prelude to action, but musical events can lead to spontaneous mobilization as well. The Carawans describe a gathering

---

*Hand out the arms and ammo/We're gonna blast our way through here. We've got to get together sooner or later/because the Revolution's here

designed to entertain and raise the spirits of striking coal miners and their families in Stearns, Kentucky, in the late 1970s:

> The music lifted people's spirits, and the songs related to coal drew enthusiastic cheers. After the rally, the visiting musicians and singers went out to the picket site and helped spark an hour-long session of singing and dancing. It was the first time that women had been to the picket site, and it set a precedent for women to begin participating in the picketing.[14]

Here a social practice that arose out of making music—the mixing of men and women as equal participants—paved the way for political practice; mobilization (of women, in this case) was actually the creation—at least in part—of musicking. Musicking may itself be the center of mobilization, the focus of activity, as in our earlier mention of the miners' strike in Buchans, Newfoundland, where roving picket lines often went to company headquarters or the homes of company officials to "song" them.[15] More commonly, musicking is used as an activity that draws people to an action.[16] And in some times and places, the act of musicking is *itself* mobilization. Think of the famous scene in the movie classic *Casablanca* in which German Nazis and French resistance fighters take turns singing *"Die Wacht am Rhein"* and *"La Marseillaise"* at each other in Rick's Café in neutral Casablanca. At that moment, musicking is not simply aiding mobilization; it *is* the political activity. This is the point of arguments that the contesting of public space by groups that are normally expected to be invisible constitutes the hidden politics of rap, just as important as lyrics.[17] As Brennan writes, "Wu-Tang's 'bass emanations bumpin' from their trunk' is a reclamation of space marked off-limits by unacceptable authority."[18]

As with all movement functions, we don't mean to say here that musicking accomplishes any of this strictly by itself. "We overestimate the ability performers have to actually bring about social change all on their own—[it's] very, very difficult," warns Billy Bragg.[19] "You are trying to inspire people and encourage people but you are by no means leading," he told us. Our claim is only that (as Bragg went on to say) "with other elements in society," musicking facilitates movement mobilization, acting as "a focus, a catalyst."

Even this may not be immediately apparent. While Paul Baker Hernandez's greatest hope for those North Americans who come to his concerts is that "they all come down to Nicaragua with me tomorrow" to help progressives there, he recognizes that

> it's a long way to that kind of dramatic action from a comfy town, isn't it? And so it would take some pretty superhuman quality to do it—right here, right now. On the other hand, it doesn't preclude, doesn't deny that one-step-at-a-time thing, and that you may enable some people to make some very critical step, not necessarily tomorrow, maybe next year.

Musicking helps mobilize in another way: It energizes and inspires those already involved in concrete movement activities to go beyond what they might otherwise have done. For example, the mass singing civil rights demonstrators engaged in before demonstrations was, in Bernice Reagon's view, not simply an accompaniment to action but absolutely necessary for it to occur: "On some level, you have an intellectual thing you have to do to be involved in struggle and know where you want to be, but the other part is ... how do you feel, do you feel like doing it? ... [When they sang] a transformation took place inside of people."[20] Sam Block, an SNCC organizer in Mississippi in the 1960s, told the Carawans this story:

> You know for so long the white man in the South used the jails to scare Negroes. They've lynched a lot of Negroes and there have been many, many cases where Negroes have been killed and their bodies mutilated, and nothing has been done about it. The Federal Government has refused to do anything. If you go to the court house and try to register they tell you, "If you live on my plantation, I'm gonna get you thrown off. And I'm gonna get the sheriff to throw you in jail and throw the key away." But in Mississippi we had a Freedom Day. One lady brought her little son. He had a sign, say: I'M TOO YOUNG TO VOTE BUT MY MOTHER WANTS TO VOTE. A policeman called him over and said, "If you don't pull off that sign and throw it away, boy, I'm gonna throw you in jail." The little boy remembered the song that we sing,* and he looked up to the policeman and said, "Mister, I ain't scared of your jail, 'cause I want my freedom."[21]

In the movement to win the eight-hour day in the late nineteenth century, singing a song of that name served as a galvanizing activity for many demonstrations:

> Throughout the nation, workers could be heard singing the song at rallies, demonstrations, and parades as the campaign reached a climax in 1886.... Few could doubt the efficacy of song-poetry's collective function when thousands sang and marched to the refrain "eight hours for work, eight hours for rest, eight hours for what we will."[22]

Musicking's ability to aid the mobilization of those who are already committed to the struggle is particularly helpful in establishing solidarity and singleness of purpose across social boundaries. Dorothy Healey, longtime Communist Party activist, tells of her experience in the 1934 Imperial Valley lettuce-pickers' strike, an important battle in the attempts to unionize agricultural laborers. As Anglo and Mexican strikers found themselves jailed together, many unable to communicate in each other's language, they discovered a commonality through singing, in their respective tongues, "The International": "It was just kind of an immediate means of communication, of identification across language barriers, across country barriers: The song that bridged all the countries of the world."[23] The Wobblies' most famous victory in the mill town of Lawrence, Massachusetts, was made possible in part through their tactic of encouraging the 25 different nationalities to share their music in mass meetings, gradually encouraging familiarity and identification with each other's culture, and building a common culture that facilitated mobilization.

This shared culture is essential for *sustaining* movements, for after all, movements are not only the moments of great upsurge, of mass demonstrations and

---

*The reference is to "I Ain't Scared a' Your Jail," words by Lester Cobb (to the melody of "The Old Gray Mare"), © 1990 Sanga Music. First verse: "I ain't scared of your jail because I want my freedom, I want my freedom.... I ain't scared of your jail because I want my freedom now."

general strikes. Some musicking energizes at the moment of engagement, when the police are moving in or the pamphlets need to be distributed in the few hours before daylight. Some musicking keeps people ready for the *next* action, serving as the link between times of more dramatic mobilizations.

This brings us full circle: When people have become educated, have developed a loyalty to a group, and have begun to engage in activities dedicated to the goals of that group, they've become members of the "committed." Yet as we said in the beginning of this discussion, commitment is not a permanent state, something movements can take for granted. On the contrary, sustaining commitment over the long term is difficult; maintaining as large a core of dedicated activists as possible is crucial.

Movement theorists aren't certain what accounts for this kind of dedication. Many factors, obviously, are involved, including family background, life experiences, social networks, organizational continuity, and so on; for some people at some times, culture—including music and musicking—plays a central role. As we've seen, much of music's power resides in its public nature, the way in which it can unify a disparate people into a group with a shared mission. But its power rests also in its portability, a memory and symbol of that public unity that we can carry with us through our private lives, reaffirming our commitment to a movement and our self-identification as a movement member. Music becomes an important repository and reminder of shared beliefs and values. With time and repetition, these become the traditions that are so crucial in "interpreting reality and giving meaning to experience; they are constitutive of collective memory and thus provide the underlying logical structure upon which all social movement activity is constructed."[24]

The ability of white power rock to educate, recruit, and mobilize disaffected white youth comes from its ability to expose them "to the raw and vitriolic language of racial and ethnic hatred" in the musical wrapping of "such powerful emotions that youths will begin to link musical messages to their focal concerns."[25] The songs of the civil rights movement mixed the comforting stability of the church, "steady, surging rhythms, their lilting melodies, ... and their simple inspirational words, repeated over and over again, [to] generate a fervor than can only be described as religious in its intensity."[26] Union organizing rallies in the South in the 1920s and 1930s invariably included a gospel chorus, "whose singing fused together class solidarity, Christian fellowship, and hopes for material gain" with a musical tradition well-known and loved by those drawn to attend.[27]

The power of musicking for movements stems in large part from its ability to weld together different spheres of human experience. Musicking weds conscious reflection and physical response, hero worship and political purpose, morality and sexuality, public and private life, everyday concerns and ideological beliefs, group traditions and personal worries—and all of these to each other. It's the resulting synergy that is so powerful. The result—given the right time, tradition, place, and person—seems to demand activity as well as agreement. Olson's free-rider dilemma is overcome.

♪

Chapter 10

How Musicking
Harms Movements

Before leaving our discussion of the functions musicking potentially plays for social movements, we need to look at one last important possibility: the ways in which musicking may be *dysfunctional* for movements. Does musicking sometimes hinder the development, growth, and maintenance of a movement?

Music may work against the interests of a movement in the first place simply because most movements seek alternatives to prevailing values and power arrangements, while much of culture—popular culture in particular—tends to reflect and perpetuate the values of the existing order, values that are typically indifferent at best and hostile at worst to the vision of the movement. So, for example, feminist groups seek to recruit members from the general population who encounter a daily diet of pop love songs that, by and large, reinforce age-old patriarchal values—"Stand by your man," "I'm a slave for you." Antiwar movements encounter a pop music environment often dominated by songs reinforcing traditional values of patriotism and support for "national defense."

Even musicking that is explicitly critical of mainstream values may express perspectives that can undermine a movement's capacity to mobilize. The values expressed in much of the countercultural music and scene of the 1960s and 1970s stressed individual freedom—"turn on, tune in, drop out"—rather than commitment to *collective* responsibilities, and encouraged a worldview that militated against collective movement activity.[1] The charity megaevents of the 1980s were criticized by some at the time for embodying an ethnocentric worldview ("Do they know it's Christmas?") that reinforced the First World dominance of other nations, which set the stage for disasters such as famine in Ethiopia.[2]

Most reaffirmation of traditional values is not expressed as conscious political comment, but appears in unspoken assumptions and unquestioned images. The idealization of the car, a central aspect of rock from Chuck Berry through Bruce Springsteen and down to the present, reaffirms Americans' love of auto culture, making environmentalists' challenge to that culture more difficult. When "The Prince of Rap" B. G. celebrates being a player, wearing lots of bling, and rolling in the most luxurious ride, the central values of contemporary capitalist society are being held up as the goals worth pursuing. Much of popular culture—and folk culture as well—doesn't hold out the promise of resisting or overthrowing the dominant culture, but of triumphing on its terms.

Even when music is not actively reaffirming hegemonic values, expressed skepticism regarding change in general and political activity in particular may discourage collective action. Much of pop culture asserts that political and social questions are irrelevant (or worse: *boring*), declaring itself to be the path instead: "There's Left, and there's Right, and there's rock 'n' roll," says Ray Davies, lead singer of the Kinks.[3] As the great social and political battles of the 1960s and 1970s unfolded, the Who declared:

And the world looks just the same, and history ain't changed....

Meet the new boss! Same as the old boss!

More recently a group of punk musickers reacted to an article in *The Nation* touting the political value of punk by writing,

> [Your correspondent] not only misconstrues the motives of punk rockers, but also attempts to pull us into the diseased game of democratic politics.... The individuals of the punk community do not and will not play the games of society and rock music.... We have no interest in allying ourselves with the progressive establishment, to "stem the rightward drift of American politics" or even in "fostering healthy, democratic community." We have no desire to support in any way the political, social and economic systems imposed on us from birth. Any punks involved in political activism do so as individuals and not as representatives of "punk politics."
>
> We have no conventional "political agenda." The community that has evolved over the decades is a mode of survival and means of enjoying life. Any attempts by well-intentioned progressives and their ilk to assimilate us into their "democracy" will be met by laughs and possibly hostility.[4]

This manifesto reminds us once again that the politics expressed by a subculture go beyond lyrics and music. The ancillary aspects of musical scenes can convey accommodative, apolitical, or antipolitical themes. Hampton argues that the image of the radical hobo rambler, first popularized by Woody Guthrie and later perfected by Bob Dylan, "glorified individualism and romanticized freedom," an "essentially apolitical and escapist" stance[5] though both artists were considered extremely important political artists at various points in their careers. The hero/tramp figure they embodied is thus read by some as a symbol of anarchist rebellion that fueled

Wobbly strikes, youthful draft resistance, and all manner of radical libertarianism, but by others as bohemian escapism.

Previously we considered arguments that musical forms themselves typically convey and/or are constructed by the listener to convey messages and meaning that reinforce an acceptance of the prevailing social world as natural and inevitable. According to Adorno and others after him, popular music in particular merely restates the familiar; the notion of alternatives is lost in a cultural form in which we all know what the next line of a song will be before we've even heard it.[6] Experiencing music doesn't result in a vitalized sense of agency on the part of the audience, but comfortable acquiescence, regardless of lyrical content or the intent of the artist. The activity in itself reproduces the social order, including existing power arrangements.

For Adorno, this was particularly true of art in a capitalist society that, as a commodity produced for sale by a culture *industry,* must meet the same market requirements as any other capitalist enterprise: Profit is the end, requiring the subordination or suppression of any quality of the music that might lead to its rejection by either consumers or other parts of the entertainment industry for violating their standardized expectations. The need for a record and artist to cross over (genres, markets, even nations) to recover the enormous costs of promotion and production and thus become profitable, at least for a major label, militates against music or musicians who offend anyone; in short, against music that has a jarring point of view and/or stimulates such a point of view in an audience. Music that once held a social significance for some local, real community—reggae for Rastafarians, hip-hop for young people of color in the Bronx—is stripped of significance as it is marketed to larger audiences, removed from the experiences of the original fans of the music and serving merely as a soundtrack for shopping or partying.

Perhaps worst of all, according to this kind of analysis: Even if some piece of thought-provoking music somehow made its way through the homogenization process, it would still be received as "just entertainment" by consumers, since the coding of art as commerce robs any single product of significance beyond consumption. All meaning is trivialized, as a musical cry for an end to government complicity in inner-city drug trade takes its turn on the radio station after a paean to girls who shake it and before a commercial for acne medicine. "In a media-saturated, capitalist society, such as ours," Bricca writes, "words and images are consumed (and produce profit) just like anything else; their utility as commodities outweighs their influence as political signifiers."[7]

In earlier chapters we reviewed some of the counterarguments to this line of thinking. The most important of these, in our view, points out that we need to look at how music—or any art form—is actually used in real situations rather than assuming that it inevitably performs any one function, regressive or progressive. Obviously, we find many situations when music has aided movement formation and opposition to the powers that be. But that doesn't mean we don't recognize the importance of the tendency Adorno and others have highlighted: Music and musicking can easily be a *diversion* from political and movement activity rather than an aid. "I would say that listening to heavy metal in high school contributed significantly to my total lack of interest in politics," one Wesleyan student wrote, expressing a sentiment reported by a number of other survey respondents.

Adorno feared that all popular art was diversionary "social cement" when created and received as a commodity, including music that declared itself to be socially significant but that was reproduced in a form that denied it social significance; Tom Frank speaks specifically of the "commodification of *dissent,*"[8] the way in which oppositional political expression becomes just one more product to buy, "turn[ing] revolt into a style."[9] Politics as fashion replaces politics with content. The vision musicking presents of the movement can easily become one in which musicking itself appears to be what the movement is about.[10] People recruited through an attraction to the scene rather than the principles of the movement (to the extent these can be separated) may adopt the latter in time—but may not. The danger here is that the movement itself will begin to reflect the values and direction of the "posers" (as they're often called) brought in by the music, rather than those most dedicated to the social and political changes sought by the movement. For example, King argues:

> [R]eggae's sudden status as an international musical sensation focused unprecedented attention on the Rastafarian movement and exacerbated tensions within the movement. Indeed, the music created whole new groups of supposed Rastafarians apparently attracted to the movement by little more than the image of the "Rastaman" and the music itself. These "pseudo" Rastafarians had little in common with traditional Rastafarian principles and beliefs.... [They] imitated the cultural trappings of Rastafari—the dreadlocks, the ganja smoking, and the lingo—without embracing its larger religious and ideological tenets. In effect, the commercialization of reggae music, in the view of more traditional Rastafarians at least, trivialized and degraded the movement. Because the popularity of the music was associated with the movement, the movement itself seemed to become more of a cultural fad than a serious religious and political movement.[11]

How exactly does this happen? In part, group decisions made more or less democratically will reflect the influx of posers who may now make up a majority of the movement. But even those who are more politically oriented, the Old Guard, may be inclined to see the movement move in ways that continue to attract new adherents, since movement growth is almost always thought to be desirable and the simple distinction of true believers from posers almost impossible to see clearly at the moment. Tactics and strategies may begin to be shaped by what is most appealing as style and fashion rather than through a sober assessment of what makes most sense politically. Rap, Street argued in the 1980s, merely gave "voice to defiance rather than to action."[12] Observing the alliance of New Left activists with culturally oriented hippies in the 1960s, Warren Hinkle wrote in alarm:

> If more and more youngsters begin to share the hippie political posture of unrelenting quietism, the future of activist, serious politics is bound to be affected. The hippies have shown that it can be pleasant to drop out of the arduous task of attempting to steer a difficult, unrewarding society. But when that is done, you leave the driving to the Hell's Angels.[13]

Just as some religions have banned music from their ceremonies, fearing it would replace religious feelings (with sensuality, or regard for the voice, for example) instead of *enhancing* them,[14] some activists fear that music and other cultural forms can become a replacement for necessary political activity. Viewing the Chinese students' movement in the wake of the government's repression of their demonstrations in Tiananmen Square in 1989, Andrew Jones observed that "rock parties, wild lyrics and slam dancing have replaced megaphones, sit-ins and rock throwing as the preferred means of protest."[15] One of our students sent us a wonderfully self-critical description of his first real demonstration, a 1999 rally held to protest the incarceration and projected execution of Mumia Abu-Jamal, the radical journalist convicted in 1982 of the murder of a police officer. As he makes his way into the hall, he's rocking out to Rage Against the Machine, which he's playing on his Walkman; this precludes his talking to anyone else coming to the rally. Actual connection to a movement right before him is replaced by an imagined connection through the music of Rage.[16]

In much the same way, socially or politically oriented music may substitute for actual experiences that might engender empathy, and perhaps lead to involvement with a movement. This is often said of the way in which middle-class whites (and some middle-class people of color) use rap: "Whereas the assimilation of black street culture by whites once required a degree of human contact between the races, the street is now available at the flick of a cable channel"[17] or the click of a mouse. Hardin writes that though "environmental" or "ambient" music may "help arouse in the urban listener an appreciation for the sounds of Nature [spurring environmental activism], at their worst they function as a placebo, a sickly substitute for the actual physical experience of interaction with the more-than-human world."[18]

Far from spurring movement activity, cultural expression through musicking can become *containment* of political activity, "ignoring the possibilities of an alternative organization of culture in favor of symbolic radicalism," as David Buxton said of rock in the 1970s;[19] musicking then functions as "a narcotic, through which the 'realization of the possibility of action substitutes for the action itself,'"[20] in Bruce Jackson's wonderful characterization. By providing an opportunity for concerned members and potential members of a movement to engage their moral concerns, political musicking risks enabling a feeling that this is all that's required.

The politically oriented band Consolidated complains:

> We play music, we sell records, we make videos, we do everything the corporations want us to do to keep the people distracted. We are even worse in some ways, because we give them politics.... They come to a Consolidated show and watch videos on racism and sexism and animal abuse and say, "wow, I've done my political duty for the month, now I can go home and watch TV."[21]

Not surprisingly, most of the musicians (and their managers) we've interviewed tend to downplay this kind of diversion as problem:

IRWIN SILBER: I think it's too cynical, it's too easy, to focus in on some individuals—and maybe a good number of them—who might say to themselves, "O.K., I've done my duty. I've gone to a Pete Seeger concert." I think it's unfair to sum it up that way.... I would put it this way: Being at such a concert and being moved by it, you would be more receptive if somebody came along and said we're gonna do this or do that. They would sign a petition or whatever is the political action.

Q: Do you think the music sometimes drains energy instead of adding energy to movements?

ODETTA: Couldn't possibly imagine that. Couldn't *possibly* imagine that. You go and have a political rally and don't have any music and see what you get.

PETER JENNER: Oh yeah, well, that's fine. You know, if that means they'd also put money in the box when someone's shaking it for the right-on cause and buy the t-shirt. Do you know what I mean? And join Greenpeace and get the magazine. And vote for the slightly better candidate. I mean, those people are very important, the casual supporters. God, if everybody you met was a political activist, wouldn't life be hell?

Q: Some people say that music just saps or diverts potential political energy. Do you ever worry about that?

ANI DiFRANCO: I don't know who those people are but they probably have to take something large out of their ass.

Political activists, however, can't just dismiss the concern that cultural activities are acting as "steam control," letting off energy in symbolic rituals that might otherwise go into more productive movement activity. Consider the now ubiquitous music-video concert scene of young fans greeting their bands with raised, clenched fists—which in earlier times symbolized collective political struggle: What happens next? Do they take those feelings of righteous anger and use them to fuel their efforts to change the world, or do they return home after the concert to a life of alienated work and private consumption, their anger satiated but their situation unchanged? Some of each occurs, no doubt. The politicizing of music, and the musicizing of politics, involves a trade-off in which movements gain a wider familiarity of their issues among the population but suffer a likely lowered shared understanding of the issues among those who "join," including the possibility that some will think the musicking is the movement.

Hero Worship

Another danger of diversion arises from the role of the artist himself. Musicking can encourage hero worship, resulting in the excessive reliance on leaders Hampton describes in *Guerilla Minstrels*. As we've briefly summarized in earlier chapters, Hampton argues that musical heroes function for movements as "totalizing agents," personifying the ideal characteristics of movement members and thus enabling "an otherwise heterogeneous mass" to come together around what seems to be a shared worldview—"social unity is synthesized out of diversity and chaos."[22] Hampton sees this as essential for movements but warns that the dangers are profound: While movement members create the mythical hero's persona by attributing to him their most esteemed characteristics, they gradually cede their own critical agency to the mythical hero they've created. We worship the star instead of the communal collectivity he originally stood for. "Collective action can be replaced by individual identification with a performer who is oppositional," Vickstrom writes in his study of Ani DiFranco fans. "Fans searching for a voice find DiFranco's instead of their own."[23] Democratic and egalitarian traditions (if they exist) are damaged, and artists gain a power in determining movement image and strategy that they may lack the knowledge, experience, and involvement to merit. Looking back on his career with the Clash, the leading politically oriented band in England in the 1970s, singer Joe Strummer said, "[I]t all seemed suddenly so adolescent to me, the way we were all gibbering away, spouting."[24]

Hero worship of musicians has grown with the growth in importance of the mass media and popular music's linkage with social movements. Songs become increasingly experienced and understood as commodities linked to individual artists rather than the collective property of a movement; stars' charisma is marketed in albums, magazines, and talk show appearances, the heroic components increasingly attributed to the personal essence of the individual hero rather than the scene of which she's representative.[25]

This danger is apparent to some musicians. Deni Frand, organizer of a 1974 benefit to raise funds for people fleeing Chile after the military coup, tells how folksinger Phil Ochs "got on stage and started screaming at the audience, 'We're not here to fuck the stars, we're here to save the Chilean refugees.'"[26] Ani DiFranco told us:

One of the circumstances of my job is that I become no longer human but symbolic, you know, and that I'm in this position that people project onto me all sorts of things. And I'm sort of pointing that out to people, or I'm trying to, if they can hear it or if they care. . . . I'm still very much doing my job and rewarded by it, but those [songs] are just me saying, like, don't forget, I'm just still a folksinger.

But many musicians (if they consider the issue at all) disagree. Says Ian MacKaye:

If they listen to my records, and something about me really inspires them, it's [because it's] a scary time in their lives. They're looking for firm footing. And they're using me for footing. Even if it means that they kind of appear to be worshiping me or whatever, it's fine. It's totally fine with me. I won't take advantage of them. But I also wouldn't disrespect them by saying they're stupid. They're not stupid. Because I listened to Jimi Hendrix like my life depended on it. . . . I even listened to Ted Nugent like my life depended on it, and what a dubious guy to depend upon. . . . They're having a hard time. We all did. And they always will. And it's just cool that I've given them a leg up, you know? I'm glad about that.

Even Hampton argues that for all the problems with hero worship,

We are left with a paradox: heroism is an evil that is necessary. In an age of mass communications, we may as well accept that charisma and star appeal must be present if any message is to reach a significant audience. Yet though this certainly implies aristocracy, it may not necessarily imply autocracy. The heroes of protest song culture are subject to accountability. To survive in the ultracompetitive world of popular music, even the superstar must perceive and respond to the wishes of fans. . . . The rock music aristocracy is pluralistically structured. Fans have a great many choices.[27]

Yet to the degree that any individual—whether music hero, religious figure, or political leader—comes to represent the totality of the movement, some democratic qualities of the movement are diminished, as collective power and responsibility are ceded to individual power and control.

This dynamic, however, is far from inevitable (as we'll discuss at greater length in Chapter 12). Some performers actively fight against this tendency. For example, Pete Seeger's intention at his legendary 1963 Carnegie Hall concert we've spoken of (as at all his concerts) was to educate and energize his audience. Seeger not only offered the culture of the civil rights movement, but took pains to inform the audience of specific actions they could take. Some audience members may have only experienced "the illusion" of participation, as Dunaway suggests, but for others (including one of the authors who was there), the concert was a kind of movement rally where connections to the movement were being developed.[28] As always, we want to resist speaking in universals. These are potential dangers we're describing, not unavoidable outcomes.

The Dangers of Solidarity

One of musicking's greatest services for movements, we've argued, is the ways in which it helps build solidarity and link movement supporters to the worldview and organizations of the movement. But this, too, has its dangers. Ensconced in their own self-contained worlds, movement members tend to lose touch with the worldviews of others. This not only makes it harder to connect with nonsupporters for purposes of winning them over to the movement's point of view but, at least as importantly, it removes a crucial reality check from the lives of movement members. When everyone around you believes what you believe, there's little reason to doubt it is the one and only Truth. This can lead to greatly distorted interpretation of political realities and serious handicaps to effective communication with the uncommitted.

Lieberman's previously mentioned critique of the 1948 Henry Wallace campaign, for example, goes beyond arguing the music was of limited help:

> The Wallace campaign singing provides another example of how the very strength of the movement culture contributed to its isolation.... One People's Songster explained frankly that the strength and enthusiasm of the campaign singing was also a weakness: "When you're singing very loudly, having a good time, it's a self-infecting kind of thing, and you imagine everybody else is also singing just as loudly and having just as good a time. It's hard to hear all the people not singing."[29]

That is, movement activists were so blinded by the strength of solidarity *within the already committed* that they failed to see how little progress they were making in moving outside their small circles. In the aftermath of Wallace's disastrous electoral showing, Woody Guthrie praised the folksingers for attracting attention to Progressive Party candidates, but asked: "Why did our songs not reach in and touch deep enough to cause the hand to push the C row in that voting booth?"[30] His answer—that the songs were "not radical enough in the proper ways"—illustrates the contradictions inherent in People's Songsters' outlook. On the one hand, they sincerely desired to take a broad approach musically and politically, to listen as well as talk to "the people." On the other hand, they assumed folk songs were obviously superior and that the people were "ready" to hear and act upon their message. Such assumptions only increased the isolation already imposed by the political climate.[31]

Ironically, the image of solidarity that musicking projects to others may also hurt recruitment. In a 1986 *Nation* article widely debated among the folksinging Left, Jesse Lemisch argued that folksinging itself had become a barrier between committed leftists and those they hoped to speak to: "What we have is a culture descended from a noble tradition of popular struggles—one whose public rehearsal is an important ritual of affirmation for those of us who grew up in it—that leaves us speaking a language that more and more Americans don't understand."[32]

This linkage (and it could just as easily be said of punk, rap, reggae, traditional ethnic musics, and so on) may then actually increase resistance to considering a movement's message. The musical trappings, signaling a worldview the noncommitted person has already heard about and relegated to the not-for-me category in her own life, may prevent any serious consideration of that view. The ability of musicking in the 1960s, for example, to weave a blanket that incorporated the threads of opposition to the war in Vietnam, of support for civil rights and national liberation, of a positive view of drugs and premarital sex, and so on, simultaneously strengthened the movement by gathering together people who endorsed only some of these views at first and *weakened* the movement by excluding others who strongly objected to any one of these views. Musical forms in themselves may produce similar reactions. Parents who hate the sound of rap, for instance, don't listen and hear what's being expressed in its lyrics; the very sound of the music strengthens their original conviction that the genre is aggressive and threatening to their age group, and perhaps class and race as well. Even those who are attracted to a movement may find that its traditions seem to exclude them, as illustrated in one of our activist interviews:

> Would you like to consider the *misuse* of music in social movements? When I was a graduate student I joined the Democratic Socialists of America. The first time I went to one of their conventions, I had to join in and sing "The International," "Joe Hill," and "Union Maid." It was very traumatic. I felt like an idiot, and since I was too young to know the context of the music, I felt permanently alienated from those old fogies.

Exclusivity, in fact, may be the point for some movement members, consciously or unconsciously. In the mid-1980s, leftist high school activists in Washington, D.C., joined with punk rockers to form Positive Force, envisioned (by the activists) as a network for coordinating political activities, with punk as its energy source, soundtrack, and recruiting tool. Within a year, however, most of the activists had left, precisely because they saw the organization becoming

> a sort of exclusive in-group of punks.... The point is this: Punk and other counter-cultural and youth subcultural expressions are *inherently* exclusive. They tend toward

creating small bands of the self-anointed, those who seek "purity" from the corrupt outside world.[33]

Internally as well, movement traditions (of all kinds) tend to narrow the perspective, and thus the range of actions, available to members. The vibrant historical traditions of the Irish conflict, kept alive most vividly in the respective Protestant and Catholic folk music cultures, Denselow suggests, created constraints on the ability of both Republican and Loyalist movement members to move beyond the traditions of the past to make progress in the present.[34]

Further, musicking can present a false sense of unanimity, encouraging movement members to feel that they're in general agreement with each other, and thus avoiding necessary discussions of important disagreements. As they encounter adversity from without and differences within, movements must be able to sustain a truly shared vision, not just the illusion of a shared vision. While the illusion is often helpful in building the movement, inevitably latent disagreements surface, and only widespread discussion and an achieved consensus can prevent these from eventually weakening the movement. The strength of music in melding together disparate factions of a movement who might not agree on all major points becomes a weakness when it substitutes for discussion. Earlier we quoted Michael Lerner on the importance of music for movements: "There was almost no form for people uniting around agreements, and no way that those agreements could fully be expressed, ... [but] song stated in ritual fashion what we all shared."[35] Read another way, however, this could mean music facilitated the illusion of agreement at the expense of actually working out agreement.

Musicking often speaks to current complaints and/or utopian impulses; neither of these, however, can substitute for the step-by-step decision making that must guide a movement. Both help that process as drawing two points defines a line—here's where we are and don't want to be; there's where we want to end up—but since movements don't travel in straight lines but a series of jagged cuts back and forth, the path along the way has to be widely considered as well. Musicking, by and large, doesn't encourage this kind of intricate consideration, but paints in broad, vibrant colors. To the extent it supplies an overly simplistic view of the world, it may discourage the kind of nuanced reasoning that political activity often requires. Did the Concert for Mandela lead the general music lover to understand the complex and long-term political struggle that would be necessary to end apartheid, Garofalo asks, or did it lead audience members to believe that raising a lot of money was all that was needed to bring it down?[36]

In the 1960s, music and related cultural activities were so successful in achieving "the communion of hippies and activists"[37] that members of both camps thought of themselves as part of "The Movement." To be sure, the two groups overlapped, sharing a range of social and political beliefs—in particular opposition to the war in Vietnam, the draft, and the government that was responsible—but it was the cultural trappings of rock and roll that most seemed to voice a shared perspective, disguising a fundamental fault line between the hippies' vision of maximum personal freedom and the activists' vision of communal responsibility. Barely more than a decade later, *Rolling Stone* gleefully informed its advertisers that a majority of the subscribers to

the magazine once seen as a voice of the cultural wing of the Movement had voted for
Ronald Reagan for president in the 1984 election. Such a finding would have been
incomprehensible to New Left activists of the late 1960s and early 1970s because the
illusion of a single unified movement had rarely been examined.[38] Musicking played
a major role in bridging—but also hiding—that crucial divide.

Similarly, in England in the 1970s, Rock Against Racism used music very
effectively to link disparate groups, usually divided along race, gender, sexual
orientation, and occupational lines. But "RAR's weakness was all the greater for
their dependence on music.... Political strategies and arguments were played out
and resolved in terms of musical choices" rather than open discussion of political
differences, and therefore "what they won in unity, they tended to lose in political effectiveness."[39] In the same era, Ospina writes, salsa became "an important
vehicle for integration and identity," promoting a generalized Hispanic identity
that broke "down ideological barriers through gaining acceptance on both left and
right ... [and] broke through the continent's territorial barriers as well."[40] Perhaps
an argument could be made that such a racial identity is a more important point
of unity than any other (though we don't agree), but in any case, there were political discussions that obviously needed to go on regarding differences of ideology,
national origin, and so on. To the extent salsa helped develop a social grouping
that debated these questions while acting in their common interest, it helped the
movement. To the extent love of the music substituted for political discussion of
these important differences, it weakened the movement.

Even musicking's role in helping to create agreement—as opposed to hiding
differences—may be dysfunctional for a movement, at least as seen by those who
believe movements are strongest when individual members have joined because
they are truly persuaded the movement will lead to a better world. As many who
attack social movements have charged (albeit often hysterically and with little
evidence to support their claims), music's ability to meld reason and emotion can
slide into what we're all tempted to call brainwashing when done by others in
accordance with values we don't like. As Warren notes, "Common affirmation of
faith, supported by rhythm and melody, is an important factor in 'whipping up a
crowd,' as any evangelist will testify."[41] The modern political rapper Talib Kweli
says, "[W]e gave the youth all the anger but yet we ain't taught them how to
express it. And so it's dangerous."[42] This power is well appreciated by politicians
who see the opportunity "to create a spontaneous and loyal following through the
use of music alone, without recourse to favors or promise or policies.... [In these
cases,] the political is parasitic upon the music. Politicians borrow its powers to
bring people together; they do not use that community or create it" to deal with
actual political problems.[43]

Survival and Resistance

Throughout the last quarter of the twentieth century, spurred by the development
of cultural studies and such seminal pieces as James Scott's *Domination and the Arts of*

Resistance (1990), scholars increasingly came to appreciate and emphasize the ways in which the ostensibly apolitical culture of oppressed groups could be "read" as resistant, typically in premovement situations before there is a free space in which openly rebellious sentiments can be voiced. Scott's work emphasized a "hidden transcript," invisible to and unheard by the oppressors, but seen and heard by the oppressed, in which the former are criticized and mocked while the latter are praised and encouraged. Slave spirituals, for example, are often said to have been a form of resistance, offering practical information for escape ("Follow the Drinking Gourd") or the solace of a promise of eventual release from captivity ("Swing Low, Sweet Chariot," "Go Down Moses"), delivered in a language the slave master couldn't decipher and expressed in a cultural activity that encouraged group solidarity. But Fisher writes that slave spirituals often helped to calm the tensions that might otherwise have brought about insurrections, as well as helping to pass on the accommodative religious ideology of Christianity.[44] The crucial question is: When do cultural forms keep the flame of resistance alive in situations where overt political resistance is not possible, and when do they merely act as safety valves, releasing tension that would otherwise manifest itself more effectively from the perspective of the oppressed group? To state this in the most provocative way: If African American slaves had not developed the rich musical forms that helped them endure slavery (and subsequently transformed American music as a whole), would they have engaged in more direct challenges to the system of slavery and achieved emancipation earlier?

In that historical moment the question was largely moot. Creating the music was not a strategic choice, and carrying out more direct forms of challenge was only rarely a debatable option. Clearly there are times, such as in the antebellum South, when power relations are so uneven that only the most nonconfrontational responses are possible (as the fate of overt slave rebellions would suggest). In the most onerous situations, when there is no intention to resist, but only to survive, we don't think it's useful to speak of resistance since the reality is forced accommodation. This isn't to diminish the importance of culture in aiding survival, or to deny that without survival in the present, there can't be any resistance in some future. It's just to say these are not the same, and conflating them just muddies our understanding of the different roles culture plays in different situations.

Even when sheer survival is not the issue, subordinated people may engage in cultural practices that help them tolerate their daily lives without directly confronting their situation. Although this can indeed be conceptualized as a psychological form of resistance—"You own my time but not my soul!"—the practical effect of this attitude of noncompliance is accommodation and acquiescence rather than resistance in the sense of opposing the conditions of daily life in some way with an eye to (eventually) altering them. Punk culture, according to Hebdige, increased the "autonomy" of disenchanted English working-class kids with dead-end futures in the 1970s, but this didn't translate into any kind of direct challenge to the political system that created that economic situation.[45] Autonomy, then, was more an illusion than an apt description of the real conditions of those in the scene, who continued to live within and thereby reproduce the confines imposed by a political economy that couldn't provide them with steady employment.

Some argue that anything that facilitates survival by helping a group endure unjust or alienating conditions should be seen as a form of resistance, even if endurance means acquiescence and accommodation.[46] By "putting sorrow to rest," for example, musical forms like the blues allow people to get on with the necessary tasks of life. Musicking is then seen as both a means and a celebration of survival. Chang defends recent rap genres that have shunned explicitly political sentiments in favor of ghettocentricity and "keeping it real" in these terms:

> For some critics, usually older and often black, such sentiments seem dangerously close to pathological, hymns to debauchery and justifications for thuggery. But the hip-hop generation recognizes them as anthems of purpose, manifestoes that describe their time and place the same way that Public Enemy's did [for the previous age cohort]. Most of all, these songs and their audiences say, we are survivors and we will never forget that.[47]

The act of artistic creation is defined in this kind of analysis as a refusal to simply live within the terms of oppression and subordination. Musicking not only proclaims the promise of eventual enjoyment of a fuller humanity, it involves one aspect of it—artistic creation—in the present. In conditions of oppression and servitude, musicking has been one of the few avenues through which those without political and social power have been able to express themselves. Slave songs, Craddock-Willis writes, "were necessary for the sustenance of African Americans. African slaves needed some means of expression, yet they could not create sculpture or even dance, for this tangible expression was forbidden by the slave master."[48] Gospel, Pratt says, provided black women with their only form of morally acceptable public artistic expression from Emancipation until World War II.[49] This is no small thing.

Moreover, even art that seems to encourage accommodation preserves a sense of we-ness that may be crucial not only for survival, but for eventual resistance. Slave songs incorporated African traditions and values within a framework acceptable to slave masters, and so preserved at least a latent sense of African identity and unity among black Americans that became an important ingredient in later, more political, challenges to white rule. And certainly, artistic expression of any kind makes a group more visible, to both itself and others, which is essential for eventual coalescence into a movement per se.

Slavery lies at one end of the dominant-subordinate continuum. For most groups, at least in the United States, the issue is not physical survival but what the quality of life will be. Here it's easier to see the weakness of the claim that any cultural activity that makes survival more likely is resistance. Music may certainly make less onerous but still oppressive situations easier to tolerate, from the song-poems developed in the nineteenth-century American labor movement to modern teenagers surviving their parents by taking refuge under the earphones of their iPod. But aiding people in survival within a dominant culture that alienates them does not demonstrate resistance unless that survival leads eventually to collective attempts to change the culture and the dominance. The saloon, Halker points out, was an oppositional cultural institution for workers in the 1800s, a refuge from the world of the owners, yet it could easily serve as a locus of consolation rather than a center of resistance that helped workers move toward a world in which their power increased vis-à-vis the boss.[50]

When, then, is musicking reinforcing existing power relations by encouraging accommodation to the status quo, and when is it in some way helping a movement or a premovement grouping form into a movement? It's not an either-or question but a continuum: Musicking can do some of each at different moments; it can affect different members differently at any one moment. But still, on balance, some musicking is more resistant than other musicking. Despite the difficulties in sorting out which factors make it so, this is not entirely random, but shows some discernable patterns.

From our perspective, musicking becomes more resistant than accommodative to the extent that it presents or preserves some sense of an *alternative* way of life. This, for instance, is Richard Dyer's defense of disco:

> [T]he movement between banality and something "other" than banality is an essential dialectic of society, a constant keeping open of a gap between what is and what could or should be. Herbert Marcuse in the currently unfashionable *One-Dimensional Man* argues that our society tries to close that gap, to assert that what is is all that could be ... or should be. For all its commercialism and containment within the to and fro between work and leisure, I think disco romanticism is one of the things that can keep the gap open, that can allow the *experience of contradiction* to continue.[51]

Lipsitz sees the same process in musics based on older traditions: "Under industrial conditions, an oral tradition serves as a collective memory of better times, as well as a means of making the present more bearable. Country music and blues bequeathed the concerns of their respective oral traditions to rock and roll, and [they] carried their subversive messages throughout society."[52]

Similarly, spirituals, which undeniably comforted slaves in the here and now and thus facilitated accommodation, nevertheless typically looked to the future, to a better world, here or in heaven, and thus maintained an element of resistance in the sense we use it. Does this mean spirituals were on balance more conducive to liberation than continued servitude? We believe so, though we're not knowledgeable (or foolhardy) enough to make a definitive statement. Our point here is to make clear our disagreement with those who assume any form of musicking to be liberating on balance if it simply helps people endure another day. Of course, if a group eventually is able to change its lot in life, it's possible to attribute a positive role to any factor that helped them survive until that day. But if that factor simultaneously delayed the arrival of liberation, it's meaningless to paint it as positive. An emphasis on surviving today—understandable and rational as it may be—can interfere with developing a consciousness of the changes and risks necessary for a better life tomorrow.

Other aspects of ostensibly accommodative music are also said to have latent value for movements. "The blues serve a cathartic function," says Pratt, "providing a means of psychological release through the substitute imagery,"[53] and perhaps this helps maintain a mental health African Americans have needed to pursue their long struggle for equality. But without a notion of an alternative to the status quo—rendered lyrically or musically, or in any aspect of musicking—the thrust of musicking is generally to reinforce existing patterns of domination and subordination. Group identity, for example, often a staple of the music of those controlled by others, is easily used by dominant groups to preserve the status quo as long as the subordinate group's members' current social and political status goes unchallenged as an intrinsic and eternal part of their identity. If African origins are accepted as "naturally" synonymous with slave status, African group solidarity carries little resistance to white slave owners. If head banger status is accepted as synonymous with working a physically draining job during the week and partying hard on the weekends, head banger solidarity carries little resistance to an economic structure in which some people are consigned to physically draining jobs on a permanent basis. The same musicking networks that might facilitate political opposition can instead act to reinforce existing patterns and impede consideration of alternative ideas.

In short, cultural expression by subordinated groups isn't inevitably resistance, resistance isn't inevitably oppositional, and even oppositional resistance can take many directions, some of which may be at odds with a movement's goals. Any structural arrangement has an infinite number of alternatives, some of which are improvements from the perspective of the movement and some of which aren't. Musicking can help oppressed people see that the status quo isn't the only possible arrangement, but the alternatives they then pick may not be those activists might wish. Doomsday cult leader Jim Jones certainly provided an alternative vision for his largely impoverished followers, yet that vision—mass suicide—didn't improve their lives. Avant garde jazz may convey that the status quo is not immutable, but the result might be a disdain for the squares who don't get it, or a patient waiting for the alien spaceship that will arrive to usher in the new order, rather than the call to black nationalism some thought so obvious in the challenge of hard bop.

If music can be functional for movements, by the same logic it can be dysfunctional: Musicking has an effect on attitudes and behavior. If it can help us move in oppositional and resistant ways, it can similarly play a role in encouraging or confirming attitudes and behaviors that perpetuate our oppression. Effective resistance isn't guaranteed by any cultural practice or form, but exists as potential, the result of an array of interacting factors. Many of these are beyond the control of the artist or activist. But as we'll discuss in the final two chapters, artists and activists can affect some of these through a conscious understanding of what's at stake, raising the chances that music will be oppositional rather than accommodative, resistant rather than merely oppositional, and, at best, resistant in ways that are in harmony with the goals of a movement.

Scott himself understood well that even cultural resistance is not enough for liberation; the hidden transcripts he wrote about should be seen as "a condition of practical resistance rather than a substitute for it."[54] The essential question remains *how?* In much of the literature, as Grossberg complains,

> The assumption that people are active and capable of struggle and resistance becomes an apparent discovery, and the important empirical questions, of the concrete and contextual effects of such practices, are left unanswered.... Domination and resistance

are assumed to be understood in advance, to operate always and everywhere in the same ways.[55]

In order to do our best to make general statements about such large topics, we need to look at some specific cases of what artists and activists have done in the past, and how it's worked from the perspective of movement members. Though we've touched on this throughout this work, we turn to it in detail in Chapter 11.

Chapter 11

What Makes a Difference?

In the first part of this book we looked at how musical meaning is constructed; in the past few chapters we've looked at the functions musicking plays—or might play—for a movement. In the concluding chapters, we'll try to draw some lessons from these investigations. Given the wide range of variables we've identified, what can be said about when musicking is more or less effective for a movement?

Participation

As we've discussed in previous chapters, the history of music in industrialized countries over the last century involved a gradual shift toward reliance on professional, specialized songwriters and performers rather than grassroots, folk, and "amateur" musical production. Today, much of the music we experience is delivered to us by mass media rather than created by us in collaboration with others with whom we are linked in any meaningful way.

On the other hand, as we've seen, audience members continually and creatively rework even the most seemingly packaged cultural materials. How different is this from performing? Is the difference between observation and performance even important? And most importantly for our purposes, does it make any difference for political practice how active we are in the musicking process? Adorno's questions arise again.

Listening to background music while conversing with friends or washing the dishes demands little active response. Active listening situations—going to a concert, attentively listening to the CD of a group you love while reading the lyrics—call forth more involvement, more attention. Singing or playing along with the music (even on air guitar) move us further along the line; we use someone else's songs but create our own ways of performing them; dancing similarly involves our own creative response to someone else's creation. Further along the continuum are creating and performing our own music. In short, while all musicking involves some active contribution from each party, some forms are more *performatively* active, involving less passive consumption and more active creation.

Movements and movement music reflect this continuum. Some movements have involved much more grassroots musicking, others more of the minstrel-audience model (while others, of course, have used comparatively little of either). The southern civil rights movement was the epitome of the former. While that movement was certainly aided by a galaxy of professional stars, its day-to-day mobilization involved mass musicking as prelude, accompaniment, and sequel to movement activities.

This tradition of ordinary activists writing and/or performing music as part of their movement activities is a long one in the United States, and worldwide. Song-poems were widely created in the labor movement of the last half of the nineteenth century; the Wobblies of the early twentieth century were famously a singing union, as evidenced by the enormous popularity of *The Little Red Songbook*; as Bird et al. have pointed out, "rather than trying to win the allegiance of artists already recognized by the dominant culture, the IWW had the audacity to believe workers could create their own art."[1] Workers' choruses, while less remembered today than the folk music of the Almanacs and their circle, were a vital part of Communist Party culture; when the party began to crumble in the 1950s under the twin pressures of government repression and the emerging revelations about Stalin's rule, the choruses were among the most important institutions preserving membership.[2] Nor is this restricted to the Left. Collective singing was an integral part of Ku Klux Klan meetings, for example, often of religious hymns, but also of songs written by and for Klan members.[3]

Certainly the development of mass media and its permeation of our lives have increased the likelihood that politically minded members will consume more than create music, but that isn't the only result. While it is easy to think that the explosion in commercially produced music inevitably stifles local music making, it's also the case that having so much music available *stimulates* people, particularly young people, to try their own hand at doing the same.[4] Typically there is a symbiotic interaction between professional and grassroots music making, and this is often productive for movements. While we think of civil rights music coming from the church, another rich source of inspiration was popular music of the day.

As we'll explore further in Chapter 12, some artists believe the benefits of participation—politically, socially, even spiritually—go beyond what's possible when audiences merely watch and listen:

> In order to be truly transformative, music must not only be heard, but actually played. Participatory music has the capacity ... to deepen our felt connection, empower our personal dance, and incite our invigorated response.... Music, like environmentalism, is most effective when experiential and participatory.[5]

Participation taps into the logic of oral traditions, Pratt argues, encouraging "a greater degree of emotional, and perhaps even physical, involvement in the environment."[6] Others argue that participation encourages greater intellectual engagement as well (hence the service-learning motto: "I hear and I forget; I see and I remember; I do and I understand").[7]

In short: Although emotional and intellectual investment in movement activity can be encouraged through all sorts of musicking, for many musickers, such investment is most likely when they are performatively involved in the music making. Many politically conscious artists mention this as their own route to greater movement commitment:

> FRED STANTON: Writing political songs was part of the process that got me seriously involved in the socialist movement; I became a singing organizer, using songs to help recruit to the cause. Some people can participate in countless hours of activity and study and discussion, but [people] really need to connect with the movement on the emotional level, too, and songs can help do that.

> PETER YARROW: As a folk singer, you don't lose your commitment because you're always there singing those songs. They reinvigorate you.[8]

The act of creation itself draws up deep feelings of investment; as with a child we've raised, we're tied to the art we've created and the meanings it has for us. But original creation may not be what is most crucial so much as the degree to which we feel ourselves participants in the art—and by extension, the movement. In some times and places, this feeling can be engendered within the formal minstrel-audience model. Rose writes:

> Public performance also provides a means by which young black women can occupy public space in ways that affirm the centrality of their voices. As Salt [of the rap group Salt-N-Peppa] observes, "The women look up to us, they take us dead seriously. It's not a fan type of thing, it's more like a movement. When we shout 'The year 1989 is for the ladies' they go crazy. It's the highlight of the show. It makes you realize that you have a voice as far as women go."[9]

But investment is often developed most powerfully in musicking experiences that don't feature the artist-audience distinction—or that deliberately overcome it in performance. Shared public performance simultaneously declares to the activist and those around him not only his willingness to be a member of a movement, but his *responsibility* for its success:

> CHARLIE KING: I think about the development of labor songs from these long anthems of the nineteenth century to the stuff that the Wobblies wrote, and then the stuff that black workers brought to it, of how the medium became ever more democratic, ever more participatory,[10] until you get a song like "Roll the Union On,"[11] and all you have to do is somebody has to start. We did this on a picket line up in Middletown last week. We sang "Roll the Union On" and it went on for about 10 minutes. Because what do you have to come up with to make a new verse? You have to come up with a name of someone you want to roll over. So everybody in the line had a name, from the governor to a superintendent to somebody who ran a nursing home, all that stuff.

And so that song is written on the spot by the people in the line. Everybody sang, they really got into it because they felt like they were creators of the song. Then the song becomes a very important metaphor for what they are doing. Every worker is an organizer, every person on this line is responsible for the struggle, is responsible for the quality of the strike, is responsible for what we get at the other end of it. When a song becomes a real participatory medium like that, it becomes the message—We are all important in this struggle.

At their most effective, these shared declarations of commitment and responsibility help to mobilize the emotional involvement that is typically necessary to overcome Olson's free-rider dilemma. It isn't enough to recognize a situation, analyze it, and "know" that a certain action is necessary; as Bernice Reagon said, "the other part is ... how do you feel, do you feel like doing it?"[12]

Participatory music making allows us to momentarily assume an identity we're thinking of taking on more permanently. It calls forth a vision of an alternative way of being and requires some of the individual qualities that will be necessary to reach that goal. But it also offers an *immediate* feeling of accomplishment. Listening to the sounds we and those around us are making, we experience a cohesiveness and a result—the aural reality of sound—that we have already constructed. The experience offers feelings of efficacy that may be lacking in daily living, and this, too, is a powerful weapon for overcoming the kinds of narrow cost-benefit analyses that animate Olson's paradox. "The role of music," an activist wrote us, "is to focus the energy and remind ourselves that we are the ones who sing; we are the ones who change the world creatively."

Again, we're not arguing that only performative musicking is participatory (since audiences are always participating to some degree in meaning construction), or even that only highly participatory music making has important movement implications. We are arguing, however, that active participation often has a particularly significant impact on musickers. Active participation in music making that is framed by political implications tends to encourage, as well as reflect, more active participation in the political struggle itself.

Musicking in Different Movements

Some movements seem to soar on the wings of song, while musicking plays a much less central role in others. Minstrels of the civil rights movement—the SNCC Freedom Singers, Guy Carawan, Odetta, and so on—encountered audiences who regarded movement songs as their own, while the music of the Almanac Singers, even when delivered to political gatherings, often "remained first and foremost entertainment, segregated largely from what went before or came after in the minds of most listeners."[13] Oi! music played a peripheral role in the skinhead movement in England where it was created, but a central role in the United States. What accounts for such differences?

The common answer to this question is "historical tradition." Sometimes this refers to cultural forms that played some kind of resistance role before a movement was possible, as with the spirituals that grew from the time of slavery, "encoded freedom songs," as Charlie King described them to us, "dynamite in a preexisting culture ... released by the civil rights movement." Sometimes "tradition" refers to previous use of explicitly political music in the communities from which the movement arose. Musicking became an integral part of IWW life, Green writes, because members were generally already

> well acquainted with two tested musical genres: formal radical fare (for example, *Socialist Songs with Music* issued by Charles Kerr, 1901); [and] traditional occupational folksong (not yet gathered in books, but present in their respective craft, regional, and ethnic communities). In short, to understand the IWW's contagious musical blend, we must hear in mind's ear rebel unionists who knew "*L'Internationale*" and "*La Marseillaise*," as well as they knew homespun shanties and ballads indigenous to forest bunkhouse, hobo jungle, or mountain-mine camp.[14]

Movement musicking is often rooted in a more general social or cultural tradition. The obvious example is the prominence of music in the group life of African Americans, itself built on African cultural traditions;[15] "I remember reading an obscure account of my people during the nineteenth century that said, 'They accompany everything they do with song,'" says Bernice Reagon; music "was already part of anything black people were doing in most of those communities. And any time that kind of community becomes engaged in a movement, it's going to be a strong singing movement."[16] Much of the singing in the early civil rights movement came straight from church life, "sung unrehearsed in the tradition of the Afro-American folk church.... The core song repertoire was formed from the reservoir of Afro-American traditional song performed in the older style of singing,"[17] a style that featured a structure of call and response. Music was similarly integral to the United Farm Workers struggle (and the larger Chicano rights struggle it helped spawn) because, Broyles-Gonzalez writes, it was already a central feature of Chicano and Mexicano culture;[18] rock audiences in Eastern Europe were primed to interpret bands politically, says Ramet, in part due to the long-standing "bard poet" tradition in those societies.[19]

Beyond the simple pervasiveness of a cultural tradition, particular embedded practices and values may be useful to the movement. For example, group rituals often invoke and celebrate solidarity in nonpolitical forms—the religious solidarity of gospel or the implied "permanent community" in the call-and-response format of soul[20]—that are then available for movement purposes. Groups with a history of collective oppression tend to develop cultural forms that speak from an artistic vision of "we," while groups with a historical past of privilege and power tend to develop traditions emphasizing the personal, individualistic vision of the artist, a much less useful form for most social movements.

All of this, however, is complicated by the multiple crosscutting traditions of which any one individual may feel a part. Mill workers in Lawrence, Massachusetts, in 1912 shared a common struggle against the owners, but were divided in their lives outside the mills by differences in national, ethnic, linguistic, and religious backgrounds. Environmental activists today may share little in common other than their environmental beliefs. Despite our tendency to think of communities, movements, and movement cultures as homogenous, most are far from that. The civil rights movement, Eyerman & Jamison remind us, needed to "build bridges between class and status groups, between blacks and white supporters, and between rural and urban, northern and southern blacks";[21] we could add age, gender, region, ethnicity, sexual orientation, and a host of other factors to most movements as well. Movement memberships are far from being products of "monocultural" traditions.

Beyond Tradition

As important as cultural inheritance may be, variation in the uses of music by movements is also heavily influenced by an array of other factors, including trends in contemporary popular and mass culture. In the past century the explosive (industry-fueled) growth of popular music in general has elevated it to become a basic resource of identity for many youth and a virtually constant accompaniment to daily activities for most, and thereby increased its relevance to social movements as well. The importance of white power rock to the American skinhead movement, for example, is due less to a historical tradition of music use within the right wing than to the centrality of rock to the social lives of contemporary teenagers generally.

As we discussed in Chapter 2, sometimes it's not the link with tradition that is most important to musickers but the *break* with tradition. The popularity and political significance of rock, and particularly punk, to Eastern Europeans in the years before the fall of the Communist parties derived not only from its link to re- bellious youth in the West, but because it so clearly broke with sanctioned musical practice and decorum in their own lands. New (or seemingly new) cultural forms often become the basis for emerging communities, the lightning rod for feelings of discontent expressed in breaks with conventional styles in music, dress, and other cultural manifestations. Such cultural transgression often preceded expression of explicitly political dissent in the communist world as well as in the West.

Movement cultures are, then, a synthesis. Past traditions are embraced or rejected, mixed with elements of other traditions, framed by current trends and fads, reworked with the values the movement is emphasizing; new members bring in their own traditions, changing the mix, as the entry of northern blacks into the civil rights movement reduced the dominance of church-based music and altered the general tenor of the southern-based movement.[22] Further, creating movement culture and initiating movement traditions become an increasingly conscious project:

> CHARLIE KING: Women's music had more of a sense of creating a new culture, inventing a new cultural form, not just what they were singing but how they set up concerts. Who was allowed to go and who wasn't, who was required to be hired as part of the technical crew, who was supposed to have access to it, who had been denied access before. It was a sense of trying to create a society, little examples of a society. You know, what kind of world do we want to live in?

Movement dynamics also affect the place of music and musicians in movement life. The prominence of rappers in recent political movements of young urban people of color, it's often said, coincides with a vacuum in other political leadership:

Thelonious Monk, Aretha Franklin, and Stevie Wonder were never asked to stand in for Thurgood Marshall, Fannie Lou Hamer, or Stokely Carmichael. But the gains of the civil rights and Black Power movements of the 1960s were being rolled back. Youths were as fed up with black leadership as they were with white supremacy. Politics had failed. Culture was to become the hip-hop generation's battlefield, and "political rap" was to be its weapon.[23]

Musicking's role is also significantly affected by the political situation a movement confronts. Street once wrote of the "interesting, if superficial connection ... between the fierceness of the regime, the vigour of the underground rock scene, and the politics of the musicians,"[24] but the relationship isn't superficial at all. When and where other forms of expression are forbidden or tightly controlled, cultural forms (or whatever avenues of communication are still available) become increasingly loaded with political significance. The importance of music in American slave culture, and then later in African American life generally and the civil rights movement specifically, was not due simply to African traditions that placed music at the center of many activities, but because few other forms of expression were permitted the slaves. Public Enemy's Chuck D explains rap's current importance similarly: "Everything else was taken away[,] so all that attitude ... leads into rap as a point of vocal expression for the black man. That's how it started out. Because black males did not have any way to express themselves."[25] A leading role for music, particularly rock and punk, has been claimed by observers and participants in a host of recent regime changes—South Africa, Argentina, Brazil, East Germany, Hungary, the Soviet Union, etc.—and in each this is largely attributed to the absence of other viable avenues of communication. In Brazil, for example, "The 'protest music' that existed before the [1964 military] coup d'état grew with the public indignation and restrictions on free speech that came with the new regime.... In the broadly conceived realm of Bossa Nova, social relevance was increasingly important after 1964."[26]

As a result, veterans of those scenes often claim, musicking becomes extremely meaningful: "'Rock,' a Soviet émigré once said, 'is a ten times more powerful emblem of freedom and fun and style in Russia than it is in the West'"[27]; rock musicians there "always viewed political protest as a central part of their role."[28] Kan & Hayes report that the much more permissive attitude toward rock of Communist Party authorities in Poland compared to other Soviet Bloc countries led to "ideological sterility" of its music scene; "only in the 1980s, during the martial law years, did Polish rock acquire the rough and hard political edge that shaped the rock culture in the other socialist countries."[29]

The importance of music as expression is most obvious when there is formal political control of communication networks, but it's also characteristic of groups that have been socially marginalized and so, largely silenced. In the early days of the civil rights movement, Bernice Reagon has written, "[M]asses of people had much to say about their condition and found the language with which to speak in the songs."[30] The importance of riot grrrl groups like Bikini Kill to teenaged girls was, in the words of one, that they "seemed driven by a desire to provide a voice for an alienated group with needs that were ill championed elsewhere."[31]

The relationship between musicking and protest can be greatly intensified if and when the music itself is targeted for repression. Where governments move to control a music, its status as "rebel music," and therefore its significance to the movement, increase; where governments tolerate or seem to champion a music, its status changes. Some governments strategically attempt to co-opt rebel music rather than censor it, as the Soviet government did with jazz (though alternating with periods of attempts at repression). This may backfire if the increased exposure allowed further mobilizes dissent, but it also often creates a dependency on the state that helps tame the musicians, if not always the reception of the audiences.[32]

The response of leadership *within* the movement is also crucial. As we've seen, musicians feel that leaders in some movements attach very little importance to their work. Fred Stanton complained to us that current

> leaders of organizations, in this country at least, have not been as comfortable with the use of songs as the civil rights leaders, with their church backgrounds, were.... Musicians are often relegated to the category of "entertainment," the last thing you think about when planning an event, rather than used as an important part of the program.

Stanton invokes the civil rights movement as the ideal, and it's invariably the example used to illustrate music playing a central role in a movement. That history stands in stark contrast to the fate of the Almanac Singers and other progressive singers on the periphery of the Communist Party in the 1930s, 1940s, and 1950s, who also believed that music should play a major role in movement life. The picture that comes down to us today is that the Communist Party leadership, influenced by the Stalinist style of Communist parties across the world, was constantly censoring and controlling the musicians and the music, sucking out its life by forcing it into a straitjacket of political correctness. But participants of the time, while granting there was occasional interference from party bureaucrats,[33] typically complain that the greater problem was being simply ignored[34] or treated, as Stanton says, as just entertainment. Despite the important organizing role the Almanacs often played in their brief tenure, many CIO officials saw them as only useful to "keep the members from leaving during intermission,"[35] and even most radicals in and around the Communist Party "did not seriously regard this new cultural emphasis as any new concrete tactical weapon in the people's arsenal."[36]

Skrewdriver's place in the right-wing skinhead movement in the United States offers us a third vision of political leadership's relation to musicking, the extreme opposite of the Almanacs' relationship with leaders of the Communist Party and the CIO. Tom Metzger, leader of the White Aryan Resistance, quite consciously used white power rock music as a recruiting tool for young people: "I saw their potential to drag the racialist movement out of the conservative right-wing mold and into a new era. I figured the music of these people could do that."[37] Metzger committed energy and resources to Skrewdriver, for instance devoting the centerfold of each issue of his organization's paper, *WAR,* to coverage of the band. Music, indeed, became arguably the single most important tool of both recruitment and mobilization for White Aryan Resistance and other American skinhead groups.[38]

Movement dynamics can create both unplanned and planned opportunities for the enhancement of musicking. The freedom rides of 1961, for instance, became "one of the most important periods for the development of movement singing [because m]ost of the freedom riders spent 40 days in jail and had lots of time to learn and sing together all the best songs that had come from many areas"; the 50-mile Selma March in the spring of 1965 "was very conducive to the spontaneous improvisation of verse after verse after verse. Many songs got started there and carried elsewhere by the 40,000 marchers across the country."[39]

Such opportunities for making movement music are more likely when preexisting institutional bases of support provide a protected space for cultural activity. In Rio de Janeiro and other Brazilian cities in the early 1960s, the explosion of politicized musicking was centered in the university-based Centro Popular de Cultura.[40] At Highlander Center, an important training center for activists in the U.S. labor, civil rights, and anti-strip-mining movements, music workshops and evening singing were standard parts of the tradition. Regional conferences, Guy Carawan told us, were always opportunities to share songs "that worked" as well as more conventional organizing information:

We started Southwide gatherings right away, which brought people from all over the South, which advertised, "What do you sing in your movement? What do you know? Come and let's hear it all together." So right away, at Gammon Theological Seminary and at Highlander and other places, we were having gatherings where the main purpose was for everybody to come and bring what they knew culturally or musically and share it and build it into a bigger repertoire for the civil rights movement.

Within such institutional free spaces, drawing on their resources and examples, musicking networks develop that spread the idea (as well as the repertoire) of a musical movement.

Sometimes the growth of movement musical networks is aided by changes in communication technology. Roscigno & Danaher show that the advent of radio in the 1920s and 1930s, bringing mill workers' music to isolated mill towns throughout the South, was a significant factor in the wave of strike activity that spread contagiously without well-established face-to-face networks.[41] In China in the late twentieth century, "governmental control [was] compromised by the empowerment of the individual listener to record and/or dub as he or she pleases,"[42] due to the availability of cassette tape and home units capable of dubbing music not sanctioned by the government, and thus not heard on radio. A clandestine radio station, *Radio Venceremos,* established by the insurgents in El Salvador, created a forum for Cutumay Camones and other rebel music makers to enter the daily lives of movement and potential movement members that would otherwise not have been possible.[43] In the post-9/11 era in the United States, particularly in the run-up to the war in Iraq, the Internet was virtually the only mass media site where antiwar music could be heard.

Musical Qualities

And what of the music itself? Our emphasis is always on musicking as process, its meaning constructed through context, as opposed to what we see as simplistic visions of music as a product with its own intrinsic qualities. Yet some characteristics of music itself do seem more or less conducive to particular movement uses. Military bands, as far as we can determine, simply do not play soft introspective ballads on the verge of battle, and the musical qualities of a piece might similarly play a role in movement use. For example, when the Carawans came to work in mining communities in Appalachia, they discovered a strong tradition there of solo ballads, in which a story is told at great length by a single singer; since the sheer number of words and verses alone limits participatory singing, such songs aren't of much use on a picket line where joint activity and solidarity need to be emphasized.

Yet as we argued previously in the "Meanings of Music" chapters, while use may have some link to the intrinsic qualities of the music, even our evaluation of what music seems to "naturally fit" a particular situation is heavily influenced by historical traditions. The very structure of call and response found in R&B, as we've seen, reinforces a collective sense, but this is the cultural product of a long tradition of collective struggle against group oppression by African Americans.[44] Irish national songs of martyrdom were probably more militarily mobilizing for the IRA than military marches, despite lacking the kind of military cadence used to rally most fighting units to battle.

Of course, neither "intrinsic" qualities of the music nor vibrant historical traditions ensure that all musickers will respond similarly. Folk music's typical emphasis on lyrics and understated beat makes it, all things being equal, more likely to serve educational purposes than mobilization. But all things are never equal, and in the right time and place, for the right person, Bob Dylan singing the extremely long folk-style ballad "The Lonesome Death of Hattie Carroll" may be far more important to mobilization than the most up-tempo rocker; the very sight of someone playing any hip-hop at all at loud volume in a public place may be more educational to a given individual than any folk song lyrics could ever be.

Working within these constellations of musical qualities, historical traditions, and individual perceptions, the kind of music used and musicking's relative importance vary by the movement activity at hand. "Zipper" songs (in which the details of the immediate situation are "zipped" into a familiar melody and format) work best in strike and demonstration situations, one current singer/activist writes, because "people engaged in struggle often have trouble listening to a lot of words, no matter how witty, but they enjoy and appreciate the feeling of solidarity and power that comes from being part of a large group singing together for a cause."[45] Hardcore's demonic energy and barely decipherable lyrics may be of little use in internal debate over tactics. The introspective tone of much of early women's music was ideally suited to the individual and group consciousness-raising that was crucial to the development of the modern women's movement, but little of it would be used in street demonstrations. As she became more politically active, Suzanne Vega told us, she began to see that

> some of my songs are *not* helpful in a political circumstance. If I go do a fundraiser for Ruth Messinger [a progressive candidate for New York City Council] and I want to sing a song to rally the troops—which is why they have me there—and I sing "Luca," I don't know if that's going to help. You know, it just makes everyone feel

sad and weird and stand around looking at their feet.... They're looking at me going, "We're here to cheer Ruth Messinger, we're not here to think about alienation at breakfast and child abuse and stuff like that." You know?

As music's role varies by activity, it varies by function (as we've defined those earlier). Experimental music may be valuable in facilitating education by shaking up worldviews, suggesting there are alternatives to ways of life taken for granted, but it probably does not mobilize very successfully for most people. The participatory singing of church-derived songs of the civil rights movement were of far greater importance in serving the committed than in educating people with a different background.

An audience's relationship to the movement is crucial, whether this is consciously considered by artists and organizers or not. Audiences of the converted want something different from musicking than neutrals who at most are wondering whether this movement has anything to do with their lives. Highly committed full-time activists may respond differently from those whose participation is more marginal; the folk music the Almanac Singers tried to import from the tradition of struggle in the rural South and Southwest never really found a home with urban workers, their primary audience, but it did profoundly affect a core of devoted activists in and around the Communist Party and the CIO (and many others a generation later).

Different kinds of movements also call for different roles for musicking. Movements that call for personal transformation as well as social change typically have a more fervent, quasi-religious tenor to them, and so the elements of ritual, including musicking, tend to be more important and more participatory. In culturally homogenous movements, a group's traditional music is likely to play a significant role, particularly in affirmation and mobilization, while movements created from more heterogeneous populations may find it harder to use music as the glue for solidarity, except where a newly emerging music itself provides the common bond, as punk did in some Eastern Bloc countries in the 1970s and 1980s.

The Role of Musicians

We began this discussion of the relative importance of music in different movements with conventional explanations that stressed cultural traditions, using the civil rights movement as perhaps the most frequently cited example of this. But musicking didn't simply arise spontaneously in the civil rights movement, nor did it always have the central role in that struggle we now celebrate. "*Since 1960* singing has been important to the movement," the Carawans wrote in 1968;[46] Branch reports that in the early days of the southern movement, the young SNCC activists were "conceded" the role of song leaders by the established leadership only "because music was of marginal importance to the normal church program."[47] The Reverend C. T. Vivian recalls:

At the beginning of the movement, we really didn't have any music that we could call "movement music." ... We also didn't realize how important a dynamic music would be to a movement. That was the beginning of a movement and we didn't know what was necessary and what wasn't. We weren't thinking about it in terms of "what is going to inspire us?"

When we did start seeking songs to use at mass meetings, the only thing we had among us that had any sense of life to it was church music. And some of the church music didn't fit at all. . . . I don't think we had ever thought of spirituals as movement material. When the movement came up, we couldn't apply them. The concept has to be there. It wasn't just to have the music, but to take the music out of our past and apply it to the new situation, to change it so it really fit.[48]

The freedom songs of the civil rights movement grew from a rich cultural tradition, but that growth required the work of dedicated songsters, typically operating out of organized groups and institutions, helping people to "discover the power in the culture they came out of," as Charlie King puts it. Activists like the SNCC Freedom Singers, James Bevel and Bernard Lafayette and their ministerial student singing quartet at the American Baptist Theological Seminary, and Guy Carawan at the Highlander Center were consciously trying to create a supportive musical environment by adapting traditional (and in some cases popular) songs to make them relevant to the movement, building on what "had been learned there during the Labor Movement—that singing could be a strong unifying force in struggle, and that commonly known songs, particularly southern gospel and religious songs with repetitive stanzas adapted to the situation, were most effective."[49] The Reverend Vivian recalls the first time he heard Carawan sing:

Guy had taken this song, "Follow the Drinking Gourd"; and I didn't know the song, but he gave some background on it and boom, that began to make sense. And little by little, spiritual after spiritual after spiritual began to appear with new words and changes—"Keep Your Eyes on the Prize," "Hold On" or "I'm Gonna Sit at the Welcome Table." Once we had seen it done, *we could begin to do it.*[50]

This kind of musicking was encouraged and spread by a series of music workshops held between 1960 and 1965, consciously designed to bring together song leaders from all over the South "to teach and learn freedom songs."[51] The seemingly spontaneous adaptation of "We Shall Overcome" as the anthem of the movement was aided considerably by the attempts by Carawan, Seeger, and others to familiarize activists with the song.

Whatever the historical tradition a movement invokes, whatever the structural framework that creates the need and provides the opportunity for it to arise, a movement is not a spontaneous, organic occurrence, but requires active humans working to make it happen. "You have to design a way to build unity," writes Chuck D. "It has to be designed. It's not going to pop up."[52] The IWW became a singing movement partially because there were cultural traditions of music among its potential members, but also because of strategic decisions made by activists within it, including the use of scarce resources to create the *Little Red Songbook*—a decision hotly debated at the time.[53]

When the Carawans went to work in Appalachian miners' communities in the late 1960s, they attempted to adapt the lessons they had learned about the use of culture in the civil rights movement. One of their first innovations was to organize "jamborees"

> to give people a chance to enjoy each other's music, dance, humor. There did not seem to be public settings for this to happen in Pike County, and later we realized that this situation was common in other mountain communities as well. . . . We experimented with group singing at the jamborees and at community meetings. We were interested in the potential of group song in the mountains, thinking of the powerful singing at mass meetings and demonstrations in the Deep South.[54]

Later, as in the civil rights movement, they organized a series of workshops devoted to using cultural expression in the mountain movement (as it was often called). There was a cultural tradition of musicking in Appalachia,[55] but just as in the civil rights movement, activist musicians needed to adapt and nurture existing traditions to transform them into important elements of movement life. Some cultural practices make this more likely, like the black musical tradition of call-and-response; some are more difficult to adapt to movement use, like the mountain tradition of long solo ballads the Carawans encountered in Appalachia.

The combination of a cultural tradition and committed musickers who want to build on it is a potent one. But what of musickers who don't have that tradition on which they can build? This, it's often claimed by both sympathizers and detractors, was the tragedy of groups like the Almanacs:

> The Almanacs assumed working-class immigrants would identify with folk songs the way they did. Unfortunately, most city dwellers didn't know "John Henry," and even if they did, the song often sounded "country" to those emigrating from the South. Instead of union songs, New Yorkers listened to their own ethnic music, or to the show tunes and pop hits the Almanacs scorned.[56]

Yet for all their failure to convert mass working-class audiences into folk music adherents —let alone revolutionary socialists[57]—the Almanacs and related groups of the 1930s, 1940s, and 1950s themselves became the historical model for a new "tradition" that exploded in the 1960s, touching far greater numbers than they could have ever dreamed. The artists and audiences who created and embraced the notion of socially conscious popular music that was so crucial in the movements of the 1960s and 1970s were invoking what *felt to them* like a historical tradition. Bob Dylan was trying to be Woody Guthrie; wanna-be folksingers in Greenwich Village in 1965 may not all have known much about Lead Belly or Florence Reece, but they had nevertheless inherited parts of their repertoire—"Rock Island Line," "Which Side Are You On?"—and something of the ethos the Almanacs constructed and embodied through their attempts to popularize that repertoire. With the coming of the cold war and the straitjacketing of cultural life in the United States, the left-wing folksingers' attempts

> to use folk song as a weapon were doomed in the short run. But the survival of a movement culture, of which the songs were an integral part, meant that the individual

self-respect, collective self-confidence, and vision required to combat the dominant culture were in some ways passed on to the next generation concerned with similar issues. Folk song as a weapon reappeared in the 1960s, playing a significant role in building, and expressing the unity and determination of, a new movement culture.[58]

The fruit of that legacy, married to other developing forms of popular music first in folk rock and then in a general linking of rock with social rebellion, went on to "modify popular consciousness as surely as if it had been introduced into the national water supply";[59] it remains one of the dominant models for "serious" popular artists today.[60]

Cultural traditions are *creations*. Over time they take on the appearance of having always existed, but they arise and develop through the practices of living, breathing people. Thus, while some political musicians have been able to use preexisting cultural traditions, others have helped to create such traditions—and many have done both.[61]

Just as our discussion of the L=ARM fallacy ultimately returned to lyrics—despite all our caveats—as still a significant factor in how musickers may construct meaning, our discussion here of the importance of the audience comes full circle to the crucial role of artists and organizers. Artist intent is only one factor in shaping the uses of music, but it's one of the few factors that can be consciously controlled. Some artists are trying to support specific movement tasks. They can't guarantee that audiences will interpret what they're doing in ways that are connected to the tasks artists and organizers believe the music is addressing. But there are undoubtedly ways that artists and organizers can make such connections more likely. We look at these in the final chapter.

Chapter 12

What Is to Be Sung (or Played)?

How do politically conscious artists create and produce music with political purpose? How do their choices affect the impact of their music on a movement? What are the relationships and dilemmas they must navigate? And how are their efforts constrained or enhanced by the particular historical contexts in which they operate?

What follows is our effort to answer such questions using the testimonies of politically concerned musicians, based on interviews we did with artists as well as drawing on previously published reflections. These musicians span a continuum of movement engagement. Some are rank-and-file members of specific organizations, involved in conventional organizing tasks when they're not musicking, as was Joe Hill in the IWW or the SNCC Freedom Singers. Others orbit such organizations, supporters on the periphery, but without actual membership or obligation (e.g., some of the Composers' Collective around the Communist Party, or Chuck D's relation to the Nation of Islam). Many more have informal links to a movement in general, but without ongoing ties to a specific party or organization (Phil Ochs, Ani DiFranco), and still others may work in relation to social and political ideas, issues, or even causes, but have little or no connection to the actual movements or organizations dealing with those issues.[1]

When we discussed songwriting with the late Joe Glazer, troubadour of the AFL-CIO for 30 years, his emphasis was always on how music could be *used* by the labor movement:

> One of the things we need always in the labor movement is good, easy-to-sing songs
> that have a lot of drive. Now there's about three or four that anybody can learn in a

minute, and they're really powerful.... I'm always looking for something like that.... If there's a situation, a strike, then I'll try to do a song.... You have to have some kind of wind-up [to a song], a kind of commercial.

Glazer voices a stance that extends back at least as far as the Wobblies of the early twentieth century, through the work of many in the "People's Songs" project in the 1940s, adopted by 1960s activists like the SNCC Freedom Singers, and by some musicians to this day. In the very first interview of a musician we did for this book, Charlie King told us:

> I do have a very ideological purpose about writing. You know, I mean it may not be that I think that I'm going to take the vast majority of American people and change the way that they view life or something like that. But I do very definitely have a purpose as a writer and a singer. And part of that purpose is that people not be confused when the song is over.... I will stay away from words that I think are confusing. You know sometimes I'm tempted by a word that has a real nice ring to it, you know, the kind of thing that in the Norton Anthology would have a footnote. But I always reject that word for clarity.... I want every song I write to have some sort of potential political impact when people hear it.

In every subsequent interview we repeated what King had said, and asked the musician what he or she thought about it. Suzanne Vega's response represents the opposite pole of the continuum: Personal artistic expression is the primary goal. How the audience then absorbs and uses that expression is a somewhat mysterious process she has little ability—or even wish—to control:

> I can only do what my instinct as an artist tells me is right and feels right to me.... [I]f you're an artist's artist, the art comes first, I think, before politics.... I would like to write about the world that we're in and show the mystery of it and the weirder sides of it. How unusual it all is, really, you know, and the power in it without explaining it to death, without making issues out of it that people can swallow whole without thinking about it.

We'll speak of these poles of *movement-orientation* and *artist-orientation* to express the continuum of possibilities rather than to classify particular artists as permanently in one camp or another. Musicians, like everyone, are affected by a range of circumstances and motives. At some times they're more dedicated to expressing their personal vision and/or pursuing their personal career, at others more interested in advancing a political position and/or supporting a political movement. To the extent their work is of importance to a movement—regardless of their own desires or motives—we refer to it as *movement music*; to the extent this is their aim, we refer to them as *movement musicians,* understanding that the line between movement musician and others interested in political questions is thin and porous.

Musicians' Aims

When talking to musicians about the issues involved in the social and political effects of their work, it's striking to see how few seem to have pondered them in much detail. "To be honest, that perpetual question, Can Music Make a Difference?, is one that I don't consider much," Billy Bragg has written;[2] Lee Hays, of the Almanac Singers, told an interviewer in 1948, "The Almanacs had a way of doing their work first, and then if anyone wanted to construct a theory about it he was welcome to do so."[3] When we asked Charlie King—among the most movement oriented of our interviewees—whether he thought his songs could translate into an actual change in the behavior of listeners, he answered, "Mostly, I don't worry about it."[4]

Musicians respond this way in part because the results are so hard to gauge: "When you write a song and send it out into the world, on radio and television, you have absolutely no idea who it will reach or what effect it will have," political rocker David Crosby has written;[5] Odetta told us: "It is difficult for any of us, whatever we are doing, to know what's going to happen. We just sort of do whatever it is that we do and then take the consequences, and hopefully those consequences are positive." Rather than dwell on Big Questions about their impact on the world, artists are much more likely to concentrate on practical questions having to do with craft. Still, when pressed by two academic sociologists,[6] their self-examinations reveal a range of aims and hopes for their work, from simply bearing witness to expressly stoking the fire of political activism.

Ballantine recounts that after a performance of the *Messiah*, "an aristocratic admirer thanked Handel for the 'noble entertainment' which he had recently given the town. 'My Lord,' replied Handel, 'I should be sorry if I only entertained them; *I wish to make them better.*'"[7] Many politically concerned musicians, however, make a point of saying that they *don't* regard themselves as capable of making others better, that they don't see themselves as more knowledgeable or competent or intelligent than their audiences. Their mission, many say, isn't to proselytize or convert, but merely to open people to different perspectives and options.

BARBARA DANE [describing her work with GIs during the Vietnam War]: The nature of art is to open up the person to think for themselves, not to tell them what to think in any instance....

ANI DiFRANCO: I don't say much, "Well, this is what you should do," so much as I say "I think you should figure it out for yourself and do it instead of sitting there." ... If anything [I] just encourage people to do for themselves.

CHUCK D: My whole motive is to tell a lot of people to be independent thinkers and think for themselves instead of leading themselves into a robotic trance—what slogans and trends might lead them into.... What people do as individuals is entirely up to them, I just want people to make an individual, independent choice to think, challenge information. That's why I said "Don't believe the hype."

Even musicians who are generally thought of as politically or socially concerned often frame their work in terms of personal testimony rather than as a weapon of organizing:

Q: Do you ever start by thinking, "We need a song about such and such and I'm going to write it"?
ANI DiFRANCO: Well, no, see that's what I don't do.... I'm sort of much more

instinctual or emotional about it. I think it's important for me, anyway, in my own writing, to really speak from what's going on inside, you know, not just a sort of cerebral, "I think I need to tell people about this."

Q: And when you write that stuff, are you thinking, "What I'm doing is expressing myself," or are you hoping for some sort of effect on a listener?

DiFRANCO: No I'm just sort of expressing myself.... I don't sit down with a sort of political agenda and say I want to write a song about this issue and try to get people educated or galvanized around an issue.

Billy Bragg goes so far as to argue that preaching a line to an audience renders the artist ineffective:

I think you have to reveal to the audience that you don't have all the answers and that you yourself are not completely sure that you know what you're doing, you're just trying to make the best of it, same as everyone else.... You *are* trying to inspire people and encourage people, but you are by no means leading.... It's not about the political artist. It's almost a cliché: It's not about offering answers, it's asking the right questions.... It's the audience that has the answers.

Yet even those artists who portray their role as expressing their personal vision rather than persuading others to embrace it still seem to harbor a hope that expressing their view will have an effect on listeners' ideas and behaviors. (This is, after all, no different from what most speakers, political or otherwise, hope when expressing an opinion in everyday conversation.) For the most movement-oriented artists, of course, this is often their explicit mission:

Q: Do you sometimes deliberately write about a topic? Do you think, "We should have a song about such-and-such" and set out to write it?

SANDY RAPP: Yeah, I do. That's exactly what I do.... "Remember Rosie" [her song condemning the cutoff of funding by Medicaid for abortions, linking it to an increase in illegal abortion–related fatalities] was the first time I sat down and said, "We need something that's catchy to sing along with while they're singing their hymns at us. I'm going to get some historical detail and going to tell a real story, and it's going to be good old-fashioned sing-along so people can remember it." And after that I've done about 25, 30 since like that.

Q: Do you think these songs can change people's minds?

RAPP: I really do. And I have had people come up to me from the other side [of the abortion debate], or from the fence, and say, "Yeah, I see what you mean. If women don't have the choice, then this woman died because she couldn't get funding."

Q: Do you have any problem deliberately crafting a song to reach an audience with a political goal in mind? You don't find that to be unproductive or damaging to your art, or anything like that?

RAPP: Not at all, not at all. I think there is something to be said for having something to say. I mean, that's a pretty good reason for writing, as far as I'm concerned.

Even when the political end is less specific or explicit, musicians all along the continuum generally have an implicit constellation of values with political implications that they're not only expressing, but often hoping others will adopt. Fred Small told Karroll:

I hope that my music will encourage people, and sometimes enable people to notice their own feelings, and the world around them.... To the extent that I can encourage people to notice how they feel, tears of joy, or relief, or sadness, or pain, that is a great gift I can give.

If I can also bring together a community of people through the medium of my songs, and remind them that they are not alone in caring about some of the issues my songs address, that is also a great gift. Because we function with so much isolation and a sense of futility.[8]

Politically minded musicians often seem to think about their social effect as a teacher might: You are doing your work in order to change people in some way. You don't expect any specific impact from a particular class or piece of writing, and trying to measure one's immediate impact is likely to be self-defeating. Instead, you do the work, trying to do your best in terms of standards you believe in, and hope at least someone out there is moved (in several meanings of that word).

The Dilemmas of Movement Musicians

Since music making is social in every sense of the word, it entails working out a series of relationships with individuals, groups, and institutions. The more identified and self-identified a musician becomes with a specific political orientation and movement, the more she finds herself with a set of dilemmas navigating those relationships, which are not typically faced by other musicians.

Relations with the State

The musician's relation to the government in power is almost invariably loaded with potential conflict since, as Street points out, the state typically does not create music itself: "[I]t has to rely on others, and in this dependence, a rival power is created."[9] This doesn't mean an adversarial relationship is inevitable. Some governments have become supporters or defenders of musicking, particularly of forms of music that don't fare well in the modern marketplace but are thought to have historical or aesthetic importance.[10] It was, for example, governmental institutions like the Library of Congress and the Smithsonian Institution that provided key resources for collecting and preserving the musics that fueled the folk revival.

Governments also have a long tradition of using music themselves, as in Nazi Germany where music was used extensively as a state-run leisure activity that reinforced desirable values. From Hausmusik—literally music to be sung in the home—to the grandest spectacles, the Nazi regime saw music as "a convenient form of cement between the rulers and their people."[11] Music instruction was integral to Hitler Youth education, valued both for its propagandistic value and for its "physical-rhythmic basic training [which] is of particular significance [for soldiers]."[12]

But frequently the relationship *is* adversarial. When governments or ruling elites feel threatened by a form of musicking, they often attempt to suppress it in one way or another. Outright banning is one method, as the Greek military junta banned all music of leftist composer Mikis Theodorakis during the years of the dictatorship (1967–1974). Censorship is another, subjecting each piece of music to the scrutiny of state authorities who decide whether it can be publicly performed or distributed, as in South Africa under apartheid (1948–1994). Musicians are then faced with bowing to this repression, finding ways to make the political implications of their work apparent to listeners while subtle enough to evade the censor, or openly defying the censorship, hoping this will undermine the legitimacy of the powers that be. In recent years, government surveillance has sometimes been evaded by use of technology that allows for self-production and underground means of wide distribution. Dubbed cassettes and CDs passed hand to hand are major examples; almost any music on the globe is now available to those with access to the Internet. All forms of technology that decentralize the production and distribution of music make state surveillance and control more difficult.

Moreover, suppression in itself carries dangers for the state, elevating the seeming political importance of the music and thus potentially turning cultural deviants into political resisters. As a result, governments often seek instead to co-opt the music and the scene around it, to channel the musicking in ways that serve their purposes. In states where the government controls access to crucial resources like recording studios or public venues, simply making these available to some musicians and not others is a powerful way of influencing bands to create music that's in line with the values the government espouses.[13] Here musicians are faced with the choice of toeing the government's ideological line or maintaining their perspective and thus facing enormous disadvantages in getting their music out to listeners.

In the United States, the state's official position has generally been one of laissez faire, as the First Amendment requires. Nevertheless, American musicians periodically have experienced state punishment for their political actions or affiliations. The case of Wobbly troubadour Joe Hill, purportedly framed and executed on a murder charge in Utah, became a worldwide cause célèbre and legend. In the fifties, congressional investigations of the entertainment industry led to blacklisting of a number of political musicians, including Pete Seeger and the other Weavers. During that period, the federal government revoked Paul Robeson's passport, preventing him from continuing his international career, while it simultaneously encouraged his blacklisting in the domestic entertainment industry. Local efforts to enforce obscenity laws led to attempts to block the sale of several rap records in some parts of the country in the 1990s.

Relations with the Music Industry

In this country, political artists' freedom is more regularly restricted by the demands and constraints of the privately controlled "cultural apparatus" and the cultural market than by the state.[14] The problem is less that corporations seek to censor ideological content that opposes their worldview than that they routinely regard political music (like other marginalized musics) as unlikely to be profitable.

This isn't a hard-and-fast rule; artists tied to a vibrant movement or political trend may thereby have a built-in audience base. There have, in fact, been periods in which political content has been seen as broadly marketable, either in times of mass mobilization like the late 1960s (when Columbia Records famously advertised its products with the hook line "But the Man can't bust our music") or when support of a specific political issue becomes popular, as environmentalism has been periodically. Particular artists, such as Rage Against the Machine, have been marketed as politically relevant. Billy Bragg's manager, Peter Jenner, argues that abandoning a critical political stance would have been "a career mistake for Billy. Because of who he is and what he is, to have something challenging about it is actually very good for him commercially." Less politically identified artists may include a few politically themed songs in their repertoire—doing so may even be thought useful for establishing their authenticity.

But, especially in the minds of industry personnel who make the decisions about what music is widely available, a reputation as first and foremost a "political" artist is conventionally thought to make the artist too didactic, too specialized, too difficult to sell:

> SANDY RAPP: I have a hard time booking myself, getting booked and getting air play. . . . I'm on the issues [and that's not seen] as user friendly or listener friendly. It's not what people expect from music, especially these days. So, there is a tension. . . . And a lot of the clubs out here don't want all this baggage. Just a general straight or mixed night club doesn't really want the fact that I had my picture on the front page of *Newsday* for a rally about abortion choice in front of a clinic a couple of weeks ago. . . . Because some of the people will complain.

When Pete Seeger and Lee Hays formed the Weavers in 1949 to carry on the work of the Almanac Singers, "the group became highly polished performers, developing a routine which permitted them to appear almost exclusively in night clubs. They took a manager, advertised in the usual ways, accepted a contract with Decca and produced a number of unexpected hits."[15] As Seeger told us, these concessions included a political price: "It was a hard period. Our manager then wouldn't let us sing at hootenannies, wouldn't let us sing 'If I Had a Hammer.'" The Weavers popularized Woody Guthrie and Lead Belly songs, but with considerable smoothing of their edginess.

Similarly, Guthrie's most famous song, "This Land Is Your Land," would almost certainly not have become the hugely popular song it became if Woody himself hadn't omitted two verses emphasizing class conflict when he first recorded it. In the first, he mocks the sanctity of private property by observing that the back of a No Trespassing sign was blank ("That side was made for you and me"); in the second he paints a picture of "my people," idle in town, dependent on "relief," and wondering "is this land made for you and me?"[16] We don't know whether Guthrie omitted these verses to make the song more commercially viable or politically inclusive (and we do know he taught these verses to his son, Arlo, to make sure they weren't lost). But there's no doubt that the version he recorded had a more universal appeal that enabled it to be printed in school songbooks and accepted as a patriotic anthem.[17]

Artists in the United States (or their management) aren't usually dealing with explicit censorship by government or the music industry. "I don't believe that there's any media that's controlling hip-hop," Russell Simmons told the *New York Times* when asked about his support of Musicians United to Win Without War, a group opposing the impending war in Iraq in early 2003. "You throw a rap record out the window, no George Bush, nobody, can stop it if it's a hit."[18] But it's taken for granted by artists that there is resistance within the industry—from record companies to radio to VH-1 to performance venues—to music and performance that disrupt audience expectations in *any* way—aesthetically, morally, or politically. Even in Public Enemy's heyday, according to lead rapper Chuck D, they had a hard time getting radio airplay, including on

> black radio. We were always in a class of our own, especially after 1990. DJs couldn't mix a Public Enemy record in an old-school set because our records are totally different. They'd be going from "I Know You Got Soul" into "My Adidas," and then they're like, "Nah, I can't mix 'Night of the Living Baseheads' [Public Enemy's extremely pointed attack on drug culture within the black community] in there."[19]

We want to avoid caricaturing those in the industry as a homogenous mass of "suits," indifferent to the music and only concerned with the bottom line. Many people within the industry are highly motivated by their love of music; some are motivated by political convictions. It's always been the case that smaller indies within the industry provide space for alternative musics of all kinds, and much of mainstream music is constituted by product that has been appropriated from musics at the margin. But by definition, industry personnel, whatever their personal commitments, operate in a market economy in which their economic survival depends on sales revenues. The more explicit the politics—or, analogously, the more radical the musical innovation—the more difficult it is to have it accepted by a broad audience, and thus the more difficult it is to convince the mainstream industry to embrace the product, especially when corporate decision makers are pressured by shareholders to maximize the bottom line.

Creating music for a market, large or small, necessarily places the artist in a web of relationships that pressure her, subtly or otherwise, to make music that can be profitably sold, whether an artist personally sees prospering financially as a main goal or not. Once she moves from true folk status to creating a product that is marketed to anyone willing to purchase it, there is always some pressure to do whatever can be done to sell to more people, including, often, pressure to dilute the political message so it won't interfere with approval and purchase by those outside the group or who otherwise might disagree with the political perspective. Whether carried by one of the majors hoping to move sales up from a million to 5 million units, or by a struggling indie hoping to sell 50,000 copies from an artist who has never sold 5,000 albums, growth in sales is almost inevitably desirable and necessary from the perspective of those with jobs or investments at stake in the production and marketing of the product.

For the artist as well, crossover is a heady temptation (and may be a deliberate political strategy, as we discuss below). Commercial success carries with it any number of benefits, from having someone else deal with schlepping the amplifiers after the gig to the perks of stardom. The drive for success almost inevitably challenges movement loyalty, creating contradictions for politically committed artists that rarely concern the average musician:

> PETER JENNER: We just did this whole tour of Borders stores. Now Borders has a very iffy, a very negative attitude to unions.... I don't think they're probably much worse than any of the other book shops or record shops or chains anyway, in that respect. But they happen to be caught in something and it's become an issue and become a symbol and—we had a lot of talking to do to explain why it was we were doing a Borders store. That was a real problem. It was a problem for the record company, and it was a problem for us because if we bitched and moaned too much about Borders and came on too hard, and said "Fuck off," then they might well say "Fuck off" to us and that would be fucking off 10 percent of our sales. Borders sells over 10 percent of our records. Exactly.... Those things cost money.

Musicians who don't aspire to radio play or arena concerts find this less of a dilemma, but the need to make a living still affects the decisions they make:

> CHARLIE KING: I don't think of myself as commercially viable, so I don't feel a tug to try to [compromise politically] ... I don't sit around and say, "How can I write a song or how could I put out a record that would break through to make me popular?" ... I don't think if I hired a real hot rock band and a great producer that I could go out there and be some [superstar]. I tend to think of myself more as a kind of self-employed tradesman who does a basic good job at a pretty simple craft, and if I deliver a good product consistently, then probably people will continue to hire me. [But] I do kind of build a repertoire that I think is useful and likely to keep me working. So, in that sense, I guess money is certainly a consideration in what I do.

Even if an artist remains true to his political agenda, even if those producing his music share his political priorities and don't urge him to sacrifice his politics (or any aspect of his musical approach) for greater sales, the very fact of being in the commercial mainstream presents a dilemma: The meaning of the music is affected by the messages being sent by the popular culture machinery surrounding it (buy this, here's what's cool right now, this is how men and women relate, buy that), whatever its original intended message.

> DAR WILLIAMS: When I did a video for "As Cool as I Am" [a relationship song with strong feminist underpinnings], I thought, "Well, I'll do a video that's a socially conscious video." But this sort of fell apart. The content was too heavy for the genre that videos are. And so when I was staying at various hotels [on tour] over the next few months, I watched videos. And I realized if you're going to be socially conscious, you're not going to make a video at all. Videos are commercials, and videos are mind zapping.[20]

Commercialization necessarily involves losing some control of one's art. As we've been arguing, no musician or composer can hope to strictly control the ways that audiences receive and use their work. But the more that work is owned and distributed by the culture industry, the more artists lose control to those *selling* the music. Audiences don't construct their meanings from an infinite number of equally presented alternative framings; how a product is received, or whether it's even received at all by more than a handful of people, is often a matter of how people other than the artist or the audience think it can be sold.

Many artists, veterans of the process, have concluded that involvement with the mainstream music industry involves so many compromises that truly meaningful work becomes impossible to produce within the industry's domain. "The Clash wanted to see if you could get to be absolutely Number One in the entire world and still have something to say," reflected their lead singer, Joe Strummer, a decade after their heyday. "The answer to that one is no, far as I can see."[21] Ian MacKaye of Fugazi sees their career in the same way:

MACKAYE: I don't believe in joining, fighting from the inside. I just don't believe you can do it.

Q: What do you think about the Clash doing that?

MACKAYE: I hated them. I thought they were sellouts from almost the word go. . . . I thought their first record was pretty great. And then I thought that after that, these guys are chumps. . . . By the time they got off the road, after they went through it all, it's like all the thorns had been rubbed off, man, like all the edges were smooth. . . .

It's why I think that from a political point of view, or from a band's point of view, that you can't do it right. You can't be a part of the machine. . . . People say, "Why didn't you guys sign to a major label?" We've been offered so many times, you know. We've always turned it down. But from my point of view, it's like, you could always be absorbed, like you can never get ahead of them. Because once you're packaged, that's it. . . .

A lot of people I know who were in bands have gone along with that. Like, "Well yeah, we're finally reaching the mainstream. We can finally effect change." But, the fact of the matter is that if you become part of the mainstream, you will never effect change. . . .

Musicians like MacKaye and his band Fugazi, or Ani DiFranco, have opted instead to be truly independent (unlike the "indie labels" now owned or controlled by the majors), controlling all aspects of production, distribution, and advertising, yet making a living through their art. By the early twenty-first century some artists with considerable previous mainstream success had decided to do the same, including Public Enemy and Michael Franti. Clearly, the Internet and digital technology in general offer more space for such attempts to bypass the industry.

But many politically oriented artists remain tied to the majors, some from a desire for commercial success, some from the belief that there's no other way to survive, but still others by ideological choice. Tom Morello, guitarist for Rage Against the Machine—the most unrelentingly political band to achieve massive success on a major label in this country—sees the effect of the Clash quite differently from Ian MacKaye:

Throughout my time in Rage Against the Machine, journalists would always ask the question, "What the hell is a band with politics of Rage doing on Epic Records?" I would often answer with long and flowery sermons about spreading an important message around the globe. But I really could have answered with two words: The Clash. I was energized and politicized and changed by the Clash. And the reason I heard about them was because Dave Vogel bought *London Calling* at Musicland Records at the local Hawthorne Mall in tiny Libertyville, Illinois. And the reason Dave could get his hands on this album at a nearby mall was because the band was on Epic Records.[22]

As he later elaborated in an interview with us,

You and I would not be sitting down doing this interview if Rage Against the Machine had not been on Sony Music [the parent company of Epic]. People in Malaysia would not be singing "Killing in the Name," they wouldn't be saying, "Fuck you, I won't do what you tell me" at the rally were it not for the band [being on a major label]....

It casts the nets wide. It reaches all the young Tom Morellos who feel isolated and alienated out there because it's in the music—it's on the cover of *Rolling Stone* and it's in the Wal-Mart.... And they get the opportunity for it to be their *London Calling* and to see, "Does this resonate with me? Am I part of something else? Can I do something about it?" ...

I honestly never saw a downside to it. It felt to me like any other path would have been turning our backs on the young versions of me.... Perhaps someday we will live in anarcho-syndicalist times and then we will be under anarcho-syndicalist labels. Until then—and I'm not saying it's the only way to go— ... I want to make music and try to stick it to the Man.[23]

Those with this perspective argue that reaching a mass audience *should* be the aim of political artists:

BOOTS RILEY: Trying to make music that moves people in some direction politically, you want it to get to as many people as possible.... You're not trying to just sell it to these 10 people that come to your show every night. You shouldn't be satisfied with that if your goal is to create music that moves a lot of people. If your goal is to make art, but you happen to have a political view that you're going to put in there, then it's fine, do whatever you want. But, I have a [political] goal, and I know what I'm doing.

BILLY BRAGG: You have to be hearty, just kind of kick through and not take no shit about the fact that you're on [the TV show] *Top of the Pops*.... I happen to think that "Between the Wars" [his prounion, antiwar hit of the mid-1980s] should be seen in 40 million homes, thank you very much, that those words should be heard. So I'm gonna go on *Top of the Pops* and don't give me no bullshit about commercialism, you know? ... Because you want your record to be in Kmart in Biloxi, Mississippi. You don't just want to be in New York and L.A. and the college towns.

Politically committed musicians understand the tension between commercial success and political efficacy to be a dilemma, particularly when signed to a major label. They look for ways to negotiate the contradictions, debating when and what compromising must go on:

BILLY BRAGG: I [rarely] get played on the radio because I'm too political. 'Cause I'm not willing to make those complete compromises and drop the s-word [socialism] from my songs. Even my most popular radio-friendly song has the word "gay" in it, you always pay a bit of a price for that. That's the reality of trying to reach the mass market. There *are* compromises to be made. You just have to make sure they're on your terms, not on the industry's terms.

Most musicians would agree that popularization almost inevitably includes the danger of some dilution of message (artistic and/or political), either through the industry's need to homogenize musical products or the artist's own attempts to widen his audience by toning down the difficult and radical aspects of his art. But artists like Bragg feel that popularization can be accomplished in ways that can advance their politics, even when their message is surrounded (and therefore potentially diluted) by ads for underarm deodorant and tips on bagging a hottie. The sacrifice of purity is outweighed by the gain in mass awareness of core issues—with the key proviso, of course, that those core issues aren't fatally corrupted in the process:

DAR WILLIAMS: In my opinion, anyone who says Lilith Fair [a series of corporate-sponsored concerts featuring only women artists] just sucks, is just corporate, does miss the point. I did the Michigan Women's Festival [a much more overtly feminist, non-corporate-backed festival] and Lilith Fair in the same week. They're very different. But I love them both for different reasons. This is where I think the roots and flowers thing comes in, because you see the flower of the success of women's music coming out in Lilith Fair. . . . I don't know who at the Lilith Fair that I played with would call herself a feminist, but all of them understood that being a self-identified woman was important.

Relations with Movements and Movement Organizations

Perhaps ironically, some of the more problematic relationships for musicians hoping to further social change are those with movements and movement organizations, imbued with fundamental questions of the relation of art and politics. Rodnitsky voices a common belief when he declares: "Art and politics are often joined, but seldom compatible";[24] critics claim that political engagement, by its very nature, limits artists' freedom of expression and capacity for truth telling. But such assumptions, stated in this form, are much too sweeping.

Some artists see no tension between their movement loyalty and their artistic mission:

GUY CARAWAN: I don't think they were in conflict. I think I had to learn what was appropriate. . . .

JOE GLAZER: No, it's not, it wasn't a problem with me. Never raised itself that way.

RONNIE GILBERT: My parents were naturalized citizens, working-class Jewish immigrants from Eastern Europe. . . . For them, activism was a normal part of life, and the distinction between music for pleasure and music in the service of social improvement hardly existed. It was an attitude I absorbed early on.[25]

But many find the relationship problematic, sometimes highly so. Some see this as a question of character types, the artistic temperament deemed incompatible with the kind of group discipline political work typically involves. Odetta told us:

> Twice I tried to belong to an organization. That is not my personality. I have no patience with the inward—or any—kind of bickering and bias: "They wore red, and they should have worn green." I don't get on very well with people. I love working for and towards the beautification and improvement of us as individuals, as groupings, but I do not understand individuals and people and the politics they have to go into. So no, I'm not an organization person [laughter].

Many movement musicians draw a distinction between being broadly politically engaged and joining a particular political organization, subject to its demands and disciplines. "I agree with everything that's happening ... but I'm not part of no movement," Bob Dylan famously told the writer Nat Hentoff in 1963. "If I was I wouldn't be able to do anything else but be in 'the Movement.' I just can't have people sit around and make rules for me. I do a lot of things no movement would allow."[26]

There are certainly musicians who have seen themselves first as members of a movement organization, and whose work has been defined by organizational imperatives. But by and large, modern musicians, including many of those who are most committed to a movement, tend not to become members of formal movement organizations. When we asked Holly Near, a famously political performer, about her ongoing relationships with movement organizations and her feelings of allegiance to them, she responded simply: "No ongoing relationships with political groups. No allegiance." When we asked Chuck D, the godfather of political rap, he mentioned groups he admired—the Nation of Islam, PUSH, the Urban League—but when asked if he felt "bound" by his connection to any of them, he replied, "I don't feel bound by anything." Though there are exceptions, these kinds of responses were far more typical of the artists we interviewed, though all were tied in some way or another to a social movement.

Many complain that political organizations give musicians little respect, using them as a come-on for generating larger crowds at rallies and demonstrations, but dismissive of them as incapable of any intellectual contribution, as the Almanac Singers discovered during their CIO support tour of 1941.[27] Sixty-five years later, Quetzal Flores told us,

> Some of the activists would say, "Oh, you guys are doing the cultural work while we're doing the real work." That would piss me off, it would just drive me *nuts* because I feel like, okay, "the *cultural* work": What the fuck does that *mean*? What exactly does that *mean*? You know, culture is *very* political. What we're doing *is* cultural work, and it's much *more* than that. And unfortunately, they couldn't see it. A lot of activists couldn't see it.

Billy Bragg was instrumental in the organization of Red Wedge, the 1980s effort to use radical political musicians to re-create the sense of the Labour Party in

England as a kind of social movement, hoping to attract great numbers of young people to the party. His manager summarizes the experience this way:

PETER JENNER: What they really wanted was Pop Stars for Labour. They wanted us to shut up, sing the songs, bring in the audience and then go in the background. Let the politicians lay on the line and the politics, and then we could go on and do our bit, and thank you very much and fuck off and here's your knighthood.... There was no willingness on the politicians' part to actually think in terms of what we were saying and taking us seriously as people with brains, who represented a constituency.

The decision to keep movement organizations at arm's length is thus often seen as necessary from a political—as well as a personal or artistic—point of view. Some distrust the "manipulation" of political organizations,[28] while others portray it less as a question of bad faith on the part of activists than the inevitable workings of organized groups. Paul Baker Hernandez has moved from his native Scotland to the United States, and now to a barrio in Nicaragua, each time explicitly to do political work. Yet he still says, "No, I'm not in an organization, I'm a freelancer essentially."

Q: Is that deliberate?
BAKER HERNANDEZ: Yeah, it is, because I've observed ... for all sorts of reasons, perfectly understandable reasons, ... the organization takes on a life of its own, and needs at certain times to suck in resources to itself so that it becomes imperialistic.... I think they all suffer from that same problem of organizationalism [though] some of them are better at dealing with it than others.

SANDY RAPP: I don't like to be affiliated too closely with any [organization] because I carry a lot of baggage. And I don't want to be told I can't sing "White Men in Black Dresses" [her most infamous song, criticizing the Catholic clergy].... You have to be careful what you say; you have to mind your tongue because you are carrying the whole organization with you.... I don't want any organization telling me what to do, so I don't have that formal position.

Belonging to a particular movement organization is actually at odds with what some artists see as their primary duty—encouraging the movement as a whole rather than advancing the claims of a particular organization:

PETER JENNER: Certainly on the left there's always a certain dividing going on and there's such sectarianism. And I think one wants to try and be above it. The role of the artist is to observe and comment on what he observes, and I think if he becomes too involved in fighting for that particular team or this team, you become too involved in such a logic chopping and taking a view, then [you] ... become negative. In order to show you're in favor of A, you diss B. And that I don't think is good.

Rather than being card-carrying members of specific organizations, many political artists remain available for fundraisers or other support work when mutually agreeable:

IAN MACKAYE: I actually don't go to meetings, I have nothing to do with that kind of stuff.... For me, it's much more the overall momentum or thrust of trying to do things that you [think can help]. That's the way this band [Fugazi] has always operated, and the way I've always operated. Like, okay—the Washington Free Clinic: If we give them $2,000, they can buy 500 HIV testing kits. That's it. That's direct grassroots operation. I feel really comfortable with stuff like that. . . . But, if someone said to me, "Hey, we want you to do a benefit album for this particular organization," we probably would not do it, because then our involvement with the organization becomes sort of stamped in a mold, it becomes kind of permanent.

Q: What about if you're doing a benefit for, say, the Free Clinic, and they come to you beforehand, they say, "Hey listen, you know, some of your songs are about AIDS, can you not do them tonight, because we've got some of these more conservative people in the audience?" Is that alright with you?

MACKAYE: That would never happen. And if it did, we would never agree to it. . . . You have to understand, this is the way we operate. If you want our input, you want our support, then you do it our way.

Still, for those who think of themselves as movement musicians, their commitment to the struggle means they must work out some mutually satisfactory arrangement that they and the movement organizations can live with:

Q: What should the relationship be between a musician and an organization? Should the organization just stay out of it or . . . ?

PETE SEEGER: It should be a continual discussion. . . . Any organization, big or small, that doesn't treasure interior discussion sooner or later will come down.

BOOTS RILEY: You get people come in with all sorts of ideas. I've had people come up to me at shows and say, "You should have said more about Palestine." And, I mean, hopefully you will at your show. . . . But I don't sense any tension because you need that kind of a push to actually make things happen. . . . I got into doing it, seriously, because I wanted it to have something to do with a movement and changing the world.

The most common concern for musicians considering their relation to movements and movement organizations is that political affiliation can constrain the artist in performing her time-honored role of minstrel, speaking the truth, regardless of whom it helps or harms:

SUZANNE VEGA: There's a part of me that says if I get involved with politics, then it's like you're tainted a bit. You know, then you're looking for someone's approval or you're sucking up to somebody and it's always been my policy not to do that to anybody in authority. I guess maybe as an artist I believe you have to be an outsider to be truthful.

The archetypal example of this dilemma, often related as a cautionary tale to illustrate the dangers of artists tying themselves to political parties, involves the Almanac Singers and the changes of policies of the U.S. Communist Party (CPUSA). In the mid-1930s the CPUSA, like Communist parties around the world, abandoned its previous policy of extreme sectarianism to create the Popular Front with all those opposed to Hitler and fascism. When the Hitler-Stalin pact of nonaggression was signed in 1939, the CPUSA made an about-face, defined the war between Hitler and Britain as a capitalist war, and advocated neutrality between the Allies and Axis powers as World War II developed. War preparations were derided as encouraging militarization; Franklin Roosevelt, who had been critically supported by the CP, became a warmonger, as in the Almanacs' "Ballad of October 16th":

> Franklin Roosevelt told the people how he felt,
> we damned near believed what he said
> He said, "I hate war, and so does Eleanor,
> but we won't be safe 'till everybody's dead"[29]

But in June 1941, Hitler invaded the Soviet Union, ending the pact, and Communist parties once again reversed directions, urging all-out war against fascism and a return to Popular Front alliances with "progressive" capitalists. Pete Seeger told Karroll:

> I said to Woody, "You mean I have to support Churchill?" Woody says, "Yup, Churchill said 'All aid to the gallant Soviet Allies.' Churchill flip-flopped, we got to flip-flop, too." So it went down in history as the great flip-flop.... I went along with them. I think it took a little persuading on my part.

The Almanac Singers, like other supporters of the Communist Party, were again faced with renouncing their previous position—and much of their previous repertoire, including the antiwar material that made up their first album, *The Ballad of John Doe*. Overnight they went from advocating class war and satirizing Franklin Roosevelt as a blood-hungry demagogue to advocating class collaboration and readiness to follow FDR to war.

The telling of this story, as in many accounts of this kind of dilemma, typically claims or implies that the musicians simply knuckled under to the party line: "To survive in closed organizations like the Party, one has to read the wind. Those preoccupied with art instead of doctrine fall behind."[30]

> JOE GLAZER: Pete [Seeger] was a good friend of mine, but you know he was tied in with the communist line. And so with that, he was in a way hedged in.... When the Communist Party said, "Sing songs about peace," he had to sing song about peace if he was going to stay with them. That was his allegiance.

Certainly there are times and places where political activists dictate to cultural workers what they should and shouldn't say or do.[31] But conformity to a party line may also derive from the artists' own principles. As Lieberman writes about the Almanacs' embarrassing shift,

> The Almanac Singers were not responding to Comintern or CPUSA directives when they changed their repertoire to match a new political situation.... They were part of a movement culture, which they helped to shape but which also defined their political outlook. The shared ideals and the dominant meanings and values of the movement culture provided the day-to-day impetus for their activity.[32]

IRWIN SILBER: That doesn't speak so much to the artist as to the nature of the political commitment that the individual has with the organization. It's not just the artist that's affected, there's lots of people. The Communist Party accepted the Nazi-Soviet pact. A lot of people quit the Party and a lot of other people may have had qualms about it but they felt, "Well, it's my party, and in general I agree with it," and some musicians would feel the same way.

Doubtless, that worldview was in some ways circumscribed by their commitments and networks. Commitment to any group helps to provide meaning and ideals, but almost inevitably results in a narrowing of viewpoint. When one is surrounded by others who share the same outlook, basic beliefs are rarely challenged; expression of doubt may be seen as a loss of commitment if not outright disloyalty. The resulting insulation restricts the artist's—and all group members'—ability to consider the widest range of possibilities. Still, the process of ensuring conformity in disciplined organizations is considerably more complicated than enforcing "blind allegiance." The weighing of imperfect alternatives is involved as well.

The very conception of art as a weapon or tool suggests an instrumental end that, even in the absence of central committee directives, can become a straitjacket. Artistic creation, Jamison has written, has "a logic of [its] own, a kind of poetic logic or rationality that cannot be mandated or be imposed. To be successful, songs have to work in their own musical terms."[33] Artistic creation, many feel, requires intellectual freedom, while political commitment erects boundaries: progressive versus regressive, politically correct versus politically incorrect, our music versus their music. "I was completely dedicated to the long-overdue celebration of women's culture, of lesbian and feminist song," Holly Near writes in her autobiography, "but women's music cramped my style in its narrow approach."[34]

Politically defined music making can run counter to artistic ambition. Many songwriters mention that the very topicality of a political song makes it likely to become dated. Some see an almost inverse relation: The more relevant a song is for a specific struggle and the greater an emotional wallop it packs for the people involved at the time, the less appeal it may have to anyone else, then or in the future. Certainly there are times when these coincide, when a piece of music achieves lasting fame because it captures a moment in history that is crucial for collective identity, or because the story it tells again illuminates contemporary reality many years after its creation.[35] But in general the political anthems that have lasted over time—"We Shall Overcome," "Imagine," "Solidarity Forever"—tend to express extremely general principles, adaptable to universal conditions. The demands of the political may be to create a piece of music that will be most relevant to a concrete struggle, but the demands of art (with the implicit judgment that the best art is that which survives over time) may point in a different direction.

Where the pure artist favors self-expression above all and the pure advocate favors serving the movement above all, the dilemma for most politically committed musicians is finding the right balance between the two:

Q: Do you feel any tensions between being an artist and having this sort of political agenda? Do those things ever come into conflict?

CHUCK D: Yeah, they always do. They come into conflict because in art you can be free to say one thing, and a certain political agenda might hold you and limit you to an existence in a box, where artist is freedom and a certain agenda is limitations. You try to mix and match. I can't wear my artist hat a lot of the time.... Sometimes you sacrifice your political stance and sometimes you sacrifice your art, but you never do it fully. You do it just with percentages, that's the only way.

The pressures that accompany a consciously political stance are often intense. Hostile critics attack you for being dull and didactic; neutral audiences suspect you will be irrelevant to their lives; supporters hold you to higher standards than anyone else (including themselves). All may expect you to operate within the narrow boundaries that "political" suggests to each. So it comes as little surprise to find that many artists, including some of those firmly committed to political movements, resist being labeled:

BILLY BRAGG: I'm not a political songwriter.... I don't let people call me—or Woody [Guthrie] for that matter—a political songwriter, just pigeonholing him. You know, he does more than that. He writes all sorts of songs, and I write all sorts of songs, so I'm much more comfortable with the idea of just being an honest, straightforward songwriter.

IAN MACKAYE: I think that kind of classification makes a band very dismissible, like: "Oh well, they're a political act, that's what they are." So then there's no real merit because that sort of explains why these guys are so angry, or that explains why they have such a passion about something—it's just because they're political. It's just a ridiculous kind of way of approaching things, but we just won't let people do that.... And so when people say, "What kind of band are you?" I say, "Well, we're a band. We play music." When they say, "What kind of music?" [I say,] "We play music. I don't think it needs to be qualified any more than that."

Indeed, bearing a political label makes it harder for musicians to accomplish one of their primary political goals—reaching out to the uncommitted and uneducated:

Once you put a prefix on an MC's name, that's a death trap," says Talib Kweli, the gifted Brooklyn-born rapper who disdains being called "conscious" [the label within the hip-hop community for socially engaged artists]. Clearly his music expresses a well-defined politics; his rhymes draw from the same well of protest that nourished the Last Poets, the Watts Prophets, and the Black Arts stalwarts he cites as influences. But he argues that marketing labels close his audiences' minds to the possibilities of his art.... At the same time, Kweli worries that being pigeonholed as political will prevent him from being promoted to mass audiences. Indeed, to be a "political rapper" in the music industry these days [late 2002] is to be condemned to preach to a very small choir.[36]

While musicians of any era may resist the loss of freedom they feel pigeonholing produces, fear of the political label is greatly affected by context, as Chang suggests in this account of Talib Kweli. Musicians, even politically committed musicians, are least willing to be seen as political in times of low levels of movement activity. It's striking to compare the comments above with those of activist musicians from the 1930s and the 1960s who came to musical maturity in times of intense movement activity. "I am an activist and define myself as such," Peter Yarrow told Karroll; "even on an immigration or customs form I'll say performer/activist."[37] When we asked Odetta if she ever "felt tension between your artistic side and your political side," she appeared puzzled by the thought:

> Never. Never. It's a very interesting question—I never even thought of it. It is because I heard of folk music that I went off into [singing] as [something] that was addressing the human side, and therefore the political side, of the reality bar in this country. So I can't even separate them. There's *no* way for me to separate them.

Those most willing to define themselves as political artists in any era are those embedded in movement cultures, surrounded by a nurturing environment that values political activity. When asked when his interest in music and politics came together, Fred Ho, a longtime activist in avowedly revolutionary organizations, replies: "They've [always] been inextricable. I've been playing the saxophone as long as I've been in the revolutionary movement. There's no separation."[38] When we asked Sandy Rapp whether she thought of herself "first and foremost as a political performer or first and foremost as a performer—does the political always come with it now?" she replied: "Yeah, the political *always* comes with it."

We've been looking at the dangers and dilemmas political commitment presents to the artist and his art, which is how political commitment is usually approached in discussions of art. But this perspective overlooks a body of evidence that points in the opposite direction: Political commitment often spurs creativity, including art of the highest quality, from Picasso's *Guernica* to the poetry of Pablo Neruda. Artistic innovation is often most pronounced in periods of social and political upheaval or repression as artists are pushed to look beyond the conventions of their everyday lives—political, personal, and artistic—and imagine new possibilities. Movements provide a range of ingredients that foster creativity, including enormous inspiration, an eager audience, and themes of great significance.[39] Despite his later turn from political commitment, much of the music Bob Dylan will be remembered for was created in reaction to the social movements transforming the United States in the 1960s. "There's something about that direct connection between what you're singing and what's happening," Bruce Springsteen said when he began singing at political events. "It's no longer abstract."[40]

Inspiration and support are not only the products of a movement in general; movement organizations often play a positive role as well, encouraging the careers of musicians and diverting resources to support them. In some cases—Woody Guthrie is often cited as an example—political commitment provides a productive discipline the artist is otherwise lacking. Boots Riley argues that this was true as well of some of the classic funk and soul music of the 1960s and early 1970s: Previously more or less apolitical artists produced some of their finest music—including James Brown's "Say It Loud (I'm Black and I'm Proud)" and Marvin Gaye's "What's Going On"—when called upon or inspired to do so by political activists and organizations within a vibrant social movement.[41] Many of the politically minded rappers who were so influential in the growth of rap in the 1980s "emerged from vibrant protest movements," Chang tells us.[42]

These benefits are at the heart of Eyerman & Jamison's vision of the connection between music and social movements. Far from being necessarily detrimental to artistic creation, movements are "cultural laboratories" that "provide social space for musical experimentation which later diffuses into the larger society."[43] Writing of the interconnection of the folk revival and social movements of the 1960s, they argue:

> The Movement provided the folksinger with more than an audience; it provided content and a sense of mission over and above the commercial. In fact, it helped justify an anticommercial attitude and foster a sense of authenticity, as well as lifestyle, that motivated an interest in folk music as such.... What made the folk revival into a social movement that had lasting repercussions for the broader culture was more than music; it was the direct connection to political activities, the fact that folk music, for a few years, could serve as an important "medium" for communicating the multifaceted message of protest.[44]
>
> One could almost say, if it were not for the movement there would not have been a folk music revival in America in the early 1960s.[45]

Although even admirers of political music warn of the dangers of "excessive" concern with sending a political message—"a point where music becomes ideology and propaganda and ceases to be art,"[46] as Eyerman & Jamison write—the same may be said of any music on any topic that strongly expresses a point of view. Is Handel's *Messiah* a compromised and lesser piece of work because above all it aims to exalt God and Jesus? Are love songs created out of the strongest feelings of affection and attachment necessarily poor love songs?

"A bad song is a bad song, whether it's on the right side or the wrong side," Odetta told us. What makes a musical work "bad" can't be simply reduced to an "excessive" devotion to a political end. The "internal logic" of a piece of music that Andy Jamison speaks of, the result of the expectations and experiences of artist and audience alike, figures highly in our evaluation of the worth of a piece of music. When it violates our sense of its logic for any reason—political proselytizing, lack of a good rhyme, poor compositional skills, obsession with revenge against an ex-spouse—the resulting piece of music is likely to be seen as a failure by listeners. Political music making, like all passionate music making, is not inferior because it *necessarily* subordinates musical ends to political ends; it's inferior *when* its political passions subvert the impact of the piece rather than contributing to it.

Our discussion of the dilemmas of artist-organization relations has also been typical in another way: We've looked at them strictly from the viewpoint of the artist. When we've discussed these issues with our students over the years, we've found they invariably take the artist's perspective, worrying how manipulative activists might misuse the artist and distort her art. It's instructive to turn this around. Most people have great respect for struggles like the civil rights movement and what they have contributed to the country; what happens if we look at these issues from the perspective of the organizations that played such an important role in their successes? What did they need, what support and resources were they giving, what were they entitled to expect from members who were, among other things, musicians? We ask our students: If you were a core member of a movement organization, what would you want and expect from the musicians?

For example, many groups (though they don't usually realize it) practice some loose form of what Lenin (the Bolshevik, not the Beatle) called "democratic central-ism": There's an expectation that once an important decision is made by the group at large, members will support that decision or leave the group. Some groups have greater degrees of postdecision debate, some less, but virtually all have some point at which chronic dissenters are advised that perhaps it's time for them to move on. Should musicians have the same limits? As members, why should they be treated differently from other members? But, of course, this means some curtailment on their artistic freedom, or at least their ability to exercise it and remain members of the organization.

In theory at least, some musicians agree with this group perspective:

> PAUL BAKER HERNANDEZ: I think if you agree to work with an organization as a part of a team, you have a responsibility to the overall goal of the organization and the strategy and the way of achieving that goal.... My Salvadoran family of friends say, "God, we hate these artist guys because they demand they've got to express them-selves, no matter what. It's like someone farting, no matter that it's going to offend everybody in the room; you do it anyway because it's freedom of expression." Artists, they say, are like that.... This big self-expression thing, nothing must stand in its way. And I personally think that's completely wrong, I think the whole role of the artist ... has to do with being a channel. You're essentially linked to the community, because where does the music come from?

All art, Baker Hernandez is arguing, is created out of a community's social legacy bequeathed to its members, and thus there's a reciprocal obligation from the art-ist to the community. In some cases the debt is even more direct. What of artists whose artistic impulse and/or popular success are directly linked to a movement, as was the case with Bob Dylan in his early years? When Dylan appeared to be publicly turning his back on political folk music, many of his fans and supporters felt betrayed. Commentaries in *Sing Out* and *Broadside,* the two leading political folk magazines of the day, charged he had "lost contact with people.... You seem to be relating to a handful of cronies behind the scenes now—rather than the rest of us out front," and compared him unfavorably to Phil Ochs, who remained in the political fold: "Meaning vs. innocuousness, sincerity vs. utter disregard for the tastes of the audience, idealistic principle vs. self-conscious egotism."[47]

An even more extreme case is that of Cutumay Camones in El Salvador, whose career was largely created and maintained through the resources of their revolu-tionary organization, the Ejército Revolucionario del Pueblo (ERP). What claim does the organization have when precious resources have been used to support the musicians, ostensibly for the benefit of the organization as a whole? Here, party control was so great that when the struggle took its final, military turn, the band was dissolved and band members were directed to join the fighting forces although this was "a decision in which not all of the musicians concurred."[48]

Financial, ethical, political, and aesthetic dilemmas all come together in this basic fact of life: Musicians need resources from somewhere. Those who aren't supported by political organizations or reject the danger of control by a political organization take their chances in the open market, where necessary compromises and self-censorship may curtail their artistic freedom (though some few may find a niche market, like the DIY punk subculture of the 1980s or the women's music movement of the 1970s, where uncompromising expression builds a paying fan base). Those who operate within a movement organization's orbit may have some of their financial (as well as political, ethical, and social) needs met, but—understandably—the organizations often claim reciprocal obligations that may also threaten artistic freedom.

Spreading the Word: The Dilemmas of Communication

Whatever an artist's actual relations with a movement or its formal organizations, public identification often brings an expectation of responsibility for and to the movement. Some find this responsibility a burden they don't want. Perhaps most famously, Bob Dylan rejected his status as the voice of the 1960s movement. "I have no message—my songs are just me talking, that's all," he told Robin Denselow in early 1965. "And I don't want to influence people either—it's other people who influence me."[49] A relatively few artists are at the other end of the spectrum, at ease in this role. When we asked Sandy Rapp if she ever felt she'd like to lay down the responsibility as Dylan did, she instantly responded, "No, I'm comfortable with what I'm doing right now." But given the weight of the responsibility, even movement musicians tend to describe themselves in somewhat self-effacing ways:

Q: Do you sometimes feel you don't want the responsibility?
HOLLY NEAR: Yes, but probably no more so than a school teacher, a parent, a minister, a health food store buyer.

To the degree movement artists seek, embrace, or just accept a responsibility to use their art as a tool of communication about social and political matters, they face a series of questions about how best to do this. One aspect of this has already come up in the Suzanne Vega–versus–Charlie King debate over whether artists should pursue their individual vision or take account of the audience's likely reaction:

Q: It's important to you that people understand the songs as you mean them?
CHARLIE KING: Yes, on first hearing! ... When I mix in the studio, I always keep the vocal way up in front. Yeah, I don't want people to be confused.

Q: Is it important to you that people understand your meaning as you intended?
SANDY RAPP: Yes, absolutely.
Q: Some artists say, "Look, the important thing is that the audience make it whatever they want. I put it out there."
RAPP: Oh no, absolutely not. No, this is not an abstract painting. No. I'm very specific with words. I do want to create a definite impression. It goes back to what I was saying about art as communication—it's not something that's done in a vacuum.

King's and Rapp's insistence on clarity of communication between artist and audience places them in a long tradition of politically concerned songsters:

> UTAH PHILLIPS: [The Wobblies] had terrific song writers like Ralph Chaplin, Richard Brazier, Joe Hill, and T-Bone Slim. Their songs are very, very simple. I've often been criticized for singing them by left-wing people who say they are too simplistic. Well, the songs were to help people define their problems and to suggest what the solutions might be.... If the songs were going to communicate, they had to be simple.[50]

Writing in *Sassafras,* the newsletter of the People's Music Network for Songs of Freedom and Struggle, civil rights veteran Matt Jones advises other artists on the best way to create music that's useful for organizing:

> First, you must know the history of your Cause and the goals of your organization. Rewrite this information in poetry and rhyme and set it to music. Rewrite in universal language understood by the people you are trying to reach. Take quotes from this material and write choruses to songs. Be sure these quotes teach what you want taught. Make the music simple, in keys easy for the average person, preferably a five-note range for the melody.... Be sure to emphasize the most important words and ideas through repetition. Say it and then say it again.[51]

Jones is extremely blunt in this prescription, but his viewpoint is shared by many other political musicians. Even Hanns Eisler, who argued for a new proletarian music that broke with traditional forms, was concerned with such clarity: "Art no longer sets out to satisfy the people's hunger for beauty, but makes use of beauty to teach the individual, to make the ideas of the working class and the actual problems of the class struggle comprehensible and attainable." This proletarian teaching function that he envisioned his music serving required Eisler to write music to be above all else clear and unmistakable in its meaning, understandable to the most unsophisticated or uneducated worker.[52]

It would be a mistake, however, to think of this debate as involving two entirely separate camps of artists, each governed by only one way of working. The dilemma for most politically minded artists is how to connect to the audience while still expressing themselves in ways they find artistically valid. "My muse is not satisfied by setting speeches to music," writes one current labor movement musician on a listserve for similar artists. "What feels powerful and convincing to me is the process of expressing the nature and reality of an issue ... using melody, rhythm, allegory, imagery, symbolism, humor, pathos, etc. in a way that brings the subject to a place deep inside where people can be moved in fundamental ways."[53] Indeed, as this comment suggests, a song doesn't work politically if it fails aesthetically. On the most practical political level, artistic concerns must come first because the fundamental task is to get people to listen, to get people to care.

> BOOTS RILEY: When I used to listen to *Purple Rain* by Prince when I was a kid, I'd be like, "Wow, I want to do that!" ... You want to be involved in all of that stuff, even though it's just normal everyday life stuff that he's talking about. But somehow

it glamorizes everything—you know, songs about heartbreak glamorize heartbreak. People listen to those songs and want to be heartbroken almost, or remember the times when they were heartbroken. Same thing with songs about love.... I want my songs to do the same thing, I want my songs to make people feel like it's cool, like it's something they want to do, to change the world—that *that* is living, that's what it's all about. It's just like every song makes you feel—every good song makes you feel like, "This is living; this is what it's all about."

Music is often most powerful when it seems to illuminate our everyday lives in ways that make them shimmer and glow as something special, something beyond what we usually perceive. The dilemma for the movement artist, wherever she is on the continuum at a given moment, is how to preserve the transcendent qualities of the music while making them applicable and useful for a concrete political struggle.

Some artists and critics believe that art's power resides in evoking an idea or emotion rather than simply declaring it. Bruce Springsteen refers to the great impact of Flannery O'Connor on him as a writer: "a big, big revelation [because] she got to the heart of some part of meanness that she never spelled out, because if she spelled it out you wouldn't be getting it."[54] Similarly, Dar Williams told us,

Usually I'll write "A" and then I'll write "C" and I'll leave "B" out, and the people who have had a similar experience will understand what that "B" is, without my having to say what it is.... Some people said, "Look, what's that line—'I will not be afraid of women' [from her song "As Cool as I Am"]—coming from? There's nothing about being afraid of women in the song." But for people who've experienced those subtle attacks on their self-esteem because their partner has compared them to other people of the same sex, they go: "Oh, I know exactly what you're talking about." And that seems like a more valuable experience for them.

Much of the most powerful and important political work, Suzanne Vega argues, derives its strength from its open-ended nature, allowing members of the audience to think, reflect, interpret. Speaking of her admiration for Dylan as a political songwriter, she says:

He didn't explain everything away, he didn't cram it down anybody's throat. The mystery and the power is in the images and in the words that he used, and it's still there. And all of that stuff was taken by this political movement, and taken in this political context, and used in a way that was political. But if you actually look at the songs themselves, and you see the images—"I saw a white ladder all covered with water"—you know, what does that mean? What does that mean politically? How could a song like that be used politically? But it *was*, and it was used effectively.... He's not saying, "No more Vietnam." He's not saying, "Vote Democrat," he's not saying any of that. He's saying, "I saw guns and sharp swords in the hands of young children." And so, you have to see that there's power in the images themselves.

As the 1960s came to a close, music critic Greil Marcus declared:

> The old-fashioned protest song has been junked, relegated to the godforsaken past.... There are many ways to get something across, though, and if the artist has any respect for his audience, and any respect for his art, he'll not make it too clear what he means.... [T]he black and white politics of [protest songs] divide the world into two sides, right and wrong.... There is nothing to understand in message lyrics of this sort, lyrics that are afraid to admit to the element of uncertainty and unpredictability that gives art—music, painting, poetry—the tension that opens up the senses.[55]

For Marcus, the problem with the Beatles' song "Revolution" wasn't that it rejected militant street actions, but that "the Beatles were giving orders and setting up rules, singing words that were perfectly intelligible, making sure nobody missed anything, singing a song that neatly caught the listener in a logical trap."[56]

Many movement musicians would agree with this kind of thinking. The great British political songster Leon Rosselson argues that the aim of political songwriters shouldn't be to provide directions about what to do or think about a specific issue, but to provide "a challenge to the status quo more subtle and complex and subversive than can be offered by a slogan or assertion."[57] "[G]ood music works through its ability to converse, not to berate," as Street summarizes his approach.[58] Pete Seeger warns of the dangers of being "teachy, preachy all the time.... An editorial in rhyme is rarely a good song."[59] Although Holly Near has been seen by some as precisely that kind of "preachy" minstrel, she now says, "I do not try to tell people what they should do, not anymore. I try to be my full best self in concert or when I'm teaching and be an example in that moment."

Musicians who want to spread a message, particularly to audiences who are not committed to a movement, know that they have to find ways to integrate education and entertainment. "When an audience comes to hear me perform," Stevie Wonder, a pioneer of commercially successful, socially concerned pop music, told a *Rolling Stone* reporter,

> they know I'm not going to put them to sleep with my moral indignation, dig it? They know I'm going to do a show, which is why they came. So I give them their show; I entertain them, because I am an entertainer, regardless of what a lot of people think. I'm not a politician or a minister, but at the same time, I can ... ah ... *enlighten* them a little.[60]

This blending of entertainment and enlightenment is easier to accomplish in some times and places than in others. In the early years of women's music, a simple love song addressed from one woman to another delivered a political message of empowerment of lesbians without needing to stray from the lyrical and musical forms that listeners were already accustomed to from hearing thousands and thousands of (nominally) heterosexual love songs. In the environmental movement, some musicians have preferred songs that "just celebrated natural beauty, rather than warning about future loss."[61]

There was ongoing debate among the Almanacs about how best to convey their political messages. Some believed their approach should be to "Say the truth as simply as you can and repeat it as many times as it has to be repeated."[62] Guthrie, in contrast, "took a classic high-culture position, arguing ... [y]ou didn't have to slam people over the head; it was more artful and effective to show them than to *tell* them."[63] Thus beyond (or coupled with) the aesthetic preference of some artists for complexity and subtlety is a strategic belief: People simply will turn off to material that is "teachy" and "preachy."

> IAN MACKAYE: I'm really not interested in just talking about something like, "I think this is fair or unfair." Saying stuff like that is sort of a flat statement that doesn't serve any purpose in my mind. I do think that trying to talk about something in a way that brings or uses some really different kind of language to reinterpret an issue does address it, does do it justice.... I don't know, I just feel like a lot of it has already been said, and secondly, I think that if you're really, really, straightforward about stuff, it makes it very easy to dismiss it.

Intrinsic to the politics of many contemporary movements is a resistance to authority that may extend to resistance to being preached at. We see this in Marcus's reaction to the Beatles "giving orders"; MacKaye recalls a similar response to his writing of "Out of Step," the song credited with launching the straight-edge movement within punk:

> The other guys in the band—we got into a tremendous argument.... The lyrics were literally: "Don't drink, don't smoke, don't fuck. At least I can fucking think." And they wanted me to put the word *I* in front of the first three lines because they thought that people would assume that was a series of directions—you know, "don't do this, don't do that." ... Then we reissued it again on another record, and in that song, I actually say "this is not a set of rules," you know, "I'm not trying to tell people what to do."

When individual survival in the most fundamental material sense is linked to the group's struggle, music that states what must be done in the clearest terms may find a more receptive audience. In groups where economic survival and security are less the issue than freedom and self-expression, preaching and teaching are much more likely to be resented and rejected. The reason pop music has been so successful in spreading information like new slang, as Christenson & Roberts have written, is precisely because it isn't *trying* to teach anything;[64] unlike school, parents, or any authority, the music just appears to *be,* and so its messages aren't resisted as restraints on freedom. "More overtly 'political' bands ... are usually less popular than bands that avoid didacticism and find indirect ways to stage fundamental social contestations and alternatives," Walser notes of the metal scene.[65] While there are exceptions to this—Rage Against the Machine and some DIY bands come to mind—these tend to succeed to the extent that they distance themselves from conventional authority.

A preference for a certain ambiguity dovetails nicely with the belief of many critics and musicians that the best an oppositional artist can or should do is problematize existing social relations, disrupting our conventional understandings so we see that alternatives are possible without necessarily specifying what these alternatives might be.[66] "Rock's politics are—at best—profound but imprecise, moving but inarticulate," declares John Street, expressing a view that might be applied to other music as well. "If singers say exactly what they mean, the musical form will collapse beneath the weight of their words. The price of accepting the constraints of the musical form, however, is that the performers can never convey quite what they mean."[67]

These are powerful arguments but, like so much of the discussion of political music, are overstated as universal truths. Are disruption and ambiguity *always* superior—politically, aesthetically, even morally? The aesthetic and moral objections to "teachy, preachy" music may assume that audiences aren't as free and competent to judge (and then accept or reject) a message in music as they are to reject or accept an argument presented in other forms, such as a critic's article.

Politically minded musicians often *do* have specific points of view and messages they would like others to adopt, just as a critic has a point of view he wants to make clear (say, that music should be ambiguous). When that's the case, disguising the message or delivering it in ambiguous terms as if they're unsure seems less like an attempt to stimulate critical reflection in the listener than deceptive manipulation. Further, preferencing disruption and ambiguity may rest on an unexamined assumption: If audiences are provoked to rethink an issue, they will come to abandon their taken-for-granted perspectives and embrace (in their own time, on their own terms) the musician's own alternative. But, of course, there are often a variety of directions for attitude change, some of which may be quite unintended by the artist. Previously unquestioned faith in established authority, once destabilized, can lead toward cynicism rather than political activism. Populist anger, once evoked, can be right-wing as well as left-.

Ambiguous art is susceptible to being used in ways counter to the artist's intent. We've previously mentioned Ronald Reagan's public co-optation of Bruce Springsteen, reinterpreting the antiwar, antiestablishment theme of "Born in the USA" as a declaration of patriotism (without even understanding the irony of doing so), apparently based on the sound of the music and the lyrics in the chorus/hook line, "Born in the USA." The extreme vagueness of lyrics used by Thomas Mapfumo to slip by the censors in the Zimbabwean civil war allowed the white minority government and its allies to eventually portray his music as supporting *their* side of the struggle: "Helicopters flew low over the rural areas, blasting out pro-Muzorewa slogans mixed with Mapfumo's song about the oversized shoe, ... a disinformation campaign that confused many of Mapfumo's followers, who concluded that he must have sold out to Muzorewa and Smith."[68]

This isn't to say that only a direct approach "works," or that ambiguity and evocation have no place in artistic presentation for the movement artist. It's to point out that this is an inherent *dilemma,* necessarily confronted by any political artist. There isn't a universal right answer to this problem (which is why it's a dilemma). The minstrel who strums his lute once on every beat and sings

> The Emperor is a fool.
> He's been tricked by two hustlers

> Though he thinks he's wearing a beautiful suit they've made him,
> He's really naked.
> They're pretending to be tailors but they really aren't

is likely to elicit a clear understanding of his message—but at what artistic price? No one will even hear that message if turned off by the art that conveys it. But the minstrel who delivers that news in an unconventional musical form that surprises and challenges the listener and in cryptic, elliptical, or poetic language—

> The king of the jungle's so vain
> About his luxurious mane
> Yet what would he do
> if he only knew
> There's naught on his neck nor his brain?

—risks having audiences misinterpret or completely miss his point. When Randy Newman released the record "Short People," intended as a parody of racial and ethnic prejudice ("They got little cars that go beep, beep, beep, they got little voices goin' peep, peep, peep/Well, I don't want no Short People 'round here"[69]), he was astounded to find he was widely attacked for being "sizist."

Questions of style and approach are particularly pressing when an artist is interested in inspiring action as well as discontent with the status quo. One approach is to tell a story meant to show how things really are, to wake people up to unjust reality of their own or others' lives. Accurate description—"keeping it real"—is highly valued in this kind of composition, though for most artists this entails not merely capturing the way things appear on the surface, but some underlying reality. Brecht and Eisler's "epic theatre," for example, "does not reproduce conditions; rather it discovers them."[70]

A different approach is to *reframe* current reality, stressing the beauty and potential of lives that now seem ugly or hopeless. John Street compares Bruce Springsteen's "Factory," a dirge-like, depressingly "realistic" view of the working life ("End of the day, factory whistle cries/Men walk through these gates with death in their eyes/And you just better believe, boy/somebody's gonna get hurt tonight/It's the working, the working, just the working life"[71]), with the Crystals' "Uptown," a bouncy love song in which a character in a similar situation is still his woman's "everything" when he returns uptown at night ("And when I take his hand there's no man that can put him down/The world is sweet, it's at his feet, when he's uptown"[72]). "Factory" may appear at first glance to be a far more politically relevant song, but the "naïve uplift" of "Uptown," Street argues, serves political opposition better because the grinding realism of "Factory" offers no hope, and thus no encouragement, for change.[73]

Indeed, it's precisely in providing an alternative space to the oppressive present, Middleton argues, that music plays its most profound political role: "To all attempts at social control through appeals to 'reality' or 'reason,' music offers a counterview, a space where rebellion is possible; and that is what explains music's immense role in political contestation and in subcultures."[74] This vision shades into a third approach: negating the present. Punk's great power, for instance, "lay in its ability to disrupt rather than to transform dominant assumptions";[75] similar claims are often made for rap, and for various kinds of experimental or avant garde music. The question here is: to what end? Street notes that even in the hands of the most political of its practitioners, punk was "the noise of anger, not observation and explanation."[76] Even much of political folk music criticizes the existing state of the world rather than suggesting concrete alternatives (hence the aptness of the label "*protest* music").

A fourth tradition goes beyond opposing present conditions to envisioning a utopian future. From "Go Down Moses" to "We Shall Overcome" to "Imagine," such visions serve both as a reminder that the present is not eternal and as a beacon illuminating the road to travel. Here the tone tends to be literally or figuratively religious, a solemn faith in a better day to come, heard in their stately melodies and contemplative pacing, as well as in their lyrics. The emphasis is on generalized goals—peace, brotherhood and sisterhood, an eventual victory of some kind.

The most difficult approach for a musician to articulate successfully is not capturing, coloring, or negating the present, or envisioning the future, but articulating some concrete path that leads from the present to the future. Here, many of the problems of political music making collide: the dangers of preaching, the difficulty of making explicit declarative statements in an art form that has many components beyond the lyrical, the extremely short period (in most musical pieces) available in which to convey complex ideas, and so forth.

As Frith has written, it's a "question about ... how people come to believe, imaginatively, in *something more than resistance*."[77] Rejecting the present, valorizing uncertainty and "horizons of possibility"[78]—these are necessary steps for a social movement, but, in our view, they're not enough. At some point—through culture, political debate, daily experiences, and myriad other factors—some framework for an alternative must be articulated and adopted by a substantial part of the movement. This need not be a single political line, a Ten-Point Program; but some general agreement, moving beyond what the movement rejects to what it wants, is necessary to arrive at a future that is not only different but better. This is not, of course, necessarily the task of musicking, but it is one possibility.

Lieberman tells us that despite constant debate among the Almanac Singers and their several years of performance in the service of a movement, "the tension between expressing people's unarticulated needs and desires on the one hand and leading people to a more radical world view on the other was never resolved."[79] Danger lies on both sides. Expressions of resistance to existing life or of general utopian hopes for a distant future are more likely to meet with a welcome reception, but the result, as Eyerman & Jamison note of the 1960s, "turned out ... to be a consciousness that was extremely difficult to transform into effective political practice."[80] On the other hand, the attempt to chart a more explicit political course risks turning off many of the people a movement artist wants to address, who recognize their complaints when an artist airs them, but don't recognize the solutions being suggested as anything familiar to them in their daily lives.

In 1984, Little Steven (Steve Van Zandt) released one of the most unabashedly and relentlessly political albums ever released on a major label, *Voice of America*. In "I Am a Patriot," he offers a list of what he isn't—not a communist or a capitalist or an imperialist or a member of any conventional political party:

> And I ain't no democrat, and I ain't no republican either
> And I only know one party and its name is freedom[81]

Perhaps this is a healthy rejection of dogmatic labels, a skepticism about ideology and labeling well warranted by the many political betrayals of the twentieth century, the crimes committed in the name of ideologies. That skepticism fits comfortably within the traditions of rock (summarized by a raised middle finger), including a youthful resistance to moving beyond opposition to prescription—which sounds like the imposition of authority.

But movements require collective action and concrete goals, which implies some acceptance of a group will, while, as Street argues, musical forms like pop emphasize individualism.[82] As he also points out, however, some forms historically linked to communities with long traditions of struggle—reggae, soul—can more readily offer prescriptions for collective action without violating conventions of the genre. This strongly suggests that the barriers to doing so are not due simply to intrinsic limitations within music itself, as is often assumed, but are the result of historical practice and thus capable of change.

Delivering the Message: Are Some Forms of Music More Appropriate Than Others?

Are there, then, general rules for music that make for more or less appropriate ways to advance political purposes? Many movement musicians and theorists have argued (or assumed) that the best musical forms are those that allow lyrics to be most easily understood. Eyerman & Jamison, for example, argue that the political effectiveness of 1960s folk music was in part due to its "quiet sounds ... [which] encouraged a focus on text as a prime source of music."[83] Seeger told us Guthrie had "a tendency to flatten out melodies [because] he didn't want a beautiful soaring melody to detract from his words."

Others have argued that complete intelligibility of lyrics is less important than using the most popular genres of the time, whatever they are, to ensure that audiences *want* to listen to what's being offered. The Almanac Singers were criticized for their folk music approach by "left-wing songwriters who wrote in the more Tin Pan Alley commercial style, who said this was the only way you could reach a mass audience," according to Irwin Silber. Urban workers liked ethnic, pop, or show music that was already familiar to them; in Dunaway's memorable phrase, "If the Almanacs wanted to reach the people, maybe they should have played saxophones or zithers instead of guitars."[84] But the Almanacs felt presenting folk music—the authentic music of the working class, as they saw it—was in itself a political statement; trying to play in the style of the popular music of the day would have been reproducing and reinforcing pop, commercial culture.[85] On one of his solo travels across the country, Guthrie wrote back to the other Almanacs that as he traveled around, he was telling working people that the popular songs of the day

> are not your songs, but songs somebody else has put in your head, and for that matter why had you ought to sing like you're rich when you ain't rich, ... why had you ought to sing like you're satisfied when you ain't satisfied, or junk like you hear over the nickel machines or over radio?[86]

Still, as Woody's biographer, Joe Klein, notes, even during their triumphant 1941 CIO tour, "As often as not, the [workers] would want to hear popular songs and had no idea what this hillbilly music was all about."[87] In the 1930s, Left artists often debated whether they should be creating art that broke the boundaries of the bourgeois and commercial or working within the genres and styles most accessible to a mass audience. There are "two rival definitions of musical 'power,'" Simon Reynolds points out, "either purity of vision or extent of influence," and this mirrors the dilemma of approach that the Left (and other nonmainstream political groups) always face in all their communications with the uncommitted.[88]

Is accessibility the highest virtue? In April 1970, Phil Ochs astounded and dismayed his Carnegie Hall audience by appearing onstage in a gold lamé suit and playing what sounded like rock and roll instead of the protest folk music for which he was known. Amidst the boos and jeers, he explained his thinking to his audience: "If there is any hope for a revolution in America, it lies in getting Elvis Presley to become Che Guevara."[89] Adorno, of course, argued just the opposite: Accessibility was a form of brainwashing, while truly progressive music challenged the audience, making them active listeners. Henry Cowell, a pioneer of avant garde music in the United States, was quoted in the Daily Worker in November 1933 saying, "One of the great faults in the field of workers' music has been that of combining revolutionary lyrics with traditional music—music which can by no means be termed revolutionary."[90] Musicians who take this debate seriously are thus charged with not only creating music that provides a break with accepted forms—thus implicitly challenging the hegemony of all existing social arrangements—but doing so in ways that are not so foreign to audiences that they're rejected as indecipherable.

The choice of presentation is further complicated by the fact that, as we've seen, musical forms and styles themselves may convey viewpoints and thus send messages. Some genres are so tied to historical moments that their use always carries implicit allusions; musical conventions are so pervasive in most societies that listeners within a social grouping will generally agree on the mood or "feeling" a piece of instrumental music expresses,[91] whether it's tied to particular times or not. Asked to compare the Sex Pistols' cover of "My Way" with the more famous Frank Sinatra original, few listeners familiar with Western music would describe the two versions in similar emotional terms. Rock, Frith & McRobbie argue, uses all its instruments to produce a percussive sound that's heavy, hard and grinding. . . . One can see how, when rock 'n' roll first came in, this must have been a tremendous liberation from popular song's disembodied eroticism—here was a really physical music, and not just mealymouthed physical, but quite clear what it was about—cock. But rock confines sexuality to cock, and this is why, no matter how progressive the lyrics and even when performed by women, rock remains indelibly phallocentric music.[92]

Cheryl Kirk-Duggan's analysis of the civil rights song "Oh Freedom" illustrates how music can support a lyric, for example by "emphasizing key words through sustained notes" or "using a moderate but steady walking tempo with percussive hand clapping, which evoked determination and a sense of redemptive hope."[93] On the other hand, as we saw in the cases of the Rolling Stones' "Street Fighting Man" and the Beatles' "Revolution," music can subvert or contradict the lyrical message, in those cases sounding far more militant than the semantic meaning in the words. Charlie Gillet argues that despite their radical political beliefs and activities, "the sound of Peter, Paul and Mary . . . was soft and easy on the ear, unlikely to stir activity in the passive pop audience."[94] Guy Carawan told us: "You had to have a good song, a good melody, . . . a good style of doing it and the words blending. You can't separate anything out of this by one. You can't talk about just the words, you've got to talk about the style in which it's sung."

Different approaches may reflect differences in the kind of impact musicians— consciously or unconsciously—seek for their work. Street compares Leon Rosselson's approach of encouraging contemplation from his audience with that of Chris Dean of the Redskins, who aims to stir emotions: "The Redskins use rock because of its public power and for its ability to carry a slogan. . . . Where Rosselson looks to the politics of private doubt and argument, the Redskins look to the politics of public certainty and action."[95]

The choice of production style also constitutes an important part of the message. "There's a world of difference between [the sound of pop star] Mariah Carey and [alternative folk rocker] Kim Deal," says Suzanne Vega, "and it's a worldview." Punk deliberately sounds ragged, expressing its DIY ethic. Those from folk traditions deliberately shun the seamless production styles of the pop world. "Underground" rap deliberately sounds different from mainstream rap.

These last debates remind us that we are speaking of musicking, and not music; "not a thing at all but an activity, something people do," as Small says.[96] Casual conversations and academic treatments alike often fall into the trap of reducing all political questions to considerations of the product—the song, the symphony, the rehearsed performance. But many musicians, including many of those most movement oriented, stress the process as equally (or more) important, in particular for the kinds of benefits of participation we sketched out in the last chapter. In line with the ideas of theorists like Adorno—though probably few would recognize that name—they try to reduce or erase the artist-audience split; encouraging the audience to be active themselves is their prime political objective.

In contrast to their Marxist contemporary, Brecht and Eisler thought this could best be done through using musical forms accessible enough to be picked up quickly by those without musical training, and musical practices that encouraged collaboration, such as the practice of some left-wing conductors of rehearsing Eisler's music with the audience, turning spectators into members of the chorus.[97] Cutumay Camones, the Salvadoran revolutionary band, set their lyrics to dance forms so people "could dance while being infused with the lyrical message."[98]

Pete Seeger is probably the best-known exponent of this view in the United States:

> When I'm out there singing, I'm bouncing some songs off of myself, ... what I'm really trying to get is the crowd singing themselves.... Even singing a sentimental old song can actually be a very political thing if people are singing together. It might be "You Are My Sunshine." Because black and white people are singing that together, getting a little harmony together, it becomes a very important thing.... When it first came out I was rather contemptuous of it—one more attempt of the ruling class to give us nice, pretty songs and forget about problems we should face up to. Well, now I see that it's not just the words of the song, but the singing of the song, which is even more important.

Some artists and groups have experimented with forms that try to minimize the artist-audience split. The industrial band Consolidated has held band-audience "rap sessions" during concerts; the Walkabout Clearwater Coffeehouse in Katonah, New York, has a tradition of preconcert sings in which audience members (and often the scheduled professional performer) teach and learn songs for an hour before the formal concert begins. The Los Angeles band Quetzal has been replicating the Veracruz, Mexico, tradition of fandango in recent years:

> QUETZAL FLORES: On this *tarima*, which is a wood platform, there can be two, three, four couples at a time. Depending on the song, it's either a woman or two women or a man and a woman.... And there are musicians surrounding the platform, rows of musicians.... There's always dancers during songs, but there's a rotating pool of dancers, and the musicians all dance too. There's no separation between musicians and dancers.... And then surrounding the musicians is our community, sitting around, hanging out, kids running around playing. It's this cross-generational community experience, gathering, fiesta, party.
> Q: And when you do it in L.A., do you have the third ring?
> FLORES: The community? Absolutely. Absolutely. It's not fandango without the community.... One of the biggest mistakes that I think has happened with organizing in the past is trying to build a movement out of an activist base. And so what we're trying to do is create a community base. A true community base—that is, people who aren't versed in this or that (theoretical approach) but people who are having these everyday experiences, and finding profundity in these everyday experiences, and creating this reciprocity between community and art.

The Artist's Role and the Question of Authenticity

Often this participatory approach includes a conscious rejection of the conception of the artist as special, different from others in the movement:

BILLY BRAGG: I'm part of the movement. I don't see my job is to create it. I'm part of it.

PETER JENNER: We're doing a job—like you go and you teach in a university, other people go off and become plumbers—but as a singer/songwriter. That's his [Bragg's] job.... We're people doing a job, which has a political overtone.

Q: Did you feel a special role for yourself, or a sense of responsibility to use your gifts [as a musician]?
ODETTA: No. I thought I could add *to,* I thought what I was doing was relevant *to.*... But nothing more than that.

But though musicians may attempt to maintain themselves as rank-and-file members of a movement and a movement organization, invariably the more successful an artist becomes, the less able she is to be involved in any specific organization on an ongoing basis. Though this is sometimes the result of changes in self-image—I'm a star, I don't have time for the grunt work—it's also a reflection of the demands of the job itself, a dilemma voiced poignantly by Ani DiFranco:

It's just the exact circumstance of my life. I'm constantly moving. When I was sort of an actual human with an actual life, living in a place—when I was living back in New York before I started touring constantly, when I would just sort of tour long weekends—I was a member of a sister cities organization that would do solidarity work with repopulated communities in El Salvador. I would spend my days there.
I've been involved in various abortion rights and feminist organizations in the past but I don't live in a place anymore ... I live on a bus if I'm lucky, or in a van, in a plane, if I'm not. So it's almost impossible to retain friendships and personal relationships, let alone political affiliations.... I think that what makes me okay with that is the fact that this is the way that I can best contribute. I think my music is for me what I can be most helpful with, and maybe move people or inspire people.... But I very much miss living in a place and being able to act locally.[99]

Can someone who isn't faced with the realities of movement life express essential concerns of those in the struggle when she doesn't share their daily experience? When the musical emphasis in the civil rights/black liberation struggle moved from the grassroots, informal musicking of activists to the commercially produced hits of professional musicians, did the music become distanced and alienated from the reality of the movement, replaced by a commercially appealing simulation of the lifeblood that was found in the original music? In short, must movement music be created by active members of the movement to be authentic—and does authenticity matter?
In Argentina, the scene that grew up around *rock nacional* played a central role in the resistance and eventual revolt against the military dictatorship that ran the country from 1976 until 1983; still, as Vila tell us:

Since its inception, the rock movement in Argentina recognized a fundamental fear ... of being co-opted, exploited, or "turned over" by the system.... To *transar* is to enter into transactions within the system.... When the young detected attitudes they suspected of being *transa,* comments arose such as "they're making commercial music now," "they've sold out," "they're taking the easy way," etc. Incorruptibility was demanded of all members of the movement, but of its leaders in particular.... For a long time the utopia of the members would seem to have been to achieve the abolition of intermediations between the music and the [politically active] public, with the idea that the music and the public made up the movement. All the other things were considered invasions, and the invasions were the system.[100]

Artists themselves often recognize this dilemma, and claim no right to the title of movement leader or activist that others would give them. "I think that what I do is commentate on activism and that puts me as a fellow traveler of activists and certainly well on their side and even within their sphere of influence," Judy Small told Jaimee Karroll. "But I don't think that what I do is direct activism";[101] Pete Seeger told her, "I'm not nearly as much of an activist as a lot of people. People like Father Daniel Berrigan, they're really active. I've *sung* to activists a lot."[102] But since audiences typically place great value on "authenticity," however that's defined, musicians who want to speak to and for a particular group often feel that they need to appear to be at least *members* of that group. Ironically, the need to appear authentic may result in inauthenticity:

Guthrie was a self-made myth. To identify with the masses, he had to remain one of the people. His power to influence, he believed, depended on his credibility. In part, his credibility depended on his continued folky ways.... Guthrie is prized as painfully honest and frank, but there was always a part of him that was pure put-on. He passed himself off as a country bumpkin.[103]

[Billy] Bragg doesn't have to sing beautifully or play the guitar impeccably to make his point. He could if he wanted to, though; he is a good enough musician that his music is sometimes deliberately simplified, deliberately amateurish, to enhance his sincerity.[104]

All of these questions are even more complex when the artist is an outsider to the community at the heart of the struggle.[105] Authenticity is questioned, commitment is questioned, understanding of the struggle is questioned. Audiences may well ask: How does this outsider have the *right* to speak in the name of our struggle (and to derive personal gain from such speaking)? Artists may ask themselves the same question:

ANI DiFRANCO: I think the music has to be of the community. I don't think Sting deciding he's going to save the rainforest and doing some kind of benefit contributing his music to the awareness of [the issue]—I mean that's like a whole other thing. But if you're talking about a community trying to effect change, then the musical expression of that community—I don't think it can be added on by well-wishers who say, "Oh, well, I'll dedicate my musical expression to this now." Because I think the people who live there, the people who know, the people who live it, are the ones who need to tell the rest of the world about it.

Outsiders who are relatively ignorant of the reality of the community and the struggle sometimes display an unconscious sense of moral superiority and ethnocentricity;[106] alternatively, outsiders may display their ignorance by "a radical romanticization ... in the Noble Savage tradition" of communities they admire but don't fully understand.[107] And what of artists who take the indigenous art of a community and its struggles and transplant it into another setting—who has the right to the music produced by a community, particularly produced by a community's struggle? The long history of those with greater power appropriating the art of those with less power makes some critics wary of the "borrowing" that goes on between groups and musics. Rap's power, for example, lay to a great extent in what Zook calls its "in-house" dialogue among African Americans, a power she sees as inevitably diluted when whites began producing the music as well.[108] By definition, imported music is always inauthentic when first introduced to a group that did not create it.

Such borrowing and re-presentation, however, is endemic in musicking. Discussing the evolution of "We Shall Overcome," Seeger says, "You know, musicians are always stealing ideas from each other. Doesn't matter where that idea comes from—you've got a good song, a good melody, a good rhythm, you're going to use it. And what this song is now is a combination of a century or more of interaction between black and white people."[109] "We Shall Overcome" has now been used in struggles around the world. As the civil rights leader Julian Bond once said, "I wouldn't be surprised if when we colonize the moon that there'll be these little green people up there, joining their antenna together. And they'll be singing or chirping something, and it will be 'We Shall Overcome.'"[110] Does this dilute its use value or, conversely, strengthen it by linking each struggle to all those that have come before it, a part of the great chain of struggles for human freedom and dignity?

Despite the dangers of co-optation of a community's music, there's no denying that those not entirely "authentic" in background or involvement in a community have nonetheless made crucial contributions to many movements. Seeger and most of the Almanacs were not working-class in origin; Dylan had only marginal contact with the civil rights movement; Chuck D didn't grow up in an inner-city ghetto; and Ani DiFranco, as she says, can't sustain a presence in any ongoing struggle. Yet they, and many others, have created and/or popularized music that has been adopted by activists as "movement music." In part this speaks to the ability of artists to take on the viewpoints of others in a way that speaks convincingly of those concerns—"Strange Fruit" was written by someone who had never seen a lynching, let alone worried about being the victim of one, just as Stephen Crane wrote the war classic *The Red Badge of Courage* without ever having seen a battle. In equal part it speaks to the malleability of "authenticity," which, as David Grazian notes, "is not so much an objective quality that exists in time and space as it is a shared belief about the nature of the places and moments most valued in any given social context."[111] What matters most is the *use* of the music by audiences, not the circumstances of its creation.

Whatever an artist's background, whatever his claims to authenticity, hero worship can render the audience passive, substituting awe of an (inevitably flawed) hero for practical activity. The most conscious political artists actively fight this tendency, as when Bragg told us, "You have to reveal to the audience that you don't have all the answers." Given the emphasis on charisma and celebrity in popular culture in general, the question of how to make one's performance serve democratic empowerment while sustaining popular appeal is fundamental. Politically conscious popular performers have dealt with this dilemma in many diverse ways: For Guthrie, the answer was to avoid commercial opportunities and venues; for Seeger, it was encouraging the audience to actively engage in mass singing; for DiFranco, it is insisting on controlling the business aspects of her work; for DIY bands, it means distributing their work through small indie labels.

The goal for political musicians is to fuse the political and cultural in ways that are mutually enhancing. Musicking, we've argued throughout this book, has the potential to make political struggle pleasurable. The question, here, is how to use the forms of delivery that culture commonly uses in the society without simply falling into serving the entertainment functions culture commonly plays, since these typically have little to do with any kind of oppositional stance and much to do with taking our minds off the problems in our daily lives. If a musician believes, as we have argued, that musicking (whether commercial or noncommercial) has both diversionary *and* mobilizing potential, the dilemma is how to encourage the latter without simultaneously negating it by encouraging the former.

Some musicians[112] assert this isn't a dilemma—recall Ani DiFranco's comment that people who worried about music diverting energy from political activity "probably have to take something large out of their ass." Chuck D told us, "I don't worry about that because music is first and foremost entertainment, and it's to enjoy. What we're adding to it is almost like an annex to whatever we do. If we're able to make people think and also add some inspiration, after they party and have a good time, I think it's a bonus."

But most (including D and DiFranco in other comments) are certainly aware of these dangers:

Q: Many people think popular music, as part of the multinational entertainment industry, is part of the problem.
TOM MORELLO: Absolutely. And frankly, when they write the history of our time, I think that's not going to be perceived as an accident. It's a crucial part of rolling the wet blanket over us.[113]

Consolidated reflects the dilemma in their song "Brutal Equation":

Being a commodity is weak, but it might be our last chance to speak
Try to get a simple point across, but too often the message is lost[114]

As Boots Riley pointed out to us, however, this is a greater problem than simply how music is used:

Q: Do you ever worry that the music diverts people from politics? That they think, "Okay, I'm listening to the Coup, that's all I have to do"?
RILEY: Yeah, I mean, I think that people do that with books also, right? I think that in this culture, anything we can do [to keep] from actually getting out there

and organizing around changing the living conditions, people are prone to do. Same way you have people that will sit around and argue whether Lenin disagreed with Marx on this or that or not, and won't organize—they'll think *that's* organizing. The same way, they think, "Okay, I'm going to support Rage Against the Machine or the Coup" and think that they're political. And what that tells you is that there is a lack of a real movement out there.

Living with the Dilemmas

While we agree with Adorno that music *may* serve a diversionary function, we stress that its actual use and effect are more complex. The same experience of musicking may encourage one person to action and rebellion and another to passivity and accommodation, or encourage the same person to rebellion at one moment and accommodation at another; complex creatures that we are, it may even encourage a person to both stances in the same listening. The lyrical content may ease our accommodation to our daily lives while the music unsettles us and makes us think of alternatives to what is. The words may cry of revolution while the way the music is distributed may hook musician and consumer alike into systems of consumer logic that overwhelm any kind of revolutionary drive within the piece itself. Given this complexity, how can a politically concerned musician make intelligent decisions about how to resolve such dilemmas?

Dilemmas don't have simple and universal answers. As Billy Bragg said to us, the contradictions are part of the situation: "You have to be a bit hearty about them, just kind of kick them through." Ironically, when we attempt to gauge the impact political musicians have had on political struggles in different times and places, it's clear that neither explicit desire to aid a movement nor intense contemplation of the kinds of dilemmas we've described here guarantees impact. There are just too many variables involved, most of which are far beyond the control of the individual musician.

It may well be that the piece of music that did the most to spread the message of black pride was James Brown's "Say It Loud (I'm Black and I'm Proud)," the work of an artist who, while familiar with and interested in racial issues, self-identified as a professional popular musician rather than as a movement musician. Yet through the percolation of freedom songs from movement participants to the greater culture, the growing dissemination of news about black consciousness through media accounts, riots and demonstrations erupting in the streets of cities outside the South, and their own direct experiences with racism, black youth in particular were more than ready to embrace that message. Obviously it wasn't that previously uninterested individuals received instant enlightenment upon hearing the song. Instead, as Dar Williams characterizes the process, it "hit the nail that's ready to be hit."

This implies an important point: Rather than argue about whether there are intrinsically superior forms of political art, we need to recognize that different musics and different approaches are more and less useful in different times and different stages of a movement, as well as to different individuals with their variety of relations to a movement (activist, participant, potential participant, opponent, etc.). Responding to Jesse Lemisch's criticism of modern-day folkies, Ernie Lieberman (who sang in the same circles as Seeger and Guthrie) protested: "[H]e ignores the history that links the distinct styles of Aretha Franklin, Steve Van Zandt and Pete Seeger. They are not in conflict. They reach different audiences, and the more effective they all are, the better for all of us.... Quality and appropriateness vary in every art form."[115]

Fifteen years after declaring that progressive political comment was impossible in rock, Leon Rosselson wrote:

> Surely no one now subscribes to [the] view that British folk music was the true culture of the working class in Britain, and that anyone who did not write in that idiom must be a renegade.... In the end we might all agree that advocating only one form of music is self-defeating. A socialist music needs to be diverse and wide-ranging, and also life enhancing, imaginative, passionate and maybe a little fun.[116]

This isn't to say that all musics are equally effective at any time and in any situation. Different approaches are like "different pitches in a baseball game," Chuck D told us: "fast ball, slider, curve, and a screwball." Just as a good pitcher knows when to throw which pitch, the task for the movement musician is to determine which answers to the various dilemmas make sense at a given moment, "a sense of appropriateness of one song [or approach] over another for the occasion," in Irwin Silber's words.

Some artists give a great deal of thought to these questions, while some give very little. The most thoughtful understand that the political value of a particular approach depends in large part on the "reach" they are trying to achieve, the appropriateness of a particular approach to a particular task and audience:

> PAUL BAKER HERNANDEZ: You try to find out about your audience: age range, political interest, etc., you know, general feel for it. And obviously input from the person organizing is really important. And then you shape, you select among your repertoire to hopefully make the best experience for that particular group.

Understanding your audience helps the artist to understand not only what will work, but what will not.[117] Since meaning is a collaboration between artist and audience (as well as the variety of other environmental factors we've discussed), artists who seek to advance a political view need to understand what meanings audience members are *likely* to draw from the artist's package. Steward & Garratt, for example, describe an ambitious attempt in political communication that apparently fails to make the band's point because the musicians don't understand how their show will be interpreted by its likely audience:

> [T]he agit-punk group, Carass, with their strident pacifist views, are even more extreme: wearing all-black, militaristic and menacing stage-clothes, they claim to be working with the contradictions of such an image, using it to attract the very audience they wish to influence. But their lyrics are inaudible live, and the lasting impression is one of violence and masculinity.[118]

Different audiences, we've said, imply different tasks. The kind of reaffirmation and spirit maintenance that are required on a picket line is served well by simple, well-known melodies expressing closed-ended certainties in simple words that everyone knows or can easily learn, the music lending itself to universal participation. The more individualistic, complex songwriting that evolved in the late 1960s (spurred, ironically, by social movements) and continues in many genres today is less appropriate to that task, but may be a valued emotional experience for tired activists seeking renewal late at night.

To the extent artists are reaching out to more mainstream audiences, their presentation needs to be oriented to efforts to inspire people to suspend apathy, distrust, or dislike, and open up enough to consider the musician's and movement's message. Blowing on the sparks of a barely lit fire requires a different approach than keeping a bonfire blazing.

Summing Up

Movements are messy matters, evolving, regressing, growing, and contracting, and far more heterogeneous in makeup and vision than they're commonly supposed (or typically present themselves) to be. As they struggle to provide music that fits these highly volatile circumstances, artists aren't likely to have a definite idea of what the result of their music making will be. "A song is just a song," Seeger once wrote. "But who knows what future souls will be strengthened by these songs?"[119] The topical folk music the Almanacs and their successors produced in the 1940s and 1950s nourished activist and organizer identity in the 1940s and 1950s, but was largely unsuccessful in attracting more than a small (if highly devoted) core of followers in its time. Yet a generation later, their work served as an inspiration and model for a music that swept the nation and became an integral part of some of the largest mass movements in U.S. history. The mainstream success of womanist (if not feminist) pop music in the 1990s was built on the pioneering efforts of lesbians and other feminists 20 years earlier. "It's not always something that happens right away—the 'Big Bang!'" Bruce Springsteen pointed out to an interviewer.[120]

Billy Bragg once wrote that his own musical heroes "didn't change the world, but they did change my perception of the world."[121] Changing perceptions and definitions, however, is necessary for changing the world, crucial to the basic task of overcoming Olson's paradox. The framing of the situation—making movement work seem necessary, viable, and *personally* rewarding—is not sufficient for determining the success of the movement, but it is one necessary ingredient. The power of musicking is often quite profound in this sense, helping to create, sustain, and circulate a general ethos that encourages, supports, and even mandates movement activity. Many factors may go into this ethos—emotions, moral beliefs, a search for purpose, rational calculations, a desire to be cool—a web of messages and meanings that together support commitment to a movement. As a bearer of tradition and coded signification, musicking preserves a group's history and recalls it to mind, organizing it, anchoring it, and reconstructing it in ways that serve the present.

As a cultural form, musicking presents an avenue for reaching some who might otherwise shun or distrust any kind of communication concerned with political or social issues. As a public declaration, it gives currency to subterranean ideas and feelings, spreading them simply by voicing and sharing them, and thus giving them a collective legitimacy through acknowledgment and celebration. As a movement activity, it serves as a collective ritual of commitment, while its portability allows it to remain part of movement members' everyday lives, reinforcing commitment even in the absence of movement peers or movement activities.

Culture in general, and musicking in particular, are crucial in making the *process* of movement activity meaningful and attractive. Of course, the eventual goal of gaining the political, social, and economic changes the movement seeks is a key motivation for action, but such goals are, in fact, "eventual." The process itself must provide payoffs of various kinds or people withdraw long before goals can be reached. Feelings of solidarity, unity, moral certainty, and historical significance are *themselves* benefits of the movement, and these feelings result from both experience and the cultural framing of that experience. Crucially, musicking brings the joy of culture—the exultation, the intoxication, the utter delight in creation—to the serious business of politics; it makes movement life more exciting, more fun.

In this sense, culture is not a luxury of a movement, but an essential component. "It is our ability to inspire that will make the difference," says longtime labor activist Joe Uehlein.[122] It may be the combination of the force of the music and the poetry of the lyrics that provides inspiration, or the activity of collectively engaging in performance; often inspiration is as derived from the persona of the musician as are her words or music, the "guerilla minstrel" serving as "the superglue that bonds the music and the protests to the culture skin" of the diverse individuals making up the movement,[123] inspiring others to themselves become active, in making music and in making change. (And in those groundbreaking moments in the development of a music and/or a movement, the opposite is true as well: The activity of everyday people may serve as inspiration and a model for the musicians.)

In all these ways and more, musicking provides ways of engendering and maintaining commitment, not only in the public moment of performance but in the many private moments of each individual's life, a piece of the movement that lives on and reminds a person that he is a part of something larger than his daily life. From singing "We Shall Overcome" with a quarter million other people in front of the Lincoln Memorial to humming it softly to ourselves, music helps carve out a free space in which a different way of life can be imagined. Central to this envisioning is a personal reconstruction as well, embracing an alternative identity in which movement participation and the values underlying that commitment are seen as integral to who we think we are. Music, with its accompaniments of style, attitude, and a general worldview, is a powerful first glimpse of alternative identities, and later a crucial marker that declares the new identity. By making that identity more visible to ourselves and others, it changes our perception and theirs, from the very fact that such identities exist to what it is they might mean socially and politically. Besieged by influences on all sides, music and musicking help to crystallize our identities, encouraging some directions and discouraging others.

At its height, a movement seems to speak to and for more than just its members or its constituency. At its height, the civil rights movement seemed to embody the dream of universal freedom and the essence of morality. At its height, the anti–Vietnam War movement seemed to speak for an end to the war, but also for an end to an entire way of life that people found violent and dehumanizing. At its height, the antiapartheid movement seemed to represent not only the struggle against apartheid in South Africa but also freedom of all oppressed peoples everywhere.

In these moments, culture, including music, often becomes the symbol of this universality, the expression of the noblest aspirations of the movement. Holly Near describes the first night of the 1976 Women on Wheels tour, a pivotal moment in the public eruption of the feminist and lesbian movements on the West Coast:

> We stood in the wings in Sonoma. More than one thousand women ... filled the hall with a vibrancy I had never felt before. ...: We were welcoming in a new era and it seemed that women's culture would never be the same again. . . . . We walked on stage. The place exploded. I thought for a moment, *My God, we are the Beatles of the women's movement!* Only when we began to play did the screaming subside so that they could hear the words. But they were too excited, and when a particularly beautiful phrase or harmony flowed out from us, they leaped to their feet again as if to grab it.[124]

In the heat of political battle, spirituals become "freedom songs," reggae becomes "Rastafarian music," rock becomes "movement music." One veteran of the communist movement in the years around World War II, now long retired from political work and quite cynical about it all, still wrote us:

> Music, all that I have heard, has in its own way led me to the belief that the emotions evoked by those songs in those tormented days and nights of wartime were immature and self-indulgent, and are ultimately fully justified, and fully elevating, when we are moved to respond to the sadness of the world with care and sacrifice.

The power of music, we've argued, rests not only on its strength in each of several dimensions, but on the way musicking melds together several at once, the way it joins head and heart and body, the way it can serve various functions simultaneously. But in arguing for music's power, we've also cautioned against exaggerating its effects, treating musical pieces and performances as "the independent and sole cause of these thoughts and acts. They depend ... on the institutional and ideological context in which they operate,"[125] as Street has written. Music itself cannot change the world—but then again, *no* form of struggle can change the world by itself. "Good singing won't do, good praying won't do, good preaching won't do," Lee Hays told an interviewer at the height of the Almanac Singers in 1941, "but if you get all of them together with a little organizing behind [them], you get a way of life and a way to do it."[126]

Musicking is most powerful when it's linked to a vibrant movement, riding that flow of energy and change as well as helping to create it. "I don't see music activism as being anything but part of the whole activist movement," says singer/songwriter Judy Small, "and without the doings the music isn't going to do a thing. But then again, without the music I think the doings would be a whole lot harder."[127] Even the ability to engage in "new knowledge production" and "diffuse" that knowledge to the wider society, which Eyerman & Jamison see as the greatest contribution of movement culture, is much more likely when the movement is successful enough to gain or create organizational and institutional spaces where such new ideas can be tried out, and where they may actually work.

Such "success," certainly, is affected by the kinds of structural and political arrangements that political opportunity theorists use to explain movement outcomes; cultural and technological trends in the greater society will play a role as well. Within these conditions, however, a politically minded artist makes—or doesn't make—strategic decisions. Given the manifold complexities, it's understandable that many artists figuratively throw up their hands and think, "I'm just going to make the art that seems right to me and hope it's helpful." And yet, we've argued, received meaning and political impact are not totally random; the input of the artist, although not determinative, is a powerful factor in the ways music may be received and used. Since they are only one part of a complex interaction, artists who would be contributors to a movement can't rely simply on artistic inclinations alone, but also on a sense of what's needed by the movement and the situation at a given time. Earlier we cited C. T. Vivian's point that it was only because civil rights songsters transformed songs from their African American past and fit them to the needs of "the new situation"[128] that they assumed the importance they did. The musicians of Cutumay Camones very consciously tailored each of their four albums to the immediate situation of the Salvadoran revolutionary movement, moving from songs describing the failure of nonviolent resistance and the alternative of armed struggle on their first album to songs offering practical instructions about armed insurrection—for example, how to shoot down a helicopter—on their last.[129]

These practical and political needs may certainly conflict with a musician's personal vision and predilections. Most movements, for example, badly need musicians to show up on a local level, yet many political musicians, like many nonpolitical performers, want to see themselves on a grander scale—Joan Baez at the March on Washington or Rage Against the Machine at the 2000 Democratic Convention—than playing on the United Food and Commercial Workers picket line in Bakersfield. A movement may need musicians to do the difficult work of education and recruitment of neutral or antagonistic audiences, while the musician may prefer the security of singing for the converted. And most poignant are situations in which artists come to feel at odds with the imperatives of a particular organization or faction, feeling torn between following their vision of the truth and their organization's vision of the necessary.

This isn't to say that only one specific musical or artistic response is appropriate in a given situation, or that artists should make art totally foreign to their own skills and vision in an attempt to be relevant. But some types of art, at any given time, may be more or less valuable to a movement, and an artist can best understand what these might be by studying her audience, thinking about the context in which its struggle is going on, and knowing something about the lessons of past movement musicians. Adept analysis doesn't guarantee political impact, of course.

This book has been filled with examples of artists who desired nothing more than to aid a movement, and yet were largely unsuccessful, and others merely following their muse (affected as it was by current events, of course) whose music took on enormous importance to a movement. Purposive musicking increases the odds of impact, but remains one of many factors in the mix.

The Role of the Movement

Finally, a word about how movements treat music and those who make it.

> HOLLY NEAR: Some [political groups] honor their singers as life savers. Others always ask the singers to come for free, don't bother to tune the piano, forget to get a sound system, offer no food, no place to rest. . . . I have been part of movement events where "the singer" is simply the one who sings during the fund pitch. I have been part of movements where the march didn't go forward until the singers and drummers arrived.

As we suggested in Chapter 11, there's a wide variation in the importance activists accord to musicking across the range of movements. Consider two drastically different examples: Although political bands (in particular Cutumay Camones) are said by Almeida & Urbizagastegui to have played "a critical role" in El Salvador's civil war, most were disbanded as the war moved into its all-out military stage in 1988 by the insurgent parties who felt "military exigencies came to outweigh . . . cultural needs."[130] In contrast, the striking mine workers of Buchans, Newfoundland, whom Narvaez has depicted were so impressed with the effect of their musicking that they diverted a part of their precious resources to create a songbook of the strike songs they were using, an endeavor strongly advocated by strike leaders.

Movement-music connections may happen spontaneously, but the political payoff is generally greater when activists in movement organizations plan how music (and other cultural forms) can best aid the movement. Looking at the women's movement in Montreal, Staggenborg & Lang argue that the political fervor cultural events help create tends to dissipate if there is no direct link to movement organizations:

> [C]ultural activities may generate solidarity and collective identity, but cultural participants do not necessarily take part in contentious political action. . . . [T]he strategies of movement organizations help to determine whether cultural events and activities serve as a conduit to contentious political activism. . . . Cultural production activity can support political activism when it is closely aligned with organizations that explicitly target the state or other institutions for political change.[131]

This alignment, in their analysis, is in large part the result of the overlapping of networks between cultural and political organizers. The point for us here is that forging these kinds of links, framing musicking in a political context and political work in a cultural context, is something activists can *decide* to do. It's a deliberate strategy of wedding them together rather than a relationship that just occurs. And as in any marriage, success requires effort on both sides. Looking back on their work in the civil rights and Appalachian mining community movements, Guy and Candie Carawan concluded:

> There is a tendency to underestimate the importance of cultural work, to feel that music and poetry, dance and humor, will naturally be a part of community life and attempts to challenge oppression or inequality. In our experience, that is not the case. The seeds for cultural expression are there, but cultivating and nurturing those seeds are also necessary. Not only is it important for individuals to seek out and encourage the richness of cultural expression; there also have to be organizations and institutions that recognize and support this work.[132]

For both activists and musicians, there is a balance to be found. Art needs room to breathe; tight control of music and musickers by political organizations is clearly counterproductive, robbing the musicking of many of the very qualities that make it so powerful. But a policy of laissez faire is also counterproductive, leaving musicians without support and musicking without the links to political practice that can concretize its effects. Music of solidarity, resistance, and even struggle will certainly be created "organically," but its power and use can be amplified by a movement that esteems culture as important and something to be nurtured. The radical tradition of music making that union organizers found in the South in the 1930s and 1940s was nurtured through institutions on the Left, such as the Highlander Center and the Commonwealth Labor College, that were consciously created to support alternative culture. In the North, however, it was never accorded the same respect, a result of different historical traditions, certainly, but also of the indifference, reluctance, or unwillingness of radical organizations to pay much attention to cultural work.

"No one can pick a song and make it an anthem of a movement," Joe Glazer warns,[133] but neither do songs become anthems purely due to their intrinsic qualities. The piece of music, the musician, the tradition, the historical context, and chance all come together; so, too, is there an important role played by the decisions movements and movement activists make or don't make about the importance of nurturing culture.

It's often said that an organizer has done her work best when she can walk away and the work she's begun continues. The same is true of a movement musician: She's most successful when her message—delivered musically, lyrically, through persona, performance, and the shared process of singing, in all these ways or in other ways—lives on for individual audience members, who, in their own ways, become performers, too. To succeed, movements need empowered actors, not audience members; participants must believe in their own sense of agency. Movements that soar on the wings of music are those in which audience members become collaborators in performance in some way. Whether we're speaking of people creating songs together on a picket line, or listening to a CD late at night, music's impact has to do with the degree to which the music—through its constituent parts—helps them to regard themselves as people who can change the world.

BRUCE SPRINGSTEEN: At your best, your most honest, your least glitzy, you shared a common history, and you attempted both to ask questions and answer them in concert with your audience. In concert. The word "concert"—people working together—that's the idea.[134]

At the height of the mass movements of the late 1960s, folk musician Artie Traum wrote in the liner notes to an album, "We are all, all of us, alienated and afraid of this monstrous, billowing junk heap; music thrives on our energy, draws our hope, purges and soothes us. It is our life, but not our solution. A small part, maybe."[135] How small or large a role music plays—from entertainment between the speeches to lifeblood of the movement—is, we've argued, the result of an extremely complex equation involving a vast array of factors over which activists and artists have only a small amount of control. But within that narrow window, the commitment to culture as an important weapon of struggle, and the work done to encourage and frame cultural forms, make a significant difference. What we decide to do matters.

Notes

Notes for Chapter 1

1. Klein 1980:199–205. Original emphasis.
2. Cited in Reuss 1971:16.
3. Dunaway 1981:87.
4. Reuss 1971:293. The FBI, however, saw the Almanacs as highly effective: One operative report of the time said, "After going through the song once, the majority of the audience joined in the singing.... They joined not from their own desire, but were led into it by mass psychology and apathy toward the utter control of the meeting by Communist officers and members" (Dunaway 1981:87–88). Pete Seeger's FBI file begins at this point.
5. Huck 1972; Gleason 1972.
6. Reynolds 1990 466.
7. Ross 1994:105.
8. Reed 1990·54 Havel does goes on to say, however, "But it can contribute to that significantly in being a part of the awakening of the human spirit."
9. For example, Eyerman & Jamison have written that "singers and songs were central to the cognitive praxis of these social movements [of the 1960s], indeed, they may be central to all social movements in their formative states" (1995:451); Ramet goes further: "[O]ne may go so far as to say that without music, there cannot be a revolution" (Ramet 1994b:1).
10. Harrington 1997:F6.
11. Quoted in Powledge 1991:343–344.
12. Quoted by Seeger in Stanton-Rich 1996:14.
13. Smith 1969:37.
14. For examples, see Moseley 1989; Silber 1973. Broadsides were also a staple of pre-Independence political life; see Dunaway 1987b:273.
15. See Flacks 1988 for a more detailed development of these propositions.
16. Olson 1965.
17. For works that do engage these questions, see McAdam, Tarrow & Tilly 2001; Klandermans 1997; Larana, Johnston & Gusfield 1994.

18. Snow et al. 1997.

19. For example, see Friedman & McAdam 1992.

20. Buechler 1997:297, characterizing the work of Castells (1983).

21. For polar examples, see Hanslick 1974:67, 70, 82, 97, and McClary 1991:20–21.

22. For example: Shepherd 1991; McClary 1991; Jones 1963; Gillett 1970.

23. Miller & Skipper 1972; Zook 1992; Ramet 1994a; Dunaway 1987b.

24. Kofsky 1970:57.

25. Eyerman & Jamison 1998:1.

26. In Esslin 1969:143.

27. For instance, Hamm reports that "the channeling of dissent and anger through the white power rock of Skrewdriver appears to raise *or* reflect a political consciousness that precipitates the long-standing subcultural style of racial violence among skinheads" [our emphasis] (1993:117); Perris comments, "The Beatles (and other popular artists) told [rebellious young people] how to view the contemporary world. Or was it the other way around? No matter" (1985:184). In other accounts the potential distinction between cause and effect is acknowledged but dismissed as not useful or meaningful (e.g., Street 1997:4; Shepherd has argued that studying movements to better understand the music *or* studying the music of movements to better understand the movement misses the degree to which the music is an inseparable *part* of the movement [and vice versa] [1991:219]).

28. People's Music Network for Songs of Freedom and Struggle Web [n.d.].

29. McClary 1991.

30. For example, see Springsteen in Percy 1998:42; Frith 1988b:466.

31. Denisoff 1983:27.

32. See in particular Jim Brown's 1989 film, *We Shall Overcome*.

33. This was not, of course, the first time folksingers had attained commercial popularity, from the Hutchinson Family in the 1800s through the political folksingers championed by Alan Lomax in the 1940s and 1950s. But it was the first time that the folksinger as a type and folk music as a genre achieved such massive attention in the commercial market.

34. Cruz 1999.

35. The Lomaxes recorded some artists in other genres as well, notably Jelly Roll Morton, a seminal figure in the creation of jazz.

36. Adorno 1950:311, cited in Denisoff 1983:201.

37. Adorno 1990:312.

38. Adorno 1990:312. Here Adorno slyly refers to "Sing Me a Song of Social Significance," the most famous song of the late 1930s hit musical *Pins and Needles*, produced by the International Ladies' Garment Workers Union to great acclaim by most leftists as well as tremendous commercial success.

39. See, for example, Nye 1988; Witkin 2000; and in Adorno's defense on some of these charges, Paddison 1982; Hamilton 1991.

40. Mills 1963.

41. See, for example, Benjamin 1999.

42. Benjamin 1973.

43. For example, Postman 1985. For a variety of perspectives from that time, see the complete volume Rosenberg & White 1957.

44. Riesman 1990:6, 9–10.

45. Becker 1963. Becker's jazz musicians, however, largely resented and regretted the "square" audience's effect on their art, complaining that musicians had to cater to mass tastes that didn't accommodate their creative impulses.

46. Riesman 1990:7–8.

47. Pratt 1990:210; Edsforth 1991:4; Fiske 1989.

48. For an excellent and seminal example, see Hall 1980.
49. Hebdige 1979:105; Hebdige borrowed the term from the work of Umberto Eco
50. Hebdige 1979.
51. Thornton 1995.
52. Negus 1996:19.
53. For a very useful review of many of these studies, see the first chapter ("Audiences") in Negus 1996.
54. Street 1986:59–60.
55. Hall 1981:235.
56. Fiske 1989; Middleton 1985; Frith 1981; Grossberg 1990.
57. Flacks 1988.
58. Garofalo 1992:19.
59. Small 1998.
60. Street 1997:43.
61. Stanton 1996:2.
62. From "Stones in My Passway" (public domain), written and performed by Robert Johnson on *King of the Delta Blues Singers* (Columbia 1961).
63. © 1959 (renewed) Folkways Music. Lead Belly wrote "Bourgeois Blues" in 1938, and recorded it several times. One version can be found on the reissue *Leadbelly: Bourgeois Blues—Golden Classics, Part 1* (Collectibles 1989).
64. Quoted in Denselow 1989:87.
65. Fiske 1989:172.
66. Frith 1996:20.
67. For example, Grossberg argues that rock's popularity is "linked to its oppositional (or in some sense political) status" (1985:452). The problem here is that its logic implies that those who don't oppose the hegemony get no pleasure from popular culture, a claim very difficult to support.
68. Lipsitz 1994:328, 327.
69. Rose 1994:61.
70. Frith 1988a:115, citing Garon 1996.
71. For example: Walser 1993:55; Rose 1994:24; McClary 1991a:29. Much of this school is obviously in debt to Foucault's work in this area. See, for example, McClary 1991a:29.
72. Frith 1996:20.
73. Of course there are many exceptions, including Street 1986; Frith 1990; Small 1998; and Negus 1995.
74. Perhaps, as some have argued, writers—who deal with words as their medium—simply can't talk about music as easily as they can talk about lyrics. For example, see Frith 1988a:105–128; Walser 1993:40.
75. This is often the case even among analysts who demonstrate a theoretical understanding of the many layers of meaning beyond lyrics (for examples, see Almeida & Urbizagastegui 1999; Kurti 1994; Wolfe & Haefner 1996:136–145; Warren 1972; Bradby 1990). For an example of an analyst who has consistently looked at *musical* (as opposed to lyrical) meaning in popular music, see the work of Philip Tagg (Tagg 1982; Tagg & Clarida 2003).
76. For an informative discussion of "why it is problematic to take fans as ordinary consumers, as models for popular cultural 'resistance,'" see Frith 1996:9.
77. In Karroll 1996:139.
78. Some SMS theorists have posited another way of evaluating success. For Eyerman & Jamison, for example, the actual fate of a movement in terms of traditional movement goals—changes in laws, representation, rights, etc.—is often less important than the ways in which the culture created by a movement becomes absorbed as part of the mainstream culture. If, for instance, an avowed feminist

revolution has not occurred, no institutional changes have been achieved, but the basic belief that women and men should have equal life chances has been generally accepted by the population, success has occurred, they would argue (e.g., Eyerman & Jamison 1991:46–48). We agree that these changes are highly significant, even essential for political struggles, but we don't agree such "cognitive" changes are meaningful unless they *eventually* lead to material, institutional changes as well. Indeed, we don't see how they could not if people's ideas are truly changing, nor how people's ideas could significantly change or be sustained without prior or simultaneous material changes supporting those views. (It appears to us that Eyerman & Jamison actually often hold this view as well. Although they sometimes argue that the production of knowledge is the key contribution of a movement, they inevitably suggest that such movement culture serves as a repository of tradition that fuels the next upsurge of movement activity in later years. It's that time lag that allows them to say that knowledge generation is itself the key thing movements do, but their evidence of this is the material change that comes later.) Nor is it only conscious ideas and ideologies that may be affected, of course. Change may be cognitive—I think differently about an issue, or I begin thinking of it *as* an issue—but it may also be emotional: I *feel* deeply about this issue, I feel *personally* about this issue.

79. For example, Horton 1957; Robinson & Hirsch 1972; Allen 1972; Gleason 1972.

80. Peterson & Berger 1972. For updates see Burnett 1993; Alexander 1996; Basu 1997; Street 1997.

81. Van Elderen 1989.

82. For example, Peterson 1972; Martin & Segrave 1988; Cloonan & Garofalo 2003.

83. For example, Gans 1969; Robinson & Hirsch 1972; Hamm 1993.

84. Denisoff 1983; Robinson & Hirsch 1972.

85. Punks: Hebdige 1979; Laing 1985. Skinheads: Hamm 1993; Moore 1993. Black ghetto dwellers: Rose 1994. Marginalized women: Robertson 1987; Petersen 1987.

86. There are exceptions, of course, including Riesman 1990; Frith & McRobbie 1990; Tsitsos 1999; Crafts et al. 1993, Finnegan 1989.

87. There could even be one more stage here, a composer hunched over a table, writing music that she then gives to the minstrel. We've combined composer and minstrel into one person, both because that's generally how minstrels have operated and to simplify the illustration.

88. Lipsitz 1993:xvi.

89. The difference in response rates might be due to several different factors. The tradition of using music is considerably stronger among leftist groups (although, as we discuss in subsequent chapters, in recent years right skinheads may present the most successful use of music by a movement); our own experiences are on the Left, and perhaps we were better able to direct our query to productive audiences in terms of yield; right-wingers who *did* have a music link may nonetheless have been less likely to respond for any number of reasons.

90. Dunaway 1987a:51.

91. For illuminating discussions of these problems, see Rose 1991a; McClary & Walser 1990; Brennan 1994.

92. Street 1997:147.

93. Shepherd 1991:116.

94. For example, see McClary & Walser 1990:279.

95. Quoted in Howard & Lyons 1957:115.

96. McClary & Walser 1990:288.

97. Brennan 1994:676.

98. McClary & Walser 1990:287.

99. Walser 1993:30.

100. McClary 1991a:26.

101. Lemisch 1986b:703.

Notes for Chapter 2

1. Small 1998, especially pp. 39–40.
2. Words and music by John Lennon & Paul McCartney, © Northern Songs 1968. As heard on *The Beatles* (Apple 1968).
3. Lyrics by David Byrne, music by Tina Weymouth, Chris Frantz, and David Byrne, © 1977 Index Music Inc., Bleu Disque Music Co. Inc. As heard on *Talking Heads: 77* (Sire 1977).
4. McClary 1991a:21.
5. McClary 1991a:4.
6. Keil 1994.
7. Small 1998:3.
8 Words and music by Otis Redding, © 1965 and 1967 by East/Memphis Music Corporation, Time Music Company, Inc., and Redwal Music Publishing Company, Inc. As heard on Franklin's *I Never Loved a Man the Way I Love You* (Atlantic 1967). Lyrics to Aretha Franklin's version come from our own listening and two websites: searchlyrics3.homestead.com/aretha_respect.html, and vivarin.pc.cc.cmu.edu/cgi-bin/lyr songs?f/Franklin.aretha/respect.gz.
9. Wexler & Ritz 1993:213.
10. These characterizations of responses to "Respect" are based mainly on years of discussing the song with students in our classes and others at talks we've given. But critics, by and large, have approached the song in the same way. For example, John Street writes: "Franklin's 'Respect' combined a gospel voice and a rhythm 'n' blues accompaniment to demand equality as a woman and a black person. The equality before God of gospel becomes equality in the home and, in the context of the civil rights campaign of the late sixties, equality at the ballot box" (1986:217).
11. Reported in Denselow 1989:230.
12. Frith 1996:164. For a recent article that claims support for the hypothesis that listening to "degrading sexual lyrics is related to advances in a range of sexual activities among adolescents, whereas this does not seem to be true of other sexual lyrics," see Martino et al. 2006. Causality, however, remains very murky in their formulation; see, e.g., Siegel 2006.
13. Ward et al. 1999:29.
14. Gleason 1972:137.
15. Huck 1972:171.
16. Gleason 1972:138.
17. Gleason 1972:142.
18. For a thorough review of many of these studies, see Christenson & Roberts 1998:153–179.
19. Rosenthal 1986a:9–10; Robinson & Hirsch 1972; Denisoff 1983:37–8; Denisoff & Levine 1972; Rosenbaum & Prinsky 1987:84–85; Leming 1987:375. The immense popularity of musics that cross language lines—North Americans listening to Brazilian bossa novas in Portuguese, Albanians listening to U.S. pop, world music in general—further suggests that semantic meaning is far from essential for enjoying music, or even finding it "meaningful." See Roberts, Christenson & Gentile 2003 for similar findings regarding "violent music."
20. Robinson & Hirsch 1972:231
21. Stipe 2001:G7.
22 Adorno 1990:312.
23. Walser 1993:26. Once this has been established, Walser integrates lyrics as well, one of the few examples of skillfully uniting lyrical and musical analysis.
24. For instance, in reviews randomly selected from recent issues of *Rolling Stone,* descriptions of music took up 22% of column lines, compared to 41% devoted to lyrics (biography and other topics took up the remaining 37%).

25. See, for example Verden, Dunleavy & Powers 1989:76. Christenson & Roberts's (1998) chapter on "Fragmented Rock" provides a good overview.

26. Nor is this limited to genres one might expect, such as folk or rap. Duany has argued that the lyrical narratives told in salsa, a genre traditionally seen as dance music, are the most meaningful elements to listeners (1984). See also Roberts, Christenson & Gentile 2003.

27. Frith 1996:242.

28. By John Prine, © 1971 (Renewed) Walden Music, Inc., and Sour Grapes Music. As heard on Bonnie Raitt's *Streetlights* (Warner Brothers 1974).

29. See Frith's discussion of Northrop Frye's comparison of the two dimensions in a poet's choice of words (1996:180).

30. Keil & Feld 1994:26.

31. Christenson & Roberts 1998:111.

32. See, for example, Qureshi 2000.829.

33. Light 1992:31.

34. McClary & Walser 1990:289.

35. Mann 1985.1–1, quoted in Mei 1998:3

36. *Music Journal* 1958, quoted in Martin & Segrave 1988:53.

37. Citron 1994:16.

38. Meyer 1956.

39. Kivy 1989:187.

40. "[Music without lyrics] manifestly cannot … give us beliefs, if it is melancholy music, that will make us melancholy and objects for our melancholy to take" (1989:157). In *Sound Sentiment* (1989:217–218), however, Kivy retreats somewhat from his position as outlined originally in *The Corded Shell*.

41. See, for example, Marcus 1972:136.

42. Castellini 1962:90

43. McClary & Walser 1990:283.

44. Meyer 1956:260.

45. Walser 1993:52.

46. Moseley 1989:71. But this is not, of course, an inevitable or "natural" connection: In the "mass song" championed by Davidenko and others in the Soviet Union of the 1920s and 1930s, all voices sang the same part, "because any superfluous polyphonic effects would detract from the desired effect on unity" (Edmunds 2000:72).

47. Willis 1990:54.

48. Frith & McRobbie 1990:374.

49. Skyvorecky 1979:3–4, quoted in Perris 1985:55–56.

50. Skyvorecky 1979:3–4, quoted in Perris 1985:56.

51. For example: "[D]istortion functions as a sign of extreme power and intense expression by overflowing its channels and materializing the exceptional effort that produces it" (Walser 1993:42).

52. Garofalo 1987:90.

53. Middleton 1985:35.

54. Street 1986:220.

55. St. Lawrence & Joyner 1991; reported in Christenson & Roberts 1998:217–218. This doesn't mean that lyrics may not *also* be a factor; see, e.g., Anderson, Carnagey & Eubanks 2003:960. But note that such perceived effects of either music or lyrics are only found in the short term in most studies.

56. Words and music by Mick Jagger and Keith Richards, © 1968 Abkco Music. As heard on the Rolling Stones' *Beggar's Banquet* (London 1968).

57. "Revolution" (© Northern Songs 1968. As heard on *The Beatles* [Apple 1968]).

58. Marcus 1972:130–131.

59. Ramet, Zamascikov & Bird 1994:207.

60. Quoted in Small 1998:102. For an extensive look into why audiences show similarities in their assessments of what a piece of music is "about," see Tagg & Clarida 2003.

61. Tramo 2001:54. Meyer, though he stressed social explanations of musical meaning, declared that all cultures privilege the octave, and most the fourth and fifth (a finding ethnomusicologists would not endorse today), thus suggesting some natural and universal aspects of music reception (1956:231).

62. Gray et al. 2001:54.

63. For instance, Gray et al., positing a universal music, note that "whales mix percussive or noisy elements in their songs with relatively pure tones, and do so in a ratio similar to that used by humans in *Western symphonic music*"; humpbacks "use musical intervals between their notes that are similar to or the same as the intervals in *our* scales.... Some birds pitch their songs to the same scale as *Western* music, one possible reason for *human* attraction to these sounds" (2001:52, our emphases).

64. Frith 1996:102.

65. Meyer 1956:259–260.

66. Qureshi 2000:815.

67. Ibid.

68. Meyer 1956:260. Wagner, however, apparently refused to reveal his system of representation to others.

69. Taffet 1997. This isn't to say that *only* traditional forms have been used by oppositional artists; witness, for example, the widespread use of what Reebee Garofalo calls "indigenized forms of rock and rap" (2009).

70. Gleason 1972:138.

71. Eyerman & Jamison 1998:75–76.

72. Eyerman & Jamison 1998:141. We were reminded of this when attending a concert given by the popular pop-punk band Blink 182 during their 2001 tour. As the curtain rose, accompanied by the portentous "2001" theme, the band was framed by a backdrop of a single word spelled out in flames. The word was *FUCK*. The crowd was very pleased, many responding with the bull's horn sign, a gesture that means "rock on, dude."

73. From the album *Okie from Muskogee* (Capitol 1969). Beginning in the mid-1970s, however, the country music terrain became increasingly contested, as "outlaw" performers like Willie Nelson asserted a countercultural perspective. These days even Merle Haggard is writing antiwar songs.

74. Light 1992:29. For a similar analysis, see Spencer 1992:446.

75. Walser 1993:55.

76. See, for example, Wicke 1992; Ramet 1994a. Rock continues to play this role in noncapitalist countries such as Cuba, where "rebellious young people have taken up hard rock as a form of opposition to the practices of established revolutionary institutions" (Tumas-Serna 1995:119).

77. Eisler 1999:75; quoted in Rozendal 1997:12. Original punctuation.

78 Quoted in Betz 1995:397.

79. Miller & Skipper 1972:32–33.

80. Ballantine 1984:125–126. Original emphasis.

81. Frith 1988a:121, 120.

82. Perris 1985:193. See also Van Deburg 1992:207.

83. Barthes 1990.

84. Though note that even in so-called classical music, which stresses composition, a major reason for the turn from classical to romantic music was to better express the composer's "true" inner feelings.

85. Frith 1992a.147. Of course, performance style is not the only way authenticity is displayed or claimed. Being from the neib, recording for an indie label, and refusing to license one's music for advertising use are others. David Samuels argues that for some rappers, "Antiwhite ... [and anti-Semitic] rhymes are a shorthand way of defining one's opposition to the mainstream.... Anti-Semitic slurs and black criminality correspond to 'authenticity' and 'authenticity' sells records" (1995:249).

86. Neither we nor Marcus can trace the original forum in which he said this (which is why we haven't quoted him directly here); as he emailed us, "It echoes something I've said at different times in different places but I can't fix where or when" (Marcus 2005).

87. "He Got Game," words and music by Carleton Ridenhour, LuQuantum Leap, and Stephen Stills, © 1998 Def Jam Music/Chrysalis Music/Cotillion Music/Ten East Music/Springalo Toones/ Richie Furay Music. As heard on Public Enemy, *He Got Game* (Def Jam 1998).

88. Cantwell 1996.

89. Rose 1991a; 1994.

90. Marcus 2000:1. Original emphasis.

91. Quoted in Denselow 1989:125.

92. Groce & Lynxwiler 1994.

93. For instance, in the days leading up to the fall of the Communist Party in the German Democratic Republic in autumn of 1989, hundreds of East German bands began their performances by reading a "declaration of concern" they had signed, criticizing the direction of the country, precipitating "an unprecedented degree of solidarity between performers and audiences" (Wicke 1992:90).

94. See, for example, Flacks 1995.

95. In some cases, the opposite is true as well: The live, shared experience is molded to replicate the recorded version as closely as possible, as when bands play their hits as faithfully to the recorded version as possible. But while this is exactly what some audience members come to see, for others it lacks the novelty and rawness—thus the "authenticity"—that they desire from a live performance.

96. Klein 1980:214.

97. Taffet 1997:95.

98. For fan testimony to this effect, see Vickstrom 1998, especially pp. 28–45.

99. Hampton 1986:201

100. McDonald 1993:6, commenting on the work of Shumway (1991).

101. For example, see McClary 1991b; Fiske 1989; Young 1991. For a critique of such views, see Harris 1992.

102. Christenson & Roberts 1998:217.

103. See Christenson & Roberts 1998:210–218 for a summary of these. There are methodological shortcomings for most of these surveys—the laboratory form, for one—as well as some conclusions drawn with which we might differ based on the data presented.

104. Videos had appeared earlier in other parts of the world, and even from time to time in the United States, but never as the kind of mandatory major-label marketing tool they became with the advent of MTV.

105. Hebdige 1988:237. Original emphasis. Hebdige, of course, was not one who worried about these changes, but welcomed them.

106. Young 1991:63. Young himself is actually a critic of postmodernism.

107. Christenson & Roberts 1998:70 MTV seems to have come to the same conclusion, as each year it provides fewer hours of video programming and more hours of conventional (if hip-appearing) "shows."

108. Goodwin 1992.

109. McClary 1991b:161.

110. Christenson & Roberts 1998:71.

Notes for Chapter 3

1. The melding of folk and commercial has an enormously long history. Negus reminds us that the creation of political broadsides—which appeared almost as soon as the printing press was invented in the mid-1400s—virtually immediately became a *commercial* venture, with the broadside writer seeking to sell his product (1996:71–73); Pratt has noted that "[m]uch of what has passed for folk music in North America is nothing more than the popular music of the past imported from the British Isles two centuries or more before" (1990:101; see González 1991 for a similar point made about "folk" in a South American setting).

2. But this is not universal, as is sometimes assumed within the industrialized countries. As Negus notes, a number of studies have shown that "while the recorded popular song is hegemonic ... it seems likely that there are vast numbers of people on this planet who ... are hearing musical sounds that have very little to do with the 'twentieth-century popular record'" (1996:54).

3 For more detailed studies see Chapple & Garofalo 1977; Negus 1996, 1999; Sanjek 1996.

4. Music & Copyright 2005:1.

5. Mooney 1972.

6. Peterson & Berger 1972.

7. More recent studies with a similar perspective include Basu 1997; Street 1997.

8. See, for example, Burnett 1993; Gottlieb 1991.

9. Some analysts don't agree, however, as we would expect from the ongoing debates regarding other industries (e g., Straw 1990). Important methodological questions are involved as well; see, for example, Alexander's (1996) critique of Peterson & Berger and their response (1996; also Peterson 1994).

10. Street 1986:102.

11. Basu 1997, citing Lewisohn 1988; Negus 1996:50.

12. Burnett 1993; Lopes 1992.

13. Street 1986:122. Kusek & Leonhard quote Clear Channel CEO Lowry Mays: "We're not in the business of providing well-researched music. We're simply in the business of selling our customers products" (2005·27).

14. Negus 1996:96. A decade later Kusek & Leonhard pointed out that it was "astonishing" that Wal-Mart was by then selling about "20 percent of all music sold in the U.S ... given that the music selection at most Wal-Mart stores is usually less than 750 titles deep" (2005:87).

15. Kusek & Leonhard 2005·87.

16. PBS [n.d.] A similar dynamic goes on in video production. As one source in the trade explained, "The reaction of [music video] channels is taken into account from the get-go in certain areas. For example, we can't show crime without retribution in a treatment. So, when we get a script which does, we'll immediately ask for a re-write. On the other hand though, if we don't know for sure that they won't accept something ... we'll usually just go ahead and shoot it and see what happens. We're forced to cater to them, but we'll only edit ourselves when we know we absolutely have to.... Although it is very rare, I have seen the channels request both artistic and content changes.... I've never seen political content removed, but then again, I haven't seen too much political content " (Linehan 2005).

17. DiCola 2006:Executive Summary 2.

18. DiCola 2006:1.

19 Quoted in Garofalo 2006:3. DiCola similarly reports that "just fifteen formats make up 76% of commercial programming.... Playlists for commonly owned stations in the same format can overlap up to 97%" (2006:Executive Summary 2). But note estimates below that over 100,000 albums are released per year, further strengthening the point.

20. Kusek & Leonhard 109.

21. Thus, despite the huge consolidation of radio station ownership just discussed, individual stations within these corporate families still aim at niche demographics.

22. Frith 1996:131, quoting Echols 1994:92.

23. Samuels, for example, argues that, "by 1988, the conscious manipulation of racial stereotypes had become rap's leading edge" (1995:247). The flip side of this is the neglect of the music of other groups. As Ma'anit has noted of World Music, "[T]he growing consumer demand for the 'authentic' musics of the South drives the industry to target certain arts to the exclusion of those which don't fit into romanticized notions of 'primitive,' 'tribal,' and 'ethnic' music" (2003:11).

24. King 1998:56.

25. In large part this is because major label contracts count all investments in artists as advances against royalties. For an acidic, passionate, and instructive look at this, see Courtney Love's declaration of independence from the recording industry (2000). Janis Ian writes, "[I]n 37 years as a recording artist, I've created 25+ albums for major labels, and I've *never once* received a royalty check that didn't show I owed *them* money" (Ian 2002; original emphases).

26. Grant 1994, citing Charters 1970.

27. Craddock-Willis 1989:35.

28. Promoter Chris Blackwell, for instance, helped propel reggae to international status by incorporating rock conventions while emphasizing the Rastafarian "as a universal symbol of rebellion and protest" (King 1998:46).

29. Wallis & Malm 1984. See in particular Chapter 9.

30. Lewis 1983:138.

31. Halker 1991:200.

32. George 1988.

33. Lipsitz 1993:xi.

34. Lipsitz 1992.

35. See, for example, Veal 2000, especially pages 11–12, 57–66, 84–90, 258.

36. Lipsitz 1994:326.

37. Gottesman 1977:64, citing data from Shaw 1964:33.

38. Disagreement about the effects of commercialization has been particularly pronounced in accounts of the development of a transnational music market, seen by some as "cultural imperialism" but by others as "transculturation," in which local music is both affected by and potentially affects the music of economically dominant countries; the result is closer to mutually enriching cultural exchange than musical imperialism (Garofalo 1992; Wallis & Malm 1990:170–180). But clearly these exchanges can't be thought of as simply equal exchanges, since the economic dominance of the multinational corporations producing the music is so profound; see Negus 1996:174–178.

39. Negus 1996.

40. For more on this theme see Shepherd 1991.

41. For a fine illustration of this see Negus's comments on the history of radio (1996:Chapter 3).

42. Schoenherr 2002.

43. Peterson 1972:241.

44. Roscigno & Danaher 2001, 2004.

45. Hamilton 1991.

46. Goodwin 1992.

47. Street 1986:120.

48. Kealy 1990:212, citing Gelatt 1965:299–300.

49. Frith 1988a:129.

50. Taylor 2001, cited in Katz 2004:159.

51. For more in-depth analyses along these lines, see Fisher 2004; Kusek & Leonhard 2004; Joyce 2009; Sandulli & Martin-Barbero 2007.

52. See, e.g., Slater & McGuire 2005. Further development of audience networking may be expected across different platforms. See, for instance, Deserto 2009.

53. Kusek & Leonhard 2005:147, 101.

54. eMarketer 2006, cited in Kinnally et al. 2008:910.

55. Kelly [n.d.]: 3,7; Joyce 2009; Sandulli & Martin-Barbero 2007; Ian 2002.

56. Hiatt & Serpick 2007; Smith 2007:E3.

57. Kusek & Leonhard 2005:6–7.

58. Smith 2007:E-3.

59. Kusek & Leonhard 2005:81. But for a tentative rejection of this argument see Walters 2008:15–16.

60. Kusek & Leonhard 2005:7, 87.

61. Walters 2008:24.

62. "Digital singles represent a massive chunk of total sales—increasing 65% between 2005 and 2006, and 45% between 2006 and 2007. Digital singles made up almost 62% of all units sold in 2007" (Walters 2008:24)

63. Kusek & Leonhard 2005:42.

64. Actual figures don't show a single trend. Clearly, it makes a difference whether the health of CD sales is gauged by number of units sold or by revenue or profits (Walters 2008). For examples of widely conflicting figures, see Smith 2007; Sandulli & Martin-Barbero 2007:64; Indie Music Stop 2009; GartnerG2 & Berkman Center 2003:18–19.

65. Joyce 2009:111.

66. Estimates of how much of the decline in sales revenue can be attributed to file sharing range from 0–30%. See Liebowitz 2003; Katz 2004.180; Oberholzer & Strumpf 2007; Pollock 2006; Anderson & Frenz 2008.

67. Joyce 2009; Ian 2002; Katz 2004:169; Kusek & Leonhard 2005:94; Anderson & Frenz 2008.

68. Katz 2004:169.

69. Ian 2002. Estimates of the number of new CDs that enter the market vary widely; Nielson SoundScan, the most knowledgeable source, tells us there were 105,575 CD releases in the United States alone in 2008 (Schwartz 2009).

70. Ian 2002.

71. Friedlander & Miller 2006:260.

72. GartnerG2 & Berkman Center 2003:17.

73. Katz 2004:161–162, citing reports by *Jupiter Research.*

74 Sandulli & Martin-Barbero 2007:68.

75. Kusek & Leonhard 2005:101.

76. Techradar 2008.

77. Kusek & Leonhard 2005:91 But note that by the time Quiring, von Walter & Atterer were writing in 2008 the official tally was over a billion downloads (2008:436).

78. Kusek & Leonhard 2005:128.

79. Quiring, von Walter & Atterer 2008.

80. Kusek & Leonhard 2005. See chapter 7 in particular. In Fisher's model (2004:Chapter 6), payment is instead through a government agency from revenue raised by taxes on ISPs.

81. Joyce 2009:112.

82. Kusek & Leonhard 2005:31.

83. See, for example, Wortham 2008; Richards 2008; Ayers 2006:4.

84. Cook 2007.

85. Pitchfork, for example, estimates it's visited by 20 million unique (i.e., different) people a month (Kaskie 2009).

86. See, for example, Dhar & Chang's study that found sales were three times as great for major label albums once they reached a threshold of 40 legitimate blog posts compared to those who failed to reach that threshold, and albums of all labels had sales 600% higher once they reached a threshold of 250 posts. They note, however, that more traditional sources, like reviews in *Rolling Stone*, are still important to sales (2007).

87. Kot 2005.

88. For differing views on whether greater availability leads listeners to wider choices, see Kusek & Leonhard 2005:67; Katz 2004:167; Ipsos-Insight 2002. Certainly both trends may happen simultaneously, with some (or most) listeners staying within their comfort zone while the more adventurous have a far wider musical palate to explore.

89. See Kun's (2009) story of how the home recording of an unknown, unsigned band—Los Pikadientes de Caborca—started circulating among friends as a ring tone, and spread so successfully that radio stations in Sonora, Mexico, began playing it regularly. Before long, "cellphone videos of people dancing to the song were flooding YouTube," the band was signed to Sony, and their 2008 album was nominated for a Grammy.

90. McEnerney 2009.

91. Kusek & Leonhard 2005:144, 170. Original emphasis.

92. Kusek & Leonhard 2005:69, 70.

93. Interviewed in the film *Money for Nothing* (Jhally 2001).

94. McEnerney 2009.

95. For discussions of Internet activism and its dangers see, for example, Kahn & Kellner 2004; Nah, Veenstra & Shah 2006; Ayers & McCaughey 2003; Trippi 2004; Biddix & Park 2008; Shapiro 2009.

96. For example, despite widespread reports of the imminent death of terrestrial radio, given historic lows in listenership, "listeners still devote approximately half of their listening time [to all forms of music] to traditional radio" (Walters 2008:32, citing McQuivey, Daily & Lawson 2008). DiCola observes that "approximately 94 percent of Americans listen to radio each week. Compare that to the 42 percent of U.S. households that had high-speed internet access as of March 2006" (2006:2).

97. Street 1986:99, 101.

98. Negus 1996:178.

99. Ramet 1994a; Wicke 1992.

100. Gitlin 1987:197. Original emphasis.

101. Riesman 1990:10.

102. For survey data supporting the notion of different levels of interest and knowledge among members of audiences often treated as homogenous (e.g., "the rock audience"), see Fox & Williams 1974; Robinson & Hirsch 1972; Verden, Dunleavy & Powers 1989.

103. Small 1998:191.

104. Denselow 1989:134–137.

105. Frith 1987:124.

106. Grant 1994:130.

107. Jones 1963.

108. Street 1986:217.

Notes for Chapter 4

1. Exceptions include Meyer 1956 and Riesman 1990. Much of the work of Walter Benjamin was focused on this very issue, and the culturalists of later generations often acknowledge their debt

to him. More recent works in this vein include Gans 1969; Street 1986; Grossberg 1985; Negus 1995, 1996; and Wolfe & Haefner 1996. Mass communication research has been both more mindful of the importance of audience reception and more grounded in actual audience-based research. See, e.g., Allor 1988; Jensen 1987; MacGregor & Morrison 1995; Morley 1980, 1993.

2. DeNora 1995:299. Original emphasis.

3. Negus 1996:192. For examples of this perspective see Hall 1980, 1981; Middleton 1981, 1985; Grossberg 1983–1984, 1993.

4. Frith 1996:203.

5. Christenson & Roberts 1998:154.

6. For examples, see Reid 1993; Gantz et al. 1978; Ramet 1994a; Fox & Williams 1974, Robinson & Hirsch 1972.

7. Gans 1969. For a more recent summary of the varying involvement with music by different social groups, see Roberts, Christenson & Gentile 2003.

8. Christenson & Roberts 1998:171.

9. Denisoff 1983:110. The account quoted is "Strike ends on note of high," *Berkeley Barb,* December 9, 1966, p. 11.

10. By John Lennon & Paul McCartney, © Northern Songs 1966. As heard on The Beatles, *Yellow Submarine* (Apple 1969).

11. Rossman 1967.

12. See, for example, Young 1991:60–66; Hebdige 1988:211; Hebdige 1990:59.

13. Christenson & Roberts 1998:179. For extensive work making the same point about music without lyrics, see Tagg & Clarida 2003.

14. See Hall 1980. Surely this comes as no surprise to anyone who has thought about advertising in the media. Negus appropriately asks, "if audiences are so active and create their own 'oppositional' messages and meanings without giving in to any 'preferred' ideas, why do entertainment corporations spend so much money on promotion, marketing, and advertising?" (1996:35). Meyer's classic account sketched a middle position: Music (by which he meant "classical music") conveys general complexes that are indeed connotative, but these are then "particularized in the experience of the individual listener" (1956:265). For a similar more recent formulation see Shepherd 1991.

15. See, for example, Schiller 1989; Postman 1985.

16. Negus 1996:178.

17. Negus 1996:52.

18. Gilroy 1993:82.

19. Bagby 1999:24.

20. Ospina 1995:56.

21. Gaines 1994:231.

22. Gaines 1991:182–183. Original emphasis.

23. Rose 1994.

24. Hotchner 1990:39, quoted in Hamm 1993:20.

25. Frith 1992b.

26. Gaines 1991:180.

27. Kofsky 1970:105–106.

28. Quoted in Crosby & Bender 2000:8–9.

29. Rozendal 1997:13.

30. Maultsby 1989:173.

31. Gaines 1991:214.

32. Tsitsos 1999:413.

33. Carawan & Carawan 1993:260.

34. Marcus 1972:128.

35. Eyerman & Jamison 1995:459.
36. In Karroll 1996:133. Of course, this technique was not limited to left movements. For descriptions of very similar uses of music by the German Nazi movement, see Warren 1972; Lidtke 1982.
37. Robertson 1987:240.
38. Sanger 1997:191–192; Reagon quoted from Williams 1987:177. This is, of course, not merely the belief of those in the civil rights movement. Environmental activist Jesse Hardin writes, "In order to be truly transformative, music must not only be heard, but actually played.... Music, like environmentalism, is most effective when experiential and participatory" (1995:107).
39. Small 1998:105.
40. Shepherd 1991:146.
41. Gleason 1972:143.
42. Gitlin 1987:205. For Gitlin, writing of the sixties, however, the modern mass media were helped enormously in this endeavor by drugs—"perhaps *the* most potent form of mass communication" (1987:205).
43. Williams 1977:132.
44. Dundes 1964:263.

Notes for Chapter 5

1. Laing 1990:335.
2. "It didn't express something else, some prior reality," Frith has written about reggae, "but *was* the structure of experience" (1981:163).
3. Shepherd 1991:107. Of course, that's not the only possible interpretation, or a necessary one. Dyer argues that the same tonality imperative operates in popular songs to give "a sense of security and containment" to passionate expressions, thus making them safer (1990:413).
4. Shepherd 1991:12. Original emphasis.
5. For example, see discussions in Grant 1994; Laing 1990; Barthes 1990.
6. McClary 1993:333.
7. Citron 1994; McClary 1991a, 1993.
8. Small 1998:164.
9. We can see this clearly through the ways in which "absolute" music changes with social context. The music of the Baroque period (1600–1750), for example, was static, one musical idea subjected to expansion, but without contrasts or opposition. Like the hegemonic political thought of the time, it "rever[ed] stability and unity." But as the social and economic system of feudalism was increasingly challenged by a growing capitalism and the first stirrings of democracy, the sonata form developed, full of "contradictions between (say) opposing tonalities, themes, rhythmic characters," and so forth, all reflecting the social thought of that revolutionary period that "against overwhelming odds, men can—and must—shape their own destinies" (Ballantine 1984:32, 33). Again, it's not necessary that composers are conscious of these connections, that they're intentionally trying to convey the spirit of the times (though some are). "Social structures," Ballantine writes, "crystallize in musical structures; ... in various ways and with varying degrees of critical awareness, the musical microcosm replicates the social microcosm" (1984:5).
10. Christenson & Roberts 1998:186–187.
11. In Percy 1998:42.
12. Gitlin 1987:215, 202.
13. Gleason 1972:143.
14. Street 1986:42, 81–82. Original emphasis.

15. Quoted in Ramet, Zamascikov & Bird 1994:209. Similar observations turn up in studies of other formerly "socialist" countries. See, e.g., Kan & Hayes 1994; Ramet 1994c.

16. Frith 1996:184. Original emphasis.

17. Marcus 1972:131.

18. Laing 1990:340.

19. Willis 1981:99, quoted in McDonnell 1992:8.

20. Perris 1985:124.

21. Feld 1994:91.

22. McDonald 1993:10.

23 In Hoover & Stokes 1998:27.

24. Hebdige 1988:213.

25. Middleton 1985:13.

26. See Feld 1994. Feld, however, sees meaning construction as typically much more fluid, "momentarily changeable and emergent, in flux as our interpretive moves are unraveled and crystallized" (Feld 1994:88), while we're interested in more stable meaning construction, because we think this is both more common and, in any case, more important for movements.

27. Those closest to our position include Garofalo, Negus, Middleton, Grossberg, and Lipsitz; others with more or less this approach include Walser, Lewis, McClary, Frith, and Keil & Feld. Aldon Morris is a good example of a social movement theorist in this tradition.

28. Hall 1980:134. Original emphasis.

29. Concert notes or other written programs, Meyer notes, serve the same function for classical forms without lyrics (1956:264).

30. Pratt 1990:184. See also Roberts, Christenson & Gentile 2003:158.

31. In Daley 2001:G8.

32. See the Jim Brown film *We Shall Overcome* (1989) for discussions of how the song evolved.

33. Quoted in Lahr 2000:121.

34. Examples may be found in Perris 1985; Riggs 1991; Ramet 1994b, 1994d. Other forms in which lyrics have been generally considered more important than musical elements include French chanson (Frith 1996:170, based on Rorem 1988), *nueva trova* in Cuba (Ospina 1995:100), calypso in Trinidad (Denselow 1989:123), and Christian rock in the United States (Reid 1993:34).

35. Ramet 1994b:5.

36. Gaines 1994:231.

37. Horton 1957:577.

38. Mondak 1988:26, 27, based on memory theorists Petty & Cacioppo's "Elaboration Likelihood Model" (1986).

39. Meyer 1956:39.

40. Negus quotes this famous Marxian dictum to explain the emergence of new musics (1996:138), but we think it fits the construction of musical meaning generally.

41. Lahr 2000:123.

42. Gleason 1972:139.

43. Gleason 1972:138.

44. Pratt 1990.

45. Frith 1996:276.

46. Miller & Román 1995:175.

47. Pratt 1990.

48. Rose 1994:124.

49. Gitlin 1987.

50. Quoted in Rozendal 1997.12.

51. Ramet 1994b:7.

52. Sanger 1997:186. Internal quote from Reagon 1975b:1. Emphases in both quotes in originals.
53. Hamm 1993:211. For similar views, see Moore 1993; Southern Poverty Law Center 1999c.
54. Ward, Lunsford & Massa 1999:29.

Notes for Chapters 6

1. Roger Manning, quoted in Ressler 1992:40.
2. In Karroll 1996:13.
3. King 1987:23, quoted in Eyerman & Jamison 1998:45.
4. Bob Cohen, Mississippi Caravan of Music director, quoted in Carawan & Carawan 1990:175.
5. Bell 1990:20.
6. Miller & Román 1995:177. Miller and Román are writing specifically about queer theatre, but their wonderful analysis holds generally for social movement artists. Snow et al. make much the same point in the language of social movement theory: "Frame alignment, once achieved, cannot be taken for granted because it is temporally variable and subject to reassessment and renegotiation" (1997:222).
7. Carawan & Carawan 1993:247–248.
8. Public domain. As performed by The Bently Boys in 1929, rereleased on *The Anthology of American Folk Music*, Smithsonian Folkways Recordings, 1997 (1952).
9. Jones 1994:9.
10. Hampton 1986:53.
11. Balch 1914:412, quoted in Smith 1969:19
12. Lerner 1991:303.
13. American Social History Project 1992:580.
14. Gitlin 1987:75–76.
15. Lieberman 1989:148.
16. Vila 1992:216–217
17. Flacks 1988.
18. Johnston, Larana & Gusfield 1997:285.
19. Honigsheim 1989:202.
20. In Sutherland 1965:150–151, quoted in Sanger 1997:188.
21. Crosby & Bender 2000:22.
22. Lester 1964:1, quoted in Sanger 1997:189.
23. Michaels & Hartford 2002.
24. Quoted in Whitman 1969:199.
25. Hardin 1995:104.
26. Reagon 1993:155.
27. Reed 1990:58.
28. In Karroll 1996:170.
29. In Vickstrom 1998:1.
30. When the union's inspiration through the workers' blood shall run,
    There can be no power greater anywhere beneath the sun.
    Yet what force on earth is weaker than the feeble strength of one?
    But the union makes us strong
    Solidarity forever! Solidarity forever! Solidarity forever! For the union makes us strong
(Ralph Chaplin, 1915, public domain.)
31. Public domain. Lyrics from Seeger & Reiser 1989:240–242.

32. Words by Alfred Hayes, music by Earl Robinson, © Leeds Music 1938. As recorded by Earl Robinson (original issue: Timely 503-A), reproduced (and lyrics reprinted, p. 72) on *Songs for Political Action* (Bear Family Records 1996).

33. Words and music by Ed McCurdy, © Richmond Organization/Almanac Music 1950 (renewed 1978), 1951 (renewed 1979), and 1955 (renewed 1983).

34. Zurofsky 2001.

35. In Karroll 1996:175–176.

36. Words and music by Phil Ochs, © Appleseed Music 1964. As performed on *I Ain't Marching Any More* (Elektra 1964).

37. Zook 1992:261. We would narrow this claim considerably since we're dubious that any group as large and varied as African Americans can be spoken of in collective expressions like "the black community." Rap obviously speaks only to a subset of that imagined community, generally younger and more urban.

38. Lyrics and music by Dana Owens and Joe Sample, © Four Knights Music 1993. As performed on Queen Latifah, *Black Reign* (Motown 1993).

39. Rose 1991b:114.

40. Words and music by Walter Cliff (Walter Gourlay). As heard on Joe Glazer and Bill Friedland, *Ballads for Sectarians* (Labor Records 1952), reproduced on Ronald Cohen and Dave Samuelson's *Songs for Political Action* (Bear Family Records 1996).

41. By Jerome Gilbert Huling, © Douglas 1970. Rereleased on the CD *The Last Poets* (Fuel 2000 Records 2002).

42. Lyrics and music by Bernice Johnson Reagon, © Songtalk Publishing 1979. As heard on Sweet Honey in the Rock's *Good News* (Flying Fish 1981; Cooked Vinyl 2003).

43. Glasser 1995:9.

44. Almeida & Urbizagastegui 1997:17–18.

45. Fisher 1953:66. According to Maurice Jackson, these meetings weren't always only religious gatherings: "Legend and considerable historical facts tell us that ... "Steal Away" may have been written by Nat Turner, who in 1831 led one of [the] largest slave revolts in North America.... The song was used as a code to convene secret meetings by Turner to plan the aborted revolt" (1995:4).

46. Almeida & Urbizagastegui 1999:32.

47. Denselow 1989:185.

48. Almeida & Urbizagastegui 1999:17, referencing Rowe & Schelling 1991.

49. Scribner 1987:61.

50. Narvaez 1986:150.

51. Christgau 1994:223.

52. Zook 1992.

53. When Band Aid folded its organization in 1992, eight years after the original event, it had raised a remarkable $144 million, only 2% of which had gone to administration (Crosby & Bender 2000:176).

54. Amnesty International [n.d]; Amnesty International USA 1986; Microsoft Encarta 2007; Giugni 2001:183. Similarly, following the Seventieth Birthday Tribute Concert for Nelson Mandela in London in 1988, membership in the British antiapartheid movement tripled (Tomaselli & Foster 1992:12).

55. Rijven & Straw 1989:209.

56. Garofalo 1992:15, 26.

57. Denisoff 1983:149.

58. For further discussions of various models, see Levine & Harig 1975.

59. For example, see Frith 1996:164.

60. Stuessy 1985.117. The evidence Professor Stuessy refers to in his testimony is actually much

274 ♪ Notes on Pages 138–141

less convincing, and frequently less relevant, than his presentation might lead one to believe. For more on this issue in general, see Martin & Segrave 1988; Cloonan & Garofalo 2003.

61. Gleason 1972:140.

62. Hamm 1993:117.

63. For example, Levine & Harig write that *all* analysts agree that "mass media and popular culture can effectively influence attitudes and behavior" (1975:196). Robert Cantwell, though in general unfriendly to the explicitly political side of folk music, writes of Pete Seeger, "His performances have changed lives" (1996:242). For similar evaluations, see Auslander 1989; Lumer 1991.

64. One key problem is the still-persistent tendency to conflate reflection and causation—or to blur the difference. For example, when Street says in his discussion of censorship that everyone agrees that "popular culture can in some way *express* political ideas" (1997:33; our emphasis), he is fudging the key question of whether it can therefore *affect* political ideas, which is the only reason governments need censors.

65. Correlation is often found, but causation is typically unclear. See Verden et al. 1989:79; Rudman & Lee 2002; Johnson & Trawalter 2000; Anderson, Carnagey & Eubanks 2003; Thora Institute 2007. Even after reviewing a wide range of studies, Christenson & Roberts can only offer a highly conditional conclusion that is more indebted to existing memory theory and intuitive logic than clear-cut evidence: "If popular music has the power to elevate [mood], it *may* also have the power to depress, or at least to exacerbate, negative emotional states.... [A]dolescents who spend a great deal of time listening to popular music or watching music videos *presumably* access typical music media schemas more often than kids who pay little or no attention to popular music or MTV. To the extent these schemas are relatively consistent in what they portray, then an adolescent's own schema structure *may* come to resemble the representations embedded in the music and the videos to which they are exposed" (1998:204, 218–219; our emphases). They conclude that "important effects need not and probably do not extend to a large proportion of the total audience" (1998:187).

66. Cott 1987:324.

67. Near 1990:141.

68. In Aronowitz & Blonsky 1964:32, quoted in Gottesman 1977:66.

69. Eisler 1999:55, quoted in Rozendal 1997:12.

70. Stanton-Rich 1996:14.

71. For example, as the musicians' antiapartheid boycott of South Africa gathered steam in the mid-1980s, Jerry Dammers, of the English ska group the Specials, fumed about bands who agreed not to tour South Africa, but still had their records sold there, telling Dammers "they were actually helping the situation by doing so. 'Talk about being self-important!' he complained. 'Some of them think their revolutionary music will help the struggle. We need less airy-fairy freedom music, and more action'" (Denselow 1989:193).

72. Sheff 1981:105.

73. In Karroll 1996:134.

74. For summaries of some of these, see Christenson & Roberts 1998; Roberts, Christenson, & Gentile 2003.

75. Stanley Gortikov, Clive Davis, quoted in Orman 1984:12–13.

76. Verden, Dunleavy & Powers 1989:73.

77. Orman 1984:57. Donna Gaines writes at one point: "A few crucial bands offered the kids a viable philosophical system which they could use to understand life. Often these bands were referred to as *crucial*" (1991:195; original emphasis), yet elsewhere she declares that "'Fuck Tha Police' [a rap song denounced by some for encouraging the 1992 Los Angeles riots] was a response, not a catalyst, to ongoing, relentless, street-based violence against young people on the basis of race and sex" (1994:228). Walser lauds heavy metal's impact in challenging gender norms, but denies it any causal impact in terms of encouraging violence or suicide (1993). John Street, who certainly sees

culture as playing an important role in persuasion, still can write polemically that "popular culture does not make people think and act in particular ways" (1997:30). Yet in the same work he writes: "Popular culture makes us feel things, allows us to experience sensations, that are both familiar and novel. It does not simply echo our state of mind, it moves us" (p. 9).

78. Walser 1993:150

Notes for Chapter 7

1. Davis & Jasinski 1994:152.

2. Marcus 1972:136. He does go on to say, "It is, at times (especially in such moments as August 1968), a way to get a feeling for the political spaces we might happen to occupy at any particular time."

3. Songs for Social Change [n.d.].

4. Letter to the Editor of *Solidarity*, December 1914, quoted in Reagon 1975a:54, reproduced in Eyerman & Jamison 1998:59. We think it likely that Hill meant "uneducated" when he said "unintelligent." Richard Frank of *New Masses* made the same point about African Americans in more politically conscious language: "Among the Negroes, it will be to a great extent through mass singing that recruiting will be done, for masses of Negro workers are held at illiteracy. Leaflets cannot appeal to them. But singing is their great form of artistic expression" (1934:30, quoted in Reuss 1971:122).

5. Quoted in Moore 1993:56.

6. Southern Poverty Law Center 2004:1.

7. Hamm 1993:219; see also Southern Poverty Law Center 2004:1. Evidence of the extreme Right's appreciation of the efficacy of the music comes in the purchase of Resistance Records for almost $250,000 by the late William Pierce of the National Alliance (at the time "America's most important neo-Nazi") in October 1998. Although dormant in recent years, "at its height it was selling an estimated 50,000 racist CDs a year and grossing, according to one of its original founders, $100,000 a month" (Southern Poverty Law Center 1999a:1; Southern Poverty Law Center 1999b:33).

8. See Sandler 2003:24 on this power in "prolife" Christian rock festivals and Crosby & Bender 2000:230 for similar comments about the Free Tibet concerts.

9. For instance, Chuck D told us: "The beauty of rap music is that ... you can actually talk to somebody and [at the same time] ride a rhythm of a music, where it won't be disturbing to them. In a subtle type of way, you're almost giving paragraphs to people."

10. Characterization by Bernice Johnson Reagon in the documentary film *We Shall Overcome* (1989).

11. The same is true of many other countries In Trinidad, for example, calypso singers were the main spokespersons for candidates for most of the twentieth century; Red Wedge was a group of leftist British pop musicians who toured in support of the Labour Party in England in the 1987 elections.

12. Among its many virtues, the choice of a rock song—instead of a more traditional Tin Pan Alley–like song, which virtually all twentieth-century campaigns had used—acted to reassure the hordes of rock fans who distrusted Gore's wife Tipper, cofounder of the Parents' Music Resource Center, that the Clintons and Gores were prorock.

13. D 1991:376.

14. Ward 2000, quoted in Harrington 2000:N40.

15 Carawan & Carawan 1990:12.

16. In Crosby & Bender 2000:23. For the most part, however, activists know that engaging those who are already hostile—whether to educate or intimidate—is very difficult and time-consuming, with little chance of fostering transformed attitudes. The real impact, we'd argue, is usually not on

enemies but on participants: If insurgents *believe* musicking has the power to educate or intimidate, it plays an important role in their own spirit maintenance.

17. Many activists believe that the increasing importance of mass media in publicizing movements—necessary in order to raise resources—has increased the importance of cultural presentations. Phil Cohen, manager of the Whiteville Apparel Choir, argues, "There is a big difference between thirty seconds and three minutes on the evening news. Producers edit tape based upon 'good copy,' entertainment value, and creative angles. Organizations and individuals who are able to deliver these consistently develop relationships within the media that not only result in more coverage, but more favorable coverage" (1997).

18. Reagon 1993:161.

19. Taffet 1997:98.

20. Words and music by Graham Land & Ray Cappo, © Roadblock Music/Govindaji Music 1995. As heard on Shelter's album *Mantra* (Roadrunner/Supersoul Records 1995).

21. Spady 1991:336.

22. See, for example, Szemere (1992) discussing Hungary and Collins (1992) discussing anti-hegemonic aspects of African popular music.

23. Gaines 1991:195.

24. Ho 1992:4.

25. "Für Chuck Berry," on Hansi Biebl, *Der Lange Weg* (AMIGA 1981), quoted in Leitner 1994:21.

26. Halker 1991.38.

27. "When Workingmen Combine," by B. M. Lawrence. Quoted in Halker 1991:123.

28. Gleason 1972:143.

29. By Leon Rosselson, © Fuse 1977. On Leon Rosselson and Roy Bailey, *Love, Loneliness and Laundry* (Fuse 1977).

30. Mills 1959.

31. In Karroll 1996:126. But for a recent argument that rap hasn't produced such results, see Thora Institute 2007.

32. By John Lennon, © Lenono Music, 1971. As performed on John Lennon, *Imagine* (Apple 1971).

33. From Paul Robeson, *Scandalize My Name* (Classics Record Library 1976).

34. Fiske 1989:190.

35. Gramsci 1992.

36. Witness this letter to *MRR*, the leading punk magazine of the 1990s: "If most *MRR* readers believe punk to be about doing constructive things they are mistaken. Punk was about tearing things down (ie, Religion, Government, Rock Star systems, fashion, school, rules). This groovie [sic] supportive alternative movement that has evolved from the northern California punk world is something else" (Mutt, *MRR* 125, October 1993, quoted in Tsitsos 1999:401).

37. Matta 1988:449.

38. Hampton 1986:58.

39. Van Deburg 1992:208.

40. In Crosby & Bender 2000:35.

41. Gitlin 1987:197–198. Original emphasis.

42. Cantwell 1996:305.

43. Riesman 1990:8.

44. Quoted in Percy 1998:42–43.

45. Ospina 1995.77.

46. Crosby & Bender 2000·138–149.

47. Southern Poverty Law Center 1999c:26. This isn't restricted to political education, of course. It was through the singing of "Luther's German Psalms and Hymns" that early followers of

the Reformation "first learned to question the usefulness of Masses, requiems, and the Catholic clergy in general" (Scribner 1987:61).

48. Moore 1993:71.
49. Alicia Dienst (of Melody and the Matriarchs). 1998.
50. Eyerman & Jamison 1991:56.

Notes for Chapter 8

1. Street 1986:60.
2. Words and music by Millard Lampell, Lee Hays, and Pete Seeger, © Stormking 1958. As recorded on The Almanac Singers, *Talking Union* (Keynote 1941).
3. Snow & Benford 1992.
4. In Karroll 1996:136. Such claims are not particular to political music, or to modern times. For example, one of the great innovations of John Wesley was to envision hymn singing as a weapon of "conversion" instead of simply one of reaffirmation.
5. Flacks 1988, 2004.
6. Vickstrom 1998:1–2.
7. Hamm 1995, quoted in Harrington 2000:40.
8. Phillips 1985.
9. Brazier 1972: 60, 64, 67.
10. See, for example, Hamm 1993:144–145. Similar claims are made in Moore 1993; Southern Poverty Law Center 1999b, 1999c; Reynolds 1999.
11. Lieberman 1989:136, 131–132. For a drastically different view expressed by someone who experienced the campaign, see the testimony of Sonny later in Chapter 8.
12. Denisoff 1983:viii.
13. In Karroll 1996:135.
14. Similar experiences occurred in the South. See, e.g., Carawan & Carawan 1990:175.
15. Rollin 1964:130, quoted in Gottesman 1977:70.
16. Temple 1999:24
17. Hamm 1993:71.
18. Eyerman & Jamison 1998:1.
19. Carawan & Carawan 1993.
20 Sanger 1997:191, 189.
21. Peter Baird, in Usher 1996:11.
22. Sanger 1997:189.
23. Note that this was Horton's point over 50 years ago about romantic life—pop songs "offer the opportunity to experiment in imagination with the roles one will have to play in the future and the reciprocal roles that will, or should be, played by the as-yet-unknown others of the drama" (1957:577).
24. Branch 1988:532.
25. Pratt 1990:25.
26. Ramet, Zamascikov & Bird 1994:181. For this view of punk, see Laing 1985; Hebdige 1979; Hamm 1993.
27. Hennion 1990:205.
28. But only sometimes! There is a tendency in some rock criticism to assume that rock groupings—"alliances"—are always antihegemonic (see, for example, Hennion 1990; Grossberg 1985; Wolfe & Haefner 1996).
29. Christenson & Roberts 1998. See, for instance, p. 60.
30. Van Deburg 1992:208.

31. Ramet 1994b:1.

32. Wicke 1992:81. But as noted in Chapter 1, some other analysts ascribe little or no role to rock and rock musicians in the toppling of the Communist Party in East Germany. See Opp and Gern 1993; Opp 1998.

33. See Thomas Carter's 1993 film, *Swing Kids.*

34. Vila 1992:209.

35. Perrone 2002.69.

36. Taffet 1997:92.

37. Lieberman 1989:42.

38. In Karroll 1996:171.

39. Flacks 1971; Cantwell 1996.

40. Hamm 1993:35.

41. (R.H.) Rosenthal 1986b:14.

42. Dorothy Cotton, quoted in Seeger & Reiser 1989.121.

43. Eyerman & Jamison 1998:35.

44. Hampton 1986.

45. Chiu 2002:16–17. The informant actually characterizes this imitation of his heroes as "rather shallow"; we've omitted the editorializing here.

46. Chiu 2002:9. Chiu in fact argues that in the hardcore/animal rights connection she studied, "[W]hile the music plays a key role, it is the community created around the music that is the most important factor.... Within this community born and bred of music, activists strengthen and solidify their identities" (Chiu 2002:30, 32).

47. Doss-Cortes 1999:2.

48. But note that participants may differ widely on what they believe this unified vision is that "all" movement participants agree with. We discuss this further in Chapter 10.

49. Eyerman 2002:450. The concerts Eyerman speaks of are often literally illegal in countries like Sweden, due to their racist content; we think, however, that his characterization of concertgoers as "co-conspirators" is typical of legal politically oriented concerts as well.

50. Small 1998:212.

51. Eyerman 2002:453, 452.

52. Eyerman 2002:450.

53. For example, see Hamm 1993:85–86.

54. But we don't mean to rule out satori experiences, or at least experiences that *feel* that way. Here's a description by Kathy Rudy: "[O]ne of my colleagues at the mental health center lent me my first Holly Near album. The issue I was supposed to connect with was farmworker rights (Near wore a UFW button in the cover photo), but the moment I listened to her articulation of alternative sexualities, I was hooked. Her resistance to heterosexual norms, her presence as a strong independent woman who loved other women, the fierceness of her politics—these things called to me, pulled me out of my cloud of unknowing, and helped me identify my true self. (Later I would theorize it differently; the words, the music, the community, the experience 'constructed' that identity. But that's certainly not how it felt at the time.)" (2001:193–194).

55. Taylor & Whittier 1997:510.

56. For example, see Taylor 1991 about such fans of Billy Bragg. Similar comments were made to us by both Bragg and his manager, Peter Jenner.

Notes for Chapter 9

1. Lott 1994:11.

2. Rosselson 1996:2.

3. Hamm 1993:160.

4. McNeil 2002:58, 59.

5. The late Joe Strummer, lead singer of the 1970s radical punk band the Clash, reflects on how well governments have understood this use: "The other week I happened to be walking down to Victoria Station through Green Park, past Buckingham Palace.... Along came mounted horsemen and along came carriages and the whole full thing, right? And there was maybe 30 bagpipers, striding along, playing, and, as they came past, I suddenly realised the truth, that I would have followed them anywhere, even over the top. If somebody had said 'Charge boys!' ... On the Somme I would have gone over the top with them, like so many did. It was too powerful. Boy, have they got it figured out.... It just shows how well they know us, how they've perfected it down to a fine art over the centuries. And how can our adolescent gibbering with a guitar ever even make a bridgehead upon this established tradition?" (Melody Maker 1986:26).

6. By Rage Against the Machine. © Retribution Music 1992. From *Rage Against the Machine* (Epic 1992).

7. As so often, the parallels to religious musicking are obvious. Dunaway points out that "John Wesley and the American Methodist movement laid a groundwork for using hymns for exhortation, particularly at camp meetings; it was no accident that later song groups ... built on this tradition and adopted hymns to political organizing" (1987b:274).

8. Over the land, over the sea/Comes the call to join the fight, the strike to be free...
Lay down your tools, leave your machine/Come up from the mines, out of the fields so green
Tie up the ships, close down the shops, Let the parasites get wise as they get lean...
No gears would work, starvation would lurk, without us nothing moves, not a single wheel...
So let us strike—strike to be free/Shed the shackles, break the chains of wage-slavery!
("General Strike Song," by Louis Burcar, *Industrial Worker*, May 4, 1934. In Industrial Workers of the World 1976:18–19.)

9. Chiu 2002:11.

10. Denselow 1989:136.

11. Indeed, it was widely reported that "Street Fighting Man" could be heard blaring from record shops in the student community of Isla Vista when residents rampaged in a riot that culminated with the burning of the Bank of America branch building in 1970 (Whalen & Flacks 1989:70).

12. By John Keen. Abkco Music, 1970. On *Hollywood Dream* (Track 1970).

13. This observation comes from 15 years of asking this question in Rosenthal's Music in Social Movements class at Wesleyan University.

14. Carawan & Carawan 1993:257.

15. Narvaez 1986.

16. Sometimes just the presence of celebrity musicians can be enough to aid mobilization, even if they don't actually perform. See, for instance, Lewis 2003:22.

17. Rose 1994.

18. Brennan 1994:672.

19. From the film *Billy Bragg and Pete Seeger: The Concert for Jobs, Peace, and Freedom* (1992).

20. Quoted in Harrington 1997:F6.

21. Carawan & Carawan 1990:150.

22. Halker 1991:35.

23. In the film *The International* (2000).

24. Eyerman & Jamison 1998:20.

25. Hamm 1993:211.

26. Sherman 1967:173–174, quoted in Denisoff 1983:56.

27. Lipsitz 1994:303.

Notes for Chapter 10

1. See Whalen and Flacks (1989) for an extended discussion of the contradictory value orientations embodied in the sixties movement, contrasting individualism and collectivism.

2. See, for example, Rijven and Straw 1989.

3. Quoted in Denselow 1989:95.

4. Ekedal et al. 1999:2.

5. Hampton 1986:213.

6. Then again, it's been argued that *all* art performs this function of diversion from real life. Consider this manifesto issued to promote an "Art Strike from January 1st 1990 to January 1st 1993": "Imagine a world in which art is forbidden! ... We could refocus our vision not on a succession of false images but on the world as it is.... Art has provided us with fantasy worlds, escapes from reality. For whatever else it is, art is not reality. Soap operas, novels, movies, concerts, the theatre, poetry. None of these are real as a starving child is real, as a town without water is real. Art is the glamorous escape, the transformation that shields us from the world we live in. .. Art has replaced religion as the opiate of the people just as the artist has replaced the priest as the spokesman of the spirit.... Artists are murderers! Artists are murderers just as surely as the soldier who sights down the barrel of a gun to shoot an unarmed civilian. Without art, life would be unendurable! We would have to transform this world.... Forbid art and revolution would follow" (Seven by Nine Squares, [n.d.]).

7. Bricca 1998:5.

8. Frank 1995. Emphasis added.

9. Marcus 1980:181, quoting the English critic George Melly. This isn't only true of musicking, naturally. See Dahl's classic discussion of some citizens' "spurious 'participation' in politics" (1961:280).

10. One example of this: Perusing the "Memories" section of a "Live Aid Home Page (www.herald. co.uk/local_info/la_memories.html), we noticed that there was almost no mention of anything that had to do with the issue Live Aid addressed; virtually all memories were about the concert qua concert.

11. King 1998:49, 40.

12. Street 1986:219.

13. Hinkle 1991:232.

14. See, for example, Perris 1985:139–140.

15. Jones 1992, quoted in Schell 1992:15.

16. Kolbe 1999.

17. Samuels 1995:251. Ice-T, a rapper who has also recorded with hardcore bands, sees it somewhat differently: "The white kids are getting something different out of it. They're getting a lot more information.... I think a lot more of them get compassion and understanding.... I think that criticism, 'Oh, the white kids are just getting off on it, and they don't care'—a lot of black kids are getting off on it, and they don't care either" (Light 1992:6).

18. Hardin 1995:98.

19. Buxton 1990:435.

20. Quoted in Cantwell 1996:305. The original editorial is from *Sing Out!* 14 (January 1964), p. 2.

21. Appnel 1991, quoted in Bricca 1992:4.

22. Hampton 1986:42, 5.

23. Vickstrom 1998:45.

24. Stud Brothers 1986:12.

25. Hampton argues that this dynamic, less developed, is also found in movements that predate the rise of the mass media and even the rise of capitalism, and in "underground" music and movements today (1986:210, 222–223).

26. Quoted in Crosby & Bender 2000:78.

27. Hampton 1986:220–221.

28. Since the entire Carnegie Hall concert appears on CD (Columbia 1989 [1963]), readers can hear for themselves how Seeger tried to deal with the contradictions.

29. Lieberman 1989:134.

30. In Lieberman 1989:134.

31. Lieberman 1989:136.

32. Lemisch 1986a:374.

33. Mattson 1999:2. Original emphasis. Mattson's account, however, is disputed by others (see Temple 1999:24). Whatever the case with this specific example, the general point of the danger of exclusivity still stands.

34. Denselow 1989:157. This isn't restricted to musicking, of course. Polletta notes that it was relatively new members of SNCC who first called attention to the pervasive sexism of the group in the mid-1960s (commonly seen as one of the key origins of the modern feminist movement), while "it was easier for women who were longtime members of the group to see an auxiliary role as consonant with the group's racially egalitarian ethos" (1999:24).

35. Lerner 1991:303.

36. Garofalo 1992.

37. Gitlin 1987:209. Gitlin is actually referring to a specific incident, the singing of "Yellow Submarine" during the 1966 student strike in Berkeley, briefly described in Chapter 4.

38. Of course other factors also militated against open discussions of this and other areas of disagreement, including the pressing needs of movement work that (as always) seemed to preclude virtually anything other than immediate tasks.

39. Street 1986:77, 78.

40. Ospina 1995:77.

41. Warren 1972:73.

42. In Chang 2003:21.

43. Street 1986:46, 50.

44. Fisher 1953, e.g., pp. 29–33.

45. Hebdige 1979.

46. Halker, for example, argues that "even a culture of consolation allows the human spirit to retain a rebellious potential" (1991:27).

47. Chang 2003:19. As Chang points out, "political rap" itself "was actually something of an invention. The Bronx community-center dances and block parties where hip-hop began in the early 1970s were not demonstrations for justice, they were celebrations of survival" (p. 17).

48. Craddock-Willis 1989:33.

49. Pratt 1990:64. See Rose 1991b for a similar argument regarding rap.

50. Halker 1991:13.

51. Dyer 1990:417. Original emphasis.

52. Lipsitz 1994:327.

53. Pratt 1990:89.

54. Scott 1990:191.

55. Grossberg 1993:337.

Notes for Chapter 11

1. Bird, Georgakas & Shaffer 1985 23.

2. See, for example, Reuss 1971: Chapter 9; Denisoff 1983:61.

3. Horwitz 2001; Lay 1992.

4. Even in an age of mass media saturation, the drive to create and perform ourselves appears quite powerful. The amount of money spent on instruments, sheet music, and new technologies to create music (such as computer software) rivals the amount spent on recorded music; by as early as 1990 an astounding 11% of American households had a member who had made music with a computer in that year (Gottlieb 1991:18, 15).

5. Hardin 1995:107.

6. Pratt 1990:85.

7. In Lazersfeld and Merton's classic account of political sociology, "mass media propaganda" was said to be most effective if significant and intelligible to the listener, and "supplemented by personal acts of involvement" (1948, quoted in Denisoff & Levine 1972:214); although they were not of the generation that thought about music—or culture generally—as integral to political mobilization, it's easy to see how musicking fits into their formulation.

8. In Karroll 1996:178.

9. Rose 1994:182.

10. The historical record would suggest the progression King is laying out here hasn't really been a straight line chronologically; earlier movements, both in the United States and elsewhere, certainly had widespread democratic participation in music making. Yet his basic point is crucial.

11. Chorus and sample verse: "We're gonna roll, we're gonna roll, we're gonna roll the union on/We're gonna roll, we're gonna roll, we're gonna roll the union on//If the boss gets in the way we're gonna roll right over him, roll right over him, roll right over him/If the boss gets in the way we're gonna roll right over him/We're gonna roll the union on."

12. Quoted in Harrington 1997:F6.

13. Reuss 1971:142.

14. Green 1997a:1.

15. For example, see Fisher 1953; Thompson 1983; Miller & Skipper 1972.

16. First clause in Karroll 1996:133; second quoted in Harrington 1997:F6.

17. Reagon 1987, quoted in Carawan & Carawan 1990:5.

18. Broyles-Gonzalez 1997.

19. Ramet 1994b.

20. Street 1986:216.

21. Eyerman & Jamison 1998:98.

22. See McAdam 1994.

23. Chang 2003:17.

24. Street 1986:25.

25. D 1991:371.

26. Perrone 2002:67.

27. Street 1986:30.

28. Ramet, Zamascikov & Bird 1994:209.

29. Kan & Hayes 1994:41.

30. Reagon 1975a:139, quoted in Sanger 1997:185.

31. Bagby 1999:2, 24.

32. For examples see Riggs 1991; Kan & Hayes 1994.

33. IRWIN SILBER: "A lot depended on the particular occasion. You know, a big Madison Square Garden rally, they poked their nose into everything. The whole world is going to see it, they hoped.... On a small level, obviously if someone gets invited to a house party, raising money for the Communist Party, nobody's gonna [care]."

BARBARA DANE: "It was political parties, it didn't matter *what* political party, just the mechanism. You have a party line . . . and the bureaucrat mentality is 'I want to reflect the party line on the program.'"

34. See Reuss 1971, especially pp. 288–293, for evidence about this. Some musickers, however, found being ignored the best situation. Irwin Silber also told us that despite the occasional interference cited above, most of the time "The Party had little to do with us. They had bigger fish to fry. . . . We were sort of like the stepchildren, which was the best thing that could have happened. Because every time we had contact with them, there was always friction."

35. Denisoff 1972:113.

36. Reuss 1971:188. Other left parties of the day displayed even less interest in music and other cultural activities. See Cohen & Samuelson 1996:12.

37. In Coplon 1989:82–83, quoted in Hamm 1993:52.

38. For supporting evidence see Hamm 1993; Moore 1993; Southern Poverty Law Center 1999b, 1999c; Reynolds 1999.

39. Carawan & Carawan 1990:5, 15.

40. Perrone 2002:66.

41. Roscigno & Danaher 2001.

42. Brace & Friedlander 1992:125.

43. Alameida & Urbizagestegui 1997:13.

44. In contrast, the rock and roll that developed from R&B and spoke to a heterogeneous and relatively more affluent population assumed an extremely individualistic stance, the alienated hero fleeing (but rarely fighting) the confinements of mainstream life. As a result, modern versions of rock have often struggled to speak in a collective voice, or to offer alternatives; even in those historical moments when such music has seemed integral to emerging social movements, there has been a noticeable tension between collective and individualistic approaches. An archetypal illustration of this clash occurred at the 1969 Woodstock Festival when political activist Abbie Hoffman leaped on stage to proclaim to the crowd that such gatherings were meaningless if they didn't lead to collective political activities such as the freeing of imprisoned activist John Sinclair; Pete Townshend, guitarist of the Who, knocked him off the stage with his guitar for interrupting their set for a non-show-related purpose. See, for example, Raskin 1997:196–197.

45. Zurofsky 2001.

46. Carawan & Carawan 1990:115. Our emphasis.

47. Branch 1988:532.

48. The Reverend C. T. Vivian, quoted in Carawan & Carawan 1990:3–4.

49. Carawan & Carawan 1990:4.

50. Carawan & Carawan 1990:4. Original emphasis.

51. Carawan & Carawan 1990:6.

52. D 1991:375.

53. Brazier 1972; Smith 1969.

54. Carawan & Carawan 1993:248.

55. Ibid.

56. Dunaway 1981:92.

57. This failure to achieve widespread conversion does not, of course, mean they were unsuccessful in achieving other movement functions. Certainly the Almanacs and similar folk musicians played a significant role in affirming the commitment of many of the inner core of long-term left activists who remained active in any number of movements, down to the current day.

58. Lieberman 1989:148.

59. Cantwell 1996:275.

60. For instance, when we interviewed Boots Riley, the most politically committed of current rappers, he placed himself (without then knowing anything about his interviewers) in that tradition,

despite his sonic distance from folk music: "In my music I talk about a lot of personal issues, and tie them to the political I'm not the first person to do that, [there are] many songwriters that are considered to be, you know, just staple political songwriters like Woody Guthrie. And Joe Hill did that, too."

61. For example, the historical tradition that Archie Green (1997a) points to that led to the Wobblies' embrace of folk songs was itself in large part due to the conscious musicking strategy of an earlier generation of radicals. In Chicago, an anarchist movement "more highly attuned to cultural activities as a tool for raising consciousness than most groups, presided over 'a secular and class culture it had created, adapted, and invented for itself'" (Halker 1991:30, quoting Nelson 1986). The less radical and militant Knights of Labor also "established group singing as a standard part of their functions" (Halker 1991.37).

Notes for Chapter 12

1. When Suzanne Vega's record "Luka" became a huge hit, for example, she was quite surprised to find herself seen as a spokesperson for the fledgling movement against child abuse: "I had no idea that it was a widespread problem, that it could be even perceived as a social problem, frankly. I was writing the way I always do, from a fairly individual point of view, as a personality.... It never dawned on me to try and write a political song, to be some part of the social movement."

2. Bragg 2000:40.

3. Quoted in Lieberman 1989:59.

4. Certainly there are important exceptions, such as among the People's Artists crowd. See Archie Green's account of Russian revolutionaries meeting on the island of Capri in 1907 debating various approaches to culture (1997b).

5. Crosby 2000:217.

6. For example, in the middle of our discussions about issues like this, Ian MacKaye said, "I can talk to you about these things.... I'm trying to articulate them and I'm trying to put them into some kind of understandable sort of form. But, I mean, keep in mind that I'm doing this for you.... Ultimately, what I do is just what I do. It's not something that I planned out."

7. Ballantine 1984.13. Original emphasis.

8. Karroll 1996:189.

9. Street 1986:44. Street actually says, "the state itself cannot make music," but, as we go on to say, there are certainly examples of that.

10. For a review of a range of governmental policies, including protection of indigenous music in Sweden and Canada, see Street 1986: Chapter 1; van Elderen 1989.

11. Kater 1997:130. See also Honigsheim 1989:201.

12. Ludwig Kelbetz, quoted in Kater 1997:142. Governments may also affect musicking in a wide variety of indirect ways, and for reasons that have little to do with their views about the music itself, from import restrictions to radio station licensing. See Edmunds 2000 for examples from the early years of the Soviet Union.

13. See, for example, Ramet, Zamascikov & Bird 1994 regarding the Soviet Union, or Wicke 1992 regarding East Germany.

14. As colorfully summarized by Richard Peterson a generation ago, "In a free mass society such as our own, ... the most potent censor of art works is not police, patron, or Pope, but profit" (1972:236).

15. Lumer 1991:53.

16. In a performance fraught with significance, these verses were included by Pete Seeger, Bruce Springsteen, and others in the "We Are One" concert at the Lincoln Memorial during the inauguration ceremonies for Barak Obama.

17. According to Michael Smith, General Manager of Woody Guthrie Publications, Woody recorded two versions of "This Land" for Asch Records in the mid-1940s, one with the radical verses (no trespassing), one without. The sanitized version was the only one released, though not until several years later; Asch and Guthrie never released the radical version, which was discovered by Smithsonian Folkways (which now owns Asch Records' inventory of tapes) in the 1990s and finally released in 1999 on The *Asch Recordings, Volume 1*. Smith points out further that the popularity of "This Land" is in great part due to Howie Richmond, the publisher who owned the rights to "This Land" and "made the smart move [in the 1950s] of allowing textbook publishers for schools to use the song at a low price or no cost at all. The song quickly spread and school children were soon singing it everywhere. The downside was that they were only singing the 'sanitized' version of the song.... Arlo Guthrie has often remarked that at one point, Woody took him aside and told him that people were singing 'This Land' but they weren't singing all the verses. Woody was afraid that they would be lost if someone was not taught them, so he taught the real version to Arlo.... As to why Howie Richmond only had the clean version published, I think the answer is more clear. No textbook publisher in their right mind would allow a song that questioned government policies and their effect on the poor (the Relief Office verse) or advocated against private property" (Smith 2004).

18. Quoted in Pareles 2003:18.

19. D 1999–2000:136.

20. Some artists have been fairly successful in using video in explicitly political ways—Little Steven's "Sun City," Jackson Browne's "Lives in the Balance," Eminem's "Mosh," for example—but these are the exceptions.

21. In Gittlins 1988:11.

22. Morello 2003.

23. But note that in recent years Morello (as "The Night Watchman") has also performed as a solo acoustic/political artist, very much in the Guthrie/Seeger mold. His argument isn't that such an approach isn't worthwhile, but that the corporate rock model reaches far more people.

24. For example, Rodnitsky declares: "Art and politics are often joined, but seldom compatible" (1999:117).

25. In Karroll 1996:149–150.

26. In Hentoff 1972:59, cited in Denisoff 1983:123. Dylan has continued to maintain this perspective all his life. Here he is in a 2004 interview with TV journalist Ed Bradley: "It was like being in an Edgar Allan Poe story. And you're just not that person everybody thinks you are, though they call you that all the time ... 'You're the prophet. You're the savior.' I never wanted to be a prophet or savior. Elvis maybe. I could easily see myself becoming him. But prophet? No.... My stuff were songs, you know? They weren't sermons" (Bradley & Dylan 2004).

27. Almanac alumnae, however, were involved in what is probably the outstanding exception to this problem in U.S. politics, the Henry Wallace campaign of 1948. Alan Lomax and Wallace's representatives negotiated "an agreement in principle that there should be a song sung for every speech made," distribution of a national song booklet of the Progressive Party so people could sing along, "a song leader at every meeting," and other similar supports for the music. All of this accorded music, especially folk music, "a far greater importance in the overall organizational scheme of its campaign than any other major election group in American history before or since" (Reuss 1971:279–280). John Kerry's presidential campaign of 2004 was by far the most music-friendly campaign since that time. See Toomey & Rosenthal 2005.

28. See, for instance, Country Joe McDonald's complaints about "'the manipulations of the left-wing' [in the 1960s], destroying his vision of 'music, fun and politics all together,'" reported in Denselow 1989:69.

29. By Millard Lampell. From *Songs of John Doe* (Almanac Records 1941). The Almanacs, however, weren't oblivious to the awkwardness of the situation. Woody immediately penned a commentary in

song, "On Account of That New Situation": "I started to sing a song/To the entire population/But I ain't a doing a thing tonight/On account of this new situation" (quoted in Dunaway 1981:86).

30. Dunaway 1981:90.

31. Similarly, though perhaps less frequently, party leaders may attempt to tell organization members which art is politically correct to enjoy and which isn't. Here's our interviewee Noah reflecting on his membership in the Revolutionary Communist Party in the late 1980s: "A lot of them listened to rap or punk at the point. It seemed like it was more for political reasons than for an actual liking of the music. I was (and still am) into heavy metal.... They would ask me questions like 'Why do you listen to Blue Oyster Cult or Slayer?' I would answer that 'I like it.' They, and over the years a lot of other leftists, would seem unable to fathom that a socialist could like *anything* that was not expressedly [sic] political. I have been told that my choice in music was 'not revolutionary' and that their music 'was revolutionary.'"

32. Lieberman 1989:56–57. Pete Seeger told us much the same: "The Communist Party never told us, [never] came up and said 'Don't sing this' or 'Do sing that.' They said, 'Have you got a song on this?' or 'Have you thought about a song on that?'"

33. Jamison 1996:12.

34. Near 1990:127.

35. For example, Woody Guthrie's "Plane Wreck at Los Gatos," which is well known among immigration activists today because of its graphic presentation of the plight of "illegal" immigrant workers.

36. Chang 2003:17.

37. In Karroll 1996:124.

38. Usher 1997:4.

39. For an excellent example of this, see Denning's (1996) description of how arts in the 1930s were galvanized by the development of a popular culture inspired and powered by the upsurge of the labor movement.

40. In Dawidoff 1997:28. See Crosby 2000 for many examples of musicians saying much the same.

41. RILEY: "James Brown made 'I'm Black and I'm Proud.' Well, he went through the whole civil rights movement, the whole black power movement without saying a word, and people were like, 'Hey, why aren't you doing this?' And he was like, 'Fuck you.' And the result of that is he finally started doing songs like that.... Marvin Gaye, he was around for that whole civil rights movement, black power movement, early seventies, it took him a long time. And then, he only came with a question: 'What's going on?' So, that push and pull. During that time, there was a concerted effort by political organizations to say, 'Hey, you know, can you make some songs? Connect it to reality a little bit?'" For an academic treatment making the same argument, see Maultsby 1989.

42. Chang 2003:17.

43. Jamison 1996:2.

44. Eyerman & Jamison 1998:118, 122.

45. Eyerman & Jamison 1995:458.

46. Eyerman & Jamison 1998:46. Similarly, despite her defense of the political work of artists around the Communist Party, Lieberman writes that "ideological purity and the subordination of aesthetic concerns to political ones certainly had a detrimental effect on some creative work" (1989:27).

47. Silber 1964; Wolfe 1972:148.

48. Almeida & Urbizagastegui 1999:33.

49. In Denselow 1989:73.

50. Phillips 1985:25.

51. Jones 1994:9.

52. Rozendal 1997:12, quoting Eisler 1999:55.

53. Korona 2000.

54. In Percy 1998:37.

55. Marcus 1972:127, 128. Similarly, Street declares that while folk music works well in a demonstration, it is "ineffective in the typical settings and moods—in private and for pleasure—in which people hear music" because of its black and white nature (Street 1986:156). This certainly must come as news to the millions of 1960s movement types who wore out the LPs of their guerilla minstrels (Seeger, Odetta, Dylan, Ochs, Paxton, Baez, etc.) late at night, burning candles (at least) and plotting the future.

56. Marcus 1972:130.

57. Rosselson 1997:28.

58. Street 1986:63.

59. In Stanton-Rich 1996:14–15.

60. In Driscoll 1987:259. Original emphasis.

61. Rodnitzky 1999:114.

62. *People's World*, August 1, 1941, p. 5, quoted in Denisoff 1972:116–117.

63. Klein 1980:208.

64. Christenson & Roberts 1998:186–187.

65. Walser 1993:165; see also Gaines 1991:204–205. "I'm hyper aware of the soapbox thing," Radiohead's Thom Yorke more recently told an interviewer. "It's difficult to make political art work. . . . If you sit down and try to do it purposefully, and try to change this with this, and do this with that, it never works" (in Burton 2003).

66. For example, Benjamin lauds the epic theater of Eisler and Brecht that "is less concerned with filling the public with feelings, even seditious ones, than with alienating it in an enduring manner, through thinking, from the conditions in which it lives" (1978 236).

67. Street 1986:157, 158.

68. Denselow 1989:137.

69. © Six Pictures Music 1977. As heard on Randy Newman, *Little Criminals* (Warner Brothers 1977).

70. Benjamin 1978:235.

71. By Bruce Springsteen, © Bruce Springsteen, 1978. As heard on *Darkness on the Edge of Town* (Columbia Records 1978).

72. By Barry Mann & Cynthia Weil, © Screen Gems–EMI Music 1961.

73. Street 1986:206–210.

74. Middleton 1981:35.

75. Street 1986:210.

76. Street 1986:210. See a similar assessment by the late Joe Strummer, lead singer and songwriter for the Clash (Melody Maker 1986).

77. Frith 1996:20. Our emphasis.

78. McClary 1991b:163.

79. Lieberman 1989:59.

80. Eyerman & Jamison 1995:459.

81. By Steven Van Zandt, © Blue Midnight Music 1983. On *Voice of America* (EMI 1984).

82. Street 1986. See chapter 11 in particular.

83. Eyerman & Jamison 1998:122.

84. Dunaway 1981:92. Such debates raged among those around the Communist Party for much of the 1930s. Charles Seeger, Pete's father, wrote in 1939 that "the farther any urban art strays from the idiom determined by the tastes and capacities of the people at large, the smaller in the long run will be the role it plays" (1939:148, quoted in Davis 2002).

85. This wasn't a simple or unanimous viewpoint, however. According to Reuss, Alan Lomax and Guthrie felt only folk music should be used, while Seeger and Lee Hays urged tolerance of other

musical forms as well (1971:265–266). Of course, as some cynics pointed out at the time, several of the Almanacs were not themselves from working-class or rural backgrounds, and thus playing the folk music of such people was inauthentic for them in any case. Jesse Lemisch leveled much the same charge at the folk musicians of the New Left and its antecedents (1986a).

86. In Klein 1980:196.

87. Klein 1980:203.

88. Reynolds 1990:467. See, for example, Taffet's discussion of radical newspapers in Chile (1997:96).

89. In Denselow 1989:110.

90. *Daily Worker*, November 21, 1933, p. 5, quoted in Reuss 1971:63. Among those in or around the Composers Collective of the 1930s—including people like Elie Siegmeister, Marc Blitzstein, and Aaron Copland—there was a general agreement that "workers' music was to be militant in terms of *both* text and tune," but "just how such an original music was to be fashioned ... was never satisfactorily spelled out in detail" (Reuss 1971:58; our emphasis). The contemporary musical theorist John Shepherd goes much further, calling for an entirely new musical framework that discards the framework of functional tonality on which Western music has been based for at least 500 years: "In order to provide a musical *alternative* as powerful as prevailing social realities and ideologies, it becomes necessary to develop musical languages capable of mediating the world in as global and extended a fashion as functional tonality, but without the centrally distanced control and alienation articulated through functional tonality music" (Shepherd 1991:143; original emphasis).

91. See, for example, Seidman 1981.

92. Frith & McRobbie 1990:415. We've removed the last clause from parentheses in the original.

93. Kirk-Duggan 1997:229.

94. Gillet 1970:297, quoted in Eyerman & Jamison 1998:122. One of our favorite examples comes not from political music, but the growing genre of Christian rock. Kauffman writes of a concert he attended. "[T]he medium is cock rock but the message is blue balls It's a supercharged sexual abstinence rally" (1994:306). Not surprisingly, many within the fundamentalist community find the message of the music so strong that it overwhelms any piety in the lyrics. One prominent critic argues, "the music is intrinsically addictive, encourages idolatry and leads teenagers to disobey their parents" (Kauffman 1994:306, summarizing the views of Bill Gothard).

95. Street 1986:65.

96. Small 1998:3.

97. Rozendal 1997:13. Thus, their approach was closer to that of Walter Benjamin, the other great Marxist cultural critic of the day, who said of writers: "This apparatus is better, the more consumers it is able to turn into producers—that is, more readers or spectators into collaborators" (1978:233).

98. Almeida & Urbizagestegui 1997:27.

99. The poignancy and irony of this excerpt might best be appreciated by contrasting it with something DiFranco said only a few years earlier to an interviewer: "I have no interest in fame or fortune. I'm more into social movements and making noise, stirring people up, traveling and communicating. I want to make a community and be based in the world, not within the corporate system of greed and amassing fame" (in Poet 1996:5, quoted in Vickstrom 1998:1).

100. Vila 1992:225.

101. In Karroll 1996:129–130.

102. In Karroll 1996:127.

103. Rodnitzky 1989:19.

104. Taylor 1991:39.

105. One special case of this dilemma concerns activist musicians forced into exile by the very fact of their activism. Matta notes that many of the most important musicians tied to the *nueva canción* movement in Latin America fled to Europe to escape the repression of rightist governments

in the 1980s, continuing to "clamor for full democracy and for the right to return to sing with their people.... [But] some doubt that the song of Latin American exile is the real expression of what it is to be Latin American now" (1988:452–453).

106. For example, those involved in "Band-Aid" were surely sincerely seeking to help build support for the efforts to bring humanitarian aid to the crisis of starvation in civil war–wracked Ethiopia. Yet, as Reid has pointed out in a commentary on the records *We Are the World* and *Do They Know It's Christmas*, these could be said to add up to the message, "We [in the West] are the world, and they [in Africa] don't even know it's Christmas" (Reid 1991).

107. Reuss 1971:390.

108. Zook 1992.

109. From the film *We Shall Overcome.*

110. Ibid.

111. Grazian 2004:32.

112. And some critics as well See Street 1997:167; Rose 1994:99–100. Neither seriously considers the question at any length, however.

113. In Powers 2003:13.

114. By Consolidated, © Amusement Control 1991. From *Friendly Fascism* (Nettwerk 1991).

115. Lieberman 1986:658.

116. Rosselson 1997:28, 29.

117. Not all of our interviewees agreed with us that this was possible, however. ODETTA: "Feeling an audience has nothing to do with it, feeling an audience is after the fact. What you are serving is the music. I've heard of people talking about feeling the audience and giving the audience what they want. I've not found the catalog to order that particular sphere that will tell me what an audience wants.... How are you going to say, 'Okay, this and this and this and this equals . .?' Not even with an abacus, you can't."

118. Steward & Garratt 1984:36–37.

119. Brochure notes to the Weavers' *Kisses Sweeter Than Wine* (Omega 1993). Quoted in Karroll 1996:16.

120. In Percy 1998:40.

121. Bragg 2000.40.

122. Uehlein 1997:10. The entire quote reads, "No matter how brilliant our attempts to inform, it is our ability to inspire that will make the difference." We see the aspects of informing and inspiring as both necessary.

123. Hampton 1986:2.

124. Near 1990:115.

125. Street 1997:32.

126. In Lowenfels 1941:7, quoted in Reuss 1971:217.

127. In Karroll 1996:130.

128. The Reverend C. T. Vivian, quoted in Carawan & Carawan 1990:4.

129. Almeida & Urbizagastegui 1997, 1999.

130. Almeida & Urbizagastegui 1999:33. Since this policy would have added a relatively tiny number of additional soldiers, it's hard to understand in light of Almeida & Urbizagastegui's claims for the music's efficacy. Perhaps they have greatly overestimated the importance of the music; perhaps their assessment is simply different from that of the insurgents' leadership. They do note that "another musical group within the ERP, Los Torogroces de Morazan, continued to function after 1989. But for Cutumay the ERP thought members could serve more important functions besides music" (Almeida 1997).

131. Staggenborg & Lang 2003:4, 5.

132. Carawan & Carawan 1993:260.

133. Glazer 1998:30.
134. In Percy 1998:42.
135. On the album *Happy & Artie Traum* (Capitol 1969).

References

Websites and List Serves

Amnesty International. [n.d.] wysiwyg://92/http://www.angelfire.com/weord/flash333/freedom/amnesty htm.

Korona, Ray. 2000. Posting to laborheritage@yahoogroups.com, July 11.

Live Aid Home Page. [n.d.] www.herald.co.uk/local_info/la_memories.html. Last accessed July 7, 2010.

People's Music Network for Songs of Freedom and Struggle. [n.d.] http://www.peoplesmusic.org. Last accessed July 7, 2010.

Seven by Nine Squares. [n.d.] "Give up art, save the starving." http://www.thing.de/projekte/7:9%23/y_Give_Up_Art.html. Last accessed July 7, 2010.

Songs for Social Change. [n.d.] Home page. http://www.globalvisions.organization/cl/sfsc.

Townshend, Pete. 2006. "Pete's diaries." http://web.archive.org/web/20061205225327/http://www.petetownshend.co.uk/diary/display.cfm?id=285&zone=diary. May 25

Zurofsky, Bennet. 2001. Posting to laborheritage@yahoo.com, October 26.

Correspondence

Almeida, Paul. 1997. Private correspondence to Rosenthal, September 10.

Cohen, Phil. 1997. Private correspondence to Rosenthal, August 9.

Dienst, Alicia. 1998. Private correspondence to Rosenthal, July 24.

Garofalo, Reebee. 2009. Private correspondence to the authors, January 25.

Kaskie, Christopher J. (Publisher, Pitchfork). 2009. Private correspondence to Rosenthal, April 14.

Kolbe, Jason 1999. Private correspondence to Rosenthal, Spring.

Linehan, Sean (Video Production Coordinator of J Records/RCA Music Group). 2005. Private correspondence to Rosenthal, June 27.

Marcus, Greil. 2005. Private correspondence to Rosenthal, September 7.

Opp, Karl-Dieter. 1998. Private correspondence to Rosenthal, October 23.
Rossman, Michael. 1967. Private communication with Flacks, April.
Schwartz, Debbie (Manager, special projects, The Nielsen Company). 2009. Private correspondence to Rosenthal, April 2.
Smith, Michael. 2004. Private correspondence to Rosenthal, November 30.

Film Recordings

Billy Bragg and Pete Seeger: The Concert for Jobs, Peace, and Freedom. 1992. Michael Uys (director). Democratic Socialists of America.
Casablanca. 1942. Michael Curtiz (director). Warner Brothers.
The International. 2000. Peter Miller (director). First run/Icarus Films.
Money for Nothing. 2001. Sut Jhally (executive producer), Kembrew McLeod (producer). Media Education Foundation.
Swing Kids. 1993. Thomas Carter (director). Hollywood Pictures.
We Shall Overcome. 1989. Jim Brown (director). California Newsreel.

Music Recordings

Almanac Singers. 1941a. *Songs of John Doe.* Almanac Records 102.
———. 1941b. *Talking Union.* Keynote #106.
A.P.P.L.E. 1994. *Neither Victims nor Executioners.* Broken Rekids BRKN 21.
The Beatles. 1969. *Yellow Submarine.* Apple SW 153.
———. 1968. *The Beatles* (otherwise known as *The White Album*). Apple SWBO 101.
Biebl, Hansi. 1981. *Der Lange Weg.* AMIGA 855 842.
Consolidated. 1991. *Friendly Fascism.* Nettwerk X2-13089.
Dobkin, Alix. 1998 [1973]. *Lavender Jane Loves Women.* Women's Wax Works 023234000127.
Franklin, Aretha. 1967. *I Never Loved a Man the Way I Love You.* Atlantic 8139.
Gabriel, Peter. 1980. *Melt.* Mercury UMER 13848.
Guthrie, Woody. 1999. *The Asch Recordings, Volume 1.* Smithsonian Folkways SFW 40100.
Haggard, Merle. 1969. *Okie from Muskogee.* Capitol ST 384.
Johnson, Robert. 1961 [1936–1937]. *King of the Delta Blues Singers.* Columbia 1654.
The Last Poets. 2002 [1970/1971]. *The Last Poets.* Douglas 3 (1970), Douglas Z-30811 (1971). Rereleased as a CD, Fuel 2000 Records 3020612262.
Lead Belly. 1989. *Leadbelly: Bourgeois Blues—Golden Classics, Part 1.* Collectibles COL5183.
Lehrer, Tom. 1965. *That Was the Year That Was.* Warner/Reprise R/RS 6179.
Lennon, John. 1971. *Imagine.* Apple SW 3379.
Little Steven & The Disciples of Soul. 1984. *Voice of America.* EMI ST 17120.
Newman, Randy. 1977. *Little Criminals.* Warner Brothers 3079-2.
Nirvana. 1994. *MTV Unplugged in New York.* Geffen 24727.
Ochs, Phil. 1966. *Phil Ochs in Concert.* Elektra EKL-310.
———. 1964. *I Ain't Marching Anymore.* Elektra EKS 7287.
Propagandhi. 1995. *I'd Rather Be Flag Burning.* Recess Records.
Public Enemy. 2002. *Revolverlution.* Koch Records.
———. 1998. *He Got Game.* Def Jam 314558130-2.
Queen Latifah. 1993. *Black Reign.* Motown 374636370-2.
Rage Against the Machine. 1992. *Rage Against the Machine.* Epic ZK 52959.

Raitt, Bonnie. 1974. *Streetlights*. Warner Brothers BS 2818.

Robeson, Paul 1976. *Scandalize My Name*. Classics Record Library 30-5647.

The Rolling Stones. 1968. *Beggars Banquet*. London PS 539.

Rosselson, Leon, and Roy Bailey. 1977. *Love, Loneliness and Laundry*. Fuse CF 271.

Seeger, Pete. 1989 [1963]. *We Shall Overcome—Complete Carnegie Hall CD*. Columbia 45312.

Shelter. 1995. *Mantra*. Roadrunner/Supersoul Records B000000H5T.

Springsteen, Bruce. 1978. *Darkness on the Edge of Town*. Columbia JC 35318.

Sweet Honey in the Rock. 2003 [1981]. *Good News*. Flying Fish LP. Rereleased as a CD, Cooking Vinyl CPPKCD 027.

Talking Heads. 1977. *Talking Heads: 77*. Sire SR 6036.

Thunderclap Newman. 1969. *Hollywood Dreams*. Track SD 8264.

Traum, Happy and Artie. 1969. *Happy & Artie Traum*. Capitol ST-586.

Various Artists. 1997 [1952] *Anthology of American Folk Music* (compiled by Harry Smith). Folkways Records FP251/252/253. Rereleased reissued as Smithsonian Folkways Recordings SFW40090.

Various Artists. 1996. *Songs for Political Action* (compiled by Ronald D. Cohen and Dave Samuelson). Bear Family Records BCD 15720 JL.

The Weavers. 1994. *Kisses Sweeter Than Wine*. Omega OCD 3021.

The Who. 1971. *Who's Next*. Decca DL7-9182/MCA-3024.

Conference Proceedings

Music and Movements Conference, University of California at Santa Barbara, February 20–22, 1997. Panel discussions.

Articles and Books

Adorno, Theodor. 1990 [1941]. "On popular music." From *Studies in Philosophy and Social Science* 9:17–48. Reprinted, pp. 301–314, in Simon Frith and Andrew Goodwin (eds.), *On Record*. New York: Pantheon.

———. 1950. "A social critique of radio music." Pp. 309–316 in Bernard Berelson and Morris Janowitz (eds.), *Reader in Public Opinion and Communication*. Glencoe, IL: The Free Press.

Alexander, Peter J. 1996. "Entropy and popular culture: Product diversity in the popular music recording industry." *American Sociological Review* 61 (1):171–174.

Allen, Gary. 1972 [1969]. "More subversion than meets the ear." Originally published as "That music, there's more to it than meets the ear," in *American Opinion* 12 (February):49–62. Reprinted, pp. 151–166, in R. Serge Denisoff and Richard Peterson (eds.), *The Sounds of Social Change*. New York: Rand McNally.

Allor, Martin. 1988. "Relocating the site of the audience." *Critical Studies in Mass Communications* 5:217–233.

Almeida, Paul, and Rubén Urbizagastegui. 1999. "Cutumay Camones: Popular music in El Salvador's National Liberation Movement." *Latin American Perspectives* 26 (March):13–42.

———. 1997. "Popular music and social movement in El Salvador: The national liberation song of Cutumay Camones." Paper presented at the Music and Social Movements Conference, Santa Barbara, February 20–22.

American Social History Project. 1992. *Who Built America? Volume II*. New York: Pantheon.

Amnesty International USA. 1986. "Conspiracy of hope." *Amnesty Action* (Summer):6–10.

Anderson, Birgitte, and Marion Frenz. 2008. "The impact of music downloads and P2P file-sharing on the purchase of music." Industry Canada. http://www.ic.gc.ca/eic/site/ippd-dppi.nsf/eng/h_ip01456.html. Last accessed July 7, 2010.

Anderson, Craig A., Nicholas I. Carnagey, and Janie Eubanks. 2003. "Exposure to violent media: The effects of songs with violent lyrics on aggressive thoughts and feelings." *Journal of Personality and Social Psychology* 84 (5):960–971.

Appnel, Timothy. 1994. "Interview with Philip Steir." *Oculus Magazine* 1 (VI):14.

Aronowitz, Alfred G., and Marshall Blonsky. 1964. "Three's company: Peter, Paul and Mary." *Saturday Evening Post,* May 30, p. 32.

Auslander, H. Ben 1989 [1981]. "If ya wanna end war and stuff, you gotta sing loud." *Journal of American Culture* 42:108–113. Reprinted, pp. 179–184, in Timothy E. Scheurer (ed.), *American Popular Music, Volume II.* Bowling Green, OH: Bowling Green State University Popular Press.

Ayers, Michael. 2006a. "Introduction " Pp. 1–8 in Michael Ayers (ed.), *Cybersounds.* New York: Peter Lang.

Ayers, Michael D. (ed.). 2006b. *Cybersounds: Essays on Virtual Music Culture (Digital Formations)* New York: Peter Lang.

Ayers, Michael D., and Martha McCaughey (eds.). 2003. *Cyberactivism.* New York: Routledge.

Bagby, Tiffany. 1999. "Exchange" (letters to the editor). *The Nation,* December 27, pp. 2, 24.

Balch, Elizabeth. 1914. "Songs of labor." *Survey* 31:14 (January 3):412.

Ballantine, Christopher. 1984. *Music and Its Social Meanings.* New York: Gordon and Breach.

Barthes, Roland. 1990 [1977]. "The grain of the voice." From *Image-Music-Text* (Stephen Heath, translation). Hill and Wang Extracted, pp. 293–300, in Simon Frith and Andrew Goodwin (eds.), *On Record.* New York: Pantheon.

Basu, Dipannita. 1997. "The economics of rap music: An examination of the opportunities and resources of African Americans involved in the business aspects of rap music." Paper presented at the American Sociological Association annual meeting, Toronto, Ontario, 1997.

Becker, Howard. 1963. *Outsiders.* New York: Free Press of Glencoe.

Bell, Desmond. 1990. *Acts of Union: Youth Culture and Sectarianism in Northern Ireland* (Youth Questions). Houndsmills, London: Macmillan Education.

Benjamin, Walter. 1999 [1936]. "The work of art in the age of mechanical reproduction." *Zeitschrift für Sozialforschung* 5(1). Pp. 219–253 in Walter Benjamin (Hannah Arendt, ed.), *Illuminations.* London: Pimlico.

———. 1978. "The author as producer." Pp. 220–239 in Walter Benjamin (Peter Demetz, ed.), *Reflections.* New York: Harcourt Brace Jovanovich.

Betz, Albrecht. 1995. "Music and politics: Theme and variations." Chapter 16, pp. 393–405, in David Blake (ed.), *Hanns Eisler: A Miscellany.* Luxembourg: Harwood Academic.

Biddix, J. Patrick, and Han Woo Park. 2008. "Online networks of student protest: The case of the living wage campaign." *New Media & Society* 10 (6):871–891.

Bird, Stewart, Dan Georgakas, and Deborah Shaffer. 1985. "Fanning the flames." Pp. 21–24 in Stewart Bird, Dan Georgakas, and Deborah Shaffer (eds.), *Solidarity Forever.* Chicago: Lake View.

Brace, Tim, and Paul Friedlander. 1992. "Rock and roll on the new long march." Chapter 7, pp. 115–128, in Reebee Garofalo (ed.), *Rockin' the Boat.* Boston: South End.

Bradby, Barbara. 1990. "Do-talk and don't talk." Pp. 341–368 in Simon Frith and Andrew Goodwin (eds.), *On Record.* New York: Pantheon.

Bradley, Ed, and Bob Dylan. 2004. "Dylan looks back" (Ed Bradley interview of Bob Dylan on *Sixty Minutes,* December 5.). http://www.cbsnews.com/stories/2004/12/02/60minutes/main658799.shtml. Last accessed July 7, 2010.

Bragg, Billy. 2000. "Can music still make a difference?" *Democratic Left* 27 (4):40.

Branch, Taylor. 1988. *Parting the Waters.* New York: Simon & Schuster.

Brazier, Richard. 1972 [1968]. "The Industrial Workers of the World's 'Little Red Songbook.'" *Labor*

History (Winter):91–104. Reprinted, pp. 60–71, in R. Serge Denisoff and Richard Peterson, (eds.), *The Sounds of Social Change.* New York: Rand McNally.

Brennan, Tim. 1994. "Off the gangsta tip: A rap appreciation, or forgetting about Los Angeles." *Critical Inquiry* 20 (Summer):663–693.

Bricca, Jacob. 1998. "The awful truth: Alternative's dead end." *Decipher* (July): 2–9.

——. 1992. "Political music in a postmodern age." Undergraduate paper, Wesleyan University, Middletown, CT. December 21.

Broyles-González, Yolanda. 1997. "The powers of music and the Chicano civil rights movement." Paper presented at the Music and Social Movements conference, University of California at Santa Barbara, Santa Barbara, CA, February 20–22.

Buechler, Steven M. 1997 [1995]. "New social movement theories." *The Sociological Quarterly* 36 (3):441–464. Reprinted, pp. 295–319, in Steven M. Buechler and F. Kurt Cylke, Jr. (eds.), *Social Movements.* London: Mayfield.

Burnett, Robert. 1993. "The popular music industry in transition." *Popular Music & Society* 17 (1):87–114.

Burton, Sarah. 2003. "Truth in the hands of artists." *AlterNet,* November 24. www.alternet.org/story/17242. Last accessed July 7, 2010.

Buxton, David. 1990 [1983]. "Rock music, the star system, and the rise of consumerism." *Telos* 57. Reprinted, pp. 427–440, in Simon Frith and Andrew Goodwin (eds.), *On Record.* New York: Pantheon.

Carawan, Guy, and Candie Carawan. 1993. "Sowing on the mountain " Chapter 12, pp. 245–261, in Stephen L. Fisher (ed.), *Fighting Back in Appalachia.* Philadelphia· Temple University Press.

——. 1990. *Sing for Freedom.* Bethlehem, PA: Sing Out.

Castellini, John. 1962. *Rudiments of Music.* New York: W. W. Norton.

Castells, Manuel. 1983. *The City and the Grassroots.* Berkeley: University of California Press.

Chang, Jeff. 2003. "'Stakes is high': Conscious rap, neosoul and the hip-hop generation." *The Nation,* January 13/20, 2003, pp. 17–21.

Chapple, Steve, and Reebee Garofalo. 1977. *Rock 'n' Roll Is Here to Pay.* Chicago: Nelson-Hall.

Charters, Samuel. 1970. *The Poetry of the Blues.* New York: Avon.

Chiu, Amanda. 2002. "Fuel to the fire: The role of hardcore in the animal rights movement." Unpublished senior thesis, Wesleyan University, Middletown, CT.

Christenson, Peter, and Donald Roberts. 1998. *It's Not Only Rock & Roll.* Cresskill, NJ: Hampton.

Christgau, Robert. 1994. "Rah, rah, sis-boom-bah." Pp. 221–226 in Andrew Ross and Tricia Rose (eds.), *Microphone Fiends.* New York: Routledge.

Citron, Marci. 1994. "Feminist approaches to musicology." Pp. 15–34 in Susan Cook and Judy Tsou (eds.), *Cecilia Reclaimed.* Urbana: University of Illinois.

Cloonan, Martin, and Reebee Garofalo (eds.). 2003. *Policing Pop.* Philadelphia: Temple University Press.

Cohen, Ronald D., and Dave Samuelson. 1996. *Songs for Political Action* (booklet accompanying the album *Songs for Political Action*). Bear Family Records BCD 15720 JL).

Collins, John. 1992. "Some antihegemonic aspects of African popular music." Chapter 11, pp. 185–194, in Reebee Garofalo (ed.), *Rockin' the Boat.* Boston: South End.

Cook, Jean. 2007. "Untangling net neutrality: One music advocate's perspective." Future of Music Coalition. www.futureofmusic.org/articles/NNWomex.cfm. Accessed April 3, 2009.

Coplon, Jeff. 1989. "The skinhead reich." *Utne Reader* (May/June):80–89.

Cott, Jonathan. 1987 [1978]. "Mick Jagger: The *Rolling Stone* interview." *Rolling Stone* (June). Reprinted, pp. 319–331, in Jann S. Wenner (ed.), *What a Long, Strange Trip It's Been: 20 Years of Rolling Stone.* New York: Friendly.

Cantwell, Robert. 1996. *When We Were Good.* Cambridge, MA: Harvard University Press.

Craddock-Willis, Andre. 1989. "Rap music and the black musical tradition." *Radical America* (October):29–40.

Crafts, Susan, Daniel Cavicchi, and Charles Keil. 1993. *My Music*. Hanover, NH: Wesleyan/University Press of New England.

Crosby, David, and David Bender. 2000. *Stand and Be Counted*. New York: HarperCollins.

Cruz, Jon. 1999. *Culture on the Margins*. Princeton, NJ: Princeton University Press.

D, Chuck. 1999–2000. "Rewind " *Blaze* (December/January):136.

———. 1991. "Chuck D lecture at the University of Pennsylvania." Pp. 364–378 in Joseph Eure and James Spady (eds.), *Nation Conscious Rap*. New York: PC International.

Dahl, Robert. 1961. *Who Governs?* New Haven, CT: Yale University Press.

Daley, David. 2001. "Something to direct the inspiration." *Hartford Courant*, December 14, p. G8.

Davis, Dennis K., and James Jasinski. 1994. "Beyond the cultural wars: An agenda for research on communication and culture." Pp. 149–157 in Mark R. Levy and Michael Gurevitch (eds.), *Defining Media Studies*. Oxford: Oxford University Press.

Davis, R. G. 2002. "Music from the left (part 2)." *US Opera* (Winter). http://www.usopeaweb.com/2002/jan/left2.htm.

Dawidoff, Nicholas. 1997. "The pop populist." *New York Times Magazine*, January 26, pp. 27+.

Denisoff. R. Serge. 1983. *Sing a Song of Social Significance*. Bowling Green, OH: Popular.

———. 1972. "Folk music and the American left." Chapter 8, pp. 105–120, in R. Serge Denisoff and Richard Peterson (eds.), *The Sounds of Social Change*. New York: Rand McNally.

Denisoff, R. Serge, and Mark H. Levine. 1972. "Brainwashing or background noise: The popular protest song." Chapter 17, pp. 213–221, in R. Serge Denisoff and Richard Peterson (eds.), *The Sounds of Social Change*. New York: Rand McNally.

Denning, Michael 1996. *The Cultural Front*. New York: Verso.

DeNora, Tia. 1995. "The musical composition of social reality? Music, action and reflexivity." *Sociological Review* 43:2 (May):295–315.

Denselow, Robin. 1989. *When the Music's Over*. London: Faber and Faber.

Deserto, Frank. 2009. "NIN set to launch iPhone application." http://blog.limewire.com/posts/13735-nin-set-to-launch-iphone-application/. April 7. Last accessed July 7, 2010.

Dhar, Vasant, and Elaine Chang. 2007. "Does chatter matter? The impact of user-generated content on music sales." IOMS: Information Systems Working Papers. http://hdl.handle.net/2451/23783. Posted October 24. Last accessed July 7, 2010.

DiCola, Peter. 2006. "False premises, false promises: A quantitative history of ownership consolidation in the radio industry." Future of Music Coalition. http://www.futureofmusic.org/article/research/false-premises-false-promises. Posted December 13. Last accessed July 7, 2010.

Doss-Cortes, Kimberly. 1999. "Exchange" (letters to the editor). *The Nation*, December 27, p. 2.

Driscoll, O'Connell. 1987 [1975]. "Stevie Wonder in New York." *Rolling Stone* (June). Reprinted, pp. 247–260, in Jann S. Wenner (ed.), *What a Long, Strange Trip It's Been: 20 Years of Rolling Stone*. New York: Friendly.

Duany, Jorge. 1984. "Popular music in Puerto Rico: Toward an anthropology of Salsa." *Latin American Music Review* 5 (2):186–216.

Dunaway, David K. 1987a. "Music as political communication in the United States." Chapter 2, pp. 36–52, in James Lull (ed.), *Popular Music and Communication*. New York: Sage.

———. 1987b. "Music and politics in the United States." *Folk Music Journal* 5 (3):268–294.

———. 1981. *How Can I Keep from Singing?* New York: McGraw-Hill.

Dundes, Alan. 1964. "Texture, text, and context." *Southern Folklore Quarterly* 28 (4):251–265.

Dyer, Richard. 1990 [1979]. "In defense of disco." *Gay Left* 8. Reprinted, pp. 410–418, in Simon Frith and Andrew Goodwin (eds.), *On Record*. New York: Pantheon.

Echols, Alice. 1994. "White faces, black masks." *Village Voice*, February 15, pp. 91–92.

Edmunds, Neil. 2000. "Music and politics: The case of the Russian Association of Proletarian Musicians." *The Slavonic and East European Review* 78:1 (January):66–89.

Edsforth, Ronald. 1991. "Popular culture and politics in modern America." Pp. 1–15 in Ronald Edsforth and Larry Bennett (eds.), *Popular Culture and Political Change in Modern America.* New York: SUNY Press.

Eisler, Hanns (Manfred Grabs, ed.). 1999 [1978]. *Hanns Eisler: A Rebel in Music.* Berlin: Seven Seas. Reprint, London: Kahn & Averill.

Ekedal, Rahsan, Emily Fox, Antonio Roman-Alcala, Gabriel Ramos, and Tania Padilla. 1999. "Exchange" (letters to the editor). *The Nation,* December 27, p. 2.

eMarketer. 2006. "Illegal downloading down." www.emarketer.com/article.aspx?R = 1003924. Posted April 17. Last accessed July 7, 2010.

Esslin, Martin. 1969. *Brecht: The Man and His Work.* Garden City, NY: Anchor

Eyerman, Ron. 2002. "Music in movement: Cultural politics and old and new social movements." *Qualitative Sociology* 25:3 (Fall):443–458.

Eyerman, Ron, and Andrew Jamison. 1998. *Music and Social Movements.* Cambridge: Cambridge University Press.

———. 1995. "Social movements and cultural transformation: Popular music in the 1960s." *Media, Culture & Society* 17:449–468.

———. 1991. *Social Movements: A Cognitive Approach.* University Park: Pennsylvania State University.

Feld, Steven. 1994. "Communication, music, and speech about music." Pp. 77–95 in Charles Keil and Steven Feld, *Music Grooves.* Chicago: University of Chicago Press.

Finnegan, Ruth. 1989. *The Hidden Musicians.* New York: Cambridge University Press.

Fisher, Miles. 1953. *Negro Slaves Songs in the United States.* New York: Russel & Russel.

Fisher, William W., III. 2004. *Promises to Keep.* Palo Alto: Stanford University Press.

Fiske, John. 1989. *Understanding Popular Culture.* Boston: Unwin Hyman.

Flacks, Marc A. 1995. "'All I want is to feel this way': Rock music and the myth of democracy." *Journal of Popular Music Studies* 7 (1):25–69.

Flacks, Richard. 2004. "Knowledge for what? Thoughts on the state of social movements studies." Chapter 10 in Jeff Goodwin and James M. Jasper (eds.), *Rethinking Social Movements.* Lanham, MD: Rowman & Littlefield.

——— 1988. *Making History.* New York: Columbia University Press.

———. 1971. *Youth and Social Change.* Chicago: Rand McNally.

Fox, William S., and James D. Williams. 1974. "Political orientation and music preferences among college students." *The Public Opinion Quarterly* 38 (3):352–371.

Frank, Richard. 1934. "Negro revolutionary music." *New Masses,* May 15, pp. 29–30.

Frank, Tom. 1995. "Alternative to what?" Pp. 109–119 in Ron Sakolsky and Fred Ho (eds.), *Sounding Off.* Brooklyn, NY: Autonomedia.

Friedländer, Paul, and Peter Miller. 2006. *Rock & Roll: A Social History.* New York: Basic Books.

Friedman, Debra, and Doug McAdam. 1992. "Collective identity and activism." Pp. 156–173 in Aldon Morris and Carol Mueller (eds.), *Frontiers in Social Movement Theory.* New Haven, CT: Yale University.

Frith, Simon. 1996. *Performing Rites.* Cambridge, MA: Harvard University Press.

———. 1992a [1987]. "Toward an aesthetic of popular music." Pp. 133–149 in Richard Leppert and Susan McClary (eds.), *Music and Society.* Cambridge, UK: Cambridge University Press.

———. 1992b. "The cultural study of popular music." Pp. 174–186 in Lawrence Grossberg et al. (eds.), *Cultural Studies.* New York: Routledge.

———. 1990 [1985]. "Afterthoughts." *New Statesman,* August 23. Reprinted, pp. 419–426, in Simon Frith and Andrew Goodwin (eds.), *On Record.* New York: Pantheon.

———. 1988a. *Music for Pleasure.* New York: Routledge.

————. 1988b. "Art ideology and pop practice." Pp. 461–475 in Cary Nelson and Lawrence Grossberg (eds.), *Marxism and the Interpretation of Culture*. Urbana: University of Illinois.

————. 1981. *Sound Effects*. New York: Pantheon.

Frith, Simon, and Andrew Goodwin (eds.). 1990. *On Record*. New York: Pantheon.

Frith, Simon, and Angela McRobbie. 1990 [1978]. "Rock and sexuality." *Screen Education* 29. Reprinted, pp. 371–389, in Simon Frith and Andrew Goodwin (eds.), *On Record*. New York: Pantheon.

Gaines, Donna. 1994. "Border crossing in the U.S.A." Pp. 227–234 in Andrew Ross and Tricia Rose (eds.), *Microphone Fiends*. New York: Routledge.

————. 1991. *Teenage Wasteland*. New York: Pantheon.

Gans, Herbert J. 1969. "The politics of culture in America: A sociological analysis." *Communications* 14:251–266.

Gantz, W., H. M. Gartenberg, M. L. Pearson, and S. O. Schiller. 1978. "Gratifications and expectations associated with pop music among adolescents." *Popular Music & Society* 6 (1):81–89.

Garofalo, Reebee. 2006. "Popular and protest music post–9/11." *Resist* 15:4 (July/August):1–3, 11.

————. 1992. "Understanding megaevents." Pp. 15–35 in Reebee Garofalo (ed.), *Rockin' the Boat*. Boston: South End.

————. 1987. "How autonomous is relative?" *Popular Music* 7 (1):77–92.

GartnerG2 & The Berkman Center for Internet & Society at Harvard Law School. 2003. "Copyright and digital media in a post-Napster world." http://cyber.law.harvard.edu/publications. Accessed March 10, 2009.

Gelatt, Roland. 1965. *The Fabulous Phonograph*. New York: Appleton-Century.

George, Nelson. 1988. *The Death of Rhythm & Blues*. New York: Pantheon.

Gillett, Charlie. 1970. *The Sound of the City*. London: Souvenir.

Gilroy, Paul. 1993. *The Black Atlantic*. Cambridge, MA: Harvard University Press.

Gitlin, Todd. 1987. *The Sixties*. New York: Bantam.

Gittlins, Ian. 1988. "Eat the rich (interview with Joe Strummer)." *Melody Maker* 64 (July 23):10–11.

Giugni, Marco G. 2001. *Political Altruism?* Lanham, MD: Rowman & Littlefield.

Glasser, Ruth. 1995. *My Music Is My Flag*. Berkeley: University of California Press.

Glazer, Joe. 1998. "Singing the gospel of brotherhood and sisterhood." *Labor's Heritage* 9:3 (Winter):22–37.

Gleason, Ralph J. 1972 [1969]. "Cultural revolution." Originally published as "The greater sound" in *Yale Drama Review* 13 (Summer):160–167. Reprinted, pp. 137–147, in R. Serge Denisoff and Richard Peterson (eds.), *The Sounds of Social Change*. New York: Rand McNally.

González, Juan-Pablo. 1991. "Hegemony and counterhegemony of music in Latin America: The Chilean pop." *Popular Music & Society* 15 (2):63–78.

Goodwin, Andrew. 1992. "Music, video, media: Why political economy and cultural pessimism are not the same thing." Talk given at the Center for the Humanities, Wesleyan University, Middletown, CT, November 23.

Gottesman, Stephen. 1977. "Tom Dooley's children." *Popular Music & Society* 5:61–78.

Gottlieb, Anthony. 1991. "The music business." *The Economist*, December 21, pp. 3–18.

Gramsci, Antonio. 1992. *Prison Notebooks*. New York: Columbia University Press.

Grant, Barry Keith. 1994. "Purple passages or fiestas in blue?: Notes toward an aesthetic of vocalese." *Popular Music and Society* 18:1 (Spring):125–143.

Gray, Patricia M., Bernie Krause, Jelle Atema, Roger Payne, Carol Krumhansl, and Luis Baptista. 2001. "The music of nature and the nature of music." *Science* 291:5 (January):52–54.

Grazian, David. 2004. "The symbolic economy of authenticity in the Chicago blues scene." Pp. 31–47 in Andy Bennett and Richard Peterson (eds.), *Music Scenes*. Nashville, TN: Vanderbilt University Press.

Green, Archie. 1997a. "Wobbly songs." Paper presented at the Music and Social Movements Conference, February 20–22, University of California at Santa Barbara.

――――. 1997b. Panel discussion on "The folk revival." Music and Social Movements Conference, February 20–22, University of California at Santa Barbara.

Groce, Stephen B., and John Lynxwiler. 1994. "The silent performance: Audience perceptions of musicians' nonverbal behavior." *Popular Music & Society* 18 (1):105–121.

Grossberg, Lawrence. 1993. "Can cultural studies find true happiness in communication?" *Journal of Communication* 43:4 (Autumn):331–339.

――――. 1990 [1986]. "Is there rock after punk?" *Critical Studies in Mass Communication* 3(1). Reprinted, pp. 111–123, in Simon Frith and Andrew Goodwin (eds.), *On Record*. New York: Pantheon.

――――. 1985. "If rock and roll communicates, why must it be so noisy?" Pp. 451–463 in David Horn (ed.), *Popular Music Perspectives 2*. Gothenburg, Sweden: International Association for the Study of Popular Music.

――――. 1983–1984. "The politics of youth culture: Some observations on rock and roll in American culture." *Social Text* 8:104–126.

Halker, Clark D. 1991. *For Democracy, Workers, and God*. Urbana: University of Illinois.

Hall, Stuart. 1981. "Notes on deconstructing the popular." Pp. 227–240 in Raphael Samuel (ed.), *People's History and Socialist Theory*. London: Routledge and Kegan Paul.

――――. 1980. "Encoding/decoding." Pp. 128–138 in Stuart Hall (ed.), *Culture, Media, Language*. London: Hutchinson.

Hamilton, Carol V. 1991. "All that jazz again: Adorno's sociology of music." *Popular Music & Society* 15 (3):31–40.

Hamm, Mark S. 1993. *American Skinheads*. Westport, CT: Praeger.

Hampton, Wayne. 1986. *Guerrilla Minstrels*. Knoxville: University of Tennessee Press.

Hanslick, Eduard. 1974 [1885]. *The Beautiful in Music*. New York: Da Capo.

Hardin, Jesse Wolf. 1995. "Deep ecology: A quarter century of earth minstrelsy." *Humboldt Journal of Social Relations* 21 (1):95–109.

Harrington, Richard. 2000. "Facing the music." *Washington Post*, September 15, p. N40.

――――. 1997. "Recalling songs' role in civil rights fight." *Los Angeles Times*, January 18, p. F6.

Harris, Daniel. 1992. "Make my rainy day." *The Nation*, June 8, pp. 790–793.

Hebdige, Dick. 1990 [1979]. "Style as homology and signifying practice." Extracted from *Subculture: The Meaning of Style* (London: Methuen). Reprinted, pp. 56–65, in Simon Frith and Andrew Goodwin (eds.), *On Record*. New York: Pantheon.

――――. 1988 *Hiding in the Light*. London: Routledge.

――――. 1979. *Subculture: The Meaning of Style*. London: Methuen.

Hennion, Antoine. 1990 [1983]. "The production of success." *Popular Music 3*. Reprinted, pp. 185–206, in Simon Frith and Andrew Goodwin (eds.), *On Record*. New York: Pantheon.

Hentoff, Nat. 1972 [1964]. "The crackin', shakin', breakin' sounds." *The New Yorker*, October 24. Reprinted, pp. 44–61, in Craig McGregor (ed.), *Bob Dylan: A Retrospective*. New York: William Morrow.

Hiatt, Brian, and Evan Serpick. 2007. "The record industry's decline." *Rolling Stone*. http://www.rollingstone.com/news/story/15137581/the_record_industrys_decline. Posted June 28. Accessed April 24, 2009.

Hinkle, Warren. 1991 [1967]. "A social history of the hippies." *Ramparts* (March). Reprinted, pp. 207–232, in Gerald Howard (ed.), *The Sixties*. New York: Paragon.

Ho, Fred Wei-han. 1992. "No longer resistance, but revolution!" Unpublished manuscript.

Honigsheim, Paul. 1989. *Sociologists and Music*. New Brunswick, NJ: Transaction.

Hoover, Michael, and Lisa Stokes. 1998. "Pop music and the limits of cultural critique." *Popular Music & Society* 22 (3):21–38.

Horton, Donald. 1990 [1957]. "The dialogue of courtship in popular songs." *American Journal of Sociology* 62:6 (May):569–578. Reprinted, pp. 14–26, in Simon Frith and Andrew Goodwin (eds.), *On Record.* New York: Pantheon.

Horwitz, Simca. 2001. "The bright fiery cross: Music and the KKK of the 1920s." Unpublished undergraduate paper. Wesleyan University, Middletown, CT.

Hotchner, A. E. 1990. *Blown Away.* New York: Simon & Schuster.

Howard, John Tasker, and James Lyons. 1957. *Modern Music.* New York: Mentor.

Huck, Susan. 1972 [1970]. "The great kid con." *Review of the News,* February 11, pp. 17–24. Reprinted, pp. 167–172, in R. Serge Denisoff and Richard Peterson (eds.), *The Sounds of Social Change.* New York: Rand McNally.

Ian, Janis. 2002. "The internet debacle—An alternative view." *Songwriter,* May 2002, www.janisian.com/article-internet_debacle.html. Last accessed July 7, 2010.

Indie Music Stop. 2009. "CD Baby pays more than 100 million dollars to independent music artists." http://indiemusicstop.wordpress.com/2009/04/01/cd-baby-payouts-surge/. Posted April 1. Last accessed July 7, 2010.

Industrial Workers of the World. 1976. *Songs of the Workers to Fan the Flames of Discontent.* Chicago: Industrial Workers of the World.

Ipsos-Insight. 2002. "File sharing and CD burners proliferate." www.ipsosna.com/news/pressrelease.cfm?id=1542. Posted June 12. Last accessed July 7, 2010.

Jackson, Maurice. 1995. Liner notes to Charlie Haden and Hank Jones, *Steal Away* (Verve 314 527 249-2).

Jamison, Andrew. 1996. "Folk music and postmodern knowledge." Paper presented at 4S/EASST conference, Bielefeld, Germany, October 9–13.

Jensen, Klaus Bruhn. 1987. "Qualitative audience research: Toward an integrative approach to reception." *Critical Studies in Mass Communications* 4:21–36.

Johnson, James D., and Sophie Trawalter. 2000. "Converging interracial consequences of exposure to violent rap music on stereotypical attributions of blacks." *Journal of Experimental Social Psychology* 36:233–251.

Johnston, Hank, Enrique Larana, and Joseph P. Gusfield. 1997. "Identities, grievances, and new social movements." Pp. 274–295 in Steven M. Buechler and F. Kurt Cylke, Jr. (eds.), *Social Movements.* London: Mayfield.

Jones, Andrew F. 1992. *Like a Knife.* Ithaca, NY: Cornell University East Asia Program.

Jones, LeRoi (now Amiri Baraka). 1963. *Blues People.* New York: William Morrow.

Jones, Matt. 1994. "Music: An organizer's tool." *Sassafras* (Fall):8–10.

Joyce, Don 2009. "Vapor music." *Culture Machine* 10:109–113.

Kahn, Richard, and Douglas Kellner. 2004. "Internet subcultures and political activism." Pp. 217–230 in Pepi Leistyna (ed.), *Cultural Studies: From Theory to Action.* Hoboken, NJ: John Wiley & Sons. http://richardkahn.org/writings/tep/internetsubculturesoppositionalpolitics.pdf. Last accessed July 7, 2010.

Kan, Alex, and Nick Hayes. 1994. "Big beat in Poland." Pp. 41–54 in Sabrina Petra Ramet (ed.), *Rocking the State.* Boulder, CO: Westview.

Karroll, Jaimee. 1996. "Twentieth-century song as an instrument of activism." Unpublished MA thesis, Mills College, Oakland, CA.

Kater, Michael H. 1997. *The Twisted Muse.* Oxford: Oxford University Press.

Katz, Mark. 2004. *Capturing Sound.* Berkeley: University of California Press.

Kaufman, L. A. 1994. "Praise the Lord, and Mammon." *The Nation,* September 26, pp. 306–307.

Kealy, Edward R. 1990 [1979]. "From craft to art: The case of sound mixers and popular music." *Sociology of Work and Occupations* 6. Reprinted, pp. 207–220, in Simon Frith and Andrew Goodwin (eds.), *On Record.* New York: Pantheon.

Keil, Charles. 1994. "Motion and feeling through music." Pp. 53–76 in Charles Keil and Steven Feld, *Music Grooves*. Chicago: University of Chicago Press.

Keil, Charles, and Steven Feld. 1994. "Getting into the dialogic groove." Pp. 1–50 in Charles Keil and Steven Feld, *Music Grooves*. Chicago: University of Chicago.

Kelly, Blair. [n.d.] "File-sharing networks." http://www.nohander.com/personal/mmedia1a03/index.htm. Accessed March 11, 2009.

King, Mary. 1987. *Freedom Song*. New York: Quill.

King, Stephen A. 1998. "International reggae, democratic socialism, and the secularization of the Rastafarian movement, 1972–1980." *Popular Music & Society* 22 (3):39–60.

Kinnally, William, Anamarcia Lacauo, Steven McClung, and Barry Sapolsky. 2008. "Getting up on the download." *New Media & Society* 10 (6):893–913.

Kirk-Duggan, Cheryl A. 1997. *Exorcizing Evil*. New York: Orbis.

Kivy, Peter. 1989. *Sound Sentiment*. Philadelphia: Temple University Press.

———. 1980. *The Corded Shell*. Princeton, NJ: Princeton University Press.

Klandermans, Bert. 1997. *The Social Psychology of Protest*. Cambridge, MA: Blackwell.

Klein, Joe. 1980. *Woody Guthrie: A Life*. New York: Knopf.

Kofsky, Frank. 1970. *Black Nationalism and the Revolution in Music*. New York: Pathfinder.

Kot, Greg. 2005. "Pitchfork e-zine tells indie fans what's hot and not." Honoluluadvertiser.com, May 8. http://the.honoluluadvertiser.com/article/2005/May/08/il/il22p.html. Last accessed July 7, 2010.

Kun, Josh. 2009. "Mexican bands hear success calling." *New York Times*, April 3. http://www.nytimes.com/2009/04/05/arts/music/05kun.html. Last accessed July 7, 2010.

Kurti, Laszlo. 1994. "'How can I be a human being?' Culture, youth and musical opposition in Hungary." Pp. 73–102 in Sabrina Petra Ramet (ed.), *Rocking the State*. Boulder, CO: Westview.

Kusek, David, and Gerd Leonhard. 2005. *The Future of Music*. Boston: Berklee.

Lahr, John. 2000. "Get happy." *The New Yorker*, December 11, pp. 120–123.

Laing, Dave. 1990 [1971]. "Listen to me." Extracted from *Buddy Holly* (London: Vista). Pp. 326–340 in Simon Frith and Andrew Goodwin (eds.), *On Record*. New York: Pantheon.

———. 1985. *One Chord Wonders*. Philadelphia: Open University.

Larana, Enrique, Hank Johnston, and Joseph R. Gusfield. 1994. *New Social Movements*. Philadelphia: Temple University Press.

Lay, Shawn (ed.). 1992. *The Invisible Empire in the West*. Urbana: University of Illinois Press.

Lazarsfeld, Paul, and Robert K. Merton. 1948. "Mass communication, popular taste, and organized social action." Pp. 78–115 in Lyman Bryson (ed.), *The Communication of Ideas*. New York: Harper.

Leitner, Olaf. 1994. "Rock music in the GDR: An epitaph." Pp. 17–40 in Sabrina Petra Ramet (ed.), *Rocking the State*. Boulder, CO: Westview.

Leming, James S. 1987. "Rock music and the socialization of moral values in early adolescence." *Youth & Society* 18:4 (June):363–383.

Lemisch, Jesse. 1986a. "I dreamed I saw MTV last night." *The Nation*, October 18, pp. 361, 374–376.

———. 1986b. "The politics of Left culture." *The Nation*, December 20, pp. 700–704.

Lerner, Michael. 1991. *Surplus Powerlessness*. Atlantic Highlands, NJ: Humanities Press International.

Lester, Julius. 1964. "Freedom songs in the south." *Broadside*, February 7, pp. 1–2.

Levine, Mark, and Thomas Harig. 1975. "The role of rock: A review and critique of alternative perspective on the impact of rock music." *Popular Music & Society* 4 (4):195–207.

Lewis, George H. 1983. "The meanings in the music and the music's in me." *Theory, Culture & Society* 1 (3):133–141.

Lewis, Miles Marshall. 2003. "Russell Simmons's rap." *The Nation*, January 13/20, pp. 21–23.

Lewisohn, Mark. 1988. *The Beatles Recording Sessions*. New York: Harmony.

Lidtke, Vernon. 1982. "Songs and Nazis: Political music and social change in twentieth-century

Germany " Pp. 167–200 in Gary D. Stark and Bede Karl Lackner (eds.), *Essays on Culture and Society in Modern Germany*. College Station: University of Texas at Arlington.

Lieberman, Robbie. 1989. *My Song Is My Weapon*. Urbana: University of Illinois Press.

Liebowitz, Stan. 2003. "Will MP3 downloads annihilate the record industry? The record so far." www.utdallas.edu/~liebowit/intprop/records.pdf. Accessed March 25, 2009.

Light, Alan. 1992. "Ice-T: The *Rolling Stone* interview." *Rolling Stone* 641 (October 15), pp. 28–32, 60.

Lipsitz, George. 1994. *Rainbow at Midnight*. Urbana: University of Illinois Press.

———. 1993. "Foreword." Pp. ix–xix in Susan Crafts, Daniel Cavicchi, and Charles Keil (eds.), *My Music*. Hanover, NH: University Press of New England.

———. 1992. "Chicano rock: Cruising around the historical bloc." Pp. 267–280 in Reebee Garofalo (ed.), *Rockin' the Boat*. Boston: South End.

Lopes, Paul D. 1992. "Innovation and diversity in the popular music industry, 1969–1990." *American Sociological Review* 57 (February):56–71.

Lott, Jeffrey. 1994. "Moral imperatives." *Swarthmore College Bulletin*, May, p. 11.

Love, Courtney. 2000. "Courtney Love does the math." *Salon*, June 14. http://dir.salon.com/tech/feature/2000/06/14/love/index.html.

Lowenfels, Lillian.1941. "One million Americans have heard 'Almanacs.'" *Daily Worker*, September 2, p. 7.

Lumer, Robert. 1991. "Pete Seeger and the attempt to revive the folk music process." *Popular Music & Society* 15 (1):45–58

Ma'anit, Adam. 2003. "Politics with soul: Rhythms of resistance can be heard all over the world." *New Internationalist* 359 (August):9–12.

MacGregor, Brent, and David E. Morrison. 1995. "From focus groups to editing groups: A new method of reception analysis." *Media, Culture & Society* 17:141–150.

Mann, Jim. 1985. "Ready to boogie, pop music: China picks up the beat." *Los Angeles Times*, February 15, Part 1, p. 1.

Marcus, Greil. 2000. "Raising the stakes in punk rock." *New York Times*, June 18, Section 2, p. 1.

———. 1980. "The Beatles." Pp. 177–189 in Jim Miller (ed.), *The Rolling Stone Illustrated History of Rock and Roll*. New York: Random House.

———. 1972. "A new awakening." Reprinted, pp. 127–136, in R. Serge Denisoff and Richard Peterson (eds.), *The Sounds of Social Change*. New York: Rand McNally.

Marcuse, Herbert. 1964. *One Dimensional Man*. Boston: Beacon.

Martin, Linda, and Kerry Segrave. 1988. *Anti-Rock: The Opposition to Rock 'n' Roll*. Hamden, CT: Archon.

Martino, Steven C., Rebecca L. Collins, Marc N. Elliott, Amy Strachman, David E. Kanouse, and Sandra H. Berry. 2006. "'Exposure to degrading versus nondegrading music lyrics and sexual behavior among youth." *Pediatrics* 118:e430-e441. http://pediatrics.aappublications.org/cgi/content/abstract/118/2/e430. Posted August 1. Last accessed July 7, 2010.

Matta, Fernando Reyes. 1988. "The 'New Song' and its confrontation in Latin America." Pp. 447–460 in Cary Nelson and Lawrence Grossberg (eds.), *Marxism and the Interpretation of Culture*. Urbana: University of Illinois Press.

Mattson, Kevin. 1999. "Exchange" (letters to the editor). *The Nation*, December 27, p. 2.

Maultsby, Portia K. 1989 [1983]. "Soul music: Its sociological and political significance in American popular culture." *Journal of Popular Culture* 17:2 (Fall):51–60. Reprinted, pp. 168–178, in Timothy E. Scheurer (ed.), *American Popular Music, Volume II*. Bowling Green, OH: Bowling Green State University Popular Press.

McAdam, Doug. 1994. "Culture and social movements." Pp. 36–57 in Enrique Larana, Hank Johnston, and Joseph R. Gusfield (eds.), *New Social Movements*. Philadelphia: Temple University Press.

McAdam, Doug, Sidney Tarrow, and Charles Tilly. 2001. *Dynamics of Contention*. Cambridge, UK: Cambridge University Press.

McClary, Susan. 1993. "Narrative agendas in 'absolute music.'" Pp. 326–344 in Ruth A. Solie (ed.), *Musicology and Difference*. Berkeley: University of California Press.

———. 1991a. "Introduction." Pp. 3–34 in Susan McClary (ed.), *Feminine Endings*. Minneapolis: University of Minnesota Press.

———. 1991b. "Living to Tell: Madonna's resurrection of the fleshly." Pp. 148–166 in Susan McClary (ed.), *Feminine Endings*. Minneapolis: University of Minnesota Press.

McClary, Susan, and Robert Walser. 1990. "Stop making sense: Musicology wrestles with rock." Pp. 277–292 in Simon Frith and Andrew Goodwin (eds.), *On Record*. New York: Pantheon.

McDonald, James R. 1993. "Rock and memory: A search for meaning." *Popular Music & Society* 17:3 (Fall):1–17.

McDonnell, Evelyn. 1992. "The feminine critique: The secret history of women and rock journalism." *Village Voice Rock & Roll Quarterly* (Fall):6–9, 18–20.

McEnerney, Charles. 2009. "[Interview with] Jeff Price of TuneCore." http://www.wellroundedradio. net/episodes/index.html. March 1. Accessed March 22, 2009.

McNeil, Donald G., Jr. 2002. "Killer songs." *New York Times Magazine*, March 17, pp. 58–59.

McQuivey, James L., Ellen Daily, and April Lawson. 2008. "The end of the music industry as we know it." Forrester Research. http://www.forrester.com/Research/Document/Excerpt/0,7211,43759,00. html. Posted February 15. Last accessed July 7, 2010.

Mei, Zi. 1998. "Rock music and the subversion of hegemony in the People's Republic of China." Unpublished undergraduate paper, Wesleyan University, Middletown, CT.

Melody Maker. 1986. "Shrink wrap." *Melody Maker* 61 (December 20–27):20–26.

Melucci, Alberto. 1996. *Challenging Codes*. Cambridge, UK: Cambridge University Press.

Meyer, Leonard. 1956. *Emotion and Meaning in Music*. Chicago: University of Chicago Press.

Michaels, Sheila, and Bruce Hartford. 2002. "Interview of Bruce Hartford." http://www.crmvtet.org/.

Microsoft Encarta. 2007. "Amnesty International." *Microsoft Encarta Online Encyclopedia*. http://encarta. msn.com/encyclopedia_761553034/Amnesty_International.html.

Middleton, Richard. 1985. "Articulating musical meaning/reconstructing musical history/locating the 'popular.'" *Popular Music* 5:5–44.

———. 1981. "Reading popular music." Unit 16 in Richard Middleton and Colin Mercer (eds.), *Popular Culture: Form and Meaning 2*. Milton Keynes, UK: Open University.

Miller, Lloyd, and James K. Skipper, Jr. 1972. "Sounds of black protest in avant garde jazz." Reprinted, pp. 26–37, in R. Serge Denisoff and Richard Peterson (eds.), *The Sounds of Social Change*. New York: Rand McNally.

Miller, Tim, and David Román. 1995. "Preaching to the converted." *Theatre Journal* 47:169–188.

Mills, C. Wright. 1963. "Mass media and public opinion." Pp. 577–598 in Irving Louis Horowitz (ed.), *Power, Politics and People*. New York: Oxford University Press.

———. 1959. *The Sociological Imagination*. New York: Oxford University Press.

Mondak, Jeffrey. 1988. "Protest music as political persuasion." *Popular Music & Society* 12 (8):25–38.

Mooney, H. F. 1972 [1968]. "Popular music since the 1920s: The significance of shifting taste." Excerpted from *American Quarterly* 20:67–85. Reprinted, pp. 181–197 in R. Serge Denisoff and Richard Peterson (eds.), *The Sounds of Social Change*. New York: Rand McNally.

Moore, Jack. 1993. *Skinheads Shaved for Battle*. Bowling Green, OH: Bowling Green State University Popular Press.

Morello, Tom. 2003. "Farewell to Joe Strummer." www.likeastone.com/articles/farewellstrummer.htm.

Morley, David. 1993. "Active audience theory: Pendulums and pitfalls." *Journal of Communication* 43:4 (Fall):13–19.

———. 1980. *The "Nationwide" Audience*. London: British Film Institute.

Moseley, Caroline. 1989 [1978]. "The Hutchinson Family: The function of their song in ante-bellum

America." *Journal of American Culture* 1:4 (Winter):713–723. Reprinted, pp. 63–74, in Timothy E. Scheurer (ed.), *American Popular Music, Volume II.* Bowling Green, OH: Bowling Green State University Popular Press.

Music & Copyright. 2005. "Recorded music sales accounted for 71% of the $61bn global music business in 2004." *Music & Copyright* 304 (September 14), pp. 1, 12–13.

Music Journal. 1958. "Editorially speaking." *Music Journal* 16 (February):3.

Nah, Seungahn, Aaron Veenstra, and Dhavan Shah. 2006. "The internet and antiwar activism." *Journal of Computer-Mediated Communication* 12 (1), article 1. http://jcmc.indiana.edu/vol12/issue1/nah.html. Last accessed July 7, 2010.

Narvaez, Peter. 1986. "The protest songs of a labor union on strike against an American corporation in a Newfoundland company town." PhD dissertation, Department of Folklore, Indiana University. Ann Arbor, MI: University Microfilms International.

Near, Holly (with Derek Richardson). 1990. *Fire in the Rain, Singer in the Storm.* New York: William Morrow.

Negus, Keith. 1999. *Music Genres and Corporate Cultures.* New York: Routledge.

———. 1996. *Popular Music in Theory.* Middletown, CT: Wesleyan University Press.

———. 1995. "Where the mystical meets the market: Creativity and commerce in the production of popular music." *Sociological Review* 43 (2):317–339.

Nelson, Bruce. 1986. "Dancing and picnicking anarchists? The movement below the martyred leadership." Pp. 76–79 in David Roediger and Franklin Rosement (eds.), *Haymarket Scrapbook.* Chicago: Charles H. Kerr.

Nye, William P. 1988. "Theodor Adorno on jazz: A critique of critical theory." *Popular Music & Society* 12 (4):69–73.

Oberholzer-Gee, Felix, and Koleman Strumpf. 2007. "The effect of file sharing on record sales: An empirical analysis." *Journal of Political Economy* 115 (1). http://www.journals.uchicago.edu/doi/abs/10.1086/511995-fn1. Last accessed July 7, 2010.

Olson, Mancur. 1965. *The Logic of Collective Action.* Cambridge, MA: Harvard University Press.

Opp, Karl-Dieter, and Christiane Gern. 1993. "Dissident groups, personal networks, and spontaneous cooperation: The East German revolution of 1989." *American Sociological Review* 58 (October):659–680.

Orman, John. 1984. *The Politics of Rock Music.* Chicago: Nelson-Hall.

Ospina, Hernando Calvo. 1995. *!Salsa!.* London: Latin America Bureau.

Paddison, Max. 1982. "The critique criticised: Adorno and popular music." Pp. 201–218 in Richard Middleton and David Horn (eds.), *Popular Music 2: Theory and Method.* Cambridge: Cambridge University Press.

Pareles, Jon. 2003. "New songs, old message: 'No War.'" *New York Times,* March 9, Section 2, pp. 1, 18.

PBS. [n.d.] "Store wars: When Wal-Mart comes to town." http://www.pbs.org/itvs/storewars/stores3_2.html. Last accessed July 7, 2010.

Percy, Will. 1998. "Rock and read: Will Percy interviews Bruce Springsteen." *Doubletake* (Spring):36–43.

Perris, Arnold. 1985. *Music as Propaganda.* Westport, CT: Greenwood.

Perrone, Charles. 2002. "Nationalism, dissension, and politics in contemporary Brazilian popular music." *Luso-Brazilian Review* 39 (1):65–78.

Petersen, Karen E. 1987. "An investigation into women-identified music in the United States." Pp. 203–212 in Ellen Koskoff (ed.), *Women and Music in Cross-Cultural Perspective.* New York: Greenwood.

Peterson, Richard A. 1994. "Cultural studies through the production perspective." Pp. 163–189 in Diana Crane (ed.), *The Sociology of Culture.* Oxford: Blackwell.

———. 1972. "Market and moralist censors of a black art form: Jazz." Reprinted, pp. 236–247, in R. Serge Denisoff and Richard Peterson (eds.), *The Sounds of Social Change.* New York: Rand McNally.

Peterson, Richard A., and David G. Berger. 1996. "Measuring industry concentration, diversity, and innovation in popular music." *American Sociological Review* 61 (1):175–178.

———. 1975. "Cycles in symbol production: The case of popular music." *American Sociological Review* 40:158–173.

———. 1972. "Three eras in the manufacture of popular music lyrics." Pp. 292–303 in R. Serge Denisoff and Richard Peterson (eds.), *The Sounds of Social Change.* New York: Rand McNally.

Petty, Richard E., and John T. Cacioppo. 1986. *Communication and Persuasion.* New York: Springer-Verlag.

Phillips, Bruce "Utah." 1985. "Bruce 'Utah' Phillips." Pp. 25–29 in Stewart Bird, Dan Georgakas, and Deborah Shaffer (eds.), *Solidarity Forever.* Chicago: Lake View.

Poet, J. 1996. "Ani DiFranco: Independent as she wants to be." *Pulse* (September). http://www.cc.columbia.edu?~marg/ani/articles/pulse-9-96/index.html.

Polletta, Francesca. 1999. "Free space in collective action." *Theory and Society* 28:1–38.

Pollock, Rufus. 2006. "P2P, online file-sharing, and the music industry." http://www.rufuspollock.org/economics/p2p_summary.html. Posted November 10, 2005, updated March 3, 2006. Last accessed July 7, 2010.

Postman, Neil. 1985. *Amusing Ourselves to Death.* New York: Viking.

Powers, Ann. 2003. "The power of music." *The Nation,* January 13/20, pp. 11–17.

Powledge, Fred. 1991. *Free at Last?* Boston: Little, Brown.

Pratt, Ray. 1990. *Rhythm and Resistance.* Washington, DC: Smithsonian Institution Press.

Quiring, Oliver, Benedikt von Walter, and Richard Atterer. 2008. "Can filesharers be triggered by economic incentives? Results of an experiment." *New Media & Society* 10 (3):433–453.

Qureshi, Regula. 2000. "How does music mean? Embodied memories and the politics of affect in the Indian *sarangi.*" *American Ethnologist* 27 (4):805–838.

Ramet, Sabrina Petra (ed.). 1994a. *Rocking the State.* Boulder, CO: Westview.

———. 1994b. "Rock: The music of revolution (and political conformity)." Pp. 1–16 in Sabrina Petra Ramet (ed.), *Rocking the State.* Boulder, CO: Westview.

———. 1994c. "Rock music in Czechoslovakia." Pp. 55–72 in Sabrina Petra Ramet (ed.), *Rocking the State.* Boulder, CO: Westview.

———. 1994d. "Shake, rattle, and self-management: Making the scene in Yugoslavia." Pp. 103–140 in Sabrina Petra Ramet (ed.), *Rocking the State.* Boulder, CO: Westview.

Ramet, Sabrina Petra, Sergei Zamascikov, and Robert Bird. 1994. "The Soviet rock scene." Pp. 181–218 in Sabrina Petra Ramet (ed.), *Rocking the State.* Boulder, CO: Westview.

Raskin, Jonah. 1997. *For the Hell of It: The Life and Times of Abbie Hoffman.* Berkeley: University of California Press.

Reagon, Bernice Johnson. 1993. "Singing for my life." Pp. 133–168 in Bernice Johnson Reagon and Sweet Honey in the Rock, *We Who Believe in Freedom.* New York: Anchor.

———. 1987. "Let the church sing freedom." *Black Music Research Journal* 7:105–118.

———. 1975a. "Songs of the Civil Rights Movement, 1955–1965." *Dissertation Abstracts International* 49, 4904A.

———. 1975b. "In our hands: Thoughts on black music." *Sing Out* (November), pp. 1–2, 5.

Reed, Lou. 1990. "To do the right thing." *Musician* 46 (October):16–17, 48–58.

Reid, John Edgar, Jr. 1993. "The use of Christian rock by youth group members." *Popular Music & Society* 17 (2):33–45.

Reid, T. V. 1991. "Music/politics/spectacle: Rock 'n' roll music and/as colonial discourse." Talk at the Center for the Humanities, Wesleyan University, Middletown, CT, April 22.

Ressler, Darren. 1992. "The politics of pop." *Option Magazine* 43 (March/April):36–41.

Reuss, Richard A. 1971. "American Folklore and Left-Wing Politics: 1927–1957." Unpublished dissertation, Indiana University. Ann Arbor, MI: University Microfilms.

Reynolds, Michael. 1999. "Hammerskin nation." *Intelligence Report* 96 (Fall):37–39.

Reynolds, Simon. 1990 [1985]. "New pop and its aftermath." *Monitor* 4. Reprinted, pp. 466–471, in Simon Frith and Andrew Goodwin (eds.), *On Record.* New York: Pantheon.

Richards, Jonathan. 2008 "YouTube chart topper provokes web backlash." *Times Online.* http://technology.timesonline.co.uk/tol/news/tech_and_web/article3582166.ece. March 19. Last accessed July 7, 2010.

Riesman, David. 1990 [1950]. "Listening to popular music." Reprinted, pp. 5–13, in Simon Frith and Andrew Goodwin (eds.), *On Record.* New York: Pantheon.

Riggs, Peter. 1991. "Up from underground: Sound technologies, independent musicianship, and cultural change in China and the Soviet Union." *Popular Music & Society* 15 (1):1–24.

Rijven, Stan, and Will Straw. 1989 [1985]. "Rock for Ethiopia." Papers presented at the 1985 International Association for the Study of Popular Music conference, Montreal, Canada.. Reprinted, pp. 198–209, in Simon Frith (ed.), *World Music, Politics, and Social Change.* New York: Manchester University Press.

Roberts, Donald F., Peter G. Christenson, and Douglas A. Gentile. 2003. "The effects of violent music on children and adolescents." Pp. 153–170 in Douglas A. Gentile (ed.), *Media Violence and Children.* Westport, CT: Praeger.

Robertson, Carol E. 1987. "Power and gender in the musical experiences of women." Pp. 225–244 in Ellen Koskoff (ed.), *Women and Music in Cross-Cultural Perspective.* New York: Greenwood.

Robinson, John P., and Paul Hirsch. 1972. "Teenage response to rock and roll protest songs." Pp. 222–231 in R. Serge Denisoff and Richard Peterson (eds.), *The Sounds of Social Change.* New York: Rand McNally.

Rodnitzky, Jerome. 1999. "The Sixties between the microgrooves: Using folk and protest music to understand American history, 1963–1973." *Popular Music & Society* 23 (4):105–122.

———. 1989 [1973]. "The mythology of Woody Guthrie." *Popular Music & Society* 2 (3):227–243. Reprinted, pp. 13–23, in Timothy E. Scheurer (ed.), *American Popular Music, Volume II.* Bowling Green, OH: Bowling Green State University Popular Press.

Rollin, Betty. 1964. "A new beat: Topical folk singers, their songs." *Vogue,* September 1, pp. 60, 82–83, 130.

Rorem, Ned. 1988. *Settling the Score.* San Diego: Harcourt Brace Jovanovich.

Roscigno, Vincent J., and William F. Danaher. 2004. *The Voice of Southern Labor.* Minneapolis: University of Minnesota Press.

———. 2001. "Media and mobilization: The case of radio and southern textile worker insurgency, 1929 to 1934." *American Sociological Review* 66 (February):21–48.

Rose, Tricia. 1994. *Black Noise.* Hanover, NH: Wesleyan/University Press of New England.

———. 1991a. "'Fear of a black planet': Rap music and black cultural politics in the 1990s." *Journal of Negro Education* 60 (3):276–290.

———. 1991b. "Never trust a big butt and a smile." *Camera Obscura* 23 (May):110–131.

Rosenbaum, Jill, and Lorraine Prinsky. 1987. "Sex, violence and rock 'n' roll: Youth's perception of popular music." *Popular Music & Society* 11 (2):79–90.

Rosenberg, Bernard, and David Manning White (eds.). 1957. *Mass Culture.* Glencoe, IL: Free Press.

Rosenthal, Rob Herbert. 1986a. "Lyric cognition and the potential for protest among punk rockers." Unpublished graduate paper, University of Hartford, Hartford, CT.

———. 1986b. "Social movements, protest, and punk rock " Unpublished graduate paper, University of Hartford, Hartford, CT.

Ross, Alex. 1994. "Generation exit." *The New Yorker,* April 25, pp. 102–106.

Rosselson, Leon. 1997. "Sound and fury." *Red Pepper* 40 (September):28–29.

————. 1996. "Letter from Leon Rosselson." *Sounds Celebrating Resistance* 2 (November):2.

————. 1982. "Mashed potato music." *New Socialist* 5 (May/June):54–55.

Rowe, William, and Vivian Schelling. 1991. *Memory and Modernity.* London: Verso.

Rozendal, Keith. 1997. "'Our singing too must be a fight': The 'classical' revolutionary music of Hanns Eisler." *Sounds Celebrating Resistance* 3 (March):12–13.

Rudman, Laurie A., and Matthew R. Lee. 2002. "Implicit and explicit consequences of exposure to violent and misogynous rap music." *Group Processes & Intergroup Relations* 5 (2):133–150.

Rudy, Kathy. 2001. "Radical feminism, lesbian separatism, and queer theory." *Feminist Studies* 27:1 (Spring):191–222.

Samuels, David. 1995. "The rap on rap: The 'black music' that isn't either." Pp. 241–251 in Adam Sexton (ed.), *Rap on Rap.* New York: Delta.

Sandler, Lauren. 2003. "Holy rock 'n' rollers." *The Nation,* January 13/20, pp. 23–25.

Sandulli, Francesco D., and Samuel Martin-Barbero. 2007. "68 cents per song: A socio-economic survey on the Internet." *Convergence* 13 (1):63–78.

Sanger, Kerran. 1997. "Functions of freedom singing in the civil rights movement: The activists' implicit rhetorical theory." *Howard Journal of Communications* 8:179–195.

Sanjeck, Russell (updated by David Sanjek). 1996. *Pennies from Heaven.* New York: Da Capo.

Schell, Orville. 1992. "Red, hot and rebellious." *Los Angeles Times Magazine,* November 15, pp. 18–22+.

Schiller, Herbert. 1989. *Culture, Inc.* New York: Oxford University Press.

Schoenherr, Steve. 2002. "Der Bingle technology." http://www.lifesaver.net/keskustelut/read. php?5,19248.

Scott, James. 1990. *Domination and the Arts of Resistance.* New Haven, CT: Yale University Press.

Scribner, R.W. 1987. *Popular Culture and Popular Movements in Reformation Germany.* London: Hambledon.

Seeger, Charles. 1939. "Grass roots for American composers." *Modern Music* 11 (March–April):143–149.

Seeger, Pete, and Bob Reiser. 1989. *Everybody Says Freedom.* New York: W. W. Norton.

Seidman, Steven. 1981. "On the contributions of music to media productions." *Educational Communications and Technology Journal* 29:1 (Spring):49–61.

Shapiro, Samantha M. 2009. "Revolution, Facebook-style." *New York Times Magazine,* January 22. www.nytimes.com/2009/01/25/magazine/25bloggers-t.html. Last accessed July 7, 2010.

Shaw, Arnold. 1964. "Guitars, folk songs, and halls of ivy." *Harper's* (November):33–43.

Sheff, David. 1981. "Interview with John Lennon and Yoko Ono." *Playboy* (January):75–114, 144. http://www.angelfire.com/pq/yesterdaysmusic/interview7.html. Last accessed July 7, 2010.

Shepherd, John. 1991. *Music as Social Text.* Cambridge, MA: Polity.

Sherman, Robert. 1967 [1963]. "Sing a song of freedom." *Saturday Review,* September 28, pp. 65–67, 81. Reprinted, pp. 173-174, in David DeTurk and A. Poulin (eds.), *The American Folk Scene.* New York: Dell.

Shumway, David. 1991. "Rock & roll as a cultural practice." *The South Atlantic Quarterly* 90 (4):753–770.

Siegel, Larry. 2006. "Correlation is not causation" (letter to the editor). *Pediatrics,* August 8. http://pediatrics.aappublications.org/cgi/eletters/118/2/e430#2217. Last accessed July 7, 2010.

Silber, Irwin. 1973. *Songs of Independence.* Harrisburg, PA: Stackpole.

————. 1964. "An open letter to Bob Dylan." *Sing Out!* (November). http://www.edlis.org/twice/threads/open_letter_to_bob_dylan.html. Last accessed July 7, 2010.

Skyvorecky, Josev. 1979. *The Bass Saxophone.* New York: Knopf.

Slater, Derek, and Mike McGuire. 2005 "Consumer taste sharing is driving the online music business and democratizing culture." http://cyber.law.harvard.edu/node/409. Posted December 13. Last accessed July 7, 2010.

Small, Christopher. 1998. *Musicking.* Hanover, NH: Wesleyan/University Press of New England.

Smith, Ethan. 2007. "Volume low on CD sales." *Hartford Courant*, March 22, p. E3.

Smith, Gibbs M. 1969. *Joe Hill.* Salt Lake City: University of Utah Press.

Snow, David, and Robert D. Benford. 1992. "Master frames and cycles of protest." Pp. 133–155 in Aldon Morris and Carol McClurg Mueller (eds.), *Frontiers in Social Movements Theory.* New Haven, CT: Yale University Press.

Snow, David, Burke Rochford, Jr., Steven K. Worden, and Robert D. Benford. 1997 [1986]. "Frame alignment processes, micromobilization, and movement participation." *American Sociological Review* 51 (August):464–481. Reprinted, pp. 211–227, in Steven M. Buechler and F. Kurt Cylke, Jr. (eds.), *Social Movements.* London: Mayfield.

Southern Poverty Law Center. 2004. "Hate-music CDs target youth." *Southern Poverty Law Center Report* 34:4 (December):1.

———. 1999a. "A generation in trouble." *Intelligence Report* 96 (Fall):1.

———. 1999b. "Money, music and the doctor." *Intelligence Report* 96 (Fall):33–36.

———. 1999c. "Youth and hate." *Intelligence Report* 96 (Fall):24–27.

Spady, James. 1991. "Chuck D [interview]." Pp. 325–363 in Joseph D. Eure and James G. Spady (eds.), *Nation Conscious Rap.* New York: PC International Press.

Spencer, Jon Michael. 1992. "Rapsody in black: Utopian aspirations." *Theology Today* 48 (4):444–451.

St. Lawrence, J. S., and D. J. Joyner. 1991. "The effects of sexually violent rock music on males' acceptance of violence against women." *Psychology of Women Quarterly* 15:49–63.

Staggenborg, Suzanne, and Amy Lang. 2003. "Culture and ritual in the Montreal women's movement." Paper presented at the Annual Meeting of the American Sociological Association, Atlanta, August 16–19.

Stanton, Fred. 1996. "A letter from Fred Stanton." *Sounds Celebrating Resistance* 1:2.

Stanton-Rich, Diane. 1996. "Being inducted into Rock and Roll Hall of Fame is no thrill for Pete Seeger." *Sassafras* (Spring):14–15.

Steward, Sue, and Sheryl Garratt. 1984. *Signed, Sealed, and Delivered.* Boston: South End.

Stipe, Michael. 2001. "Sometimes lyrics are just notion." *Hartford Courant*, October 14, p. G7.

Straw, Will. 1990. "Characterizing rock music culture: The case of heavy metal." Pp. 97–109 in Simon Frith and Andrew Goodwin (eds.), *On Record.* New York: Pantheon.

Street, John. 1997. *Politics and Popular Culture.* Philadelphia: Temple University Press.

———. 1986. *Rebel Rock.* New York: Basil Blackwell.

Stud Brothers. 1986. "Once a hero." *Melody Maker* 61 (October 18):12–13.

Stuessy, Joe. 1985. "Testimony in hearing before the Committee on Commerce, Science, and Transportation, United States Senate (99th Congress), on the contents of music and the lyrics of records." *U.S. Congress Hearings* 99 (1):117–127. Washington, DC: U.S. Government Printing Office.

Sutherland, Elizabeth (ed.). 1965. *Letters from Mississippi.* New York: McGraw-Hill.

Szemere, Anna. 1992. "The politics of marginality: A rock musical subculture in socialist Hungary in the early 1980s." Pp. 93–114 in Reebee Garofalo (ed.), *Rockin' the Boat.* Boston: South End.

Taffet, Jeffrey. 1997. "'My guitar is not for the rich': The new Chilean song movement and the politics of culture." *Journal of American Culture* 20:2 (Summer):91–103.

Tagg, Philip. 1982. "Analysing popular music: Theory, method and practice." Pp. 37–67 in Richard Middleton and David Horn (eds.), *Popular Music 2: Theory and Method.* Cambridge, UK: Cambridge University Press.

Tagg, Philip, and Bob Clarida. 2003. *Ten Little Title Tunes.* New York: Mass Media Music Scholars' Press.

Taylor, Timothy D. 2001. *Strange Sounds.* New York: Routledge.

———. 1991. "Resigning mass culture: Billy Bragg's 'There is power in a union.'" *Popular Music & Society* 15 (Summer):35–48.

Taylor, Verta, and Nancy Whittier. 1997 [1992]. "Collective identity in social movement communities." In Aldon D. Morris and Carol McCLurg Mueller (eds.), *Frontiers in Social Movement Theory*

(New Haven, CT: Yale University Press). Reprinted, pp. 505–523, in Steven M. Buechler and F. Kurt Cylke, Jr. (eds.), *Social Movements*. London: Mayfield.

Techradar. 2008. "Facebook, MySpace statistics." http://techradar1.wordpress.com/2008/01/11/facebookmyspace-statistics/. January 11. Last accessed July 7, 2010.

Temple, Johnny. 1999. "Exchange" (letters to the editor). *The Nation,* December 27, p. 24.

Thompson, Robert Farris. 1983. *Flash of the Spirit*. New York: Random House.

Thora Institute. 2007. "Will white rap fans help or hurt black America?" *Black Directions* 2 (6):1–6.

Thornton, Sarah. 1995. *Club Cultures*. Hanover, NH: University Press of New England.

Tomaselli, Keyan, and Bob Foster. 1993. "Mandela, MTV, television, and apartheid." *Popular Music & Society* 17 (2):1–19.

Toomey, Jenny, and Rob Rosenthal. 2005. "Music for change." *The Nation,* January 31, pp. 14–16.

Tramo, Mark Jude. 2001. "Music of the hemispheres." *Science* 291 (January 5):54–56.

Trippi, Joe. 2004. *The Revolution Will Not Be Televised*. New York: Regan Books.

Tsitsos, William. 1999. "Rules of rebellion: Slamdancing, moshing, and the American alternative scene." *Popular Music* 18 (3):397–413.

Tumas-Serna, Jane. 1995. "Mass-mediated popular music and cultural change: The Cuban new song movement." *Journal of Communication Inquiry* 19:1 (Spring):111–125.

Uehlein, Joe. 1997. "Art & action." *Democratic Left* 6.10–12.

Usher, Craig. 1997. "An interview with revolutionary Chinese-American composer and saxophonist Fred Ho." *Sounds Celebrating Resistance* 3 (March):4–5.

———. 1996. "A discussion with members of the Sacramento Labor Chorus and Melody and the Matriarchs." *Sounds Celebrating Resistance* 2:8–11.

Van Deburg, William L. 1992. *New Day in Babylon*. Chicago: University of Chicago Press.

van Elderen, P. L. 1989 [1985]. "Pop and government policy in the Netherlands." Paper presented at the 1985 International Association for the Study of Popular Music conference, Montreal, Canada. Reprinted, pp. 190–197, in Simon Frith (ed.), *World Music, Politics, and Social Change*. New York: Manchester University Press.

Veal, Michael E. 2000. *Fela: The Life & Times of an African Musical Icon*. Philadelphia: Temple University Press.

Verden, Paul, Kathleen Dunleavy, and Charles H. Powers. 1989. "Heavy metal mania and adolescent delinquency." *Popular Music & Society* 13 (1):73–82.

Vickstrom, Erik. 1998. "Willing to fight: Understanding Ani DiFranco fans as a collective actor." Senior honors thesis, Wesleyan University, Middletown, CT.

Vila, Pablo. 1992. "*Rock nacional* and dictatorship in Argentina." Pp. 209–230 in Reebee Garofalo (ed.), *Rockin' the Boat*. Boston: South End.

Wallis, Roger, and Krister Malm. 1990 [1984]. "Patterns of change." Extracted from *Big Sounds from Small Peoples* (London: Constable). Pp. 160–180 in Simon Frith and Andrew Goodwin (eds.), *On Record*. New York: Pantheon.

———. 1984. *Big Sounds from Small Peoples*. London: Constable.

Walser, Robert. 1993. *Running with the Devil*. Hanover, NH: Wesleyan/University Press of New England.

Walters, Doug. 2008. "Causes and solutions for the recent decline in recorded music sales." Senior honors thesis, Wesleyan University, Middletown, CT.

Ward, Andrew. 2000. *Dark Midnight When I Rise*. New York: Farrar, Straus and Giroux.

Ward, Eric K., Jonn Lunsford, and Justin Massa. 1999. "Sounds of violence." *Intelligence Report* 96 (Fall):28–32.

Warren, Roland L. 1972 [1943]. "The Nazi use of music as an instrument of social control." *Journal of Abnormal and Social Psychology* 38:96–100. Reprinted, pp. 292–303, in R. Serge Denisoff and Richard Peterson (eds.), *The Sounds of Social Change*. New York: Rand McNally.

Wexler, Jerry, and David Ritz. 1993. *Rhythm and Blues.* New York: Knopf.

Whalen, Jack, and Richard Flacks. 1989. *Beyond the Barricades.* Philadelphia: Temple University Press.

Whitman, Wanda Willson (ed.). 1969. *Songs That Changed the World.* New York: Crown.

Wicke, Peter. 1992. "'The times they are a-changin': Rock music and political change in East Germany." Pp. 81–92 in Reebee Garofalo (ed.), *Rockin' the Boat.* Boston: South End.

Williams, Juan.1987. *Eyes on the Prize.* New York: Viking.

Williams, Raymond. 1977. *Marxism and Literature.* Oxford: Oxford University Press.

Willis, Ellen. 1981. *Beginning to See the Light.* New York: Knopf.

Willis, Paul. 1990 [1978]. "The golden age." Extracted from *Profane Culture* (London: Routledge and Kegan Paul). Reprinted, pp. 43–55, in Simon Frith and Andrew Goodwin (eds.), *On Record.* New York: Pantheon.

Witkin, Robert. 2000. "Why did Adorno 'hate' jazz?" *Sociological Theory* 18 (1):145–170.

Wolfe, Arnold S., and Margaret Haefner. 1996. "Taste culture, culture classes, affective alliances, and popular music reception: Theory, methodology, and an application to a Beatles song." *Popular Music* 20 (Winter):127–155.

Wolfe, Paul. 1972 [1964]. "The 'new' Dylan." *Broadside* 53 (December 20). Reprinted, pp. 147–150, in R. Serge Denisoff and Richard Peterson (eds.), *The Sounds of Social Change.* New York: Rand McNally.

Wortham, Jenna. 2008. "Cheating fans give Avril Lavigne a YouTube life." *Wired.* http://blog.wired.com/underwire/2008/06/avril-lavigne-f.html. June 24. Last accessed July 7, 2010.

Young, Stephen E. 1991. "Like a critique: A postmodern essay on Madonna's postmodern video, *Like a Prayer." Popular Music & Society* 15 (1):59–68.

Zook, Kristal Brent. 1992. "Reconstruction of nationalist thought in black music and culture." Pp. 255–266 in Reebee Garofalo (ed.), *Rockin' the Boat.* Boston: South End.

Index

Dundes, Alan, 101
Dyer, Richard, 194
Dylan, Bob, 44, 51, 59, 62, 68, 71, 98, 100, 105, 112, 148, 152, 171, 174, 182, 206, 209, 223, 229, 231–232, 234, 246

East Germany, 86, 163, 203
Eisler, Hans, 8, 57, 96–97, 139, 151, 233, 238, 242–243
Ejercito Revolucionario del Pueblo (ERP), 231
El Salvador, 134, 231, 243–244, 253–254
Ellington, Duke, 149
EMI Records, 71
England. See Great Britain
environmental movement, 126, 128, 201, 217, 235
Epic Records, 221
escapism, 23, 182–183
Etheridge, Melissa, 61
ethnocentrism, 53, 181
Eve of Destruction, 25, 86
Eyerman, Ron, 7–8, 55, 98, 126, 155, 160, 167, 169, 202, 230, 239–240, 253

Facebook, 77
Factory, 238
fandango, 33, 243
Farm Aid, 88
Farmer Is the Man, The, 167
Federal Inspection Office for Writing Endangering Youth, 140
Feld, Steven, 47, 108
feminism and feminist movement, 21, 33, 35, 63, 87, 98, 100, 108, 127, 136, 138, 151, 153, 168, 181, 219, 222, 227, 244, 250, 252; Respect and, 42–43, 58, 103–104, 109
file sharing, 32, 76–82
Finian's Rainbow, 8
Fireside Book of Folk Songs, The, 146
Fisher, Miles, 192
Fiske, John, 18, 150
Fitzgerald, Ella, 47
Fletcher, Andrew, 3
Flores, Quetzal, 33, 60, 223, 243
folk music, 9, 18, 22, 26, 52, 60, 62, 67–69, 73, 87, 94, 96, 103, 108, 160, 165, 168, 170–171, 190, 197, 206, 209, 229, 240, 249; and the Communist Party, 4, 100,

207; and the folk process, 10–11, 23; and the folk revival of the 1950s and 60s, 60, 73, 153, 215, 230; and its political uses, 20, 31, 54, 55, 126, 131, 146, 149, 152, 187–189, 210, 239, 241, 250; and popular culture, 12–14, 19, 56, 218, 231, 242
Folk Song Army, The, 24
Follow the Drinking Gourd, 134, 192, 208
framing, 6–8, 28, 109–110, 115–116, 124, 143, 238, 250–251, 254
Frand, Deni, 187
Frank, Tom, 184
Frankfurt School, 14–15
Franklin, Aretha, 42, 48, 58, 62, 103, 107, 110, 114, 203, 249
Franti, Michael, 220
Free Nelson Mandela concert, 135
free rider dilemma, 5–6, 158, 179, 200
free space, 116–117, 150–151, 153, 168, 192, 205, 251
Freedom Summer of 1964, 144, 160
Frith, Simon, 18, 22–23, 43, 45, 53–54, 58–59, 76, 88, 91, 95, 106, 116, 239, 241
Fugazi, 34, 220, 225
functional tonality, 104
funk music, 54, 229
Future of Music Coalition, 32, 36, 83, 85

Gabriel, Peter, 147
Gaines, Donna, 94–95, 97, 113, 147
Gang of Four, 109
Gans, Herbert J., 92
Garofalo, Reebee, 19, 190
Garon, Paul, 22
Garratt, Sheryl, 249
Gay and Lesbian Rights Movement, 35, 117, 168, 171, 250, 252; music and performers of, 98, 170, 227, 235
Gaye, Marvin, 229
gender, 42, 71, 92, 191, 202; and equality, 87, 132; and gender roles, 9, 20, 124, 151; presentation of, 21, 104
George, Nelson, 73
Germany, 140, and atonality, 57; and music under Nazism, 50–51, 127, 163, 215. See also East Germany
Gil, Gilberto, 21
Gilbert, Ronnie, 222

About the Authors

Rob Rosenthal is the John E. Andrus Professor of Sociology at Wesleyan University. He has written widely on housing and homelessness (including *Homeless in Paradise* (1994) and the use of music in social movements. He has played in bands for over forty years, including The Fuse, which recorded his rock opera *Seattle 1919* in 1986.

Dick Flacks is Emeritus Professor of Sociology at University of California–Santa Barbara. His work focuses on the roots and strategies of social movements and the American Left (*Making History: The American Left and the American Mind*, 1988), the social psychology of political activism (*Beyond the Barricades*, 1989), and culture and social movements. He's produced a weekly radio program on music and politics since 1982.

CPSIA information can be obtained at www.ICGtesting.com
Printed in the USA
LVOW05s1050040414

380349LV00009B/98/P